FROMMER'S

COMPREHENSIVE TRAVEL GUIDE

TAMPA &
ST. PETERSBURG

3RD EDITION

W9-BTF-467

by Patricia Tunison Preston
and John J. Preston

MACMILLAN TRAVEL

U.S.A.

*Dedicated to Dorothy A. Tunison
who always makes us feel "at home"
in the St. Petersburg/Tampa Area*

Macmillan Travel
A Prentice Hall Macmillan Company
15 Columbus Circle
New York, NY 10023

ISBN 0-671-88382-8
ISSN 1047-7896

Design by Robert Bull Design
Maps by Geografix Inc.

SPECIAL SALES
Bulk purchases (ten or more copies) of Frommer's Travel Guides are available to corporations at special discounts. The Special Sales Department can produce custom editions to be used as premiums and/or for sales promotion to suit individual needs. Existing editions can be produced with custom cover imprints, such as corporate logos. For more information, write to Special Sales, Prentice Hall, 15 Columbus Circle, New York, NY 10023.

Manufactured in the United States of America

CONTENTS

LIST OF MAPS

ACKNOWLEDGMENTS

We would like to acknowledge the tremendous help and enthusiasm of the many dedicated people who work long and hard for the various tourism organizations and chambers of commerce in the St. Petersburg/Tampa area. In particular, we extend a big "thank you" to Lee Daniel of the St. Petersburg/Clearwater Area Convention & Visitors Bureau, and to Mary Lou Janson and Stacey Rosseter of the Tampa/Hillsborough Convention and Visitors Bureau. Thank you also to Marilyn Wood and her great "team" for making this book a reality, and especially to our editor for this edition, Peter Katucki.

INVITATION TO THE READERS

In researching this book, we have come across many fine establishments, the best of which we have included here. We're sure that many of you will also come across recommendable hotels, inns, restaurants, guesthouses, shops, and attractions. Please don't keep them to yourself. Share your experiences, especially if you want to comment on places that we have covered in this edition that have changed for the worse. You can address your letters to us:

Pat Tunison Preston and John J. Preston
Frommer's Tampa & St. Petersburg
c/o Macmillan Travel
15 Columbus Circle
New York, NY 10023

A DISCLAIMER

Readers are advised that prices fluctuate in the course of time and travel information changes under the impact of the varied and volatile factors that affect the travel industry. The authors and the publisher cannot be held responsible for the experiences of the readers while traveling. Readers are invited to write to the publisher with ideas, comments, and suggestions for future editions.

SAFETY ADVISORY

Whenever you're traveling in an unfamiliar city or country, stay alert. Be aware of your immediate surroundings. Wear a moneybelt and keep a close eye on your possessions. Be particularly careful with cameras, purses, and wallets, all favorite targets of thieves and pickpockets.

CHAPTER 1

INTRODUCING TAMPA & ST. PETERSBURG

1. HISTORY OF THE TAMPA BAY AREA
• **DATELINE**
2. RECOMMENDED BOOKS

Tampa and St. Petersburg, two totally different cities joined by Tampa Bay, comprise one of the fastest-growing metropolitan areas in the United States. Each has its own distinctive history and layout, but together they are synonymous with sunshine and the good life. Rimmed by the Gulf of Mexico on Florida's west coast, these two cities are in the center of the state, within easy reach of other Florida destinations—just over 80 miles from Orlando and less than 270 from Miami.

Tampa, once considered little more than a landing port for banana boats from Colombia, or a cigar-making enclave, has been rejuvenated as a city in the last 20 years. The once-dingy downtown area is humming with new skyscrapers, financial centers, high-tech industries, and entertainment facilities.

St. Petersburg, on the other hand, was known for years primarily as a winter haven for seniors, but in the past decade, the city has been revived with new industries, an influx of younger citizens, and exciting downtown developments.

With a year-round warm climate and miles of sandy beaches, it's not surprising that tourism is the number-one industry for both cities. More than three million visitors, about one-third from overseas, flock to the Tampa Bay area annually.

Just 15 miles apart, these two cities are served by Tampa International Airport, one of the best in the nation and often touted as an attraction in itself. Tampa and St. Petersburg are connected by three bridges that span Tampa Bay: the Courtney Campbell, the Howard Frankland, and the George Gandy. The combined Tampa–St. Petersburg Metropolitan area has a population of 2,107,271, ranking 20th in the nation.

1. HISTORY OF THE TAMPA BAY AREA

EARLY HISTORY

The Tampa Bay area was first inhabited by large settlements of Native Americans, particularly the Tocobaga and Timucuan tribes.

DATELINE

• **1521–39** Spanish arrive.

(continues)

DATELINE

- **1750s** Pirates patrol the area.
- **1757** Tampa Bay charted.
- **1763–83** British take over.
- **1824** Fort Brooke established.
- **1842** First citrus fruit planted.
- **1848** John's Pass formed by flooding.
- **1855** Tampa incorporates.
- **1875** John Williams begins building new city.
- **1884** Railroad comes to Tampa.
- **1888** St. Petersburg named.
- **1891** Tampa Bay Hotel opens.
- **1896** Belleview Hotel opens.
- **1897–98** Rough Riders train in Tampa.
- **1903** St. Petersburg incorporates.
- **1910** St. Pete nicknamed "Sunshine City."
- **1914** First commercial airline flight.
- **1920–26** Building boom.
- **1959** Busch Gardens unveiled.
- **1971** Tampa International Airport brings new focus to area.
- **1988** The Pier is reborn.
- **1990** ThunderDome dazzles.

(continues)

The first Europeans arrived in the 16th century. From 1521 to 1539, Spanish adventurers and explorers Juan Ponce de León, Pánfilo de Narváez, and Hernando de Soto explored the area. While searching for gold, de Soto discovered five mineral springs near a large Tocobaga village in what is now Safety Harbor, north of St. Petersburg and west of Tampa. He named the large body of water near the village (Tampa Bay) "La Bahía del Espíritu Santo" or "Bay of the Holy Spirit" since the Native Americans believed the springs had healing qualities—a legend that persists today.

The first use of the name Tampa is usually attributed to a shipwrecked Spaniard named Fountaneda, who spent time living among the natives in the late 1570s. He referred to the area by the Native American name: "Tanpa," variously defined to mean "a town near the bay" or "sticks of fire." Early cartographers apparently changed the spelling to Tampa.

Almost 200 years later, in 1757, a Spanish expedition led by Don Francisco María Celi charted the first detailed map of Tampa Bay and the surrounding waterways. At about the same time, pirates are said to have been active along the Florida coastline and Caribbean waters.

In 1763 the region came under British rule when the Spanish traded Florida for Havana. Within a decade, Lord Hillsborough, a British colonial secretary of state, lent his name to the river, bay, and county on the east side of Tampa Bay.

FLORIDA — THE 27TH STATE

In the early 1820s Florida became a territory of the U.S., and Gen. Andrew Jackson took charge as the region's first governor. In 1824, after the first American settlers had arrived in the Tampa Bay area, Col. George Brooke built a U.S. Army post, known as Fort Brooke, at the mouth of the Hillsborough River (today the site of downtown Tampa). Ten years later the County of Hillsborough was established by the Territorial Legislature.

On the west side of Tampa Bay, in an

area now called Safety Harbor, Dr. Odet Phillipe, a former surgeon in the French navy under Napoléon, established a plantation in 1842. With citrus stock brought from the Bahamas, Phillipe cultivated Florida's first grapefruit grove. Florida became the 27th state of the Union in 1845.

DATELINE

1995 Florida Aquarium and Garrison Seaport Center open.

In 1848, U.S. Army Lt. Col. Robert E. Lee surveyed the area for possible coastal defense installations. He recommended Mullet Key, a site later used as a military post in both the Civil and Spanish-American wars. In that same year, a 90-m.p.h. gale ripped across the area, with waters rising from the gulf to Tampa Bay. All islands and keys were inundated and John's Pass (the narrow strip of water between the southern tip of Sand Key Island and the northern end of Treasure Island) was created.

Meanwhile, a thriving settlement had grown up around the site of Fort Brooke, an important center for trade and transportation. In 1855 this settlement was incorporated as the town of Tampa.

Twenty years later, Gen. John Williams, son of the first mayor of Detroit, headed for Florida. Ordered by his doctor to find a milder climate to cure his asthma, Williams bought 1,600 acres west of Tampa Bay and the already-thriving Tampa. After failing as a farmer because his northern methods were unsuited for the semitropical region, Williams set out to build a new city—what would become St. Petersburg.

RAILROADS, CIGARS & HOTELS

In 1884 Tampa became even more accessible for travel and trade when railroad tycoon Henry B. Plant brought his narrow-gauge South Florida Railroad to Tampa. The following year, 1885, Tampa residents organized a board of trade (predecessor of today's chamber of commerce). That same year, a prominent physician, Dr. W. C. Van Biber of Baltimore, drew international attention to the area west of Tampa Bay (where Williams was building his city) when he presented a paper, "Where Should a Health City Be Built," to a meeting of the American Medical Society in New Orleans. This spot, he declared, had all the elements to be regarded as the "healthiest place on earth."

Shortly thereafter, in 1886, recognition of a different sort came to the area. Vincente Martínez Ybor, an immigrant from Cuba via Key West, established Tampa's first cigar factory in what eventually became known as Ybor City, and Tampa became the "cigar capital of the world."

John Williams was well into his task of building a city when, in 1887–88, Russian immigrant Peter Demens (Petrovich A. Demenshev) and three partners extended their Orange Belt Railroad from Sanford, northeast of Orlando, to the western Tampa Bay area. Popular legend has it that, when the railroad was complete, Williams and Demens drew lots to determine which of them would get to name their new community. Demens won, and christened the new

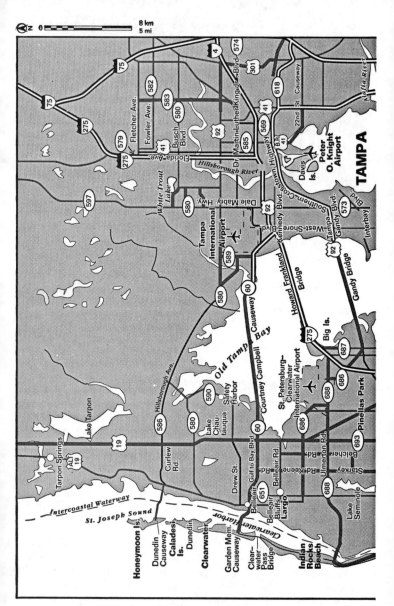

city St. Petersburg, after his hometown in Russia. As a consolation, Williams erected the city's first commercial building—the 40-room Detroit Hotel—and named it after his hometown.

In Tampa, Henry B. Plant opened the Tampa Bay Hotel, a fashionable winter resort for the rich and famous, in 1891. Touted at the time as "the world's most elegant hotel," it had over 500 rooms filled with antiques and art from around the world, with a striking Moorish facade topped by 13 silver minarets. Plant followed this

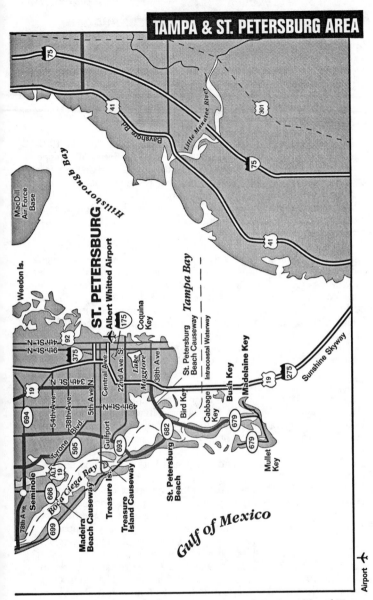

achievement by spreading his influence to the other side of Tampa Bay during 1893–96, when he took over the Orange Belt Railroad and built the huge Belleview Hotel (later to become the Belleview Biltmore) north of St. Petersburg, overlooking Clearwater Harbor.

In 1897–98 the U.S. became involved in the Spanish-American War, and Tampa became a staging point for 30,000 troops. One of the officers based here was Teddy Roosevelt, who set up his headquarters at the commandeered Tampa Bay Hotel. He trained his

Rough Riders on the hotel's grounds. On the St. Pete side, Fort DeSoto was built on Mullet Key to protect Tampa Bay during the war—but the war ended before construction was finished and the fort's cannons were never fired.

THE 20TH CENTURY

In 1903 St. Petersburg became an incorporated city, and in 1907 Noel Mitchell, a St. Pete real estate salesman, ordered 50 orange benches for people who wished to rest and enjoy the sun on the city's streets. Other businesses followed suit, but the many benches they installed differed in size and color. Eventually, Mitchell sponsored an ordinance that standardized the color of all city benches, thus beginning the era of St. Petersburg's green benches (a city trademark that lasted until 1969).

Another colorful bit of St. Pete history began in 1910, when the *St. Petersburg Independent,* a newspaper founded four years earlier, made its famous "sunshine offer"—a pledge to distribute free newspapers on any day when the sun didn't shine. This inspired the nickname "Sunshine City" for St. Pete. A year later, in 1911, Tampa and St. Petersburg were separated into two different counties when Pinellas County was created out of the western portion of Hillsborough County.

The area won a place in the history of aviation in 1914 when the first commercial airline service in the U.S. was inaugurated between St. Pete and Tampa by pioneer aviator Tony Jannus. The fare was $400, a small fortune at the time, for a 23-minute flight.

As the 1920s roared in, a building boom exploded in the region, with St. Petersburg adding 12 major hotels, including the posh Don CeSar, still in operation today. In Tampa, the Davis Islands were created by dredging Hillsborough Bay, and became one of Tampa's most attractive residential sections. In 1924 the first bridge (the $3-million George Gandy Bridge) opened between Tampa and St. Petersburg.

The World War II–era had a dramatic impact on Tampa Bay. Many major St. Petersburg–area hotels, such as the Don CeSar, the Vinoy, and the Belleview Biltmore, were taken over by the military for use as hospitals during World War II. The legendary Tampa Bay Hotel was annexed permanently by the University of Tampa. MacDill Air Force Base was established on Hillsborough Bay.

In the 1950s and 1960s the Tampa Bay area began to perk up again. The first Sunshine Skyway bridge, then the longest open-water crossing in the United States, was built in 1954, linking St. Petersburg with the Bradenton/Sarasota area; the area's first television station, WSUN, began broadcasting; St. Pete unveiled a new Museum of Fine Arts and the Bayfront Center; and Tampa became the site of Busch Gardens. The population of both cities began to soar, and the Howard Frankland Bridge, the third of the overwater links between them, opened.

The last two decades have been equally positive for the Tampa Bay area, starting in 1971 with the opening of the state-of-the-art Tampa International Airport, increasing tourist access. Downtown St.

Petersburg launched the Bayfront Center, an entertainment and sports complex, plus the Dalí Museum and a new Pier which has revitalized the waterfront as well. Downtown Tampa blossomed too with dozens of new skyscrapers and a Performing Arts Center; and Harbour Island was developed as a new recreational and residential focal point for the city.

In the 1990s expansion has continued, with the opening of the ThunderDome in St. Petersburg and a brand-new riverside convention center in Tampa. Future developments in St. Petersburg include a new nine-block, $200-million waterfront shopping district and the debut in 1995 of the Florida International Museum. Across the bay, Tampa is the future site for the $94-million waterfront Florida Aquarium, a new four-story marine-science center, set to debut in 1995 and the centerpiece of the Port of Tampa's new Garrison Seaport Center. In addition, plans call for a new $25-million music dome amphitheater, a promenade, and a new downtown hockey stadium.

2. RECOMMENDED BOOKS

Anderson, Robert. *Guide to Florida Wildlife and Nature Series.* Altamonte Springs: Winner Enterprises, 1984–92.

—*Saltwater Fishing.* St. Petersburg: Great Outdoors, 1989.

Arsenault, Raymond. *St. Petersburg and the Florida Dream.* Norfolk: Donning Co., 1988.

Boone, Floyd E. *Florida Historical Markers and Sites.* Houston: Gulf Publishing Co., 1988.

Branyon, Max. *Florida Saltwater Fishing Guide.* Orlando: Sentinel Communications Co., 1988.

Burnett, Gene M. *Florida's Past,* Vols 1–3. Sarasota: Pineapple Press, 1986, 1988, 1991.

Doyle, Larry J., et al. *Living with the West Florida Shore.* Durham: Duke University Press, 1984.

Dunn, Hampton. *Yesterday's Clearwater.* Miami: E. A. Seaman, 1973.

—*Yesterday's St. Petersburg.* Miami: E. A. Seaman, 1973.

—*Yesterday's Tampa.* Miami: E. A. Seaman, 1977.

Fotheringham, Nick, and Brunemeister, Susan. *Beachcomber's Guide to Gulf Coast Marine Life.* Houston: Gulf Publishing Co., 1989.

Fuller, Walter P. *St. Petersburg and Its People.* St. Petersburg: Great Outdoors, 1972.

Golenbock, Peter. *The Forever Boys.* New York: Birch Lane Press, 1991.

Lewis, Gordon. *Florida Fishing: Fresh and Saltwater.* St. Petersburg: Great Outdoors, 1957.

Marth, Del, and Marth, Martha. *Florida Almanac.* Gretna: Pelican Publishing Co., 1992.

Mormino, Gary R., and Pozetta, George E. *Immigrant World of Ybor City.* Chicago: University of Illinois Press, 1987.

Neill, Wilfred. *The Story of Florida's Seminole Indians.* St. Petersburg: Great Outdoors Publishing, 1964.

O'Sullivan, Maurice, and Lane, Jack C. *The Florida Reader.* Sarasota: Pineapple Press, 1991.

Roosevelt, Theodore. *The Rough Riders.* New York: Charles Scribner and Sons, 1906.

Young, June Hurley. *Florida's Pinellas Peninsula.* St. Petersburg: Byron Kennedy & Son, 1983.

Waggoner, Holly. *Skyway to the Stars.* Sarasota: Omnigraphics, 1988.

CHAPTER 2

PLANNING A TRIP TO TAMPA & ST. PETERSBURG

1. INFORMATION
2. WHEN TO GO
- TAMPA & ST. PETERSBURG CALENDAR OF EVENTS
3. WHAT TO PACK
4. TIPS FOR SPECIAL TRAVELERS
5. GETTING THERE
- FROMMER'S SMART TRAVELER: AIRFARES

This chapter is devoted to the where, when, and how of your trip—the advance-planning issues required to get it together and take it on the road. This chapter will also resolve such other important questions, as when to go and where to obtain more information about the destination.

To get the most for your money, consider traveling to the St. Petersburg/Tampa area in the off-season: the months of May and June, September through November, and, to a lesser extent, July and August.

1. INFORMATION

While you are planning your trip, you can obtain helpful brochures and information by contacting tourist offices in advance.

For the St. Petersburg Area

- St. Petersburg/Clearwater Area Convention & Visitors Bureau, St. Petersburg ThunderDome, 1 Stadium Dr., Suite A, St. Petersburg, FL 33705-1706 (tel. 813/892-7892, or toll free 800/951-1111 for an information guide, or toll free 800/354-6710 for advance hotel reservations; fax 813/582-7949).
- Canadian Office: 102 Bloor St. W., Suite 460, Toronto, ON M5S 1M8, Canada (tel. 416/927-1505; fax 416/927-7809).
- U.K. Office: 182/184 Addington Rd., 1st floor, Selsdon, Surrey CR2 8LB, England (tel. 081/651-4742; fax 081/651-5702).
- Central Europe Office: Alt-Erlenbach 25, 60437 Frankfurt am Main, Germany (tel. 06101/44052; fax 06101/4524).

For the Tampa Area

- Tampa/Hillsborough Convention and Visitors Association, 111 Madison St., Suite 1010, Tampa, FL 33602-4706 (tel. 813/223-2752, or toll free 800/44-TAMPA; fax 813/229-6616).

2. WHEN TO GO

THE CLIMATE

The Tampa/St. Petersburg area has a warm and wonderful tropical climate year round, just perfect for vacationing. St. Petersburg boasts an average of 361 days of sunshine each year, with an average temperature of 73.6°F, while Tampa's average temperature is 72.2°F. The annual average water temperature along the beaches is 75°F.

There can be extremes, with high humidity and heavy thunderstorms, particularly during the summer months. In January and early February, temperatures can dip to freezing levels at night, but this rarely happens more than once every few years.

Average Tampa Temperatures & Rainfall

	Jan	Feb	Mar	Apr	May	June	July	Aug	Sept	Oct	Nov	Dec
Avg. High (°F)	70	71.0	76.0	82.0	87.0	90.0	90.0	90.0	89.0	84.0	77.0	72.0
Avg. Low (°F)	50.0	50.0	56.0	61.0	67.0	72.0	74.0	74.0	73.0	65.0	56.0	51.0
Avg. Rain (in.)	2.2	3.0	3.5	1.8	3.4	5.3	7.3	7.6	6.2	2.3	1.8	2.1

Average St. Petersburg Temperatures & Rainfall

	Jan	Feb	Mar	Apr	May	June	July	Aug	Sept	Oct	Nov	Dec
Avg. High (°F)	70.0	71.0	76.2	81.9	87.1	89.5	90.0	90.3	88.9	83.7	76.9	71.6
Avg. Low (°F)	49.5	50.4	56.1	61.1	67.2	72.3	74.2	74.2	72.8	65.1	56.4	50.9
Avg. Rain (in.)	2.2	2.8	2.1	2.3	3.1	6.9	7.7	8.0	6.6	2.6	1.6	2.1

TAMPA & ST. PETERSBURG CALENDAR OF EVENTS

JANUARY

☐ **Hall of Fame Bowl,** Tampa. Two of the nation's top college teams meet at Tampa Stadium in this highly rated annual bowl game. Jan 1.

☐ **Feast of the Epiphany,** Tarpon Springs. Day-long celebration of Greek Orthodox traditions that includes a dive for the cross, releasing a white dove of peace, ethnic foods, music, and dancing in this Greek enclave 35 miles north of St. Petersburg. Jan 6.

○ *TREASURES OF THE CZARS* *Heralding the debut of St. Petersburg's new Florida International Museum, this special exhibit will bring one of the largest collections of royal family treasures ever to leave Russia to the U.S.*

Where: Florida International Museum, downtown St. Petersburg. When: Jan 11–July 11, 1995. How: Tickets, tentatively priced at $11 for adults and $3 for students, will be available by advance application only, for specifically assigned time and date. Contact the Florida International Museum, 101 Third St. N., St. Petersburg, FL 33701 (tel. 813/824-6734).

FEBRUARY

☐ **GTE Suncoast Classic,** Tampa. The greatest players on the Senior PGA tour tee off in this $500,000 tournament at the Cheval Golf and Country Club. First or second week in Feb.

○ *GASPARILLA PIRATE INVASION, PARADE & FESTIVAL* *In a spirit akin to Mardi Gras, Tampa's leading business executives don the garb of legendary buccaneer José Gaspar and his band of pirates, and sail into the harbor on a triple-masted galleon. This signals the start of a month-long program of parades, concerts, fiestas, races, and art festivals.*

Where: Tampa Convention Center, Bayshore Boulevard, and downtown Tampa. When: Early Feb. How: For complete details, contact Tampa/Hillsborough Convention and Visitors Association, 111 Madison St., Suite 1010, Tampa, FL 33602 (tel. 813/223-1111, or toll free 800/44-TAMPA).

○ *FLORIDA STATE FAIR* *Just about anything that grows in Florida—from blue-ribbon livestock to fine foods and wines—is on display at this gathering, along with craft demonstrations, circus acts, carnival rides, horse shows, rodeos, alligator wrestling, and entertainment by top stars of country-and-western music.*

Where: Florida State Fairgrounds, 4800 U.S. 301, Tampa. When: Second week of Feb. How: Tickets available at the gate: $6 for adults, $3 for children 6 to 11. Contact the Florida State Fair Authority, P.O. Box 11766, Tampa, FL 33680 (tel. 813/621-7821).

○ *ST. PETERSBURG GRAND PRIX* *The streets of downtown St. Petersburg surrounding the ThunderDome*

are transformed into a 1.75-mile high-speed course for this annual Sports Car Club of America event, attracting top international drivers.
    Where: *Downtown St. Petersburg.* ***When:*** *Last weekend of Feb or first weekend of Mar.* ***How:*** *For advance program and other information, contact the St. Petersburg Area Chamber of Commerce, 100 Second Ave. N., St. Petersburg, FL 33731 (tel. 813/821-4069).*

MARCH

☐ **St. Petersburg International Folk Fair (SPIFFS),** St. Petersburg. A three-day festival, held since 1975, featuring the cultural customs of more than 40 countries. Second weekend in Mar.

✪ *FLORIDA STRAWBERRY FESTIVAL & PARADE*
This is not only a feast of luscious berries (on shortcake, in milk shakes, etc.), but also an array of rides, amusements, and top-name country music entertainment. It's held 25 miles east of Tampa at Plant City, known as the "winter strawberry capital of the world."
    Where: *Florida Strawberry Festival Fairgrounds, Fla. 574, off Exit 10 or 11 of I-4, Plant City.* ***When:*** *First 11 days of Mar.* ***How:*** *Tickets at the gate: $5 for adults, free for children under 10 if accompanied by an adult. Contact the Florida Strawberry Festival, P.O. Drawer 1869, Plant City, FL 34289-1869 (tel. 813/752-9194).*

✪ *ST. PETERSBURG FESTIVAL OF THE STATES* St.
Pete plays host to award-winning high school bands from around the country, with more than 100 events, from parades and pageantry to a windsurfing competition, fishing tournament, regatta, air show, jazz fest, and antique-car rally.
    Where: *Downtown St. Petersburg.* ***When:*** *End of Mar and first week of Apr for 17 days.* ***How:*** *Most events are outdoors and free. Contact Suncoasters of St. Petersburg, P.O. Box 1731, St. Petersburg, FL 33731 (tel. 813/898-3654).*

☐ **Winter Equestrian Festival/American Invitational,** Tampa. Top riders and jumping horses of the world at the Florida State Fairgrounds. Last two weeks in Mar.
☐ **Spring Arts and Crafts Festival,** Tampa. Artists from around the country display jewelry, pottery, paintings, and more at Ybor Square. Last weekend in Mar.

APRIL

☐ **Mainsail Art Show,** St. Petersburg. Festival of sights, sounds, and images, with live theater, art shows, antique-auto shows, and outdoor concerts. Last week in Apr or early May.

- **Fun 'n' Sun Festival,** Clearwater. Includes a band competition, parades, boat regatta, and sportsfest; a tradition since 1953. Last two weeks in Apr.
- **St. Anthony's Tampa Bay Triathlon,** St. Petersburg. Florida's largest swim-bike-run meet. Last weekend in Apr.

MAY

- **American Stage in the Park,** St. Petersburg. Live productions of Shakespearean plays are performed outdoors at Demens Landing on the waterfront. Throughout May.
- **Seminole Bluegrass Folk and Arts Festival,** Seminole. A day of continuous bluegrass and folk music at the Seminole City Park, north of downtown St. Petersburg. Mid-May.

JUNE

- **Kid's Week,** Clearwater Beach. A week-long series of special events designed exclusively for kids including plays, magic shows, arts and crafts, beach activities, fishing tournament, marine and environmental programs, variety shows, and dances. Third week of June.

JULY

- **Pirate Days and Invasion,** Treasure Island. A celebration of the island's colorful history, in conjunction with Independence Day weekend. First week in July.
- **Summer Arts and Crafts Festival,** Tampa. Artists from around the country display jewelry, pottery, paintings, and more at Ybor Square. One weekend in mid-July.

SEPTEMBER

- **International Festival,** Tampa. A medley of crafts, music, and foods from many lands, along the downtown riverwalk. Last weekend in Sept.

OCTOBER

- **Fall Arts and Crafts Festival,** Tampa. Artists from around the country display jewelry, pottery, paintings, and more at Ybor Square. First weekend in Oct.

✪ *GUAVAWEEN Based on Tampa's nickname of "The Big Guava," this is a Latin-style celebration of Halloween. A parade of costumed revelers led by "Mama Guava" is followed by a giant street party with ethnic foods and live music—from rock to reggae—on six stages. The event attracts 200,000 people.*

Where: Ybor City. When: Last Sat of Oct. How: Tickets: $2 donation is encouraged. For more information, *contact the Ybor City Chamber of Commerce, 1800 E. Ninth Ave., Tampa, FL 33605 (tel. 813/248-3712).*

✪ ***JOHN'S PASS SEAFOOD FESTIVAL*** *One of the most popular seafood festivals on Florida's west coast. Music, arts and crafts, and enormous quantities of fresh fish are the star attractions at this rustic waterfront village west of St. Petersburg.*
    Where: *John's Pass Village and boardwalk, Madeira Beach.* ***When:*** *Last weekend of Oct.* ***How:*** *Most events are free. Contact Gulf Beaches Chamber of Commerce, 501 150th Ave., Madeira Beach, FL 33108 (tel. 813/391-7373).*

☐ **Clearwater Jazz Holiday,** Clearwater. A four-day extravaganza featuring some of the nation's top jazz musicians. Mid-Oct.

NOVEMBER

☐ **Kahlua Cup International Yacht Races,** Clearwater. Annual event that draws craft from around the world. Second weekend in Nov.
☐ **Florida Classic Football Game,** Tampa. Bethune-Cookman College vs. Florida A&M—one of the longest-running college football rivalries, which fills Tampa Stadium. Last Sat in Nov.
☐ **Ybor Arts Open House Gallery Walk,** Tampa. Streets of Ybor City are lined with candles as local artists open their studios and galleries to the public. Last Sat in Nov.
☐ **Snowfest and Holiday Fantasy,** St. Petersburg. A month-long tradition of beautiful decorations, choirs of carolers, holiday entertainment, a major Christmas parade, and other special events. Last week of Nov and all of Dec.

DECEMBER

☐ **Christmas Boat-a-Cade,** Madeira Beach. A holiday highlight for more than 25 years, with lighted and decorated boats parading at night in Boca Ciega Bay. Last weekend before Dec 25.
☐ **The Holidays in Tampa.** Celebrations and seasonal activities ranging from *Nutcracker* ballet performances and concerts to festivals of trees and lights, Victorian Christmas strolls, a jingle-bell fun run, and an arts-and-crafts show. Throughout Dec.

3. WHAT TO PACK

The Tampa–St. Petersburg lifestyle is informal and relaxed and so is the dress. Casual and comfortable clothing is acceptable almost everywhere.
    For men, ties and jackets are usually not required, but it's wise to

pack at least one of each if you plan to patronize some of the finer restaurants or cultural events. For women, a couple of dressy outfits might also come in handy for special outings, but on the whole, slacks and shorts are recommended. Be sure to bring along a light linen jacket, blazer, or sweater for the ubiquitous air-conditioning. If you are traveling in the summer months, when the probability of a quick thunder shower is high, pack a collapsible umbrella or a light raincoat or shell.

With sunshine guaranteed just about every day of the year, this area is a natural for outdoor sports, so be sure to bring along whatever gear you enjoy using, from running shoes to golf clubs and tennis rackets. Take several pairs of comfortable shoes or sneakers for walking along the beaches or bayfronts. If you'll be fishing or boating, a light windbreaker always comes in handy. And, above all, don't forget your bathing suit, suntan lotion, and sunglasses.

4. TIPS FOR SPECIAL TRAVELERS

FOR THE DISABLED Two local companies in the Tampa/St. Petersburg area specializing in services for disabled travelers are **Wheelchair Transport Services** (tel. 813/586-2111), and **Wheelchair Getaways** (tel. toll free 800/348-9424).

FOR SENIORS There are many services for retirees in the St. Pete area including **AARP** (American Association of Retired Persons), at 330 Fifth St. N., St. Petersburg (tel. 892-5420), and the **St. Petersburg Office on Aging,** Sunshine Center, 330 Fifth St. N., St. Petersburg (tel. 893-7101).

In Tampa, the office of **Better Living for Seniors,** is at 419 Pierce St. (tel. 684-6434); in Ybor City the location is 2015 N. 15th St., 2nd floor (tel. 272-5250).

FOR WOMEN In St. Petersburg, the **Rape Crisis Hotline** is 344-5555. In Tampa, organizations helping women include the Tampa chapter of **NOW** (National Organization for Women; tel. 961-8507).

FOR GAYS & LESBIANS The Pinellas County Gay Hotline can be reached by calling 586-4297, or by writing to The Line, P.O. Box 14323, St. Petersburg, FL 33733. *Womyn's Words,* a monthly publication for lesbians and feminists is produced by the Womyn's Energy Bank Collective of St. Petersburg; *Visions* is a newsletter published by the Metropolitan Community of Churches in Pinellas County.

Gay and lesbian publications in the Tampa area include *A Friendly Voice,* a weekly bar and social guide, *The Gazette,* a monthly magazine, and *Reach Out,* a newsletter published by the Metropolitan Council of Churches in Hillsborough County.

5. GETTING THERE

BY PLANE

AIRLINES   One of the most accessible destinations in the U.S., the Tampa/St. Petersburg area is served by more than two dozen major scheduled airlines with nonstop or single-plane service from over 65 cities. Both scheduled and charter services also operate from major gateways in Canada and Europe.

Airlines flying into Tampa International Airport include: Air Canada (tel. toll free 800/776-3000), American (tel. toll free 800/433-7300), America West (tel. toll free 800/247-5692), Cayman Airways (tel. toll free 800/422-9626), Canadian Airlines International (tel. toll free 800/426-7000), Continental (tel. toll free 800/525-0280), Delta (tel. toll free 800/221-1212), Midwest Express (tel. toll free 800/452-2022), Northwest (tel. toll free 800/441-1818), Trans World (tel. toll free 800/438-2929), United (tel. toll free 800/241-6522), and USAir (tel. toll free 800/428-4322).

The following are among the charter carriers flying into Tampa International from domestic and foreign gateways: American Trans Air, Condor, Martinair Holland, and Odyssey International.

In addition, scheduled and charter services operate into St. Petersburg–Clearwater International Airport. Carriers providing

---

**ⓕ FROMMER'S SMART TRAVELER:
AIRFARES**

VALUE-CONSCIOUS TRAVELERS SHOULD
TAKE ADVANTAGE OF THE FOLLOWING:

1. Shop all the airlines that fly to Tampa International Airport and check if any charters go from your area into St. Petersburg–Clearwater International Airport.
2. Always ask for the lowest-priced fare, not just for a promotional fare.
3. Keep calling the airline of your choice—availability of reduced-priced seats changes daily. Airlines would rather sell a seat at a low price than have it fly empty. As the departure date nears, additional low-cost seats often become available.
4. Be flexible with your time and days of departure—getting the best price usually means flying midweek, and sometimes it requires departing at off-peak hours.
5. Avoid holidays and other high-traffic periods, such as Thanksgiving, Christmas, and Easter. Fares are at their highest during these times, and discount fares are often subject to "blackout" restrictions.

scheduled services include American Trans Air and Eagle Airlines. Check with a travel agent for information about charter flights.

TYPICAL FARES   Because the St. Petersburg/Tampa area is one of the most popular destinations in the southeastern U.S., the airlines offer a wide choice of flights and have many seats to fill. For this reason, promotional fares are usually plentiful, particularly in the off-season when carriers seek to stimulate traffic. Generally speaking, except for holiday periods, fares are at their lowest from May through early December.

Of all the carriers with a heavy presence in the Tampa/St. Petersburg market, Continental usually sets the trend by offering slashed-rate fares in the slack seasons, and invariably the other airlines match them. From the Northeast, fares go as low as $99 one way, based on a round-trip purchase; from the Midwest, $139; and from the West Coast, $159. Of course, these fares are highly restricted, subject to change without notice, and must be purchased in advance, but if you're looking for a bargain, you can usually find one, unless you want to travel at Thanksgiving, Christmas, or from mid-February to mid-April.

If you are not lucky enough to qualify for a promotional fare, then it can cost you at least $400 to $500 to fly round-trip between Tampa/St. Petersburg and most Northeast and Midwest destinations, or as high as $500 to $1,000 from most western cities. Two good rules to remember: Plan in advance and shop around.

For more information, consult a travel agent or contact the airlines directly, by using toll-free numbers.

BY TRAIN

Amtrak offers daily service between East Coast cities and Tampa (with a bus connection to St. Petersburg) via its *Silver Star* and *Silver Meteor* trains. From New York, the trip takes approximately 26 hours, with intermediate stops at Philadelphia, Washington, D.C., Savannah, Jacksonville, and other East Coast points. From the Midwest, you can transfer to these trains at Philadelphia or Washington, and from the West Coast you can connect in Jacksonville from the weekly *Sunset Limited* (Los Angeles/Miami service).

Individual ticket prices vary, but by using Amtrak's "All Aboard America" fares, you'll pay one flat fee for round-trip travel within one region or among the three regions of the United States. For example, you can travel between Florida and any East Coast city for between $179 and $199, from the Midwest to the eastern corridor for $229 to $279, or from the West Coast to the East for $259 to $339. These fares allow you to make up to three stops, if you wish. The lowest rates are available in the winter and spring, with a validity period of up to 180 days. If you are from Europe and plan to do a lot of traveling beyond Tampa/St. Petersburg, inquire from your travel agent about a USA Rail Pass, available only to overseas visitors.

If you prefer to bring your own car, reserve space on Amtrak's Auto Train, operating daily between Lorton, Virginia, about one hour south of Washington, D.C., and Sanford, Florida, an hour northeast of Orlando. You'll travel in comfort and style while your car (with baggage safely stored inside) is professionally handled and secured in enclosed car carriers. Your ticket also provides you with a seat for the overnight journey, and complimentary buffet dinner and breakfast. Depending on the date of travel, one-way fares range from $49 to $155 for adults, $24.50 to $77.50 for children aged 2 to 15, $115 to $175 for your car and $150 to $210 for your van.

For more information on all Amtrak services and rates, call toll free 800/872-7245 (800/USA-RAIL) or write Amtrak Distribution Center, P.O. Box 7717, Itasca, IL 60143.

BY BUS

Greyhound Trailways operates bus service from many U.S. cities to both Tampa and St. Petersburg. Fares vary according to point of origin (from New York the regular fare is $109 one way, $207 round-trip).

The best deals can be obtained by making an advance purchase: save 15% by buying 3 days in advance, save 25% by buying 7 days in advance, save 35% by buying 14 days in advance, or save 50% by buying 21 days in advance. Check with your local Greyhound office for the latest details and prices.

BY CAR

Situated in the heart of central Florida's west coast, the Tampa/St. Petersburg area can easily be reached by car. In the winter season, you'll see thousands of license plates bearing the imprints of many U.S. states and Canadian provinces.

The main arteries leading to the Tampa Bay area are I-75, I-275, I-4, U.S. 19, U.S. 19A, U.S. 41, U.S. 92, U.S. 301, and Fla. 60.

To help you plan, here are some approximate driving distances from selected cities (in miles):

Atlanta	470	Montréal	1,520
Boston	1,390	New Orleans	635
Chicago	1,230	New York City	1,150
Cleveland	1,120	Orlando	85
Detroit	1,230	Pittsburgh	1,040
Miami	275	Toronto	1,480

BY BOAT

Rimmed by the waters of the Gulf of Mexico and Tampa Bay, the Tampa/St. Petersburg region is a popular port of call for boaters. If you decide to navigate your own craft to this area, there are many marinas catering to visiting boaters. However, be forewarned that some marinas have waiting lists and limits on the length of stay, so be sure to make arrangements to dock in advance. Among the marinas that welcome short-term or out-of-state visitors are:

- St. Petersburg Municipal Marina, 300 Second Ave. SE, St. Petersburg (tel. 813/893-7329).
- Harborage at Bayboro, 1110 Third St. S., St. Petersburg (tel. 813/821-6347).

- Maximo Moorings, 4801 37th St. S., St. Petersburg (tel. 813/867-1102).
- Harbour Island Marina, The Waterwalk, Harbour Island, Tampa (tel. 813/229-5324).

FOR THE FOREIGN TRAVELER

Although American fads and fashions have spread across Europe and other parts of the world so that America may seem like familiar territory before your arrival, there are still many peculiarities and uniquely American situations that any foreign visitor will encounter. This chapter is meant to clue you in on what they are.

1. PREPARING FOR YOUR TRIP

NECESSARY DOCUMENTS Canadian nationals need only proof of Canadian residence to visit the United States. Citizens of Great Britain and Japan need only a current passport. Citizens of other countries, including Australia and New Zealand, usually need two documents: a valid **passport** with an expiration date at least six months later than the scheduled end of their visit to the United States and a **tourist visa** available at no charge from a U.S. embassy or consulate.

To get a tourist or business visa to enter the United States, contact the nearest American embassy or consulate in your country; if there is none, you will have to apply in person in a country where there *is* a U.S. embassy or consulate. Present your passport, a passport-size photo of yourself, and a completed application, which is available through the embassy or consulate.

You may be asked to provide information about how you plan to finance your trip or show a letter of invitation from a friend with whom you plan to stay. Those applying for a business visa may be asked to show evidence that they will not receive a salary in the United States.

Be sure to check the length of stay on your visa; usually it is six months. If you want to stay longer, you may file for an extension with the Immigration and Naturalization Service once you are in the country. If permission to stay is granted, a new visa is not required unless you leave the United States and want to reenter.

MEDICAL REQUIREMENTS No inoculations are needed to enter the U.S. unless you are coming from, or have stopped over in, areas known to be suffering from epidemics, especially of cholera or yellow fever. Applicants for immigrants' visas (and only they) must undergo a screening test for AIDS under a law passed in 1987.

If you have a disease requiring treatment with medications containing narcotics or drugs, carry a valid, signed prescription from your physician to allay any suspicions that you are smuggling drugs. Ditto for syringes.

TRAVEL INSURANCE All such insurance is voluntary in the U.S.; however, given the very high cost of medical care, we cannot too strongly advise every traveler to arrange for appropriate coverage before setting out. There are specialized insurance companies that will, for a relatively low premium, cover loss or theft of your baggage, trip-cancellation costs, guarantee of bail in case you are sued, sickness or injury costs (medical, surgical, and hospital), and costs of an accident, repatriation, or death. Such packages (for example, "Europe Assistance" in Europe) are sold by automobile clubs at attractive rates, as well as by insurance companies and travel agencies.

2. GETTING TO THE U.S.

Travelers from overseas can take advantage of the **APEX (Advance Purchase Excursion) fares** offered by all the major U.S. and European carriers. Aside from these, attractive values are offered by **Icelandair** on flights from Luxembourg to New York or Orlando; and by **Virgin Atlantic** from London to New York/Newark or Miami.

Some large airlines (for example, TWA, American Airlines, Northwest, United, and Delta) offer travelers on their transatlantic or transpacific flights special discount tickets under the name **Visit USA,** allowing travel between any U.S. destinations at minimum rates. They are not on sale in the U.S., and must therefore be purchased before you leave your foreign point of departure. This system is the best way of seeing the U.S. at low cost. You should obtain information well in advance from your travel agent or the office of the airline concerned, since the conditions attached to these discount tickets can be changed without advance notice.

For further information about travel to and around Tampa/St. Petersburg, see "Getting There" in Chapter 2, and "Getting Around" in Chapters 4 and 8.

FAST FACTS **FOR THE FOREIGN TRAVELER**

Accommodations See Chapters 5 and 9.
Automobile Rentals See "Getting Around," in Chapters 4 and 8.
Business Hours See "Fast Facts," in Chapters 4 and 8.

Climate   See "When to Go," in Chapter 2.

Currency and Exchange   The U.S. monetary system has a decimal base: one dollar ($1) = 100 cents (100¢). The most common bills (all green) are the $1 ("a buck"), $5, $10, and $20 denominations. There are also $2 (seldom encountered), $50, and $100 bills (the two latter are not welcome when paying for small purchases). There are six denominations of coins: 1¢ (one cent, or "penny"); 5¢ (five cents, or "nickel"); 10¢ (ten cents, or "dime"); 25¢ (twenty-five cents, or "quarter"); 50¢ (fifty cents, or "half dollar"); and the rare—and prized by collectors—$1 piece (both the older, large silver dollars and the newer, small Susan B. Anthony coin).

If they are denominated in *dollars,* traveler's checks are accepted at most hotels, motels, restaurants, and large stores. But as any experienced traveler knows, the best place to change traveler's checks denominated in other currencies is at a bank, for which there will be a charge.

However, the method of payment most widely used is the credit card or charge card: VISA (BarclayCard in Britain), MasterCard (EuroCard in Europe, Access in Britain, Diamond in Japan), American Express, Diners Club, and Carte Blanche, in descending order of acceptance. You can save yourself trouble by using "plastic money," rather than cash or traveler's checks, in 95% of all hotels, motels, restaurants, and retail stores (except for those selling food or liquor). A credit card can serve as a deposit for renting a car, as proof of identity (often carrying more weight than a passport), or as a "cash card," enabling you to draw money from banks that accept them.

Note: The "foreign-exchange bureaus" so common in Europe are rare even at airports in the U.S., and nonexistent outside major cities. Try to avoid having to change foreign money, or traveler's checks denominated other than in U.S. dollars at a small-town bank, or even a branch bank in a big city; in fact, leave any currency other than U.S. dollars at home—it may prove more nuisance to you than it's worth. If you do bring foreign currency to Tampa/St. Petersburg, there is a currency-exchange desk at Tampa International Airport, on the Third Level, and most major banks exchange currency.

Customs and Immigration   Every adult visitor may bring in, free of duty: one liter of wine or hard liquor; 200 cigarettes or 100 cigars (but *no* cigars from Cuba) or three pounds of smoking tobacco; and $400 worth of gifts. These exemptions are offered to travelers who spend at least 72 hours in the U.S. and who have not claimed them within the preceding six months. It is altogether forbidden to bring into the country foodstuffs (particularly cheese, fruit, cooked meats, and canned goods) and plants (vegetables, seeds, tropical plants, etc.). Foreign tourists may bring in or take out up to $10,000 in U.S. or foreign currency with no formalities; larger sums must be declared to Customs on entering or leaving.

The visitor arriving by air, no matter what the port of entry—Tampa, New York, Boston, Miami, Honolulu, Los Angeles, or the rest—should cultivate patience and resignation before setting foot on U.S. soil. The U.S. Customs service is among the slowest and most suspicious on earth. On some days, especially summer weekends, you may wait two hours or more to have your passport stamped at major international airports. Add the time it takes to clear Customs and you will see that you should make very generous allowance for delay in planning connections between international and domestic flights— an average of two to three hours at least.

In contrast, for the traveler arriving by car or by rail from Canada, the border-crossing formalities have been streamlined to the vanishing point. And for the traveler by air from Canada, Bermuda, and some points in the Caribbean, you can sometimes go through Customs and Immigration at the point of *departure,* which is much quicker and less painful.

Electric Current U.S. wall outlets give power at 110–115 volts, 60 cycles, compared to 220 volts, 50 cycles, in most of Europe. Besides a 110-volt transformer (sometimes incorrectly called a converter), small appliances of non-American manufacture, such as hairdryers or shavers, will require a plug adapter with two flat, parallel pins.

Embassies and Consulates All embassies are located in the national capital, Washington, D.C.; some consulates are located in major cities, and most nations have a mission to the United Nations in New York City.

Listed here are the embassies and consulates of the major English-speaking countries—Australia, Canada, Ireland, New Zealand, and the United Kingdom. If you are from another country, you can get the telephone number of your embassy by calling "information" in Washington, D.C. (tel. 202/555-1212). There is no consular representation in the Tampa Bay area for Australia, Canada, Ireland, or New Zealand, but there is a British consulate in Miami (see below).

The embassy of Australia is at 1601 Massachusetts Ave. NW, Washington, DC 20036 (tel. 202/797-3000). The nearest Australian consulates are at 303 Peachtree St. NE, Atlanta, GA 30308 (tel. 404/880-1700); and in the International Bldg., 636 Fifth Ave., New York, NY 10111 (tel. 212/245-4000). Other Australian consulates are in Honolulu, Houston, Los Angeles, and San Francisco.

The embassy of Canada is at 501 Pennsylvania Ave. NW, Washington, DC 20001 (tel. 202/682-1740). The nearest Canadian consulates are: One CNN Center, Suite 400, South Tower, Atlanta, GA 30303 (tel. 404/577-6810); 2 Prudential Plaza, 180 N. Stetson Ave., Suite 2400, Chicago, IL 60601 (tel. 312/616-1860); Illuminating Building, 55 Public Sq., Cleveland, OH 44113 (tel. 216/771-0150); and 1251 Ave. of the Americas, New York, NY 10020 (tel. 212/768-2400). Other Canadian consulates are in Boston, Buffalo (N.Y.), Dallas, Detroit, Los Angeles, Minneapolis, and Seattle.

The embassy of Ireland is at 2234 Massachusetts Ave. NW, Washington, DC 20008 (tel. 202/462-3939). The nearest Irish consulates are: 535 Boylston St., Boston, MA 02116 (tel. 617/267-9330); 400 N. Michigan Ave., Chicago, IL 60611 (tel. 312/337-1868); and 345 Park Ave., New York, NY 10154 (tel. 212/319-2555). There's another Irish consulate in San Francisco.

The embassy of New Zealand is at 37 Observatory Circle NW, Washington, DC 20008 (tel. 202/328-4800). The only New Zealand consulate in the U.S. is in Los Angeles.

The embassy of the United Kingdom is at 3100 Massachusetts Ave. NW, Washington, DC 20008 (tel. 202/462-1340). The nearest

British consulate is at 1001 S. Bayshore Dr., Miami, FL 33131 (tel. 305/374-1522). The next nearest are at 245 Peachtree Center Ave., Suite 912, Atlanta, GA 30303 (tel. 404/524-5856); 33 N. Dearborn St., Chicago, IL 60602 (tel. 312/346-1810); and 845 Third Ave., New York, NY 10022 (tel. 212/745-0200). There are other British consulates in Houston and Los Angeles.

Emergencies In all major cities you can call the police, an ambulance, or the fire brigade through the single emergency telephone number 911. Another useful way of reporting an emergency is to call the telephone-company operator by dialing 0 (zero, *not* the letter "O"). Outside major cities, call the county sheriff or the fire brigade at the number you will find in the local telephone book.

If you encounter such travelers' problems as sickness, accident, or lost or stolen baggage, call Travelers Aid, an organization that specializes in helping distressed travelers, whether American or foreign. The office in the Tampa/St. Petersburg area can be reached by calling 813/273-5936.

Holidays On the following legal national holidays, banks, government offices, post offices, and many stores, restaurants, and museums are closed: January 1 (New Year's Day), third Monday in January (Martin Luther King Day), third Monday in February (Presidents' Day, Washington's Birthday), last Monday in May (Memorial Day), July 4 (Independence Day), first Monday in September (Labor Day), second Monday in October (Columbus Day), November 11 (Veterans Day/Armistice Day), last Thursday in November (Thanksgiving Day), and December 25 (Christmas Day).

The Tuesday following the first Monday in November is Election Day, and is a legal holiday in presidential-election years.

Information See "Information," in Chapter 2.

Legal Aid The foreign tourist, unless positively identified as a member of the Mafia or of a drug ring, will probably never become involved with the American legal system. If you are pulled up for a minor infraction (for example, exceeding the speed limit on a highway), never attempt to pay the fine directly to a police officer; you may wind up arrested on the much more serious charge of attempted bribery. Pay fines by mail, or directly into the hands of the clerk of the court. If accused of a more serious offense, it is wise to say and do nothing before consulting a lawyer. Under U.S. law, an arrested person is allowed one telephone call to a party of his choice. Call your embassy or consulate.

Liquor Laws See "Fast Facts: St. Petersburg," in Chapter 4.

Mail If you want your mail to follow you on your vacation, you need only fill out a change-of-address card at any post office. The post office will also hold your mail for up to one month. If you aren't sure of your address, your mail can be sent to you, in your name, "c/o General Delivery" at the main post office of the city or region where you expect to be. The addressee must pick it up in person, and produce proof of identity (driver's license, credit card, passport, etc.).

Postal rates in the United States, at this writing, are 19¢ for postcards, 29¢ for letters up to 1 ounce. Rates to foreign countries vary; again at this writing, 40¢ for letters to Canada, 40¢ for postcards and 50¢ per half-ounce for letters to most (but not all) other countries. Consult a post office for verification.

Generally to be found at intersections, mailboxes are blue with a red-and-white logo, and carry the inscription U.S. MAIL. If your mail is addressed to a U.S. destination, don't forget to add the five-figure ZIP Code, after the two-letter abbreviation of the state to which the mail is addressed (FL for Florida).

Measurements and Sizes   While most of the rest of the world is on the metric system, for nonscientific purposes the United States still adheres to its own units of measurement. For tables to help you with conversions of standard measurements, see the Appendix.

Medical Emergencies   See "Emergencies," above.

Newspapers and Magazines   See "Fast Facts," in Chapters 4 and 8.

Post   See "Mail," above.

Radio and TV   There are 6,500 radio stations in the U.S.; small communities have access to about half a dozen, each broadcasting talk shows or a particular kind of music—classical, country, jazz, pop, gospel—punctuated by news broadcasts and frequent commercials.

Television plays a major part in American life. The three coast-to-coast networks—ABC, CBS, and NBC—were joined in recent years by the Public Broadcasting System (PBS), the Fox network, and the cable network CNN. There are 1,200 local stations throughout the country. In the big cities, viewers have a choice of about a dozen channels, many of them transmitting 24 hours a day. In small towns the choice may be limited to four TV channels. Numerous cable stations (which cost extra) broadcast everything from wrestling to the latest movies. For radio and TV stations in Tampa/St. Petersburg, see "Fast Facts," Chapters 4 and 8.

Safety   In general, the U.S. is safer than most other countries, particularly in rural areas, but there are "danger zones" in the big cities which should be approached only with extreme caution.

As a general rule, isolated areas such as gardens and parking lots should be avoided after dark. Elevators and public-transport systems in off-hours, particularly between 10pm and 6am, are also potential crime scenes. You should drive through decaying neighborhoods with your car doors locked and the windows closed. Never carry on your person valuables like jewelry or large sums of cash; traveler's checks are much safer.

Taxes   In the U.S. there is no VAT (Value-Added Tax), or other indirect tax at a national level. Every state, and each city in it, is allowed to levy its own local tax on all purchases, including hotel and restaurant checks, airline tickets, etc. It is automatically added to the price of certain services such as public transportation, cab fares, phone calls, and gasoline. It varies from 4% to 10% depending on the state and city, so when you are making major purchases such as photographic equipment, clothing, or high-fidelity components, it can be a significant part of the cost.

The sales tax rate is 7% for St. Petersburg and 6.5% for Tampa.

Telephone, Telegraph, and Telex   Pay phones are an integral part of the American landscape. You will find them everywhere: at street corners, in bars, restaurants, public buildings, stores, service stations, along highways, etc. Outside the metropolitan areas, public telephones are more difficult to find. Stores and gas stations are your best bet. In the Tampa/St. Petersburg area, local calls cost 25¢.

For long-distance or international calls, stock up with a supply of quarters; the pay phone will instruct you when, and in what quantity, you should put them into the slot. For direct overseas calls, first dial 011, followed by the country code (Australia, 61; Republic of Ireland, 353; New Zealand, 64; United Kingdom, 44; and so on), and then by the city code (for example, 71 or 81 for London, 21 for Birmingham) and the number of the person you wish to call. For long-distance calls in Canada and the U.S., dial 1 followed by the area code and number you want.

Before calling from a hotel room, always ask the hotel phone operator if there are any telephone surcharges. These are best avoided by using a public phone, calling collect, or using a telephone charge card.

For reversed-charge or collect calls, and for person-to-person calls, dial 0 (zero, *not* the letter "O") followed by the area code and number you want; an operator will then come on the line, and you should specify that you are calling collect, or person-to-person, or both. If your operator-assisted call is international, ask for the overseas operator.

For local directory assistance ("information"), dial 411; for long-distance information dial 1, then the appropriate area code and 555-1212.

Like the telephone system, telegraph and telex services are provided by private corporations like ITT, MCI, and above all, Western Union. You can bring your telegram in to the nearest Western Union office (there are hundreds across the country), or dictate it over the phone (a toll-free call, 800/325-6000). You can also telegraph money, or have it telegraphed to you, very quickly over the Western Union system.

Telephone Directory   See "Yellow Pages," below.

Time   The U.S. is divided into six time zones. From east to west, these are: eastern standard time (EST), central standard time (CST), mountain standard time (MST), Pacific standard time (PST), Alaska standard time (AST), and Hawaii standard time (HST). Always keep changing time zones in mind if you are traveling (or even telephoning) long distances in the U.S. For example, noon in New York City (EST) is 11am in Chicago (CST), 10am in Denver (MST), 9am in Los Angeles (PST), 8am in Anchorage (AST), and 7am in Honolulu (HST). Tampa/St. Petersburg is in the *eastern* time zone.

Daylight saving time is in effect from 1am on the first Sunday in April until 2am on the last Sunday in October (except in Arizona, Hawaii, part of Indiana, and Puerto Rico).

Tipping   See "Fast Facts: St. Petersburg," in Chapter 4.

Toilets   Foreign visitors often complain that public toilets are hard to find in most U.S. cities. True, there are none on the streets, but the visitor can usually find one in a bar, restaurant, hotel, museum, department store, or service station—and it will probably be clean (although the last-mentioned sometimes leaves much to be desired). Note, however, a growing practice in some restaurants and bars of displaying a notice that "toilets are for the use of patrons only." You can ignore this sign, or better yet, avoid arguments by paying for a cup of coffee or soft drink, which will qualify you as a patron. The cleanliness of toilets at railroad stations and bus depots may be more open to question, and some public places are equipped with pay toilets, which require you to insert one or two 10¢ coins (dimes) into a slot on the door before it will open.

Yellow Pages   There are two kinds of telephone directory available to you. The general directory is the "white pages," in which private and business subscribers are listed in alphabetical order. The inside front cover lists emergency numbers for police, fire, and ambulance, and other vital numbers (like the Coast Guard, poison control center, crime-victims hotline, etc.). The first few pages are devoted to community-service numbers, including a guide to long-distance and international calling, complete with country codes and area codes.

The second directory, the yellow pages, lists all local services, businesses, and industries by type, with an index at the back. The listings cover not only such obvious items as automobile repairs by make of car, or drugstores (pharmacies), often by geographical location, but also restaurants by type of cuisine and geographical location, bookstores by special subject and/or language, places of worship by religious denomination, and other information that the tourist might otherwise not readily find. The yellow pages also include city plans or detailed area maps, often showing postal ZIP Codes and public transportation routes.

GETTING TO KNOW ST. PETERSBURG

Sitting on a sheltered curve of land between Tampa Bay and the Gulf of Mexico, St. Petersburg blends the businesslike pulse of a city with the relaxed rhythm of a resort. Sleek new office towers rise beside historic Spanish-style landmarks, wide and busy thoroughfares edge shady palm-tree-lined parks, and huge building cranes hover over the skyline as sailboats breeze by. Even the layout is diverse—the compact downtown business district hugs the bayfront, surrounded by huge residential areas reaching toward the beaches. Houses range from hacienda-style villas to contemporary sun-roofed cottages, clusters of condominiums, or endless rows of mobile homes.

St. Pete, as it is fondly known, is home to over 250,000 people, with more new residents settling in every day. Long favored by senior citizens because of its idyllic climate, it is now a mecca for people of all ages who seek economic opportunity and the good life under fair skies.

1. ORIENTATION

ARRIVING

BY PLANE

AIRPORTS The **Tampa International Airport,** off Memorial Highway and Fla. 60, Tampa (tel. 813/870-8700), approximately 16 miles northeast of downtown St. Petersburg, is the gateway for all scheduled domestic and international flights. Currently handling more than 10 million passengers a year, it has been voted the best airport in the U.S. in various passenger polls. Services include a small shopping mall, six restaurants, three lounges, an art gallery, duty-free shops, and a complete international arrivals/Customs facility. The 71 landing gates (Airside) are connected to the main terminal (Landside) and baggage-claim areas via high-speed "people movers" that shuttle passengers in 40 seconds.

✔️ WHAT'S SPECIAL ABOUT ST. PETERSBURG

Beaches
☐ Pass-A-Grille, for its panoramic vistas and quiet off-
the-main-road location.
☐ Treasure Island, for its wide,
sandy shore.

Natural Spectacles
☐ Sunsets from Fort DeSoto
Park with views of both
Tampa Bay and the Gulf of
Mexico.
☐ Watching pelicans take flight
after a recuperative stay at
the Suncoast Seabird Sanc-
tuary, the largest wild-bird
hospital in the U.S.

Parks and Gardens
☐ Sand Key Park, with vistas
of the Gulf of Mexico and
Clearwater Pass.
☐ DeSoto Park, five islands off
the coast with bird, plant,
and animal sanctuaries.

Architectural Highlights/Buildings
☐ The ThunderDome, a slant-
roofed stadium that is the
first cable-supported dome
of its kind in the U.S. and
one of the largest of its type
in the world.
☐ The Belleview Mido, the
world's largest occupied
wooden structure.

Museums
☐ Salvador Dalí Museum,
housing the world's largest
collection of works by the
surrealist Spanish artist.

Events/Festivals
☐ Festival of the States, a winter celebration with 17 days
of parades, pageantry, and
outdoor fun.
☐ John's Pass Seafood Festival. Tons of the "local catch"
dominate this fun-filled
weekend at one of the St.
Pete area's top fishing
spots.

For the Kids
☐ Boyd Hill Nature Park, for
an up-close view of sea
birds, reptiles, and other na-
tive species.
☐ Adventure at sea aboard
Captain Memo's Pirate
Cruise Ship.

Activities
☐ Swimming, sunning, shelling,
or shore-walking along St.
Petersburg's strip of sandy
white beaches.
☐ Sailing aboard a ketch,
sloop, yacht, or windjammer
from St. Pete Beach or
Clearwater Harbor.

Shopping
☐ The Gas Plant Antique Arcade, showcase for 100 area
dealers.
☐ Evander Preston Contemporary Jewelry, for one-of-a-
kind hand-hammered gold
pieces.
☐ Wagon Wheel Flea Market,
the area's largest open-air
market.

St. Petersburg–Clearwater International Airport, on
Roosevelt Boulevard (Fla. 686), Clearwater (tel. 813/535-7600),
approximately 10 miles north of St. Petersburg, is primarily a charter
facility, serving over 500,000 domestic and international passengers

annually. It has a new international arrivals facility for Customs, Immigration, and agriculture inspections.

Albert Whitted Municipal Airport, 108 Eighth Ave. S., St. Petersburg (tel. 813/893-7654), located downtown on the bayfront, serves as a landing strip for private planes.

GETTING TO/FROM THE AIRPORTS The Limo Inc., 11901 30th Court N., St. Petersburg (tel. 813/572-1111, or toll-free 800/282-6817), offers 24-hour door-to-door service between Tampa International Airport or St. Petersburg–Clearwater airport and any destination (hotel, condo, private home, mobile-home park, or otherwise) via a fleet of air-conditioned vans. No reservations are required on arrival; just proceed to any Limo desk outside of each baggage-claim area. Departures to most destinations are every 20 minutes or less. For a return trip to the airport, reservations for pickup should be made at least six hours prior to flight departure and preferably a day in advance. Flat-rate fare one-way is $12 per person from Tampa International Airport or $10 from St. Petersburg–Clearwater airport, to any St. Pete or gulf beach destination.

Red Line Limo Inc. (tel. 813/535-3391), also provides daily 24-hour van service from Tampa International Airport or St. Petersburg–Clearwater airport to St. Petersburg or any other destination in Pinellas County. The cost is only $10.75 per person from Tampa International Airport and $9 from St. Petersburg–Clearwater airport, but reservations are required 24 hours in advance. There are no arrivals desks at the airports; passengers are met according to prebooked reservations. If you have not made a reservation, then you must call from a pay phone in the arrivals hall to check if pickup arrangements can be made.

Yellow Cab Taxis (tel. 813/821-7777) line up outside the baggage-claim areas; no reservations are required. Average fare from Tampa International Airport to St. Petersburg or any of the gulf beaches is approximately $25 to $35 per taxi (one or more passengers). Travel time is a half hour to 45 minutes, depending on exact destination and traffic. The fare from St. Petersburg–Clearwater airport is approximately $15 to $20, depending on the final destination; travel time can be 15 minutes to a half hour.

BY TRAIN

Amtrak trains from points north terminate at the **Tampa Amtrak Station,** 601 Nebraska Ave. N., Tampa (tel. 813/221-7600). However, if your destination is St. Petersburg, shuttle-bus service meets all trains and transfers passengers to the St. Petersburg Amtrak Station, 33rd Street North and 37 Avenue North, St. Petersburg, (tel. 813/522-9475) or Clearwater Amtrak Station, 657 Court St. (tel. 441-1793).

BY BUS

Greyhound/Trailways buses from destinations around the United States arrive at the carrier's downtown depot at 180 Ninth St. N., St. Petersburg (tel. toll free 800/231-2222).

BY CAR

The St. Petersburg area, is linked to the Interstate system and is accessible from I-75, I-275, I-4, U.S. 19, and Fla. 60.

TOURIST INFORMATION

Once you have arrived, you'll find many local visitor information offices, such as the following:

- **St. Petersburg Area Chamber of Commerce,** 100 Second Ave. N., St. Petersburg, FL 33701 (tel. 813/821-4069), open Monday through Friday from 9am to 5pm.
- **Suncoast Welcome Center,** 2001 Ulmerton Rd. (at the juncture of I-275 and Fla. 688), Clearwater, FL 34622 (tel. 813/573-1449), open daily from 9am to 5pm.
- **The Pier Visitor Information Center,** 800 Second Ave. NE, St. Petersburg, FL 33701 (tel. 813/821-6164), open daily from 10am to 8pm.
- **St. Petersburg Beach Chamber of Commerce,** 6990 Gulf Blvd., St. Petersburg Beach, FL 33706 (tel. 813/360-6957), open Monday through Friday from 9am to 5pm.
- **Treasure Island Chamber of Commerce,** 152 108th Ave., Treasure Island, FL 33706 (tel. 813/367-4529), open Monday through Friday from 8am to 4:30pm.
- **The Gulf Beaches on Sand Key Chamber of Commerce,** 501 150th Ave., Madeira Beach, FL 33708 (tel. 813/391-7373); and 105 Fifth Ave., Indian Rocks Beach, FL 34635 (tel. 813/595-4575), both open Monday through Friday from 9am to 5pm, and mid-January to April also on Saturday from 9am to 3pm.
- **The Greater Clearwater Chamber of Commerce,** 128 N. Osceola Ave., Clearwater, FL 34615 (tel. 813/461-0011), open Monday through Friday from 8:30am to 5pm.
- **Welcome Center** (on Courtney Campbell Causeway), 3350 Gulf-to-Bay Blvd., Clearwater, FL 34619 (tel. 813/726-1547), open daily from 9am to 5pm. Look for another Welcome Center on the beach at 40 Causeway Blvd., Clearwater Beach, FL 34630 (tel. 813/446-2424), open daily from 9am to 5pm.

CITY LAYOUT

St. Petersburg is laid out according to a grid system, with streets running north to south and avenues running east and west. **Central Avenue,** a wide four-lane thoroughfare that cuts across the city from Tampa Bay to Treasure Island on the Gulf of Mexico, is the dividing line for north and south addresses.

Downtown With the exception of Central Avenue, most streets and avenues downtown are one-way. As a rule, south of Central Avenue, even-numbered **avenues** go west and odd-numbered avenues go east; north of Central Avenue, even-numbered

Albert Whitted Municipal
  Airport **20**
Belleair **4**
Belleair Beach **5**
Belleair Bluffs **6**
Belleair Shores **7**
Clearwater **2**
Clearwater Beach **1**
Gulfport **18**
Indian Rocks Beach **9**
Indian Shores **10**
Largo **8**
Madeira Beach **15**
North Redington Beach **12**
Pinellas Park **22**
Redington Beach **14**
Redington Shores **11**
Sand Key **3**
Seminole **13**
St. Petersburg **21**
St. Petersburg Beach **19**
St. Petersburg-Clearwater
  International Airport **23**
South Pasadena **17**
Treasure Island **16**

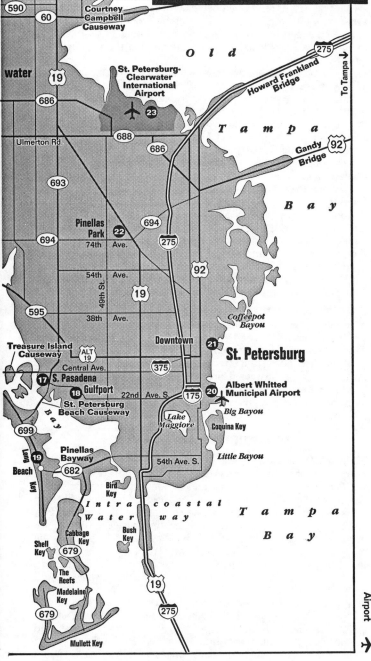

590 · 60 · Courtney Campbell Causeway · 275 · To Tampa

Old

water · 19 · St. Petersburg-Clearwater International Airport · Howard Frankland Bridge

686 · Tampa

23 · Gandy Bridge · 92

688 · 686

Ulmerton Rd.

693 · Bay

694 · Pinellas Park · 694 · 22 · 74th Ave. · 275

54th Ave. · 19 · 92

595 · 38th Ave. · 49th St.

Coffeepot Bayou

Treasure Island Causeway · ALT 19 · Downtown · 21

Central Ave. · 375 · St. Petersburg

17 · S. Pasadena · Albert Whitted Municipal Airport

18 · Gulfport · 175 · 20

22nd Ave. S. · Big Bayou

St. Petersburg Beach Causeway · Lake Maggiore · Coquina Key

699 · Little Bayou

Pinellas Bayway · 54th Ave. S.

19 · Beach · 682

Long Key · Bird Key

Intra coastal Water way · Tampa

Shell Key · Cabbage Key · Bush Key · Bay

679

The Reefs

Madelaine Key

679 · 19

275

Mullett Key

Airport ✈

avenues go east and odd-numbered avenues go west. In the case of **streets,** most even-numbered streets go south and most odd-numbered streets go north. If it sounds confusing, it is—but if you spend a few hours walking, you'll catch on to the pattern pretty quickly.

The main exceptions are thoroughfares along the bayfront, such as **Bayshore Drive** and **Beach Drive,** where two-way traffic is permitted. These streets are curved or diagonal and not strictly part of the grid. The Pier, which extends out into the bay, is on a street that is an eastward extension of Second Avenue North, so that address is indicated by Second Avenue NE.

Two-way traffic is also permitted on **boulevards,** usually diagonal thoroughfares west or north of downtown, such as Tyrone Boulevard, Gandy Boulevard, and Roosevelt Boulevard.

Along the Beaches Along the beach strip, west of St. Petersburg, **Gulf Boulevard** is the main two-way north-south thoroughfare, and most avenues, which cross in an east-west direction, have two-way traffic. Avenues are numbered in continuous fashion, starting with First Avenue at the southern tip of the Pass-A-Grille section of St. Petersburg Beach and extending north to 200th Avenue at the top of Indian Shores; at the Indian Rocks Beach city line, the numbers start again from First Avenue and go upward as Gulf Boulevard continues north through Belleair Beach.

FINDING AN ADDRESS First determine if the address is north or south; the rest is just a matter of following numbers. For instance, we know that 101 Second Avenue North is two avenues north of Central Avenue. The street number, 101, tells us it is in the 100 block, between First and Second Streets North, just as no. 305 on the same avenue would be between Third and Fourth Streets North.

On the beach strip, the addresses on Gulf Boulevard correspond to the numbering of avenues. For example, 5500 Gulf Boulevard is at 55th Avenue.

NEIGHBORHOODS IN BRIEF

THE CITY The **bayfront** area, overlooking Tampa Bay, is the major focus of St. Petersburg's downtown district. Here you will find the Pier, all the major museums, the Bayfront performing arts center, Al Lang Stadium, hotels, restaurants, and leading shops, as well as the city's playgrounds—Spa Beach, Demens Landing, Bayboro Harbor, and Straub Park. Walk inland along Central Avenue and you'll see many of the city's old landmark buildings as you approach the modern ThunderDome. This downtown core of the city is also home to leading churches, an open-air post office, and Mirror Lake, a sylvan setting just right for sitting on a bench and having a restful moment.

Fanning out from the bayfront, the city of St. Petersburg is composed of various residential clusters. Some radiate great success and others reflect a leaner lifestyle. Two of the more popular inland neighborhoods include **Pinellas Park** and **Seminole,** both of which have large stretches of small one-story houses, condominium dwellings, or mobile-home parks. One of the most exclusive neighborhoods is **Snell Isle,** a little over a mile north of the Pier. This section is composed of upscale waterfront homes overlooking Tampa Bay. Similarly, south of the Pier, the homes on **Tropical Shores** and **Coquina Key** also overlook Tampa Bay, while newer sections such as **Gulfport** and **Pasadena,** to the southwest of midtown, overlook Boca Ciega Bay.

NEIGHBORING BEACH DISTRICTS Mention St. Pete and most people will say "beach." Among the many beach communities in the area, the 7½-mile stretch known as **St. Petersburg Beach** is the leader. Just west of mainland St. Petersburg, nestled between Boca Ciega Bay and the Gulf of Mexico, it's lined with motels, hotels, restaurants, and all types of shops and water-sports attractions. The lower tip, known as Pass-A-Grille, has some lovely old houses and has been attracting visitors for over 150 years. The beachfront is dominated by the "Pink Palace," the landmark Don CeSar Hotel, listed on the National Register of Historic Places.

Treasure Island, like its literary namesake, was once reputed to be the site of buried pirate treasure and a hideout for a band of buccaneers. Located just north of St. Petersburg Beach, it's 3½ miles in length. It has a wide sandy beach, lined with motels, restaurants, and other attractions including Kingfish Wharf and the Empress Cruise Lines dock.

The 12-mile-long **Sand Key Island** sits north of Treasure Island, extending from John's Pass to Sand Key Park. The most southerly of its communities is **Madeira Beach,** often called "Mad Beach" because it's busy and popular with all age groups. A center for deep-sea fishing, Madeira Beach offers many places to stay and eat overlooking either the gulf or Boca Ciega Bay. It is also home to the *Europa FunKruz* cruise ship and the only McDonald's in the world on a floating dock.

North of Madeira is a cluster of beaches: **Redington Beach,** with a casual "old Florida" atmosphere and a row of small cottages tucked amid palms and pines; **North Redington Beach,** often called the "Million-Dollar Mile" because it's lined with high-priced condominiums and apartments; and **Redington Shores,** the site of the Redington Long Pier, extending over 1,000 feet into the Gulf of Mexico.

Next is **Indian Shores,** home of the Suncoast Seabird Sanctuary, a unique hospital for pelicans and other injured seabirds. To the north is **Indian Rocks Beach,** a narrow strip edged by the Intracoastal Waterway as well as the gulf, and **Belleair Beach,** one of the most exclusive residential areas on the coast. This strip ends with **Sand Key Park,** a public beach and park nestled between the Gulf and Clearwater Harbor.

Clearwater Beach, with a wide sandy stretch of beachfront, lies on an island linked to downtown Clearwater by a causeway and to the north end of Sand Key Island by a bridge. The beach is popular with young and old alike, and the marina offers a wide array of fishing party boats, sightseeing vessels, sailing rentals, and all sorts of water-sports activity. Clearwater Beach is about 20 miles northwest of St. Petersburg, and 20 miles west of Tampa.

MAPS

The St. Petersburg Chamber of Commerce is a good source for up-to-date maps of the downtown area. The chambers of commerce along the beach will likewise supply you with free maps of their particular areas. To buy a good map either in advance by mail or on the spot, the best source is Haslam's Book Store, 2025 Central Ave., St. Petersburg, FL 33713 (tel. 813/822-8616).

2. GETTING AROUND

BY PUBLIC TRANSPORTATION

BY BUS   The **Pinellas Suncoast Transit Authority/PSTA** (tel. 530-9911) operates regular bus service in the downtown St. Petersburg area and throughout Pinellas County. The system is very popular with the locals who use it for transport to shopping malls or for commuting from residential areas. Several routes go toward the beaches and connect with local beach transport. Buses run Monday through Saturday; hours vary, according to route. The fare is 90¢; a weekly "Super Pass," for $11, allows unlimited rides.

   BATS City Transit, 5201 Gulf Blvd., St. Petersburg Beach (tel. 367-3086), offers bus service along the beach strip, from Pass-A-Grille northward along Gulf Boulevard and via the St. Petersburg Beach Causeway to the South Pasadena Shopping Center, where a connection can be made to the PSTA buses to downtown. Buses run hourly Monday through Saturday from 7:45am to 6pm and on Sunday from 7:45am to 6pm, but phone to check exact schedule. The fare is $1.

   Treasure Island Transit System, c/o City Hall, 120 108th Ave., Treasure Island (tel. 360-0811), is an hourly bus service along the Treasure Island strip, making stops at several hotels, motels, and shopping centers. It also connects with PSTA routes for service to downtown St. Pete and other parts of Pinellas County. Buses run Monday through Saturday from 8:15am to 5pm. Fare is $1.

BY MOTORIZED TROLLEY   The **Clearwater Beach Trolley** is operated by the PSTA (tel. 530-9911) in the Clearwater Beach area along Mandalay Avenue, Gulf Boulevard, and South Gulfview Boulevard. It runs continuously from Bay Esplanade Resort, making an intermediate stop near Pier 60 in the center of the beach district. The trolley runs Monday through Sunday from 10am to midnight. The ride is free.

BY WATER TAXI   The **Clearwater Express,** Drew Street Dock, Clearwater (tel. 442-RIDE), is a water taxi service connecting downtown Clearwater with Clearwater Beach (making stops at both the Clearwater Beach Marina and the South Beach north and south ends of the beach). Ferries operate Tuesday through Sunday, but schedules vary. The fare is $2. Service is also available from Clearwater and Clearwater Beach to neighboring Caladesi Island for $6.05 round-trip.

BY TAXI

Taxis in St. Petersburg do not normally cruise the streets looking for passengers, but they do line up at hotels and bus and train depots. If you need a taxi, it's best to ask at your hotel or call either **Yellow Cab** (tel. 821-7777), **St. Pete Taxi** (tel. 327-3600), or **Independent Cab** (tel. 327-3444).

Along the beach, the major cab company is **BATS Taxi,** 5201 Gulf Blvd., St. Petersburg Beach (tel. 367-3702). In the Clearwater area, call **Clearwater Yellow Cab** (tel. 799-2222).

BY CAR

RENTALS   Renting a car is the way to go in the St. Petersburg area. You really need a car to reach the various attractions, hotels, and restaurants, especially in the evening hours.

All major firms are represented at the airports and in the St. Pete area, including Avis (tel. 813/867-6662), Dollar (tel. 813/367-3779), Hertz (tel. 813/360-1631), and National (tel. 813/530-5491). Local car-rental companies include Pinellas (tel. 813/535-9891) and Suncoast (tel. 813/393-3133).

Rental rates, although always changing, are very competitive and can often be $100 a week or less with unlimited mileage, depending on the time of year. You can also rent a great variety of vehicles in this area, from economical subcompact cars to classy convertibles and sports cars such as the Le Baron (available from Avis).

Note: Under Florida law, rental-car agencies are required to charge drivers $2.05 per car per day (or part of a day) to help finance drug education for young people and for law enforcement. This rule applies to all rentals up to a maximum of 30 days.

PARKING   Parking is plentiful in downtown St. Petersburg, as most streets provide both free and metered parking (25¢ an hour). Meter rules are strictly enforced (maximum two hours, 8am to 6pm on weekdays).

Parking lots and garages charge an average of 50¢ to $1 per hour or $2 to $5 for all day.

Along the beach strip, meters are the rule, with a charge of 25¢ per 15 minutes or per half hour, enforced daily from 9am to 5pm.

DRIVING RULES   It is legal to turn on red at traffic lights, after coming to a complete stop. Pedestrians in crosswalks have the right of way; automobiles must stop if someone is in a crosswalk.

The speed limit in most downtown or beach areas is 25 or 30 m.p.h. unless otherwise indicated. Seat belts are mandatory for the driver and front-seat passenger; children under 5 must be in protective seats.

CAUSEWAYS & BRIDGES   The St. Petersburg mainland (downtown) is connected to St. Petersburg Beach and the other gulf beaches via a series of causeways and bridges. Some are free and others require a toll (in each direction). Here is a run-down, from the most southerly point northward:

Pinellas Bayway (50¢) links St. Petersburg (54th Avenue South) with St. Petersburg Beach (Gulf Boulevard).

St. Petersburg Beach Causeway (free) links St. Petersburg (South Pasadena district) with St. Petersburg Beach (Corey Avenue).

Treasure Island Causeway (50¢) links St. Petersburg (Central Avenue) with Treasure Island (Gulf Boulevard).

Tom Stewart Causeway (free) links St. Petersburg (38th Avenue North) with Madeira Beach (Gulf Boulevard).

Park Boulevard Causeway (free) links Pinellas Park/ Seminole area (north of St. Petersburg) with Indian Shores (Gulf Boulevard).

Indian Rocks Bridge (free) links Largo area and Fla. 688 (north of St. Petersburg) with Indian Rocks Beach (Gulf Boulevard).

Belleair Causeway (free) links Largo/Belleair Bluffs area and Fla. 686 (north of St. Petersburg) with Belleair Shore, Belleair Beach, and Sand Key Beach/Park (Gulf Boulevard).

Clearwater Pass Bridge (75¢) links the north end of Sand Key Island (Gulf Boulevard) to the southern tip of Clearwater Beach (Gulfview Boulevard).

Memorial Causeway (free), links downtown Clearwater and Rte. 60 with Clearwater Beach and Marina (Gulfview Boulevard and Mandalay Avenue).

Note: Plans call for replacing Clearwater Pass Bridge, an old structure that is sometimes closed without advance warning, with a new bridge. The construction, which began in late 1993, may cause further delays. In any case, the speed limit of 15 m.p.h. across the bridge is *strictly* enforced.

FAST ST. PETERSBURG

Airports   See "Orientation," in this chapter.

Area Code   The telephone area code is 813.

Babysitters   With a few hours' advance notice, most hotels can arrange for babysitters. Otherwise, call the Family Care Referral Service (tel. 527-7386) or the Babysitter Service of St. Petersburg (tel. 525-1094).

Buses   See "Getting Around," in this chapter.

Business Hours   Most businesses are open Monday through Friday from 9am to 5pm; shops and stores are open from 9am to 6pm or later Monday to Saturday downtown and daily at the malls and along the beach strip. Banks are open Monday through Friday from 9am to 4pm; some banks are open on Friday until 6pm and others are open on Saturday mornings.

Car Rentals   See "Getting Around," in this chapter.

Climate   See "When to Go," in Chapter 2.

Currency and Exchange   See "Fast Facts: For the Foreign Traveler," in Chapter 3.

Dentists   For 24-hour emergency services or referrals, call the Pinellas County Dental Society (tel. 323-2992).

Doctors   Most hotels have a doctor on call; if not, contact the Pinellas County Physician Information Line (tel. 585-PHIL). The Bayfront Medical Center, in downtown St. Petersburg, operates a doctor referral service (tel. 893-6112). Along the beach strip, there are several walk-in medical offices including The Doctors Inn, 13495 Gulf Blvd., Madeira Beach (tel. 391-4100); and the Clearwater Beach Medical Clinic, 37 Baymount St., Clearwater Beach (tel. 461-4644).

Documents Required   See "Preparing for Your Trip," in Chapter 3.

Driving Rules   See "Getting Around," in this chapter.

Drugstores   Eckerd Drugs is the leading pharmacy chain in the area, with many stores throughout downtown and the beaches, including a 24-hour branch at the Tyrone Gardens Shopping Center, 900 58th St. N., St. Petersburg (tel. 345-9336). For more locations, consult the yellow pages under "Pharmacies."

Embassies and Consulates   See "Fast Facts: For the Foreign Traveler," in Chapter 3.

Emergencies   For police, fire, or ambulance emergency, dial 911 (free at any pay phone).

Eyeglasses   Many national optical chains operate in the St. Petersburg area, including LensCrafters, Pearle Vision Center, and Sears Optical. For exact locations, consult the yellow pages under "Optical Goods: Retail."

Hairdressers and Barbers   Hair-care businesses for men and women are plentiful, with some of the best shops located in such department stores as Sears and J. C. Penney, all shopping malls, and at the larger full-service hotels such as the Don CeSar and Breckenridge. Chains with several locations include Fantastic Sam's, Joseph's, ManTrap, and Silver Scissors. For locations nearest to you, consult the yellow pages under "Barbers," "Beauty Salons," and "Hair Styling."

Holidays   See "When to Go," in Chapter 2, and also "Fast Facts: For the Foreign Traveler," in Chapter 3.

Hospitals   The Bayfront Medical Center, 701 Sixth St. S., St. Petersburg (tel. 823-1234); St. Anthony's Hospital, 1200 Seventh Ave. N., St. Petersburg (tel. 825-1100); St. Petersburg General Hospital, 6500 38th Ave. N., St. Petersburg (tel. 384-1414); and Morton F. Plant Hospital, 323 Jeffords St., Clearwater (tel. 462-7000).

Information   See "Orientation," in this chapter.

Laundry and Dry Cleaning   Most hotels supply same-day laundry and dry cleaning service. Reliable local firms include Pillsbury Cleaners, at 1800 Fourth St. N. (tel. 822-3456) and five other locations, and Rogers Cleaners and Laundry, at 1700 Central Ave. (tel. 822-3869) and 2018 Fourth St. N. (tel. 894-0706).

Libraries   The St. Petersburg Main Library is at 3745 Ninth Ave. N., St. Petersburg (tel. 893-7724), with five branches spread throughout the city. In addition, other convenient libraries are located at 365 73rd Ave., St. Petersburg Beach (tel. 363-9238), and at 12345 Starkey Rd., Clearwater (tel. 535-7979).

Liquor Laws   The legal drinking age is 21. No liquor may be sold prior to 1pm on Sunday. All alcoholic beverages are available in liquor stores; beer and wine are also sold in grocery stores. It is unlawful to consume liquor in public places such as beaches or streets or to have an open container of alcohol in any moving vehicle. In St. Petersburg, most lounges serve alcohol until 2am.

Lost Property   If article is lost or found at a hotel, restaurant, shop, or attraction, contact the management; if lost or found in public areas, contact the police.

Mail   The main post office is at 3135 First Ave. N., St. Petersburg (tel. 323-6517), open Monday through Friday from 8am to 6pm and on Saturday from 8am to 12:30pm.

Maps   See "Orientation," in this chapter.

Money   See Currency in "Fast Facts: For the Foreign Traveler," in Chapter 3.

Newspapers and Magazines   The *St. Petersburg Times* is the city's award-winning daily newspaper; the best periodical covering the area is *Tampa Bay,* a monthly magazine.

Photographic Needs   Eckerd Express Photo Services offers one-hour processing at several St. Petersburg area locations including 7900 Gateway Mall, St. Petersburg (tel. 579-4257); Dolphin Village, 4685 Gulf Blvd., St. Petersburg Beach (tel. 360-0818); and 467 Mandalay Ave., Clearwater Beach (tel. 796-1854). For general photographic or video equipment repairs, contact Southern Photo Technical Service, 1750 Ninth Ave. N., St. Petersburg (tel. 896-6141).

Police   See "Emergencies," above. To report lost or stolen goods, call 893-7560 (St. Petersburg) or 587-6200 (Pinellas County).

Radio and TV   Local radio stations include WFLA-AM 970 (ABC), WHNZ-AM 570 (CNN, CBS), WSUN-AM 620 (A.P.), and WAMR-AM 1320 (NBC, Mutual). WAMA-AM 1550 broadcasts Spanish-language programs.

The local TV stations are WTSP-TV Channel 10 (ABC), WTVT-TV Channel 13 (CBS), WFLA-TV Channel 8 (NBC), WFTS-TV Channel 28 (Fox), WTOG-TV Channel 44 (independent), WEDU-TV Channel 3 (PBS).

Religious Services   There are hundreds of houses of worship in the St. Petersburg area; inquire at the front desk of your hotel or consult the yellow pages under "Churches," "Religious Organizations," and "Synagogues."

Restrooms   All hotels, restaurants, and attractions have restrooms available for customers. A unique and historic (dating to 1927) public comfort station is located downtown on the approach to the Pier, next to the Waterfront Historical Museum.

Safety   Be mindful of money and valuables in public places; do not leave wallets or purses unattended on the beach; lock car doors and trunks at all times.

Shoe Repairs   Two handy downtown locations are Bill's Shoe Service, 454½ First Ave. N. (tel. 822-3757), and Holmes Shoe Repair, 17 Sixth St. N. (tel. 898-7930). Others are listed under "Shoe Repairing" in the yellow pages.

Taxes   Local taxes can add quite a bit to your costs, so keep them in mind when you figure your budget. There's a 10% tax on hotel room charges, a 7% tax on restaurant bills, and a 7% general sales tax on purchases. If you leave the area by plane on an international flight, you'll be hit with a $6 airport departure tax.

Taxis   See "Getting Around," in this chapter.

Time Zone   Eastern. For more information, see "Fast Facts: For the Foreign Traveler," in Chapter 3.

Tipping   For good restaurant service, 15% is usual; a few establishments automatically add 12% to 18% to a bill (be sure to check). It's customary to leave $1 to $2 per person a day for hotel housekeeping staff; tip bellmen and doormen as services are provided. Tip taxi drivers 10% to 15%; porters at airports, $1 per bag.

Transit Information   Dial 530-9911.

Weather   Dial 645-2506.

ST. PETERSBURG ACCOMMODATIONS

As a city surrounded by bays and beaches and as a developing commercial center, St. Petersburg offers a great variety of accommodations. From full-service hotels catering to businesspeople to sprawling surf-and-sand resorts or informal mom-and-pop motels, you are bound to find something to fit both your style and your budget. The lodgings that we have selected here represent a sampling of what we consider to be the best in the hotel and motel categories, as well as in bed and breakfasts.

A stay in "the St. Petersburg area" can mean many types of locations. It can mean downtown (along the bayfront), or north or south of the city center in residential or industrial areas. To most people, however, a stay in St. Petersburg means heading west to the gulf beach strip—St. Petersburg Beach, Treasure Island, the Island of Sand Key, and Clearwater Beach.

Rates are at their highest during the high season, from December or January through April. If you want to stay on the beach during this period, you can sometimes expect to see "minimum stay" requirements of three to five nights. Rates are also set per room or unit, so that you'll pay the same price for single or double occupancy.

On the plus side, many units, particularly along the beach, offer much more than an average room—usually with small kitchens, minibars, refrigerators, and often separate living, dining, and sleeping rooms. This is ideal if you want to make your own breakfast or lunch.

Better rates are offered during June, July, and August, but if you want the best of bargains, plan to come during May, September, October, or November, when rates are as much as 50% lower than in the high season. And the hotels catering to businesspeople, primarily in downtown St. Petersburg and its business corridors, offer lower rates on weekends throughout the year.

The rates that we specify below give you the spectrum, ranging from the lowest in the off-season to the highest in the peak months. A room that will cost you $125 in February might set you back only $65 or $75 in May.

In addition, at all times of the year you'll pay an extra **10% tax** on the price of a room—7% for Florida state and county taxes and 3% resort tax. Tipping is normally at your own discretion for daily maid service, etc., unless otherwise specified.

The following guidelines apply for high-season room prices (per night, double occupancy) in the St. Petersburg area hotels. In the low season, almost *all* properties have rooms in the moderate or budget range.

Very Expensive	Over $175
Expensive	$125–$175
Moderate	$65–$125
Inexpensive	Under $65

Reservations   are a *must* in the high season and certainly recommended at other times, although you'll often find a special offer on the spot in the low-season months, if you don't mind shopping around. Better yet, shop around by phone before you travel by using the toll-free reservations numbers provided by most hotels.

1. DOWNTOWN

For a city of over 250,000 inhabitants, St. Petersburg has surprisingly few world-class hotels or major chain properties. Not that there aren't many places to stay—there are hundreds of apartments and boardinghouses for retirees throughout the city, but for the most part, these establishments cater to seniors who stay the entire winter season, or even year-round.

St. Pete's accommodations for vacationers, like its attractions, are spread out in all directions. In addition to the downtown area near the bayfront, you'll find good hotels in the areas to the north and south. There are also dozens of small family-run motels along major routes, such as U.S. 19, U.S. Alt. 19, and U.S. 92. See "South of Downtown" and "North of Downtown," below, for information on accommodations in these areas.

The listings below represent the best choices for short-term vacationers.

VERY EXPENSIVE

STOUFFER VINOY RESORT, 501 Fifth Ave. NE, St. Petersburg, FL 33701. Tel. 813/894-1000, or toll free 800/HOTELS-1. Fax 813/822-2785. 360 rms, 28 suites. A/C MINIBAR TV TEL

$ Rates: $119–$399 single or double. AE, CB, DC, DISC, MC, V. **Parking:** Self $6, valet $9.

Standing out along the bay front, this sprawling property is undoubtedly the "grande dame" of St. Petersburg's downtown hotels. It's located between Beach Drive and Bay Shore Drive, directly north of Straub Park and the entrance to the Pier. Dating back to 1925 and originally known as the Vinoy Park, it has been meticuously restored and totally refurbished to the tune of $93 million. With an elegant Mediterranean-style peach-toned facade, this seven-story resort overlooks Tampa Bay and is within walking distance of the Pier, Central Avenue, museums, and other attractions.

Ⓕ FROMMER'S SMART TRAVELER: HOTELS

VALUE-CONSCIOUS TRAVELERS SHOULD
TAKE ADVANTAGE OF THE FOLLOWING:

1. Low prices during off-season months: May, September, October, and November.
2. Reduced-rate package deals that may apply for the time you want to stay.
3. Low weekend rates at hotels downtown and along business corridors.

QUESTIONS TO ASK IF YOU'RE ON A BUDGET

1. Is there a parking charge? In St. Petersburg, this is usually free, but some places charge for valet service.
2. Is the 10% hotel tax included in the price quoted?
3. Is continental breakfast included in the quoted price?
4. Is there a surcharge on local and long-distance telephone calls? At some hotels, local calls are free.
5. Is there a discount for cash payment?

All the guest rooms and suites, most of which enjoy lovely views of the bayfront, are designed to offer the utmost in comfort and include three phones, an additional TV in the bathroom, a hairdryer, and more; some units in a newly constructed wing have individual Jacuzzis and private patios/balconies.

Dining/Entertainment: The signature restaurant is Marchand's Grille, a classy room named after the original Vinoy's first chef, Henri Marchand; it specializes in steaks, seafood, and chops, in a setting overlooking the water. The Terrace Room is the main dining room for breakfast, lunch, and dinner. Casual lunches and dinners are available at the gazebo-style AlFresco near the pool deck and at the Clubhouse at the golf course on Snell Isle. There are also two bar/lounges.

Services: Concierge, 24-hour room service, shuttle service to gulf beaches, laundry, tour desk, babysitting, complimentary coffee and newspaper with wake-up call.

Facilities: Two swimming pools, 14-court tennis complex (nine lighted), 18-hole championship golf course (on nearby Snell Isle), private 74-slip marina, two croquet courts, fitness center (with sauna, steam room, spa, massage, and exercise equipment), access to two bayside beaches, hair salon, gift shops, meeting rooms.

EXPENSIVE

PRESIDENTIAL INN, 100 Second Ave. S. (P.O. Box 57306), St. Petersburg, FL 33701. Tel. 813/821-7117. Fax 813/821-7818. 30 rms. A/C TV TEL

$ Rates (including continental breakfast): $85–$130 single or double. AE, CB, DC, MC, V. **Parking:** Free adjacent covered self-parking.

An unusual concept, this hotel occupies the fifth floor of City Center, a 12-story office complex on the bayfront, at the corner of First Street South, opposite Al Lang Stadium. Under the same management as the adjacent Hilton Hotel, it caters primarily to business travelers, but discriminating vacationers who prefer a quiet out-of-the-way setting consider this a real find.

Guest rooms, each with a different view of the bay or city, are individually decorated with traditional "Old Europe"–style furnishings, dark woods, silk wall hangings, and tasteful artworks; bathrooms have separate phone extensions, and eight rooms have private whirlpools.

Dining/Entertainment: Guests have access to the Hilton Hotel's restaurants and room-service system.

Services: Laundry valet service.

Facilities: Living room–style lounge/reading room.

ST. PETERSBURG HILTON AND TOWERS, 333 First St. S., St. Petersburg, FL 33701. Tel. 813/894-5000, or toll free 800/944-5500. Fax 813/821-5943. 333 rms. A/C TV TEL

$ Rates: $84–$139 single or double; $129–$169 concierge level, single or double. AE, CB, DC, MC, V. **Parking:** Free outdoor self-parking or valet parking.

⭐ Situated opposite the Bayfront Center and Al Lang Stadium, this 15-story tower overlooks the bayfront, between Fourth and Third Avenues South, and is within walking distance of major attractions such as the Pier and Dalí Museum. A favored choice for business travelers, it's also an ideal place to stay if you plan to attend concerts or sporting events. The high ceiling and soft lighting of the lobby reflects the tone of this well-maintained hotel, with a rich decor of marble, crystal, and tile, antiques and artwork, leafy potted trees and plants.

The guest rooms, with wide-windowed views of the bay, are accessible by computer-card keys and furnished in a modern art deco style of traditional dark woods, floral fabrics, and seascape art, with one king-size or two double beds, and an executive desk. The 15th-floor concierge-level rooms provide shoeshine machines, personal bathrobes, and a mini-TV/radio in each bathroom.

Dining/Entertainment: There are two full-service restaurants, Charmene's, for American cuisine, and Eli's, a steak house. For light fare, try the First Street Deli; for a quiet drink with a piano background, settle into Brandi's Lobby Bar; and for a lively evening, it's Wings lounge with a biplane suspended from the ceiling.

Services: Room service, concierge, valet laundry, babysitting.

Facilities: Outdoor heated swimming pool, patio deck, Jacuzzi, health club, gift shop, meeting rooms.

MODERATE

BEACH PARK MOTEL, 300 Beach Dr. NE, St. Petersburg, FL 33701. Tel. 813/898-6325. 26 units. A/C TV TEL

St. Petersburg

 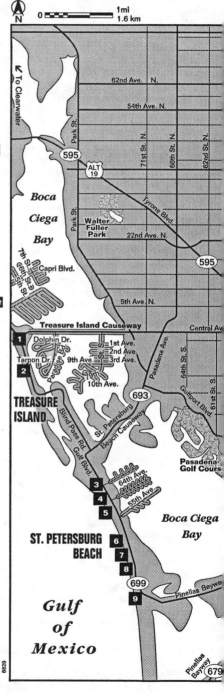

6629

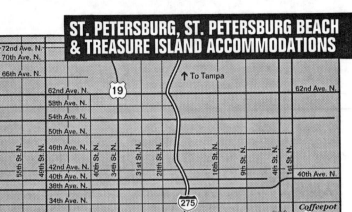

ST. PETERSBURG, ST. PETERSBURG BEACH & TREASURE ISLAND ACCOMMODATIONS

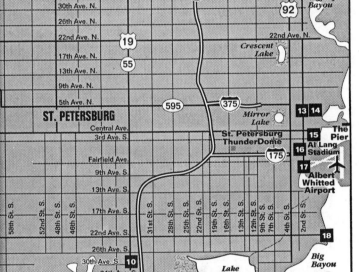

↑ To Tampa

72nd Ave. N.
70th Ave. N.
66th Ave. N.
62nd Ave. N.
58th Ave. N.
54th Ave. N.
50th Ave. N.
46th Ave. N.
42nd Ave. N.
40th Ave. N.
38th Ave. N.
34th Ave. N.
30th Ave. N.
26th Ave. N.
22nd Ave. N.
17th Ave. N.
13th Ave. N.
9th Ave. N.
5th Ave. N.

19
275
92
19
55
595
375

62nd Ave. N.
40th Ave. N.

Coffeepot Bayou

Crescent Lake

22nd Ave. N.

ST. PETERSBURG

Central Ave.
3rd Ave. S.
Fairfield Ave.
9th Ave. S.
13th Ave. S.
17th Ave. S.
22nd Ave. S.
26th Ave. S.
30th Ave. S.
34th Ave. S.
38th Ave. S.

Mirror Lake

St. Petersburg ThunderDome

595 | 375
175

13 **14**

The Pier

15

16 Al Lang Stadium

17

Albert Whitted Airport

18

10

11

12

Clam Bayou

Lakeview Country Club

Lake Maggiore

Lake Maggiore Park

Big Bayou

Boyd Hill Nature Park

45th Ave. S.

54th Ave. S.
58th Ave. S.
Royhanna Dr. | 62nd Ave. S.

Little Bayou

Pinellas Point Dr.

682

19
275

Tampa Bay

Airport ✈

$ Rates: $40–$45 single; $45–$55 double; $50–$65 efficiency. AE, DISC, MC, V. **Parking:** Free outdoor parking.

This well-maintained two-story motel right in the heart of downtown, across from Straub Park and the Fine Arts Museum, has views of the bayfront or the Pier. Guest rooms have one or two double beds, or one king-size bed, with a decor of light woods and bright Florida colors. Each has a small balcony or sitting area; 11 have small kitchenettes, and the rest have a small refrigerator and coffee maker. There are no dining facilities, but dozens of eateries are within walking distance.

THE HERITAGE/HOLIDAY INN, 234 Third Ave. N., St. Petersburg, FL 33701. Tel. 813/822-4814, or toll free 800/283-7829. Fax 813/823-1644. 75 rms. A/C TV TEL

$ Rates (including continental breakfast): $49.50–$110 single or double. AE, CB, DC, MC, V. **Parking:** Free, outdoors.

With a sweeping veranda, fountains, French doors, and tropical courtyard, this hotel in the heart of downtown has the feel of a southern mansion. Situated on a quiet street in a residential neighborhood three blocks north of Central Avenue, at the corner of Second Street North, yet within three blocks of the business district or bayfront, the Heritage dates back to the early 1920s. Previously known as the Martha Washington, it was completely restored in the late 1980s. Furnishings include period antiques in the public areas and in the guest rooms.

Dining/Entertainment: The Heritage Grille, with a unique decor of light woods, modern art, and an antique wooden bar from the Jefferson Davis mansion, offers a creative menu of "nouveau American" light regional cuisine (see Chapter 6, "St. Petersburg Dining").

Services: Room service, valet laundry.

Facilities: Outdoor heated swimming pool, Jacuzzi, meeting rooms.

INEXPENSIVE

BEACH DRIVE HOTEL, 656 Beach Dr. NE, St. Petersburg, FL 33701. Tel. 813/823-7055. 8 units (all with bath). A/C TV

$ Rates: $45–$65 single or double. AE, DISC, MC, V. **Parking:** Free.

Nestled in a quiet residential area five blocks north of the Pier and across from the landmark Stouffer Vinoy Resort, this little hotel has the ambience of an intimate inn. Although there is no restaurant here, each of the individually decorated units has a kitchen and a coffee maker, so guests can cater for themselves—or walk across the street to the Vinoy for meals. Dating back to the turn of the century and built in the Colonial-Revival style, the hotel has been completely refurbished and decorated with antiques, curio pieces, and original oil paintings. Facilities include a heated spa, outdoor barbecue grills, guest laundry, porches with rocking chairs, and a tropically landscaped central courtyard. There is a public phone in the lobby, and plans call for a private phone to be installed in each room. Beverly Raymond is the innkeeper.

BED & BREAKFAST

BAYBORO BED AND BREAKFAST, 1719 Beach Dr. SE, St. Petersburg, FL 33701. Tel. 813/823-4955. Fax 813/823-4955. 3 rms, 1 suite (all with bath). A/C TV **Directions:** Head south to 22nd Ave. S.; turn left and proceed east five blocks to Tampa Bay; turn left on Beach Dr. SE and the house is on the left.

$ Rates (including continental breakfast): $75–$85 single or double; $375 per week one-bedroom suite. MC, V. **Parking:** Free, outdoors.

This city of beautiful old homes is surprisingly short on good bed-and-breakfast inns. This little gem, the pride and joy of proprietors Gordon and Antonia Powers, is situated in a residential area a few minutes south of Bayboro Harbor and the Port of St. Petersburg. A historical landmark three-story Victorian, it looks right out onto the bay opposite Lassing Park, a stretch of natural terrain with a small beach. An Old South ambience prevails here, from the wide veranda with rockers and a swing to the cozy upstairs bedrooms with antique beds and armoires, fine linens, lace and embroidery, and quilts. Each guest room has a different view and an individual theme and decor (the Yellow Room, the Rose Room, the Captain's Room); there is also an apartment-size suite with separate sitting area and kitchen. Breakfast is served each day in the dining room; wine and soft drinks are served in the afternoon. Smoking is permitted on the veranda, but not in the house.

MANSION HOUSE, 105 Fifth Ave. NE, St. Petersburg, FL 33701. Tel. 813/821-9391. Fax 813/821-9754. 6 rms (all with bath). A/C

$ Rates (including breakfast): $60–$70 single or double. MC, V. **Parking:** Free.

Reputed to have been the home of the first mayor of St. Petersburg, this cozy two-story bed-and-breakfast home is located downtown on a residential street, within walking distance of Beach Drive, The Pier, and other attractions. Rooms are decorated in southern turn-of-the-century style, and a sumptuous English-style breakfast is served each morning. Public rooms include a screened-in porch, TV/library room, and sitting room.

2. SOUTH OF DOWNTOWN

A largely residential area and the home of Eckerd College, this section of St. Petersburg has a number of standard motels along the I-275 and U.S. 19 corridors. The advantage of staying in this area is that you'll have ready access to the Sunshine Skyway Bridge, linking St. Petersburg with Bradenton, Sarasota, and points south, and to the

Pinellas Bayway, a causeway connecting the city of St. Petersburg to St. Petersburg Beach.

EXPENSIVE/MODERATE

DAYS INN MARINA BEACH RESORT, 6800 34th St. S., St. Petersburg, FL 33711. Tel. 813/867-1151, or toll free 800/DAYS-INN. Fax 813/864-4494. 157 rms, 11 lodges. A/C TV TEL **Directions:** Take I-275 south to Pinellas Point Dr. (Exit 3).

$ Rates: $49–$115 single or double; $99–$131 one-bedroom lodge; $148–$259 two- or three-bedroom lodge. AE, CB, DC, MC, V. **Parking:** Free, outdoors.

Located on the southern tip of the city, this sprawling two-story hotel seems to have it all. Offering quick access to downtown, it sits in a tropical setting on 14 acres along the Tampa Bay shoreline just north of the Skyway Bridge. For good measure, it's also a year-round base of the Annapolis Sailing School.

Guest rooms have an airy decor with light woods, pastel tones, ceiling fans, plants, and private balconies or patios. Lodges also offer kitchenettes. The highest-priced rooms face the bay, while others have views of the garden or pool.

Dining/Entertainment: Restaurant, beach bar, lounge, and snack bar.

Facilities: Private bayside beach, two outdoor swimming pools (one heated), Jacuzzi, seven tennis courts, fishing pier, marina, shuffleboard and volleyball courts, water-sports rentals, games room, children's playground, meeting rooms, coin-operated laundry.

MODERATE/INEXPENSIVE

HOLIDAY INN—ST. PETERSBURG, 4601 34th St. S., St. Petersburg, FL 33711. Tel. 813/867-3131, or toll free 800/HOLIDAY. Fax 813/867-2025. 134 rms. A/C TV TEL **Directions:** Take I-275 south to Exit 4, at the intersection of U.S. 19 and 46th Ave. S.

$ Rates: $49–$99 single or double. AE, CB, DC, DISC, MC, V. **Parking:** Free, outdoors.

Even though this basic two-story hotel is on the busy U.S. 19 corridor, it's set back from the main road in a convenient and quiet setting, across from a marina and midway between downtown and the Sunshine Skyway Bridge, with easy access to the beaches. The Maximo Moorings branch of the famous Leverock's Restaurant is just a block away.

Bedrooms are furnished in contemporary style, with dark woods, brass fixtures, and light pastel fabrics and carpeting. The bathroom includes a spacious and well-lit vanity area.

Facilities include Duke's Country Western and Music Lounge, a snack bar, guest laundry, outdoor swimming pool, patio, and shuffleboard.

HOWARD JOHNSON HOTEL, 3600 34th St. S., St. Petersburg, FL 33711. Tel. 813/867-6070, or toll free 800/654-2000. Fax 813/867-6591. 168 rms. A/C TV TEL **Directions:**

Take I-275 south to Exit 6, and then take U.S. 19 south for one mile; the hotel is on the left.

$ Rates (including continental breakfast): $52–$90 single or double. AE, CB, DC, DISC, MC, V. **Parking:** Free, outdoors.

Set back from the busy U.S. 19 corridor, this hotel has an impressive, almost Coliseum-like facade, with a pillared entry ramp and lush tropical landscaping. The public areas and guest rooms are pure Florida style, with wicker and light-wood furnishings, lots of hanging plants, and pastel tones.

Dining/Entertainment: The Celebrity Lounge offers live music, while the Tiki Bar provides outdoor snacks and refreshment.

Facilities: Outdoor swimming pool, patio, lighted tennis court, games room, vending room, meeting rooms.

SUNCOAST EXECUTIVE INN, 3000 34th St. S., St. Petersburg, FL 33711. Tel. 813/867-1111, or toll free 800/458-8671. Fax 813/867-7068. 120 rms. A/C TV TEL **Directions:** Take I-275 south to Exit 6, at the intersection of U.S. 19 and 22nd Ave. S.

$ Rates: $38–$60 single; $44–$85 double. AE, DC, MC, V. **Parking:** Free, outdoors.

Situated in the Suncoast Village office and retail center, this three-story hotel sits between the busy corridors of U.S. 19 and I-275, with easy access to downtown and the beaches. The public areas and guest rooms are furnished in contemporary style, with bright Florida colors and fabrics.

This hotel is an ideal choice for tennis buffs, since there is a nine-court rooftop tennis complex and resident pro on the premises. Other facilities include an outdoor swimming pool, tropical courtyard, restaurant, and lounge.

3. NORTH OF DOWNTOWN

Over half a dozen fine hotels are clustered north of downtown St. Petersburg on Fla. 688 (Ulmerton Road), just after you cross over the Howard Frankland Bridge on I-275 heading south. Called the "gateway" area, this section is an entry corridor for traffic heading to St. Petersburg from the airport, from Tampa, and from points north, and the site of several large office parks, including Gateway Industrial Park. The St. Petersburg–Clearwater airport is also smack in the middle of this busy hub. This hotel strip is wedged between north St. Petersburg and south Clearwater. The establishments listed here actually have Clearwater addresses, but, for all practical purposes, their location is most readily identified as "north St. Petersburg." For these reasons, we are describing these hotels here rather than in the Clearwater section, which, for the most part, concentrates on beachside accommodations.

And why would you want to stay on the northern rim of St. Petersburg, rather than downtown or near the beaches? First, there's the location: This is an ideal base if you want to fan out in several directions, dividing your time between St. Petersburg and Tampa attractions, all within a half-hour drive from this central point. Then there are the prices: Even the best choices fall into the moderate range. And since all these hotels are geared primarily to weekday business traffic, you can also find some good bargains here on weekends or at other times (such as holiday periods) when business travel is low.

MODERATE

COMFORT INN, 3580 Ulmerton Rd., Clearwater, FL 34622. Tel. 813/573-1171, or toll free 800/228-5150. Fax 813/572-8736. 120 rms, 8 suites. A/C TV TEL **Directions:** On Route 688 directly across from the Showboat Dinner Theater.

$ Rates (including continental breakfast): $53–$80 single; $59–$90 double; $65–$90 suite. AE, CB, DC, MC, V. **Parking:** Free, outdoors.

This three-story hotel on Fla. 688, directly across from the Showboat Dinner Theater, has a futuristic architecture with geometric designs, wide columns, concealed lighting, and glass-walled elevators. The bedrooms, each with a king- or queen-size bed, have sand and sea tones, light woods, modern art, and large work areas with desks. Most rooms have patios or balconies that overlook a lushly landscaped central courtyard or the pool.

Dining: Palo's, a two-tiered café and lounge, serves American dishes.

Facilities: Outdoor heated swimming pool, whirlpool, exercise room, meeting rooms, complimentary airport transport.

COURTYARD BY MARRIOTT, 3131 Executive Dr. (at Ulmerton Rd.), Clearwater, FL 34622. Tel. 813/572-8484, or toll free 800/321-2211. Fax 813/572-6991. 137 rms, 12 suites. A/C TV TEL **Directions:** Take I-275 to Exit 18; the hotel is on Fla. 688, just west of the Howard Frankland Bridge.

$ Rates: $54–$68 single or double; $76–$84 suite. AE, CB, DC, DISC, MC, V. **Parking:** Free, outdoors.

Opened in late 1989, this is one of the newest hotels along this strip. Set back from the road, it follows the usual layout for hotels in this chain, with guest rooms surrounding a well-landscaped central courtyard and lobby with café/lounge. Most of the bedrooms, furnished in light woods and pastel colors, have one king-size bed, but about one-third have two double beds. Suites have refrigerators.

Facilities: Outdoor heated swimming pool, indoor whirlpool, exercise room, coin-operated guest laundry.

DAYS INN, 3910 Ulmerton Rd., Clearwater, FL 34622. Tel. 813/573-3334, or toll free 800/DAYS-INN. Fax 813/573-3334, ext. 163. 120 rms. A/C TV TEL

$ Rates (including continental breakfast and local phone calls): $39–$69 single; $45–$75 double. AE, DC, DISC, MC, V. **Parking:** Free, outdoors.

On Fla. 688, one-half mile west of the Showboat Dinner Theater, this modern four-story hotel is short on frills but offers good value. Guest rooms, with standard furnishings, have two double beds or one queen-size bed, and some have sofa sleepers or recliners, as well as microwave ovens and refrigerators. The decor emphasizes contemporary sea-patterned fabrics and Florida art. There are no dining facilities on the premises, but a 24-hour restaurant is adjacent.

Facilities: Outdoor heated swimming pool, sun deck, meeting rooms, guest laundry.

HOLIDAY INN, 3535 Ulmerton Rd., Clearwater, FL 34622. Tel. 813/577-9100, or toll free 800/HOLIDAY. Fax 813/573-5022. 174 rms. A/C TV TEL

$ Rates: $75–$90 single or double. AE, CB, DC, DISC, MC, V. **Parking:** Free, outdoors.

This five-story hotel on Fla. 688, next to Showboat Dinner Theater, is the largest along this busy strip, but set back from the main traffic flow. The high-ceilinged atrium-style lobby is impressive. Guest rooms are equally contemporary, with light colors and woods, most with two double beds and standard amenities. Some rooms have a king-size bed, work area, and a large desk.

Dining/Entertainment: The Cascades Restaurant, on the lobby level, specializes in buffets. The Club Marbles lounge has live entertainment Tuesday through Saturday.

Services: Complimentary shuttle to Tampa airport, laundry/dry cleaning.

Facilities: Outdoor heated swimming pool, whirlpool, lighted tennis court, exercise room, car-rental desk, gift shop, coin-operated guest laundry.

INEXPENSIVE

HAMPTON INN, 3655 Hospitality Lane (at Ulmerton Rd.), Clearwater, FL 34622. Tel. 813/577-9200, or toll free 800/HAMPTON. Fax 813/572-8931. 118 rms. A/C TV TEL

$ Rates (including continental breakfast and local phone calls): $49–$69 single; $54–$75 double. AE, CB, DC, DISC, MC, V. **Parking:** Free, outdoors.

Situated next to the Holiday Inn, in a convenient location on Fla. 688, just west of the Showboat Dinner Theater, the Hampton Inn has limited services. It does have well-equipped contemporary guest rooms as well as an outdoor heated swimming pool, whirlpool, sauna, lighted tennis court, exercise room, and coin-operated guest laundry. Restaurants are adjacent and nearby.

LA QUINTA INN, 3301 Ulmerton Rd., Clearwater, FL 34622. Tel. 813/572-7222, or toll free 800/531-5900. Fax 813/572-0076. 118 rms. A/C TV TEL

$ Rates (including continental breakfast): $47–$61 single; $53–$73 double. AE, CB, DC, DISC, MC, V. **Parking:** Free, outdoors.

This well-kept three-story hotel, on Route 688 just east of the Showboat Dinner Theater, offers contemporary-style rooms all with standard appointments and a choice of bed sizes. Rooms are decorated in the contemporary Southwestern theme characteristic of this popular chain. There is no dining facility on the premises, but a restaurant is adjacent. Facilities include an outdoor heated swimming pool, sauna, Jacuzzi, and exercise room.

4. ST. PETERSBURG BEACH

VERY EXPENSIVE

THE DON CeSAR BEACH RESORT, 3400 Gulf Blvd., St. Petersburg Beach, FL 33706. Tel. 813/360-1881, or toll free 800/637-7200 or 800/282-1116. Fax 813/367-6952. 277 rms, 51 suites. A/C TV TEL **Directions:** Take the Pinellas Bayway via the toll bridge west to Gulf Blvd. (Fla. 699).

$ Rates: $140–$265 single or double; $220–$645 suite; $750–$1,000 penthouse suite. AE, CB, DC, MC, V. **Parking:** Free, outdoors.

Often referred to as the Pink Palace, this local landmark sits majestically on 7½ acres of beachfront, rising to 8 and 10 stories in separate wings. A blend of Moorish and Mediterranean architecture and fairy-tale whimsy, it was built in 1928 by Thomas Rowe, a successful land speculator born in Boston but reared in Ireland—hence the structure's castlelike turrets, towers, and trim. Rowe named the hotel after his favorite hero, Don Caesar de Bazan, a character in the English opera *Maritana*. In its heyday, "the Don" was frequented by F. Scott Fitzgerald, Babe Ruth, Lou Gehrig, and countless other celebrities, but then it fell on hard times. Eventually restored and totally refurbished in the 1980s (for a reputed $15 million) and renewed again in 1993–94, it is today in a class by itself. On the National Register of Historic Places, it's a showcase of classic high windows and archways, crystal chandeliers, marble floors, and original artworks.

Guest rooms, most of which offer spectacular views of the Gulf of Mexico or Boca Ciega Bay, are first-rate, with high ceilings, traditional furnishings, marble bathrooms, and a decor blending rich tones of rose, teal, mauve, and sea green. Some rooms have balconies, and, for ultimate luxury, there are two penthouse suites with private terraces.

Dining/Entertainment: The King Charles Restaurant is the place to splurge on a sumptuous Sunday brunch. Other choices include the Maritana Grille for fresh seafood, Zelda's Seaside café for casual fare, and the Beachcomber Bar and Grille for light snacks and drinks served outdoors.

Services: 24-hour room service, concierge, valet laundry, children's program.

Facilities: Beach, outdoor heated swimming pool, Jacuzzi, exercise room, sauna, steam room, whirlpool, resident masseuse, lighted tennis courts, volleyball, gift shops, meeting rooms, rentals of water-sports equipment.

TRADEWINDS, 5500 Gulf Blvd., St. Petersburg Beach, FL

33706. Tel. 813/367-6461, or toll free 800/237-0707. Fax 813/360-3848. 370 rms, 207 suites. A/C MINIBAR TV TEL **Directions:** Take Pinellas Bayway to Fla. 699 (Gulf Blvd.); turn right at the light and head north; the hotel is at 55th Ave.

$ Rates: Single or double room mid-Dec to end-Jan $135–$190, Feb–Apr $175–$209, May to mid-Dec $115–$190; one-bedroom suite mid-Dec to end-Jan $169–$239, Feb–Apr $245–$305, May to mid-Dec $147–$239. AE, CB, DC, DISC, MC, V. **Parking:** Free valet or self-parking.

An oasis unto itself, this resort sits amid 18 acres of beachfront property, sand dunes, and tropical gardens, with rambling brick paths, meandering channels of water, boardwalks, Victorian gazebos, and wooden footpaths. Guests can glide along the waterways in motorized gondolas to their rooms or to dinner.

The guest units, in six- and seven-story buildings, look out on the gulf or the extensive grounds. All have up-to-date kitchens or kitchenettes, contemporary furnishings, and private balconies. Two- and three-bedroom suites are also available on request, at higher rates.

Dining/Entertainment: The top spot for lunch or dinner is the Palm Court, with an Italian bistro atmosphere; for dinner, there is also Bermudas, a casual family spot with a tropical atmosphere in a pastel gingerbread setting. Other food outlets include the Flying Bridge, a beachside floating restaurant in Florida cracker-house style, the Fountain Square Deli, and Tropic Treats. Bars include Reflections piano lounge, B. R. Cuda's with live entertainment and dancing, and the poolside Salty's Beach Bar.

Services: Room service, concierge, valet laundry, children's program.

Facilities: Three heated outdoor and one indoor swimming pools, whirlpools, sauna, fitness center, four tennis courts, racquet-ball, croquet, water-sports rentals, gas grills, guest laundry, video-game room, general store.

EXPENSIVE

RADISSON SANDPIPER BEACH RESORT, 6000 Gulf Blvd., St. Petersburg Beach, FL 33706. Tel. 813/360-5551, or toll free 800/333-3333. Fax 813/360-3848. 36 rms, 123 suites. A/C MINIBAR TV TEL **Directions:** Take Pinellas Bayway to Fla. 699; turn right at the light and head north; the hotel is on the left at 60th Ave.

$ Rates: $69–$174 single or double; $109–$229 suite. AE, CB, DC, DISC, MC, V. **Parking:** Free.

A well-landscaped tropical courtyard separates the two wings of this six-story hotel set back from the main road: The older wing sits right on the beachfront and the newer wing is slightly to the side.

Rooms in the older wing have the best views of the beach, but rooms in the newer wing have private balconies. Pleasantly furnished with light woods, pastel tones, and touches of rattan, most units have two double beds (some have one king- or queen-size bed) as well as coffee makers, toasters, and small refrigerators. Suites have separate living rooms with sofa bed and full kitchen.

Dining/Entertainment: Piper's Patio is a casual café with indoor and outdoor seating; the Sandbar offers frozen drinks and snacks by the pool. Also part of the hotel is Tucson's Family Grill and Bar, a local chain restaurant and lounge.

Services: Room service, concierge, valet laundry, babysitting.

Facilities: Beachfront heated swimming pool; enclosed heated swimming pool; two air-conditioned courts for racquetball, handball, and squash; supervised children's activities; volleyball; exercise room; shuffleboard; games room; gift shop/general store.

ST. PETERSBURG BEACH HILTON INN, 5250 Gulf Blvd., St. Petersburg Beach, FL 33706. Tel. 813/360-1811, or toll free 800/HILTONS. Fax 813/360-6919. 152 rms. A/C TV TEL **Directions:** Take Pinellas Bayway to Fla. 699; turn right at the light and head north; the hotel is on the left between 52nd and 53rd Aves.

$ Rates: $90–$160 single or double. AE, CB, DC, DISC, MC, V.
Parking: Free, covered and outdoors.

Set back from the main road, this 11-story hotel stands out along the beachfront with a circular facade, a glass-walled elevator, and a revolving rooftop lounge. Guest rooms are furnished in contemporary light woods, bright colors, and some rattan touches, all with private balconies and expansive views of the Gulf of Mexico or Boca Ciega Bay.

Dining/Entertainment: C. Chan's Restaurant on the lobby level features tableside cooking and frequent buffets. Schooner's Beach Bar and Grill serves snacks by the pool, and the revolving Bali Hai Lounge on the rooftop is the place to go for sunsets from every angle as well as for drinks and entertainment into the wee hours (Tuesday through Saturday).

Services: Room service, lifeguard, valet laundry.

Facilities: Outdoor heated swimming pool, whirlpool, games room, meeting rooms, beach rentals for parasailing and water sports.

MODERATE

BON-AIRE MOTEL, 4350 Gulf Blvd., St. Petersburg Beach, FL 33706. Tel. 813/360-5596. Fax 813/367-6489. 10 rms, 40 efficiencies, 30 apartments. A/C TV TEL **Directions:** Take Pinellas Bayway to Fla. 699; turn right at the light and head north; the motel is on the left between 43rd and 44th Aves.

$ Rates: $41–$88 single or double; $49–$95 efficiency; $66–$130 apartments. MC, V. **Parking:** Free.

A sprawling motel complex with more than a dozen wings, this beachfront property offers a wide choice of size and type of accommodations, including basic motel rooms; half or full efficiency units with kitchenettes; deluxe apartments with separate bedroom and living room; and various other combinations. Rooms with waterfront views are the most in demand and command the highest rates. Some units can accommodate families of up to eight people.

Dining/Entertainment: Sandbar Bill's Bar and Grille offers food and drink in a casual setting.

Facilities: Two outdoor heated pools, sun deck/terrace, barbecue grills, four shuffleboard courts, coin-operated laundry.

COLONIAL GATEWAY INN, 6300 Gulf Blvd., St. Petersburg Beach, FL 33706. Tel. 813/367-2711, or toll free 800/237-8918. Fax 813/367-7068. 200 units. A/C TV TEL **Directions:** Take Pinellas Bayway to Fla. 699; turn right at the light and head north; the hotel is on the left at 63rd Ave.

$ Rates: $67–$120 single or double. AE, CB, DC, DISC, MC, V. **Parking:** Free.

Spread over a quarter mile of beachfront, this U-shaped complex of one- and two-story units is a favorite with families. Rooms, most of which face the pool and a central landscaped courtyard, are contemporary, with light woods and beach tones; about half the units are efficiencies with kitchenettes.

Dining/Entertainment: The White Horse Café is well known for its breakfast buffets, Etchings Lounge is a popular nightspot for music and occasional comedy shows, and the Swigwam beach bar offers light refreshments.

Facilities: Outdoor heated swimming pool, children's pool, shuffleboard, games room, parasail and water-sports rentals.

DAYS INN ISLAND BEACH RESORT, 6200 Gulf Blvd., St. Petersburg Beach, FL 33706. Tel. 813/367-1902, or toll free 800/DAYS-INN. Fax 813/367-4422. 102 rms. A/C TV TEL **Directions:** Take Pinellas Bayway to Fla. 699; turn right and head north; the hotel is on the left at 62nd Ave.

$ Rates: $79–$159 single or double; $89–$169 efficiency. AE, CB, DC, DISC, MC, V. **Parking:** Free.

Located right on the gulf beachfront, this two-story complex sits on five acres of tropical property. Formerly the Beachcomber, it was totally renovated and refurbished under the Days Inn banner in the early 1990s. Guest rooms, furnished in light woods and pastel tones, have picture-window views of the beach or a central courtyard with the pool, lush greenery, and fountains. About half the units (48) are efficiencies with kitchenettes.

Dining/Entertainment: Players Bar and Grille offers meals as well as evening sporting events on wide-screen TV or live music and dancing, and Dilligaf's beach bar provides outdoor refreshment and evening entertainment.

Facilities: Outdoor heated swimming pool, volleyball, shuffleboard, games room.

THE INN ON THE BEACH, 1401 Gulf Way, St. Petersburg Beach, FL 33706. Tel. 813/360-8844. 8 units. A/C TV TEL **Directions:** Take the Pinellas Bayway to Fla. 699; turn left at the light and take Pass-A-Grille Way south to 14th Ave.; turn right, go one block to Gulf Way, and the inn is between 14th and 15th Aves.

$ Rates: $35–$125 single or double. No credit cards. **Parking:** Free.

Situated across the street from the wide and sandy beachfront, this two-story pastel-toned property exudes an "Old Florida" charm. One of the few motels in the mostly residential strip at the southern tip of St. Pete Beach, it has a bright, airy, and plant-filled decor. Each unit is decorated with ceramic tile floors, wicker furniture, brass accents, and antique pieces. All units have kitchens, and most have private decks or courtyards. Facilities include free use of outdoor gas grills, beach chairs, umbrellas, and bicycles. The best views are from the second-floor units.

INEXPENSIVE

ISLAND'S END RESORT, 1 Pass-A-Grille Way, St. Petersburg Beach, FL 33706. Tel. 813/360-5023. Fax 813/367-7890. 6 cottages. A/C TV TEL **Directions:** Take Pinellas Bayway to Fla. 699; turn left at the light and take Pass-A-Grille Way south to its end; the resort is on the left.
$ Rates: $68–$99 one-bedroom cottage; $160 three-bedroom cottage. MC, V. **Parking:** Free.

Nestled in the quiet southern tip of Pass-A-Grille where the Gulf of Mexico meets Tampa Bay, this resort was well named by owners Millard and Jone Gamble. It's also an ideal lodging choice for those who want a residential nonhotel atmosphere—six contemporary cottages in a shady setting on the water's edge. Each cottage has a dining area, living room with sofa bed, kitchen, bathroom, and bedroom (one unit has three bedrooms and a private pool). Facilities include a lighted fishing dock, patios, decks, landscaped walkways, barbecues, and hammocks. There's no swimming from the seawall on the edge of the property, but the public beach is less than a block away. Most guests consider it a "home away from home" and settle in for a week or month (at substantial savings), returning yearly.

5. TREASURE ISLAND

MODERATE

BILMAR BEACH RESORT HOTEL, 10650 Gulf Blvd., Treasure Island, FL 33706. Tel. 813/360-5531, or toll free 800/826-9724. Fax 813/360-2362. 63 rms, 105 efficiencies with one or two bedrooms. A/C TV TEL **Directions:** From downtown St. Petersburg, take Central Avenue west; continue straight over the Treasure Island Causeway to Treasure Island and Gulf Blvd.; turn left and the hotel is on the right.
$ Rates: $70–$125 single or double; $105–$150 one-bedroom efficiency; $128–$189 two-bedroom efficiency. AE, CB, DC, MC, V. **Parking:** Free.

Stretching for over 500 feet along the beachfront, this huge hotel stands out on the Treasure Island strip, with a complex of three-, four-, and eight-story buildings standing side-by-side. Most of the units have balconies or patios and most have kitchenettes.

Dining: An Old English theme dominates the decor and menu at the Grog Shoppe Restaurant and Lounge; light fare is also available outdoors at the Beach Bar Café.

Services: Room service, babysitting.

Facilities: Two outdoor heated swimming pools, sun decks, hot tub, boutique, meeting rooms.

INEXPENSIVE

CAPTAIN'S QUARTERS INN, 10035 Gulf Blvd., Treasure Island, FL 33706. Tel. 813/360-1659, or toll free 800/526-9547. 6 rms, 3 suites. A/C TV TEL **Directions:** From downtown St. Petersburg, take Central Ave. west; continue straight over the Treasure Island Causeway to Treasure Island and Gulf Blvd; turn left and travel south for six blocks; the hotel is on the right.

$ Rates: $45–$70 single or double; $60–$95 one-bedroom suite. MC, V. **Parking:** Free.

 In the endless row of motels along this small island, this is a real find—well-kept accommodations on the gulf at inland rates. It's owned and operated by Ron and Mickey McCaughan, who maintain it in a nautical theme. Six rooms are efficiencies with new mini-kitchens (including microwave oven, coffee maker, and wet bar or sink), and three units have a separate bedroom and a full kitchen. The complex sits on 100 yards of beachfront and quiet tropical gardens, a much-favored vantage point for watching the sun set each evening.

Facilities: Outdoor solar-heated freshwater swimming pool, sun deck, boat dock on the bay, guest barbecues, library, guest laundry.

6. THE ISLAND OF SAND KEY

MADEIRA BEACH

EXPENSIVE

HOLIDAY INN, 15208 Gulf Blvd., Madeira Beach, FL 33708. Tel. 813/392-2275, or toll free 800/HOLIDAY. Fax 813/392-2275, ext. 143. 147 rms. A/C TV TEL **Directions:** Take Tom Stewart Causeway (Fla. 666) to Gulf Blvd. (Fla. 699), turn right, and go one block; the hotel is directly on the left.

$ Rates: $75–$145 single; $90–$160 double. AE, CB, DC, DISC, MC, V. **Parking:** Free.

Well-maintained and dependable, this four-story hostelry sits on 600 feet of gulf beach, on the north end of the Madeira strip. Guest rooms are contemporary in style, a blend of light woods and floral fabrics, most with two double beds, some with one king-size bed. All have balconies or patios, with full beach views or side views.

Dining/Entertainment: Maxie's Restaurant overlooks the pool and the gulf and frequently offers seafood buffets. Bob's Sports Bar enjoys the same views and is popular at sunset. Try the Tiki Bar by the pool for snacks and tropical beverages.

Services: Room service, valet laundry, babysitting.

Facilities: Outdoor heated swimming pool, lighted tennis court, meeting room; rentals of cabanas, beach lounge chairs, and watersports equipment.

INEXPENSIVE

AU-RENDEZVOUS MOTEL, 160 145th Ave., Madeira Beach, FL 33708. Tel. 813/347-5330. 9 units. A/C TV

Directions: From downtown St. Petersburg, take Tom Stewart Causeway (Fla. 666) to Gulf Blvd. (Fla. 699); turn left, go five blocks, and then turn left onto 145th Ave.; the motel is mid-block on the left.

$ Rates: $45–$55 one-bedroom unit for one or two; $55–$70 two-bedroom unit. No credit cards. **Parking:** Free.

A half block from Gulf Boulevard, this small family-run motel, though not on the beach, is within two blocks of the gulf beach to the west and Boca Ciega Bay to the east. The Pesovich family, owners since 1989, have refurbished each room with new carpeting and furniture, tiled bath with shower, and fully equipped kitchen and dining area. The guest units surround a central courtyard, with orange trees, gardens, and a shuffleboard court.

NORTH REDINGTON BEACH

EXPENSIVE

NORTH REDINGTON BEACH HILTON, 17120 Gulf Blvd., N. Redington Beach, FL 33708. Tel. 813/391-4000, or toll free 800/HILTONS or 800/447-SAND. Fax 813/391-4000, ext. 7777. 125 rms. A/C MINIBAR TV TEL **Directions:** Take Tom Stewart Causeway (Fla. 666) to Gulf Blvd. (Fla. 699), make a right, and go north to the hotel.

$ Rates: $85–$145 single; $125–$185 double. AE, CB, DC, DISC, MC, V. **Parking:** Free.

 This six-story Hilton is one of the newest full-service hotels along the Redington Beach/Shores strip. Set on 250 feet of beachfront, surrounded largely by private homes and condominiums, it is built such that every room has a balcony and enjoys a water view of either the Gulf of Mexico or Boca Ciega Bay. Guest rooms, accessible by computer-card keys, are decorated in pastel tones, with extra-large bathrooms, separate dressing areas, and full-length mirrored closets.

Dining/Entertainment: The multilevel Jasmine's Steak House offers outdoor and indoor dining (see Chapter 6, "St. Petersburg Dining"). The poolside Tiki Bar is popular each evening for its sunset-watching festivities.

Services: Room service, valet laundry.

Facilities: Outdoor heated swimming pool, sun deck, meeting rooms.

INDIAN ROCKS BEACH

MODERATE

ALPAUGH'S GULF BEACH MOTEL APARTMENTS, 68 Gulf Blvd., Indian Rocks Beach, FL 34635. Tel. 813/595-2589. 16 rms. A/C TV TEL **Directions:** Take Fla. 688 west to Gulf Blvd.; turn left for the first location and right for the second location.

$ Rates: Gulf front $60–$80 single or double; courtyard $56–$72 single or double. DISC, MC, V. **Parking:** Free.

A long-established tradition in the Indian Rocks area, this well-maintained and family-oriented motel is owned by Bob and Kay Alpaugh. There is another branch at 1912 Gulf Blvd., Indian Rocks Beach (tel. 813/595-9421), which has 17 rooms and 1 cottage. Both properties sit beside the beach, with grassy central courtyard areas and fountains on each site. The rooms offer homey motel-style furnishings, and all units have a kitchenette and dining area. (At 1912 Gulf Blvd., the one-bedroom cottage costs $68 to $86, and some two-bedroom suites go for $74 to $98.) Units facing the courtyards are less expensive than gulf-front units. Facilities at each location include coin-operated laundry, lawn games, picnic tables, and shuffleboard.

INEXPENSIVE

PELICAN EAST & WEST, 108 21st Ave., Indian Rocks Beach, FL 34635. Tel. 813/595-9741. 13 units. A/C TV **Directions:** Take Fla. 688 west to Gulf Blvd.; turn north and go to 21st Ave.; units are on the right and left side of the street.

$ Rates: $35–$55 single or double at Pelican East; $55–$75 single or double at Pelican West. MC, V. **Parking:** Free.

"P.D.I.P." ("Perfect Day in Paradise") is the motto at this dependable motel complex owned and operated for over 25 years by Mike and Carol McGlaughlin. Depending on your budget, you have a choice of two settings. Pelican East, which has four units, each with bedroom and separate kitchen, offers the best rates, but it's on the bay side of the road, 500 feet from the beach with no water views. Pelican West sits right on the gulf beachfront, offering four apartments, each with living room, bedroom, kitchen, and small patio, and unbeatable views of the gulf. Either choice gives you access to the beach in a quiet, mostly residential neighborhood, but close to restaurants and shops in either direction.

BELLEAIR BEACH

MODERATE

BELLEAIR BEACH RESORT MOTEL, 2040 Gulf Blvd., Belleair Beach, FL 34635. Tel. 813/595-1696, or toll free 800/780-1696. 42 units. A/C TV **Directions:** Take the Belleair Causeway to Gulf Blvd. and turn right at the light; the hotel is 10 blocks north, on the left between 20th and 21st Sts.

$ Rates: $39–$68 single or double motel room; $45–$72 standard efficiency; $55–$100 gulf-front efficiency; $49–$77 one-bedroom apartment. AE, MC, V. **Parking:** Free.

Belleair is undoubtedly the most unspoiled of all the beaches on Sand Key Island, with only a handful of motels discreetly placed along a mile-long corridor of spectacular and secluded gulf-front homes. Shaded by leafy foliage and palms, this two-story complex is set back from the road, right on the beach. The well-kept units, about two-thirds of which are equipped with kitchens, face either the central courtyard and outdoor pool or the gulf. Other facilities include a patio sun deck, shuffleboard, barbecue grills, picnic tables, and coin-operated guest laundry.

7. CLEARWATER BEACH

EXPENSIVE

ADAM'S MARK CARIBBEAN GULF RESORT, 430 S. Gulf-view Blvd., Clearwater Beach, FL 34630. Tel. 813/443-5714, or toll free 800/444-ADAM. Fax 813/442-8389. 207 rms. A/C TV TEL **Directions:** Take Fla. 60 and Memorial Causeway west to Clearwater Beach; turn left at Mandalay Ave., then bear right to Gulfview Blvd.

$ Rates: $64–$179 single or double. AE, DISC, MC, V. **Parking:** Free.

Sitting just south of the Clearwater public beach, this 14-story property makes good use of limited ground space. The building is divided into three sections—the lobby, restaurant, and lounges are on the ground floor, then there are three levels of parking, and the bedrooms occupy the upper floors. It does not have its own beach, but all its rooms have balconies that overlook the gulf waters.

   Dining/Entertainment: Calico Jack's restaurant has a Caribbean-style ambience, with rattan chairs and lots of leafy plants. Jack's Place lounge offers live music as well as backgammon tables; for outdoor refreshment, try the Calypso Galley or the Tiki Bar, both of which also offer steel drum music.

   Services: Room service, valet laundry.

   Facilities: Outdoor heated swimming pool, whirlpool, children's pool, sun deck, games room, gift shop, meeting rooms.

Ⓕ FROMMER'S COOL FOR KIDS: HOTELS

Days Inn Marina Beach Resort (see p. 50) Offers a games room and water-sports rentals.

Don CeSar (see p. 54) Supervised children's activity programs, beachfront location, and water-sports rentals.

Innisbrook Hilton Resort (see p. 70) Has a super-vised children's activity program, children's play area, games room, and pool.

Tradewinds (see p. 54) On the beach; operates full-time children's and teens' programs including barbecues and movies at night, plus paddleboats, bicycles, water sports, and life-size chess and checkers sets.

CLEARWATER BEACH HOTEL, 500 Mandalay Ave., Clearwater Beach, FL 34630. Tel. 813/441-2425, or toll free 800/292-2295. Fax 813/449-2083. 136 rms, 21 suites. A/C TV TEL **Directions:** Take Fla. 60 and Memorial Causeway west to Clearwater Beach; turn right at Mandalay Ave.

$ Rates: $90–$175 single or double; $140–$195 suite. AE, CB, DC, MC, V. **Parking:** Free valet or self-parking.

Dating back more than 80 years but renovated and updated in 1988, this is one of the few hotels on Clearwater Beach that offers an old-world atmosphere. The complex, which directly overlooks the gulf, consists of the main six-story building plus smaller two- and three-story wings. The guest rooms are decorated with floral fabrics and light woods or caned pieces, mirrored closets, and separate vanities; some have small kitchens. The types of rooms vary, and so do the rates, according to location and views; some have balconies.

Dining/Entertainment: The Dining Room offers a continental menu and views of the gulf, as does the Schooner Lounge with its nautical decor, classic cherrywood bar, and brass foot rail. Outdoor service is provided at the Pool Bar.

Services: Room service, valet laundry.

Facilities: Heated outdoor swimming pool, meeting rooms.

CLEARWATER BEACH HILTON, 715 S. Gulfview Blvd., Clearwater Beach, FL 34630. Tel. 813/447-9566, or toll free 800/HILTONS. Fax 813/447-9566, ext. 2168. 210 rms, 5 suites. A/C MINIBAR TV TEL **Directions:** Take Fla. 60 and Memorial Causeway west to Clearwater Beach; turn left at Mandalay Ave., and bear right onto Gulfview Blvd.

$ Rates: $69–$139 single or double; $205–$235 one-bedroom suite, $305–$425 two-bedroom suite. AE, CB, DC, DISC, MC, V. **Parking:** Free.

Situated on the southernmost end of the beach strip and next to the Sand Key Bridge, this beachfront hotel is a favorite spot for watching the boats pass between the gulf and Clearwater Harbor. The complex consists of a 10-story tower and a 2-story beachfront lanai wing. The guest rooms, which have balconies or patios, are a pleasant blend of light woods, pastel tones, sea art, and plants. Units on the upper floors that offer a gulf view cost more than rooms on the lower levels or those with views of the boulevard. Some rooms have refrigerators, and the one- and two-bedroom suites have parlor/sitting rooms.

Dining/Entertainment: The main restaurant indoors is Pippindale's, while Lane's Landing offers drinks and live music on a tropical outdoor deck by the pool. The Café provides outdoor dining.

Services: Room service, valet laundry, babysitting.

Facilities: Outdoor heated swimming pool, children's pool, exercise room, fitness center, volleyball court, dock, playground, gift shop, meeting rooms, water-sports equipment rentals.

HOLIDAY INN GULFVIEW, 521 S. Gulfview Blvd., Clearwater Beach, FL 34630. Tel. 813/447-6461, or toll free 800/HOLIDAY. Fax 813/443-5888. 288 rms. A/C TV TEL **Direc-**

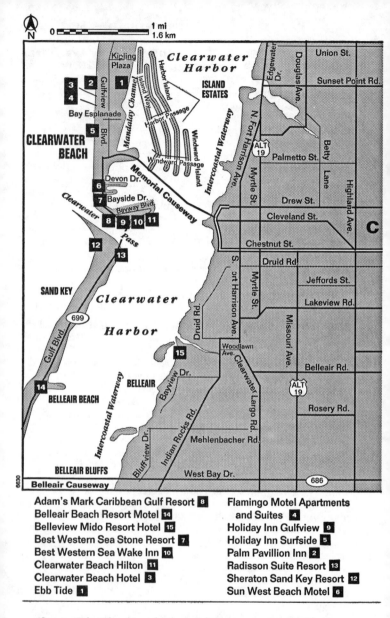

Adam's Mark Caribbean Gulf Resort **8**	Flamingo Motel Apartments and Suites **4**
Belleair Beach Resort Motel **14**	Holiday Inn Gulfview **9**
Belleview Mido Resort Hotel **15**	Holiday Inn Surfside **5**
Best Western Sea Stone Resort **7**	Palm Pavillion Inn **2**
Best Western Sea Wake Inn **10**	Radisson Suite Resort **13**
Clearwater Beach Hilton **11**	Sheraton Sand Key Resort **12**
Clearwater Beach Hotel **3**	Sun West Beach Motel **6**
Ebb Tide **1**	

tions: Take Fla. 60 and Memorial Causeway west to Clearwater Beach; turn left at Mandalay Ave., then bear right onto Gulfview Blvd.

$ Rates: $89.50–$149.50 single; $99.50–$159.50 double. AE, CB, DC, DISC, MC, V. **Parking:** Free.

At the south end of Clearwater Beach, this property overlooks Clearwater Pass and the Gulf of Mexico, but is not directly on the beach. The guest rooms, spread over a seven- and a nine-story wing,

have light woods, fabrics in sea tones, and two double beds or one king-size bed. Most rooms have balconies.

Dining/Entertainment: Choices include the Waffle House, the poolside Tiki Bar, and Fanny's Lounge for DJ music and dancing.

Services: Room service, valet laundry.

Facilities: Outdoor heated swimming pool, children's pool, gift shop, barber and beauty salons, games room, car-rental desk, meeting rooms.

HOLIDAY INN SURFSIDE, 400 Mandalay Ave., Clearwater Beach, FL 34630. Tel. 813/461-3222, or toll free 800/ HOLIDAY. Fax 813/461-0610. 427 rms. A/C TV TEL **Directions:** Take Fla. 60 west and Memorial Causeway to Clearwater Beach; turn right onto Mandalay Ave.; the hotel is on the left.

$ Rates: $89.50–$174.50 single; $129.50–$214.50 double. AE, CB, DC, DISC, MC, V. **Parking:** Free valet or self-parking.

This nine-story hotel dominates the north end of the Clearwater Beach strip, with 10 acres of beachfront property. It's also a center for water-sports equipment rentals, beach events, and tournaments. The guest rooms, most of which have balconies, are decorated in tones of sea green or sandy beige, with light-wood furniture. The largest rooms offer king-size beds and separate work or sitting areas.

Dining/Entertainment: The main restaurant is Reflections, while Café Mandalay serves breakfast. Bob's Sports Bar & Grill and the Sand Bar offer snacks and drinks, the Lobby Bar has a piano lounge, and the Surf Club is a multilevel state-of-the-art disco.

Services: Room service, concierge, valet laundry.

Facilities: Outdoor heated swimming pool, sun deck, volleyball, gift shop, car-rental desk, meeting rooms; equipment rentals for windsurfing, parasailing, and other water sports.

RADISSON SUITE RESORT, 1201 Gulf Blvd., Clearwater Beach, FL 34630. Tel. 813/596-1100, or toll free 800/ 333-3333. Fax 813/595-4292. 220 suites. A/C MINIBAR TV TEL **Directions:** Take the Belleair Causeway to Gulf Blvd.; turn right and follow Gulf for approximately three miles to the top of Sand Key Island; the hotel is on the right.

$ Rates: $119–$235 single or double. AE, CB, DC, DISC, MC, V. **Parking:** Free valet or self-parking.

 Although technically at the northern tip of Sand Key Island, this 10-story all-suite hotel is considered part of the Clearwater Beach corridor. It is situated next to the Shoppes at Sand Key, a new bayside complex of 30 shops and restaurants, including the Clearwater Beach branch of the famous Tampa-based Spanish restaurant, the Columbia. Opened in early 1990, this hotel is an expansive $40-million seven-acre property overlooking Clearwater Harbor, with the Gulf of Mexico just across the street.

Each suite, accessible by computer-card key, has a bedroom with balcony offering harbor views, as well as a complete living room with sleep sofa, microwave oven, coffee maker, and video entertainment unit. The decor, of mostly pink and teal tones, includes mirrored closets, miniblinds, and bathrooms with cultured marble accoutrements.

Dining/Entertainment: On the lobby level, the Harbor Grille specializes in barbecues and buffets. The Harbor Lounge, with indoor and outdoor seating, features a piano bar, while Kokomo's by the pool offers light fare and tropical drinks.

Services: Room service, valet laundry, shuttle to Sand Key Park and beaches, child-care program.

Facilities: Outdoor heated free-form swimming pool with waterfalls, sun deck, sauna, exercise room, waterfront boardwalk, meeting rooms, guest laundry, 60-slip marina.

SHERATON SAND KEY RESORT, 1160 Gulf Blvd., Clearwater Beach, FL 33515. Tel. 813/595-1611, or toll free 800/325-3535. Fax 813/596-8488. 390 rms. A/C TV TEL **Directions:** Take the Belleair Causeway to Gulf Blvd.; turn right, and follow Gulf for approximately three miles to the top of Sand Key Island; the hotel is on the left.

$ Rates: $88–$148 single; $98–$158 double. AE, CB, DC, DISC, MC, V. **Parking:** Free.

Situated along 32 gulf-front acres of Sand Key Island's northern tip, this nine-story resort overlooks a 650-foot beach and is a favorite with water-sports enthusiasts.

Guest rooms offer standard beach-toned decor with light-wood furniture; accessibility is via computer-card keys. Despite the high-rise layout, ground-floor accommodations are available near the pool. All units have a balcony or patio with views of the gulf or the harbor.

Dining/Entertainment: Rusty's Restaurant, just off the lobby, serves breakfast and dinner; for lighter fare, try the Island Café, at the east end of the lobby, or the Sundeck or Gazebo Bar outdoors.

Services: Valet laundry, babysitting.

Facilities: Outdoor heated freshwater swimming pool, health club, Jacuzzi, three lighted tennis courts, volleyball court, newsstand, games room, children's pool, playground, meeting rooms, rooms equipped for disabled guests; water-sports rentals.

MODERATE

BEST WESTERN SEA STONE RESORT, 445 Hamden Dr., Clearwater Beach, FL 34630. Tel. 813/441-1722, or toll free 800/444-1919 or 800/528-1234. Fax 813/449-1580. 65 rms, 44 suites. A/C TV TEL **Directions:** Take Fla. 60 west and Memorial Causeway to Clearwater Beach; at Mandalay Ave., bear left onto Coronado Dr.; at Brightwater Dr., make a left and then the next right onto Hamden Dr.

$ Rates: $59–$119 single or double; $94–$186 suite. AE, CB, DC, DISC, MC, V. **Parking:** Free.

Formerly two properties, known individually as the Best Western Sea Stone Suites and the Gulfview Inn, this is now one resort on the bayfront, connected by a pool and sun deck. The focus is on the Sea Stone Suites, a six-story building of classic Key West–style architecture, opened in 1988 with 43 one-bedroom suites. A few steps away, the older five-story Gulfview wing has been revamped with a matching exterior and 65 refurbished bedrooms. The suites have kitchenettes and a living room; all rooms have a refrigerator.

Dining/Entertainment: Marker 5 Restaurant is on the lobby level of the suite complex, offering indoor and outdoor seating, and a lounge.

Facilities: Heated outdoor swimming pool, Jacuzzi, boat dock, coin-operated guest laundry, meeting rooms.

BEST WESTERN SEA WAKE INN, 691 S. Gulfview Blvd., Clearwater Beach, FL 34630. Tel. 813/443-7652, or toll free 800/444-1919 or 800/528-1234. Fax 813/461-2836. 60 rms, 50 efficiencies. A/C TV TEL **Directions:** Take Fla. 60 west and

Memorial Causeway to Clearwater Beach, turn left at Mandalay Ave., then bear right to Gulfview Blvd.

$ Rates: $91–$129 single or double; $101–$139 efficiency. AE, CB, DC, DISC, MC, V. **Parking:** Free.

This six-story property is on the southern tip of the strip, with its own beach. Its relatively small size provides a homey atmosphere but with all the modern and up-to-date amenities of a larger complex. It offers rooms with views of the water or of the boulevard; all units have refrigerators, most have balconies, and some have small kitchens.

Dining/Entertainment: Lenora's Restaurant, with inside and outdoor seating, is especially popular at sunset and for its menu of dishes prepared at the table. Lenora's Lounge offers nightly music, and the outdoor Tiki Bar serves snacks and tropical drinks.

Services: Valet laundry, children's program.

Facilities: Outdoor heated swimming pool, sun deck, gift shop, meeting rooms, cabana rental.

INEXPENSIVE

EBB TIDE, 621 Bay Esplanade, Clearwater Beach, FL 34630. Tel. 813/441-4421, or toll free 800/635-0620. Fax 813/443-4804. 17 units. A/C TV TEL **Directions:** Take Fla. 60 west and Memorial Causeway to Clearwater Beach; turn right onto Mandalay Ave., go six streets north, and turn right onto Bay Esplanade.

$ Rates: $48–$86 one-bedroom unit for one or two; $75–$115 two-bedroom unit for up to four guests (three-day minimum). MC, V. **Parking:** Free.

Situated in the quiet northern end of Clearwater Beach in a mostly residential area, this two-story motel overlooks the bay, with its own fishing pier and boat dock. The rooms are furnished with standard motel-style pieces including two beds, plus some comfortable Florida-style rockers, rattan furniture, and tiled bathrooms. Each apartment has a kitchen and a balcony or patio that overlooks the bay as well as the on-site gardens. Facilities include an outdoor swimming pool, shuffleboard, and barbecue grills.

SUN WEST BEACH MOTEL, 409 Hamden Dr. S., Clearwater Beach, FL 34630. Tel. 813/442-5008. 4 rms, 10 efficiencies. A/C TV TEL **Directions:** Take Fla. 60 and Memorial Causeway west to Clearwater Beach; at Mandalay Ave., turn left onto Coronado Dr.; at Fifth St., make a left and then turn right onto Hamden Dr.

$ Rates: $40–$61 single or double; $48–$79 efficiency. DISC, MC, V. **Parking:** Free.

 Overlooking the bay and yet only a two-block walk from the gulf beach, this modern one-story motel is a good value at any time of year, thanks to careful maintenance by owners Pat and John Joniec. The rooms, which face either the bay, the pool, or the sun deck and shuffleboard area, have contemporary resort-style furnishings. The motel rooms have small refrigerators and the apartment/efficiencies have kitchens. The larger units have microwaves and ceiling fans. Facilities include a heated pool, fishing/boating dock, sun deck, shuffleboard, and guest laundry room.

FLAMINGO MOTEL APARTMENTS AND SUITES, 450 N. Gulfview Blvd., Clearwater Beach, FL 34630. Tel. 813/ 441-8019, or toll free 800/821-8019. Fax 813/446-6599. 28 suites, 29 efficiencies. A/C TV **Directions:** Take Fla. 60 and Memorial Causeway west to Clearwater Beach, turn right onto Mandalay Ave., go one block north to Papaya St. and turn left; then turn right onto Gulfview Blvd. and the hotel office is on the left.

$ Rates: $30–$65 efficiency; $60–$100 suite. DISC, MC, V. **Parking:** Free.

On a quiet street in the northern section of the beach strip, this two-story multiwing motel has been owned and operated by the Fletcher family for over 30 years. It sits on 300 feet of beachfront, with three buildings directly on the gulf and another smaller building with two cottages, outdoor pool, and sun deck on the opposite side of the street. All units have kitchenette facilities and can accommodate up to four adults. The rates depend on the location and size of rooms. In addition to the pool, facilities include a whirlpool, exercise room, barbecue grills, shuffleboard, and children's playground.

PALM PAVILION INN, 18 Bay Esplanade, Clearwater Beach, FL 34630. Tel. 813/446-6777, or toll free 800/ 433-PALM. Fax 813/446-4255. 27 rms, 2 efficiencies. A/C TV TEL **Directions:** Take Fla. 60 and Memorial Causeway west to Clearwater Beach, turn right onto Mandalay Ave., and go six streets north; the hotel is on the left, next to the firehouse.

$ Rates: $49–$95 single or double; $64–$95 efficiency. AE, MC, V. **Parking:** Free.

A stroll along the beachfront is bound to draw your attention to this three-story art deco building, recently restored and artfully trimmed in pink and blue. The lobby and guest rooms are also art deco. Rooms in the front of the house face the gulf, and those in the back face the bay; four units have kitchenettes. Facilities include a rooftop sun deck, direct access to the beach, and complimentary coffee in the lobby.

8. NEARBY RESORT & SPA HOTELS

VERY EXPENSIVE/EXPENSIVE

BELLEVIEW MIDO RESORT HOTEL, 25 Belleview Blvd. (P.O. Box 2317), Clearwater, FL 34617. Tel. 813/442-6171, or toll free 800/237-8947. Fax 813/441-4173 or 813/443-6361. 292 rms, 47 suites. A/C MINIBAR TV TEL **Directions:** Take Fla. 60 west to downtown Clearwater and turn left at Fort Harrison Ave.; travel south on Fort Harrison for one mile to Belleview Blvd.; turn right and follow Belleview to the entrance.

$ Rates: $85–$175 single; $130–$195 double; $220–$385 suite for one, $240–$405 suite for two. AE, CB, DC, DISC, MC, V. **Parking:** Free.

Perched on a high bluff above Clearwater Bay, this massive multigabled white clapboard Victorian hotel enjoys an out-of-the-way setting amid lofty native pines, water oaks, cabbage palms, palmettos, citrus trees, orchids, holly, and jacarandas. Opened in 1897 with great fanfare by railroad magnate Henry Plant, it quickly became the favored western-Florida oasis for steel magnates, industrial barons, and such international celebrities as the Duke of Windsor. Today, almost a century later, the "Queen of the Gulf" is a landmark—it's listed on the National Register of Historic Places as the largest occupied wooden structure in the world. Although the exterior and much of the interior (like the Tiffany stained-glass windows, crown moldings, crystal chandeliers, and brass fixtures) have been carefully preserved, there are also modern overtones, such as a futuristic glass-filled entrance and circular atrium-style lobby.

The high-ceilinged guest rooms, for the most part unchanged, are decorated in Queen Anne style, with dark-wood period furniture including four-posters, armoires, and rich fabrics. Suites have sun parlors or balconies.

Dining/Entertainment: The main restaurants are the informal indoor/outdoor Terrace Café for breakfast, lunch, or dinner overlooking the pool; and Madame Ma's for gourmet Chinese cuisine in an artistic Far East atmosphere. There is also a pub, lounge, and poolside bar.

Services: Room service, dry cleaning, valet laundry, nightly bed turndown, currency exchange, business-office services, babysitting.

Facilities: 18-hole par-72 championship golf course, four red-clay tennis courts, indoor and outdoor heated swimming pools, Jacuzzi, sauna, Swiss showers, workout gym, jogging and walking trails, access to a private Cabana Club on the Gulf of Mexico, bicycle rentals, fishing and sailboat charters, gift shops, art gallery, newsstand, meeting rooms.

INNISBROOK HILTON RESORT, P.O. Drawer 1088, Tarpon Springs, FL 34688. Tel. 813/942-2000, or toll free 800/456-2000 or 800/HILTONS. Fax 813/942-5576. 1,000 units. A/C MINIBAR TV TEL **Directions:** From St. Petersburg, take U.S. 19 north, about eight miles past the intersection with Fla. 60. The complex is south of Klosterman Rd. between U.S. 19 and U.S. 19A; there are entrances on U.S. 19 and on Klosterman.

$ Rates: $86–$189 single or double; $121–$225 one-bedroom suite; $167–$355 two-bedroom suite. Two-, three-, and five-night packages and meal plans available. AE, CB, DC, MC, V. **Parking:** Free.

Situated on 1,000 acres of rolling hills in upper Pinellas County, this sprawling resort sits between two very busy thoroughfares, yet it's in a world by itself. No traffic sounds are heard, just the sounds of birds and the peaceful hum of rustling natural foliage, the ripples of the lakes, the stirring of nearby wildlife. All this, and world-class golf and tennis facilities, too (it's the home of the Innisbrook Golf Institute).

Accommodations are spread throughout the complex in 28 three-story mansard-roofed lodges, each named for a famous golf course around the world (from St. Andrews and Royal Aberdeen, to

Augusta and Pine Valley). All units have balconies or patios, and are nestled around the resort's three golf courses, one of which (the Copperhead Course) is ranked among the top courses in the world. Each unit also has a fully equipped kitchen and living area, and the larger layouts have one or two separate bedrooms.

Dining/Entertainment: Each golf clubhouse offers a full-service dining room, a café-style facility for light meals, and a bar/lounge with evening entertainment. For northern Italian cuisine, the top spot is Toscana in the Island Clubhouse. For mesquite-grilled or barbecued dishes, try the Copperhead Grille and Lounge; the Sandpiper Dining Room is known for its elaborate seafood meals. (*Note:* Meals and lounge services are available only to overnight guests.)

Services: Complimentary on-site tram service and beach-shuttle service, airport shuttle service ($18), concierge, room service, valet laundry, children's activity program, babysitting.

Facilities: One 27-hole championship golf course and two 18-hole championship courses, practice tee, driving range, six outdoor heated swimming pools, health club, three clubhouses and pro shops, and a tennis and racquetball center with 15 courts (7 lighted), children's play area, games room, fishing-rod and bicycle rentals, jogging track, nature trails, exercise classes, massage therapy, gift shops, unisex hair salon, meeting rooms.

SAFETY HARBOR SPA AND FITNESS CENTER, 105 N. Bayshore Dr., Safety Harbor, FL 34695. Tel. 813/726-1161, or toll free 800/237-0155. Fax 813/726-4268. 212 rms. A/C TV TEL **Directions:** Take U.S. 19 north to Fla. 60 and turn right (east); after one mile, turn left onto Bayshore Blvd., which eventually becomes Bayshore Dr., and travel north for two miles; the spa is on the right.

$ Rates (including all meals and unlimited daytime tennis and on-site golf driving range): $226–$312 single; $169–$232 per person double. Four- and seven-day fitness packages, tennis packages, and beauty makeover plans available, as well as two-night fitness or beauty weekends. AE, CB, DC, MC, V. **Parking:** Free.

Founded in 1926 and completely renovated in the late 1980s, this modern 35-acre spa on Old Tampa Bay is not just another artificial fitness complex—it's a health resort built around five natural sulfur-filled springs, reputed to have been discovered in 1539 by Hernando de Soto and named Espíritu Santo or "Springs of the Holy Spirit." For many centuries, believers seeking cures were drawn to these mineral waters.

Today you can take part in a program of up to 35 different activities. The regimen includes swimming, rowing, walking, tennis, golf, and bicycling, as well as water exercise, low-impact aerobics, stretch classes, and circuit weight training.

Most of the accommodations are in a six-story main building and three-story wing, many with patios or balconies overlooking the bay; 20 additional rooms with kitchenettes are available across the street in a newly renovated building. Rooms are decorated in tropical style, with original artwork, rattan furnishings, and brilliant colors.

Dining/Entertainment: Enjoy nutritious international spa cuisine or order à la carte in the skylit dining room with an exotic bird mural. Other choices include a juice bar and a lounge where evening concerts, movies, lectures, and seminars are held.

Services: Complimentary airport shuttle, room service, valet laundry.

Facilities: Heated indoor and outdoor swimming pools, Finnish saunas, Turkish steam baths, Jacuzzis, seven clay and two asphalt tennis courts, exercise equipment, golf driving range, full-time medical staff, on-premises Clarins Institut de Beauté, meeting rooms, fashion boutique, gift shop/newsstand, and coin-operated guest laundries.

ST. PETERSBURG DINING

From elegant candlelit dining rooms to panoramic waterfront restaurants or casual cafés, St. Petersburg has a wide variety of good eating experiences. There is plenty of international fare—from Japanese steak houses to Swiss fondue places, as well as the cuisines of Italy, France, Germany, Spain, Scandinavia, and all parts of the U.S., especially regional southern dishes.

But most of all, the St. Petersburg area is outstanding for seafood—fresh from gulf waters and beyond. You'll have a choice of local favorites like grouper, pompano, snapper, stone crabs, or rock shrimp, as well as piscatorial delights from other shores, such as Maine lobster, Louisiana crayfish, and crab legs and salmon from the Northwest. Many restaurants sell so much seafood that they operate their own fishing boats, and literally take the day's catch from the dock to the kitchen in a matter of hours. Fresher fish is hard to find anywhere. Stick with the daily specials and you'll always have something to rave about.

Before you set out to satisfy your appetite, here are some points to remember:

Reservations Particularly for dinner, reservations are always advised and often required at the more elegant establishments. However, a good number of the moderate or inexpensive restaurants do not take reservations. They base their operations on high volume, requiring a first-come, first-served policy. You might have to stand in line, but it's usually well worth the wait.

Taxes All restaurant charges are subject to 7% state and county tax.

Tipping A few of the older and more formal restaurants in the St. Petersburg area add a gratuity or service charge to the bill, usually 15% to 18%. If this is the case, it will be clearly stated on the menu. Always ask if you're in doubt.

Alcoholic Beverages Most restaurants serve cocktails, wine, and other alcoholic beverages with meals, and many also have separate bar/lounge areas. If a place serves only beer and wine, or does not serve alcoholic beverages but permits guests to bring their own, this is specified in our description.

PRICES In dollar terms, St. Pete–area restaurants run the gamut—you can spend $50 and up for a dinner at the top spots, or confine the tab to under $10 with no problem at all. For the restaurants we describe, we have used the following guidelines for average prices of most main courses on the menu:

Very Expensive	Over $25
Expensive	$17–$25
Moderate	$10–$17
Inexpensive	Under $10

In the majority of St. Petersburg–area restaurants, the price of a main course includes a house salad or soup, breads or rolls, vegetables, and potato, rice, or pasta. To estimate the price of a complete meal with appetizer, dessert, coffee, tax, and tip, you can usually double the cost of the main course. So, if your main course is $12, a complete dinner will probably be around $24 for one or about $50 for two.

"Early-Bird" Dining Like many Florida cities, St. Petersburg is a great exponent of the "early-bird dinner"—a three- or four-course evening meal at a fixed price, usually costing $5.95 to $9.95 and served between 3:30pm and 6:30pm. Menu choices may be limited, but by being an "early bird," you can sample even the most expensive restaurants and rarely pay more than $12 for a complete dinner. As a rule, such specials and rates change often, so we have not specified early-bird prices for the restaurants we describe. The best strategy is to inquire about early-bird policies when calling for a reservation. Although most restaurants are eager to feature these special prices to draw customers before peak dining hours, a few places may not tell you about early-bird specials unless you ask.

1. DOWNTOWN

EXPENSIVE

BASTA'S CANTINA D'ITALIA RISTORANTE, 1625 Fourth St. S. Tel. 894-7880.
   Cuisine: NORTHERN ITALIAN/CONTINENTAL. **Reservations:** Recommended, especially for dinner. **Directions:** South of Central Ave. between 16th and 17th Aves. S.
$ **Prices:** Appetizers $2.95–$7.95; main courses $5.95–$9.95 at lunch, $13.95–$22.95 at dinner. AE, CB, DC, MC, V.
   Open: Lunch Mon–Fri 11:30am–3pm; dinner Mon–Sat 5–10pm.

Situated southwest of the Dalí Museum, this classy little enclave is slightly off the beaten track but worth a detour. The decor, a blend of art deco and Mediterranean influences, is capped with fine linens and soft lighting. The main attraction, of course, is the food, and chef/owner Frank Basta earns frequent accolades for using natural ingredients and fresh herbs, making all pastas on the premises, and cooking all food to order. His specialties include seafood Porto Fino (lobster, shrimp, clams, scallops, and crab legs poached in white sauce over angel-hair pasta), and filet mignon Napoléon (filet of beef topped with mozzarella cheese, mushrooms, and herbs, and sprayed with brandy), as well as veal saltimbocca, shrimp scampi, lobster tails, steak Diane, and rack of lamb.

HERITAGE GRILLE, in the Heritage Hotel/Holiday Inn, 256 Second St. N. Tel. 823-6382.

Cuisine: AMERICAN. **Reservations:** Recommended.

$ Prices: Appetizers $3.95–$6.95; main courses $5.95–$8.95 at lunch, $16.50–$22.50 at dinner. AE, DC, MC, V.

Open: Lunch Mon–Fri 11:30am–2:30pm; dinner Mon–Thurs 5:30–10pm, Fri–Sat 5:30–11pm.

Housed in the hotel of the same name, this restaurant is three blocks north of Central Avenue at the corner of Third Avenue North, in the heart of downtown St. Pete. It has the charm of a country inn, with a decor of stained-glass windows, ornate wood carvings, French doors, and original paintings by local artists. There are four eating areas, including an airy tropical room and a small patio for al fresco dining. No matter what setting you choose, however, the food is the real attraction, expertly prepared and presented with a creative and colorful flair.

Main courses include grilled strip loin of beef with Gorgonzola fondue; pan-roasted chicken with butterscotch beans; parsley-roasted rack of lamb; pan-seared scallops with Pinot Noir butter and oyster mushrooms; and crab cakes with andouille, spinach, and Créole mustard béarnaise sauce. Lunch choices include seafood salads, burgers, pastas, and creative sandwiches.

MODERATE

APROPOS, 300 Second Ave. NE. Tel. 823-8934.

Cuisine: AMERICAN. **Reservations:** Accepted for dinner.

$ Prices: Appetizers $2.95–$6.95; main courses $4.95–$7.95 at lunch, $8–$15 at dinner. CB, DC, MC, V.

Open: Lunch Tues–Sat 11am–3pm; dinner Thurs–Sun 6pm–midnight; brunch Sun 8:30am–2pm.

Always known for its good food, now this trendy art deco–style restaurant also has picture-perfect waterside views. Originally downtown, it moved in 1992 to its new location right on the marina at the corner of Bayshore Boulevard, on the approach to the Pier. There is both air-conditioned seating indoors and patio-style seating on an outdoor deck.

The menu, which features light foods spiked with fresh herbs, includes dinner main courses such as rosemary chicken, vegetarian

A.J.'s Deli Café 19
Apropos 22
Arigato Japanese
 Steakhouse 4
Basta's Cantina d'Italia
 Ristorante 27
Captain Kosmakos 6
Cha Cha Coconuts 24
Chuck E. Cheese's 5
The Columbia 23
Crabby Bill's 12
Fourth Street Shrimp Store 16
Le Grand Café 21
Heritage Grille 17
Hooters 3
Keystone Club 18
Kinjo 13
Leverock's (37th Street) 28
Leverock's
 (St. Petersburg Beach) 10
Leverock's
 Waterfront Steakhouse 1
Melting Pot 15
Mulligan's Sunset Grille 8
Nick's on the Water 25
Ollie's Grill 20
Outback Steakhouse 2
Sea Critter Café 14
Silas Dent's 11
Sunset Beach Café 7
Tavern on the Green 26
Ted Peters' Famous
 Smoked Fish 9

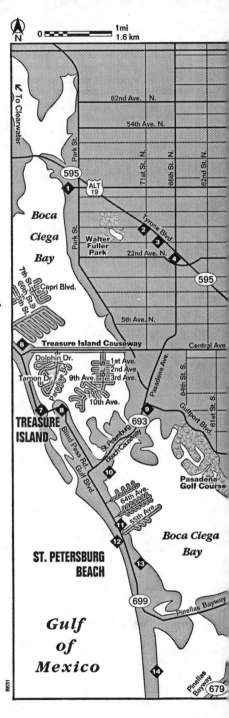

ST. PETERSBURG, ST. PETERSBURG BEACH & TREASURE ISLAND DINING

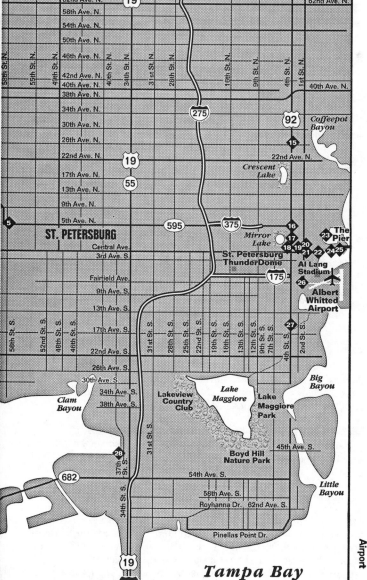

↑ To Tampa

72nd Ave. N.
70th Ave. N.
66th Ave. N.
62nd Ave. N.
58th Ave. N.
54th Ave. N.
50th Ave. N.
46th Ave. N.
42nd Ave. N.
40th Ave. N.
38th Ave. N.
34th Ave. N.
30th Ave. N.
26th Ave. N.
22nd Ave. N.
17th Ave. N.
13th Ave. N.
9th Ave. N.
5th Ave. N.

62nd Ave. N.
40th Ave. N.

ST. PETERSBURG

Central Ave.
3rd Ave. S.
Fairfield Ave.
9th Ave. S.
13th Ave. S.
17th Ave. S.
22nd Ave. S.
26th Ave. S.
30th Ave. S.
34th Ave. S.
38th Ave. S.
45th Ave. S.
54th Ave. S.
58th Ave. S.
Royhanna Dr. 62nd Ave. S.
Pinellas Point Dr.

Coffeepot Bayou
Crescent Lake
Mirror Lake
The Pier
St. Petersburg ThunderDome
Al Lang Stadium
Albert Whitted Airport
Big Bayou
Clam Bayou
Lake Maggiore
Lakeview Country Club
Lake Maggiore Park
Boyd Hill Nature Park
Little Bayou

Tampa Bay

Airport

platters, lamb chops, pepper steak, and fresh seafoods like lobster. Lunch choices range from tomato-basil tarts to salads, sandwiches, and fruit and cheese plates.

THE COLUMBIA, 800 Second Ave. NE. Tel. 822-8000.
  Cuisine: SPANISH. **Reservations:** Recommended for dinner.
  Directions: Follow signs to the Pier; the restaurant is on the 4th floor.
$ **Prices:** Appetizers $1.95–$4.95; main courses $4.95–$8.95 at lunch, $7.95–$16.95 at dinner. AE, CB, DC, MC, V.
  Open: Mon–Thurs 11am–10pm, Fri–Sat 11am–11pm, Sun noon–10pm.

 Opened in 1988, this branch of the landmark Tampa restaurant occupies a prime position in the St. Pete Pier complex. Although it may lack some of the charm and antique decor of the original location, it excels in offering unequaled views of the Gulf of Mexico and the St. Petersburg skyline. See Chapter 10, "Tampa Dining: Ybor City," for a description of the cuisine.

KEYSTONE CLUB, 320 Fourth St. N. Tel. 822-6600.
  Cuisine: AMERICAN. **Reservations:** Recommended.
$ **Prices:** Appetizers $1.95–$6.95; main courses $4.95–$12.95 at lunch, $8.95–$17.95 at dinner. MC, V.
  Open: Lunch Mon–Fri 11am–2:30pm; dinner Mon–Thurs 5–10pm, Fri–Sat 5–11pm.

In a city that basks in fine seafood, this fairly new downtown restaurant, between Third and Fourth Avenues North, prides itself on its beef, served in the clubby atmosphere of a Manhattan-style chophouse. Specialties include roast prime ribs of beef, New York strip steaks, and filet mignon as well as lamb chops, calves' liver, chicken, and veal. Seafood also makes an appearance on the nightly special menu, with choices such as salmon filet with dill sauce, crab imperial, broiled grouper, and stuffed lobster tail. Lunch specials often include hearty fare such as meat loaf, chicken pie, beef Stroganoff, and roast pork.

LE GRAND CAFE, 247 Central Ave. Tel. 821-6992.
  Cuisine: CONTINENTAL. **Reservations:** Recommended.
$ **Prices:** Appetizers $3.95–$7.95; main courses $4.95–$7.95 at lunch, $10.95–$18.95 at dinner; complete prix-fixe dinners $20–$30. AE, DC, MC, V.
  Open: Lunch Mon–Sat 11:30am–3pm; dinner Mon–Thurs 6–10pm, Fri–Sat 6–10:30pm, Sun 1–9pm.

This stylish restaurant brings a little bit of Paris to the city's main thoroughfare, between Second and Third Streets in the heart of downtown, with an art-filled bistro interior, French background music, and a sidewalk café outside. The menu blends classic with creative cooking, offering dishes such as pot au feu; pepper steak; filet of lamb with mushrooms, rosemary, honey, and herbs; roast duck with raspberry-shallot sauce; ground buffalo with chestnut sauce; and

---

**ⓕ FROMMER'S SMART TRAVELER:
RESTAURANTS**

QUESTIONS TO ASK IF YOU'RE ON A BUDGET

1. Is there an "early bird" dinner? If so, what are the prices and the hours of service?
2. Is the service charge included in the bill's total?
3. Is the 7% state and county tax included in the total?
4. Are there any specials today? What are the prices?
5. If you're traveling with kids, is there a children's menu?

---

chicken breast with hazelnut liqueur, nuts, and cream. Salads, omelets, and croissant or baguette sandwiches prevail at lunchtime. In the grand old French tradition, prix-fixe four-course menus are also available.

NICK'S ON THE WATER, The Pier, 800 Second Ave. NE. Tel. 898-5800.

Cuisine: ITALIAN/AMERICAN. **Reservations:** Recommended for dinner.

$ Prices: Appetizers $1.95–$6.95; main courses $3.95–$8.95 at lunch, $6.95–$14.95 at dinner. AE, CB, DC, MC, V.

Open: Sun–Thurs 11:30am–10pm, Fri–Sat 11:30am–11pm.

Located on the ground level of the Pier, this relatively new and informal restaurant offers expansive views of downtown St. Petersburg and the bayfront marina. The menu features a variety of pizzas and pastas, along with a half-dozen veal dishes including Nick's Chef Special (médaillons sautéed with mushrooms, white wine, and lemon, and topped with prosciutto and mozzarella cheese), lamb chops, and steaks. Signature dishes include Nick's Angel Hair (in a tomato cream sauce, basil, peas, and prosciutto), penne pomodoro (with plum tomatoes, garlic, and basil), and seafood combination (sautéed shrimp, calamari, scungilli, clams, scallops in a spicy marinara sauce on a bed of linguine).

OLLIE'S GRILLE, 111 Second Ave. NE. Tel. 822-6200.

Cuisine: AMERICAN. **Reservations:** Recommended.

$ Prices: Appetizers $2.50–$5.50; main courses $3.95–$7.95 at lunch, $5.95–$16.95 at dinner. MC, V.

Open: Lunch Mon–Fri 11am–2:30pm; dinner Mon–Thurs 5–9pm, Fri–Sat 5–10pm.

Situated on the mezzanine level of the Plaza Courtyard shopping complex on the approach to the Pier, this convenient restaurant is a local favorite at lunchtime. It offers a clubby bi-level interior with views of the city and seating under umbrellas overlooking an interior plant-filled courtyard. The menu features all-American favorites such as pot roast, lamb chop mixed grill, prime rib of beef, burgers, omelets, barbecued spareribs, jumbo beer-battered shrimp, lobster tail, and N.Y. strip steaks. Lunch items also include sandwiches, burgers, soups, fresh-fruit platters, and salads.

INEXPENSIVE

A.J.'S DELI CAFE, 111 Second Ave. NE. Tel. 821-4151.

Cuisine: AMERICAN/DELI. **Reservations:** Not required.

$ Prices: All items $2.50–$4.95. No credit cards.

Open: Mon–Fri 7:30am–2:30pm, Sat–Sun 8am–1:30pm.

For light meals, snacks, or take-out picnic ingredients, try this downtown spot on the ground level of the Plaza courtyard, between First and Second Streets North (shop no. 106). Service is fast and friendly and the decor is bright and airy, with Florida prints on the walls. There is seating at tables and around a central counter. Menu items include hot and cold sandwiches, salads, hoagies, chili, and homemade baked goods.

CHA CHA COCONUTS, 800 Second Ave. NE. Tel. 822-6655.

Cuisine: AMERICAN/CARIBBEAN. **Reservations:** Not required. **Directions:** Follow signs to the Pier and take the elevator to the 5th floor.

$ Prices: Appetizers $2.95–$4.95; main courses $3.95–$5.95 at lunch or dinner. AE, CB, DC, MC, V.

Open: Mon–Thurs 11am–midnight, Fri–Sat 11am–1am, Sun noon–10pm.

Billed as a tropical bar and grill, this informal spot sits on the top floor of the Pier complex, offering panoramic views of both the Gulf of Mexico and the St. Petersburg skyline. It's a great vantage point from which to watch the fishermen and boaters or to sip a tropical drink as the sun sets. Live music is usually on tap after dark and the menu is appealing at any hour of the day—burgers, fish sandwiches, chowders and chilis, and finger foods such as peel-and-eat shrimp, and chicken wings. All items on the menu are also available for takeout. For other locations, see "Clearwater Beach," below in this chapter, and Chapter 10, "Tampa Dining: Harbour Island."

TAVERN ON THE GREEN, 121 Seventh Ave. S. Tel. 821-1418.

Cuisine: AMERICAN. **Reservations:** Not required.

$ Prices: All items $1.50–$4.90. No credit cards.

Open: Mon–Fri 11am–11pm, Sat 11am–3pm.

On the University of South Florida campus, between First and Second Streets South, this typical campus eatery sports a decor of posters and memorabilia. There is seating indoors and outside on picnic tables overlooking the university buildings and the adjacent Albert Whitted Airport; the Salvador Dalí Museum is just a block away as well. The all-day menu features sandwiches named after literary greats, from a "Shakespeare" (ham, turkey, and Swiss) and "Hemingway" (tuna, Swiss, and tomato) to a "James Joyce" (corned beef, sauerkraut, and melted cheese). Salads, nachos, hot dogs, and made-to-order sandwiches are also available. Beer and wine only.

2. SOUTH OF DOWNTOWN

MODERATE

THE GOOD TIMES, 1130 Pinellas Bayway, Tierra Verde. Tel. 867-0774.
  Cuisine: CONTINENTAL. **Reservations:** Recommended. **Directions:** From downtown, take I-275 south to Pinellas Bayway and travel south on Fla. 679; the restaurant is at 13th St. W.
$ **Prices:** Appetizers $1.95–$5.95; main courses $10.95–$15.95. No credit cards.
  Open: Dinner only, Tues–Sat 5–9pm.

Located in a small shopping center, this restaurant is an unexpected surprise—a European bistro tucked between the waters of the Gulf of Mexico and Tampa Bay. The Czech proprietors use recipes reflecting French, Austrian, Swiss, Czech, Hungarian, and Russian traditions amid a decor of beer barrels, wine racks, and vines. Main courses include steak au poivre vert, beef Stroganoff, Bohemian sauerbraten with lingonberries, veal schnitzel à la Holstein, and roast pork with sauerkraut and knedliky (dumplings). Save room for dessert, a tempting assortment of rich treats such as Black Forest cake, apple strudel, and strawberry Romanov ice-cream pie.

LEVEROCK'S, 4801 37th St. S. Tel. 864-3883.
  Cuisine: SEAFOOD. **Reservations:** Not accepted. **Directions:** Take U.S. 19 south to 46th Ave. S. and turn right; go one block to 37th St. S. and turn left.
$ **Prices:** Appetizers $1.95–$3.95; main courses $3.95–$6.95 at lunch, $6.95–$14.95 at dinner. AE, CB, DC, DISC, MC, V.
  Open: Daily 11:30am–10pm. **Closed:** Thanksgiving and Christmas.

Dating back to 1948 and synonymous with the freshest of seafoods at affordable prices, Leverock's now operates five fish houses, each unique in its way, in the St. Petersburg area. In our view, this location on the Maximo Moorings is the best. Wide floor-to-ceiling windows frame views of Boca Ciega Bay and the yachts along the docks. If you like seafood, you won't be disappointed here (the chain has its own fleet of fishing boats). You may have to wait on line at busy times.

Selections range from 12 different shrimp dishes, to sautéed snapper, grouper Florentine, salmon stir-fry, and crab cakes, to a "captain's platter" of shrimp, scallops, fish, crab legs, and petite lobster tails. Only lobster tails, surf-and-turf, and king crab legs are slightly higher than the general main course price range. Steaks, chicken Cordon Bleu, and baby back ribs round out the menu. The lunch choices include burgers, salads, and sandwiches (don't miss Leverock's version of the traditional "club," stuffed with tender bay shrimp).

Surprisingly, the original Leverock's is not on the water at all, but north of downtown St. Petersburg at 7000 U.S. 19 at Park Boulevard,

Pinellas Park (tel. 526-9188), convenient if you're traveling between St. Pete and Tampa. The other three locations are on the water and are described later in this chapter (see "St. Petersburg Beach," "Island of Sand Key," and "Clearwater Beach").

INEXPENSIVE

TED PETERS' FAMOUS SMOKED FISH, 1350 Pasadena Ave. S. Tel. 381-7931.
Cuisine: SMOKED SEAFOOD. **Reservations:** Not accepted.
Directions: Take Fifth Ave. N. west and turn left at Pasadena Ave.; the restaurant is south of the Pasadena Shopping Center, on the approach to the Corey Ave. Causeway leading to St. Petersburg Beach.

$ Prices: Appetizers $1.25–$4.50; main courses $3.95–$11.95 at lunch or dinner. No credit cards.
Open: Wed–Mon 11:30am–7:30pm.

Your nose tells you when you are near this rustic little roadside stand and its adjacent smokehouse—aromas of smoking fish fill the air. The menu is limited, basically just smoked salmon, mackerel, or mullet, but people drive for miles to get their fill. It's totally informal and casual, with seating at picnic tables or along the counter. The smoked fish is served with German potato salad. If you feel like something lighter, there are sandwiches filled with smoked-fish spreads. The spreads are so popular that they're sold by the quart. Burgers are also available, as is beer.

3. NORTH OF DOWNTOWN

MODERATE

ARIGATO JAPANESE STEAKHOUSE, 3600 66th St. N. Tel. 343-5200.
Cuisine: JAPANESE. **Reservations:** Recommended on weekends. **Directions:** Northwest of downtown at 38th Ave. N., near the Tyrone Boulevard shopping area.

$ Prices: Appetizers $2.95–$4.95; main courses $8.95–$17.95. AE, CB, DC, DISC, MC, V.
Open: Dinner only, Mon–Sat 5–10pm, Sun 4–9pm.

 A fun place for adults and kids alike, this is a typical Japanese steak house where the chef is also the star performer. Groups of 10 guests sit around a teppanyaki table for each meal. You may not know all the people at your table as the meal begins, but such formalities certainly don't prevent you from sharing a memorable dining experience. A chef assigned to your table then prepares hibachi steak, sukiyaki chicken, shrimp, lobster, scallops, or whatever you order right before your eyes, with a dash of spice and a flash of cutlery. A favorite selection is ichiban, a mix of filet mignon, shrimp, and chicken. In all, seven courses are served, including appetizer, soup, salad, rice, and vegetables.

This restaurant is northwest of downtown, at 38th Avenue North near the Tyrone Boulevard shopping area. Other locations in the area include one at 1500 U.S. 19N., Clearwater (tel. 799-0202), and one in Tampa (see Chapter 10, "Tampa Dining").

LEVEROCK'S WATERFRONT STEAK HOUSE, 8800 Bay Pines Blvd. N. Tel. 345-5335.

Cuisine: AMERICAN. **Reservations:** Not accepted. **Directions:** Follow Tyrone Blvd. north toward the causeway to Madeira Beach; the restaurant is between Lighthouse Point Marina and Veterans Memorial Park.

$ Prices: Appetizers $1.95–$3.95; main courses $3.95–$6.95 at lunch, $6.95–$17.95 at dinner. AE, CB, DC, DISC, MC, V.
Open: Daily 11am–10pm. **Closed:** Thanksgiving and Christmas.

In a prime waterfront location, this restaurant was taken over in early 1990 by the Leverock's group, known primarily for fine seafood at moderate prices. The company decided not to convert it into another seafood house, but to put the focus on choice western beef, at affordable prices. So if you've enjoyed any of the Leverock's other locations for seafood, this place is the ideal alternative when you have a craving for beef. Best of all, it's not just another steak house setting—there are expansive views of Boca Ciega Bay from every table.

The menu features three different cuts of prime rib, two sizes of filet mignon, and four types of steaks, plus chopped steak, beef kebabs, and four variations of surf-and-turf. Just for variety, baby back ribs, chicken, and two or three seafood items round out the menu. Alaskan crab legs and lobster are also available, at higher prices.

MELTING POT, 2221 Fourth St. N. Tel. 895-6358.

Cuisine: SWISS. **Reservations:** Recommended.
$ Prices: Appetizers $2.95–$4.95; main courses $8.95–$14.95. AE, MC, V.
Open: Dinner only, Sun–Thurs 5–11pm, Fri–Sat 5pm–midnight. The fondue craze of the past is alive and thriving at this rustic chalet-style spot north of downtown, between 21st and 22nd Avenues North and two blocks north of Sunken Gardens.

The menu is simple, with emphasis on bubbling pots of Swiss and Cheddar cheeses and baskets filled with bite-size pieces of bread, fruit, and vegetables. You simply skewer a piece of bread, a grape, green bean, or various other choices, and then submerge and coat it with the creamy melted cheeses. Alternatively, lighter fondue-style cooking is also offered, using traditional court bouillon or peanut oil, to cook chicken, beef, seafood, or vegetables, accompanied by a selection of spicy and piquant dipping sauces. Top off the meal with a selection from a variety of white- and dark-chocolate fondues for dessert ($5.50 to $6.95 for two people).

OUTBACK STEAKHOUSE, 4088 Park St. Tel. 384-4329.
   Cuisine: AUSTRALIAN/AMERICAN. **Reservations:** Not accepted.
$ Prices: Appetizers $1.95–$5.95; main courses $7.95–$16.95. AE, DC, MC, V.
   Open: Dinner only, Sun–Thurs 4:30–10:30pm, Fri–Sat 4:30–11:30pm.

If you're a *Crocodile Dundee* fan, you're sure to enjoy this casual, come-as-you-are Aussie-theme restaurant. In fact, you'll probably catch yourself saying "G'day" before the meal's end. The menu features such down-under dishes as chicken and ribs grilled "on the barbie," Jackeroo pork chops, the Melbourne (a hefty porterhouse steak), Brisbane shrimp sauté, and "Botany Bay fish o' the day." The libation list includes lots of imported beers and wines from Australia.

This steak house is northwest of downtown, at the junction of Tyrone and Bay Pines Boulevards. Farther north, between St. Pete and Clearwater, there's another location at 3690 E. Bay Dr., Largo (tel. 538-9499), and there are branches both north and south of Tampa Airport (see Chapter 10, "Tampa Dining").

PEPIN, 4125 Fourth St. N. Tel. 821-3773.
   Cuisine: SPANISH. **Reservations:** Recommended.
$ Prices: Appetizers $2.95–$5.95; main courses $4.95–$15.95 at lunch, $10.95–$19.95 at dinner. AE, MC, V.
   Open: Mon–Fri 11am–11pm, Sat 5–11pm, Sun 5–10pm.

A mainstay of fine dining along the busy Fourth Street corridor, north of downtown between 41st and 42nd Avenues North, this inland restaurant offers a setting that is reminiscent of an Iberian villa, with lots of red tones and dark wrought-iron trim.

The menu reflects the restaurant's motto of *"Al pan, pan y al vino, vino,"* which roughly translated means food in its purest form, with no artificial ingredients or additives. The bread is freshly baked on the premises every morning, the fish comes from nearby waters, and the meats are aged and cut daily. Specialties include Spanish favorites such as shrimp Almendrina (with orange-mustard sauce), paella, and chicken with yellow Valencia rice, as well as local and international fare from whole Florida lobster and pompano en papillote, to chateaubriand and rack of lamb. Tapas, which can be a meal in themselves at lunch, range from $3.95 to $5.95.

INEXPENSIVE

CHUCK E. CHEESE'S, 1024 58th St. N. Tel. 345-3736.
   Cuisine: AMERICAN. **Reservations:** Not required
$ Prices: Most items $1.95–$6.95; large pizza with all the trimmings $15.95. AE, MC, V.
   Open: Sun–Thurs 11am–10pm, Fri 11am–11pm, Sat 10am–11pm.

Espousing the theme "where a kid can be a kid," this place in the Tyrone Gardens shopping mall, at the intersection of Ninth Avenue North, caters to the little ones. The food—pizza is the focal point—is only part of the attraction. Kids eat when they're not enjoying the rides, songs, games, videos, and shows by puppets and performing animated animals. Besides the pizza, the limited menu offers a help-yourself salad bar and a variety of sandwiches. If you're traveling with youngsters, don't miss this place.

FOURTH STREET SHRIMP STORE, 1006 Fourth St. N., between 10th and 11th Aves. N. Tel. 822-0325.
Cuisine: SEAFOOD. **Reservations:** Not accepted.
$ Prices: Appetizers $1–$3; main courses $4–$11 at lunch or dinner. No credit cards.
Open: Mon–Thurs and Sat 11:30am–8:30pm, Fri 11am–9pm, Sun noon–8pm.

 This Old Florida–style fish market and restaurant offers seafood at rock-bottom prices. Step inside and take a seat at one of the two dining rooms; there are no views of the water, but lots of nautical memorabilia, from fish nets and crab traps to three-dimensional fish art. Whimsical murals, old St. Petersburg street signs, and sports pennants round out the eclectic decor.

The tablecloths, utensils, and glasses are plastic and the plates are made of paper, but the seafood is the real thing—heaping servings of fresh grouper, smelts, frogs' legs, shrimp of all sizes, oysters, and crab. Many of the main courses come with mallets, so you can crack open the crustaceans on your own. Full dinners, platters, and baskets of fish are available throughout the day, as are seafood sandwiches, beef burgers, chicken wings, and steaks. Beer and wine available.

HOOTERS, 2901 Tyrone Blvd. Tel. 343-4947.
Cuisine: AMERICAN. **Reservations:** Not accepted.
$ Prices: Appetizers $1.95–$4.95; main courses $2.95–$14.95 at lunch or dinner. AE, MC, V.
Open: Mon–Fri 11am–midnight, Sat 11am–1am, Sun noon–10pm.

Though located along a busy shopping corridor northwest of downtown, opposite the Tyrone Square Mall shopping center, and far from the beaches, this establishment maintains a year-round beach-party atmosphere. For a description of the decor and the menu, see the entry for the original Hooters in Clearwater under "Nearby Dining," below in this chapter. For branches in Tampa, see Chapter 10, "Tampa Dining."

PEP'S SEA GRILL, 7610 Fourth St. N. Tel. 521-1655.
Cuisine: SEAFOOD. **Reservations:** Not accepted.
$ Prices: Appetizers $1.95–$3.95; main courses $5.95–$12.95. No credit cards.
Open: Dinner only, Mon–Sat 4–10pm, Sun 11:30am–9pm.

Located about a mile south of Gandy Boulevard and the Gandy Bridge approach, north of downtown between 76th and 77th Avenues North, near the Gateway Mall Shopping Center, this is a small, almost dinerlike eatery, with a cheery art deco decor. It is known for serving fresh seafood at rock-bottom prices. The menu items vary with the local catch, but specials often include salmon and snow crab, stone crabs, and a hearty one-pound shrimp feast. Beer and wine available.

Another branch is located in St. Petersburg Beach at 5895 Gulf Blvd. (tel. 367-3550). It's open Sunday through Thursday from 4 to 10pm and Friday and Saturday 4 to 10:30pm.

4. ST. PETERSBURG BEACH

MODERATE

HURRICANE, 807 Gulf Way. Tel. 360-9558.

Cuisine: SEAFOOD. **Reservations:** Not accepted. **Directions:** From downtown, take the Pinellas Bayway to Gulf Blvd.; turn left at the Don CeSar, go south to Eighth Ave., and turn right and then right again onto Gulf Way; the restaurant is between Eighth and Ninth Aves.

$ Prices: Appetizers $3.95–$9.95; main courses $2.95–$5.95 at lunch, $6.95–$17.95 at dinner. MC, V.

Open: Daily 8am–1am.

If you're a fan of Florida black grouper or even if you've never tasted it before, here's *the* spot to try it. Overlooking Pass-A-Grille beach, this informal, three-story, indoor-outdoor restaurant serves more than 5,000 pounds of grouper in an average week.

Main courses range from grouper Florentine and grouper parmesan to grouper au gratin, grouper Oscar, or grouper amandine, to name a few. And if you tire of grouper, there's always crab legs and claws, shrimp, scallops, and swordfish, as well as barbecued ribs and steaks. Lunch offers a choice of nine different grouper sandwiches, grouper chowders, and grouper salads, as well as conch fritters, barbecued shrimp, hot vegetable sandwiches, and burgers. The most popular eating times seem to be around sunset, when the view from the outside deck is mesmerizing, and after 9pm Wednesday, Friday, Saturday, and Sunday, when there's a live jazz band inside.

KINJO, 4615 Gulf Blvd. Tel. 367-6762.

Cuisine: JAPANESE. **Reservations:** Not accepted.

$ Prices: Appetizers $2.95–$5.95; main courses $7.95–$16.95. CB, DC, MC, V.

Open: Dinner only, Sun–Thurs 5–10pm, Fri–Sat 5–10:30pm.

A glass elevator whisks you to the second floor of this modern restaurant in the center of St. Petersburg Beach, at 46th Avenue, in the Dolphin Landing shopping center, overlooking Boca Ciega Bay. Seating, which is both Western style (at tables) and tatami style (on the floor), is on a first-come, first-served basis, so it is wise to arrive early.

The menu offers a selection of sushi and sashimi, acclaimed as first-rate by local newspaper critics, as well as a variety of beef, chicken, seafood, and vegetables cooked according to your preference (teppanyaki style on a grill, deep-fried as tempura, or stir-fried).

LEVEROCK'S, 10 Corey Ave. Tel. 367-4588.

Cuisine: SEAFOOD. **Reservations:** Not accepted.

$ Prices: Appetizers $1.95–$3.95; main courses $3.95–$6.95 at lunch, $6.95–$14.95 at dinner. AE, CB, DC, DISC, MC, V.

Open: Daily 11:30am–10pm. **Closed:** Thanksgiving and Christmas.

 One of five Leverock's in the St. Petersburg area, all known for fresh seafood at affordable prices, this location on the north end of St. Petersburg Beach, to the right of the entrance to the Corey Avenue Causeway, is convenient to both downtown and the beaches, so it's understandably popular. Overlooking Boca Ciega Bay, it offers lovely waterside views. The only drawback is waiting on line at peak dining times, so get here early. The food and views are definitely worth the wait.

For a description of the menu, see "South of Downtown," earlier in this chapter.

MULLIGAN'S SUNSET GRILLE, 9524 Blind Pass Rd. Tel. 367-6680.

Cuisine: SEAFOOD/AMERICAN. **Reservations:** Not accepted.

$ Prices: Appetizers $3.95–$7.95; main courses $4.95–$10.95 at lunch, $8.95–$19.95 at dinner. AE, MC, V.

Open: Daily 11am–11pm; brunch Sun 11am–3pm.

Overlooking the waters of Boca Ciega Bay, this informal restaurant is at the north end of St. Pete Beach, at 95th Avenue beside the bridge and Blind Pass Park. It has a nautical decor, with oak tables, captain's chairs, and bi-level seating offering views of the water and the park. In addition, there is outdoor waterfront dining overlooking the bay. The straightforward menu offers steamed seafood platters, stone crabs in season, and seafood combination pots for two people (with steamed oysters or mussels, snow crab, shrimp, corn on the cob, and more), as well as mesquite-smoked ribs, steaks, Southwest-style chicken, and pastas.

SILAS DENT'S, 5501 Gulf Blvd. Tel. 360-6961.

Cuisine: REGIONAL/SEAFOOD. **Reservations:** Recommended.

$ Prices: Appetizers $2.95–$7.95; main courses $7.95–$18.95. AE, CB, DC, MC, V.

Open: Dinner only, Sun–Thurs 5–10pm, Fri–Sat 5–11pm.

With a rustic facade of driftwood and an interior of palm fronds and cedar poles, this restaurant at 55th Avenue, opposite the TradeWinds Resort, seeks to replicate the home of a popular local folk hero, Silas Dent. Known as the "hermit of Cabbage Key," he inhabited a nearby island for many years earlier in this century and often rowed his boat over to St. Pete Beach, to the delight of the local residents.

The menu aims to reflect Silas's diet of local fish and vegetation, using such ingredients as alligator, amberjack, grouper, and squid, as well as current favorites, such as Dungeness crab and lobster tails, seafood fettuccine, coconut shrimp, sea bass with dill sauce, scallops primavera, and Jamaica paella, as well as prime ribs, filet mignon, and chicken Silas (with red bell pepper sauce).

INEXPENSIVE

CRABBY BILL'S, 5100 Gulf Blvd. Tel. 360-8858.

Cuisine: SEAFOOD. **Reservations:** Not accepted.

$ **Prices:** Appetizers $2.95–$4.95; main courses $3.95–$16.95. MC, V.

Open: Mon–Thurs 11am–10pm, Fri–Sat 11am–11pm, Sun 1–10pm.

Set back from the main road, this beach house–style restaurant overlooks the gulf and offers great views amid a casual picnic-table-style decor and crustacean-cracking ambience. An offshoot of a long-established restaurant of the same name about 15 miles up the beach strip, this place is known for its crabs—steamed blue crabs, garlic crabs, stone crab claws, soft-shell crabs, and crab cakes. In addition, there's an ever-changing selection of other fresh seafoods, from oysters, clams, and mussels to shrimp, mahimahi, and catfish. The original Crabby's is at 401 Gulf Blvd., Indian Rocks Beach (tel. 595-4825), and nearly always has a line out the door, so come early to either location.

SEA CRITTERS CAFE, 2007 Pass-A-Grille Way. Tel. 360-3706.

Cuisine: AMERICAN. **Reservations:** Not accepted.

$ **Prices:** Appetizers $2.95–$5.95; main courses $2.95–$6.95 at lunch, $5.95–$13.95 at dinner. MC, V.

Open: Sun and Tues–Thurs noon–10pm, Fri–Sat noon–11pm.

The decor and theme of this informal eatery focus on sea critters of all types but especially caricatures of catfish. The management even goes so far as to publish a sort of tongue-in-cheek booklet, "How to Properly Feed Catfish," and encourages guests to venture outside to the dock after dark to feed the passing sea critters. With table seating on the dock, deck, or inside, this restaurant enjoys a lovely location on the Pass-A-Grille Channel of the Intracoastal Waterway at the Vina Del Mar Bridge. The same menu is in effect all day, offering salads, finger foods (from nachos to chicken wings), hot and cold sandwiches, beef burgers and clamburgers, pastas, steaks, Jamaican jerk chicken, and seafood platters, such as the house specialty of "shellfish lover's feast" (snow crab legs, broiled shrimp, and scallops with drawn butter, red beans, and rice).

5. TREASURE ISLAND

MODERATE

CAPTAIN KOSMAKOS, 9610 Gulf Blvd. Tel. 367-3743.

Cuisine: AMERICAN/INTERNATIONAL. **Reservations:** Recommended. **Directions:** Follow Blind Pass Rd. north from St. Pete Beach; the restaurant is on the bay side at 96th Ave.

$ **Prices:** Appetizers $1.95–$5.95; main courses $8.95–$21.95. AE, CB, DC, MC, V.

Open: Daily 3pm–1am.

The setting is eye-catching—a large glass building on concrete stilts, with the restaurant on the upper level overlooking the waters between

St. Pete Beach and Treasure Island. There are two big and open dining rooms, which are sometimes noisy.

But the big draw is the food, an eclectic blend of American, Greek, and Italian dishes, all served in hefty portions. The menu includes Florida grouper and snapper, Maryland crab cakes, Alaskan crab legs, Maine lobster, and pan-fried squid, as well as chicken cacciatore, veal marsala or parmesan, shrimp Créole, shish kebab, pasta, prime rib, and steaks.

INEXPENSIVE

SUNSET BEACH CAFE, 9701 First St. E. Tel. 367-3359.
   Cuisine: AMERICAN. **Reservations:** Not required.
$ **Prices:** Appetizers $1.25–$8.95; main courses $2.95–$5.95 at lunch, $5.95–$9.95 at dinner. CB, DC, DISC, MC, V.
   Open: Daily 7am–9:30pm.

Located at the corner of Gulf Boulevard across the road from the beach on the southern tip of Treasure Island, this family-run restaurant exudes a continental feeling, with reproduction art by Renoir and Monet on the walls, but the wraparound windows add unmistakably Florida views on all sides. The all-day menu includes a variety of freshly prepared salads, burgers, sandwiches, omelets, Belgian waffles, pastas, and pizzas, as well as dinner choices of baby back ribs, steaks, scallops scampi, fried chicken, coconut shrimp, fried or broiled grouper, and stir-fry dishes. For those with room for dessert, key lime pie is a specialty.

6. THE ISLAND OF SAND KEY

MADEIRA BEACH

MODERATE

BALLOON PALACE, 14995 Gulf Blvd. Tel. 393-2706.
   Cuisine: AMERICAN. **Reservations:** Not accepted.
$ **Prices:** Appetizers $1.95–$4.95; main courses $2.95–$6.95 at lunch, $4.95–$9.95 at dinner. AE, MC, V.
   Open: Mon–Thurs 11am–midnight, Fri–Sat 11am–2am, Sun 1–11pm.

Just south of the entrance to the Tom Stewart Causeway (Fla. 666), in the Madeira Commons shopping center, this restaurant is a fun spot with a beach-party atmosphere. The decor is dominated by dozens of models and miniatures of hot-air balloons.

The menu is straightforward, with emphasis on steaks, barbecued ribs, local seafoods, and the house specialty, Buffalo-style chicken wings. Servings range from a five-piece taster portion to 20 pieces or more, with extra sauce or celery on the side. You can also get a take-out bucket of 50 wings for beach parties. Lunch items include pizza fingers, peel-and-eat shrimp, nachos, salads, beer-battered grouper fingers, burgers, and sandwiches.

FRIENDLY FISHERMAN, 150 128th Ave. Tel. 391-6025.
Cuisine: SEAFOOD. **Reservations:** Not accepted.
$ Prices: Appetizers $1.95–$4.95; main courses $2.95–$6.95 at lunch, $7.95–$19.95 at dinner. MC, V.
Open: Sun–Thurs 7am–10 or 11pm, Fri–Sat 7am–midnight.

The centerpiece of John's Pass Village, this restaurant on the boardwalk at the southern tip of Madeira Beach, is the outgrowth of a busy fishing business launched over 50 years ago by Capt. Wilson Hubbard, who is indeed a "friendly fisherman" and hence the name. You'll often see the captain strolling from table to table making sure that customers are happy—you'll recognize him by his yachting cap and his red-and-green socks, a trademark. The restaurant offers indoor and outdoor seating, with waterside views in both cases.

The seafood is brought in fresh daily by the captain's own fleet, and served smoked, steamed, fried, or broiled. Dinner choices range from amberjack and mullet to stone crabs, shrimp, grouper, snapper, and flounder, as well as lobster tails and four kinds of surf-and-turf. Lunch choices are seafood samplers, sandwiches, and salads, as well as burgers and smoked meats.

LEVEROCK'S, 565 150th Ave. Tel. 393-0459.
Cuisine: SEAFOOD. **Reservations:** Not accepted.
$ Prices: Appetizers $1.95–$3.95; main courses $3.95–$6.95 at lunch, $6.95–$14.95 at dinner. AE, CB, DC, DISC, MC, V.
Open: Daily 11:30am–10pm. **Closed:** Thanksgiving and Christmas.

Situated east of Gulf Boulevard, to the right of the entrance to the Tom Stewart Causeway, off the main beach stretch on the marina overlooking Boca Ciega Bay, this is one of five Leverock's in the St. Petersburg area. All are known for fresh seafood at affordable prices, and are understandably very popular, even though the no-reservations policy can often mean standing in line to wait for a table, but the food and views are well worth the wait.

For a menu description, see "South of Downtown," above in this chapter.

INEXPENSIVE

OMI'S BAVARIAN INN, 14701 Gulf Blvd. Tel. 393-9654.
Cuisine: GERMAN. **Reservations:** Recommended.
$ Prices: Appetizers $2.95–$5.95; main courses $6.95–$15.95. MC, V.
Open: Dinner only. Wed–Mon 3–9:30pm.

This little restaurant in the center of Madeira Beach, four blocks south of the Tom Stewart Causeway, on the bay side, is a small patch of Germany on the gulf. Specialties include a choice of various schnitzels, sauerbraten and Schweinebraten (roast pork), chicken paprikash, beef goulash, Bavarian bratwurst, and stuffed pepper. A variety of seafoods and steaks is also on the menu. Beer and wine available, including many European imports.

NORTH REDINGTON BEACH
EXPENSIVE

THE WINE CELLAR, 17307 Gulf Blvd. Tel. 393-3491.
   Cuisine: CONTINENTAL. **Reservations:** Highly recommended.
$ Prices: Appetizers $2.75–$9.75; main courses $11.75–$27.50. AE, DC, DISC, MC, V.
   Open: Dinner only, Tues–Sun 4:30–11pm.

⭐ Considered by locals to be the top choice in the St. Pete area despite its lack of a water view, it's on the bay side about two miles north of the Tom Stewart Causeway, between 173rd and 174th Avenues. With its culinary reputation, it doesn't need views. There are seven dining rooms, each with a distinctive European theme, such as a village boulevard of shops, a wine vault, or a country-garden conservatory.

With tuxedoed waiters and live background music, this is an atmosphere conducive to a big splurge. Why not start your meal by indulging in fresh Russian caviar ($45 for two ounces), Swedish smoked salmon ($6.95 a serving), or perhaps a hearty soup (Hungarian goulash or Swiss cheese soup, $3.50 to $4.50). The main courses present the best of Europe and the United States, with such dishes as North Carolina rainbow trout, red snapper Waleska, frogs' legs provençal, various cuts of prime rib, wienerschnitzel, beef Wellington, rack of lamb, and chateaubriand. There are also vegetarian and low-calorie dishes and a nightly "surprise dinner" when the chef selects a "culinary adventure" from appetizer through dessert.

MODERATE

JASMINE'S GULFFRONT STEAK HOUSE, in the North Redington Beach Hilton, 17120 Gulf Blvd. Tel. 391-4000.
   Cuisine: AMERICAN. **Reservations:** Recommended.
$ Prices: Appetizers $2.95–$9.95; main courses $4.95–$14.95 at lunch, $9.95–$19.95 at dinner. AE, CB, DC, DISC, MC, V.
   Open: Lunch daily 11:30am–2:30pm; dinner daily 5–10pm.

This lobby-level hotel restaurant has a tropical atmosphere, with indoor and outdoor seating overlooking the Gulf of Mexico. It's just under two miles north of the Tom Stewart Causeway, between 171st and 172nd Avenues. The specialty of the house is T-bone steaks, with a variety of other choices, such as shrimp Diane, barbecued ribs, key lime chicken, pork chop teriyaki, and surf-and-turf. Lunch items range from sandwiches and salads to design-your-own omelets, seafood, and pastas. Even if you can't dine here, it's worth stopping by for a drink and the nightly "sunset celebration" on the deck.

REDINGTON SHORES
EXPENSIVE

LOBSTER POT, 17814 Gulf Blvd. Tel. 391-8592.
   Cuisine: SEAFOOD. **Reservations:** Highly recommended.

$ Prices: Appetizers $2.95–$9.95; main courses $12.95–$27.95. AE, CB, DC, MC, V.

Open: Dinner only, Mon–Sat 4:30–10pm, Sun 4–10pm.

Don't judge this restaurant by its exterior. Housed in a rustic-looking building with a plain exterior and no waterside views, it has a charming nautical decor inside with fine linens, crystal, and candlelight. Above all, you'll quickly discover why this spot is considered a benchmark among the gulf coast's seafood houses.

First and foremost this is a lobster house, with 22 varieties of lobster offerings, including specimens from Maine, Florida, South Africa, and Denmark, tails or whole, in sauces and au naturel, all sold at market prices. In addition to lobster, there is a wide selection of grouper, snapper, salmon, swordfish, shrimp, scallops, crab, and even Dover sole, prepared simply or in elaborate sauces. If you can't decide, try one of the dishes designed "for those who want it all," such as lobster potpourri, bouillabaisse, and Neptune's delight. Filet mignon, steaks, and chicken round out the menu. The restaurant is located on the gulf side, about 2½ miles north of the Tom Stewart Causeway, between 178th and 179th Avenues.

INEXPENSIVE

THE FRIENDLY TAVERN, 18121 Gulf Blvd. Tel. 393-4470.

Cuisine: AMERICAN. **Reservations:** Not accepted.

$ Prices: Appetizers $1.95–$4.95; main courses $2.95–$9.95. AE, MC, V.

Open: Daily 11am–1am.

Situated opposite a public beach about three miles north of Tom Stewart Causeway, between 181st and 182nd Avenues, this indoor-outdoor spot is convenient for casual dining after a swim or a walk on the beach. You can watch the traffic go by on Gulf Boulevard as you sip a tropical drink or try some finger foods such as fried vegetables or cheese sticks. Other items on the menu include beer-steamed shrimp (sold by the pound or half pound), plus burgers, hot dogs, sandwiches, chili, soups, seafood salads, and steaks. To quench a thirst, there are also 50 beers from 14 countries.

SHELLS, 17855 Gulf Blvd. Tel. 393-8990.

Cuisine: SEAFOOD. **Reservations:** Not accepted.

$ Prices: Appetizers $1.95–$4.95; main courses $4.95–$13.95. AE, MC, V.

Open: Sun–Thurs 11:30am–10pm, Fri–Sat 11:30am–11pm.

Closed: Thanksgiving and Christmas.

 Shells is a local institution. The first Shells restaurant opened in Tampa in 1985 and this location followed soon after, as have over 20 other branches in Florida and beyond. This is one of the nicer settings, overlooking Boca Ciega Bay about 2½ miles north of Tom Stewart Causeway, between 178th and 179th Avenues. For a description of the decor and the menu, see Chapter 10, "Tampa Dining: Airport/West Shore."

Another branch in the St. Pete area is at 1190 34th St. N., St. Petersburg (tel. 321-6020).

INDIAN SHORES

MODERATE

CHATEAU MADRID, 19519 Gulf Blvd. Tel. 596-9100.
   Cuisine: SPANISH/CONTINENTAL. **Reservations:** Recommended. **Directions:** Take Park Blvd. Causeway (Fla. 694) west to Gulf Blvd.; turn right and the restaurant is five blocks north on the Intracoastal Waterway side.
   $ Prices: Appetizers $3.95–$6.95; main courses $8.95–$18.95. AE, CB, DC, MC, V.
   Open: Dinner only, Sun–Thurs 4–10pm, Fri–Sat 4–11pm.

Set back from the main road, this contemporary-style hacienda overlooks the waters of the Narrows, along the Intracoastal Waterway. Like its sister restaurant of the same name (see "Nearby Dining," below), it conveys the ambience of an Iberian villa. The menu features a variety of traditional dishes from Spain including paella valenciana, arroz con pollo (chicken with rice), whole pompano a la sal, and a signature dish of "Ternera Château Madrid" (veal, shrimp, and mushrooms in brandy cream sauce). There are also dishes associated with other parts of Europe, such as veal marsala, wienerschnitzel, rigatoni à la vodka, rack of lamb flamed in brandy, shrimp provençal, and chateaubriand. A pianist plays international background music in the lounge on Friday through Sunday evenings.

SCANDIA, 19829 Gulf Blvd. Tel. 595-5525.
   Cuisine: SCANDINAVIAN. **Reservations:** Recommended. **Directions:** Take the Park Blvd. Causeway (Fla. 694) west to Gulf Blvd.; turn right and the restaurant is eight blocks north on the Intracoastal Waterway side.
   $ Prices: Appetizers $2.95–$6.95; main courses $4.95–$7.95 at lunch, $6.95–$19.95 at dinner. DISC, MC, V.
   Open: Lunch Tues–Sat 11:30am–3pm; dinner Tues–Sat 4–9pm, Sun noon–8pm.

Unique in decor and menu along the gulf coast, this chalet-style restaurant brings a touch of Hans Christian Andersen to the beach strip. There are five cozy dining rooms, all decorated with Royal Copenhagen pottery, paintings of Denmark, chiming clocks, and other handcrafted bric-a-brac.

   The menu offers Scandinavian favorites, from smoked salmon and pickled herring to roast pork, sausages, schnitzels, and Danish lobster tails, as well as a few international dishes such as curried chicken, surf-and-turf, roast leg of lamb, and local seafood choices—jumbo shrimp, scallops, grouper, flounder, and more. Many of the items served—red cabbage, sausage, soups, salad dressings, and baked goods—are also available for purchase in the adjacent shop.

INEXPENSIVE

HUNGRY FISHERMAN, 19915 Gulf Blvd. Tel. 595-4218.
   Cuisine: SEAFOOD. **Reservations:** Not accepted. **Directions:** Take the Park Blvd. Causeway (Fla. 694) west to Gulf Blvd.; turn right and the restaurant is nine blocks north on the Intracoastal Waterway side.

$ Prices: Appetizers $1.95–$4.95; main course $2.95–$5.95 at lunch, $5.95–$16.95 at dinner. No credit cards.
  Open: Daily 11:30am–10pm.

There's nothing fancy about this restaurant, but you'll regularly see people lined up outside the door. It has to be doing something right, and in this case, the secret is serving a tremendous variety of fresh seafood at remarkably low prices. With the exception of multi-item seafood platters and steaks, all dinner main courses come in well below the $10 mark. The menu includes over 40 seafood choices from white fantail gulf shrimp to Alaskan salmon, grilled halibut, grouper, snapper, Danish lobster tails, Dungeness crab, frogs' legs, and deep-sea scallops. The lunch menu offers much of the same, as well as seafood platters, salads, and casseroles, beef or fish burgers. Get there early.

INDIAN ROCKS BEACH

MODERATE

GUPPY'S ON THE BEACH, 1701 Gulf Blvd. Tel. 593-2032.
  Cuisine: AMERICAN/SEAFOOD. **Reservations:** Not accepted. **Directions:** Take Fla. 688 west to Gulf Blvd. and turn right; the restaurant is just over a mile north, between 17th and 18th Aves., on the Intracoastal Waterway side.
$ Prices: Appetizers $2.95–$6.95; snack items $3.95–$8.95; main courses $7.95–$15.95. AE, CB, DC, MC, V.
  Open: Sun and Tues–Thurs 11:30am–10:30pm, Fri–Sat 11:30am–11pm.

Formerly known as "La Cave" and then "Café Martinique," this restaurant has been reborn with new owners and a tropical Caribbean-style decor of bright pink, teal, and white furnishings inside, and splashy pastel umbrellas outside on the patio. The main attraction, however, is the seafood, served fresh daily and prepared to order, from swordfish and snapper to scampi, as well as amberjack, mahimahi, grouper, tuna, and cobia. The menu, which is the same throughout the day, also includes upper potato crust salmon, fried shrimp with pineapple jalapeño salsa, crab cakes with brandy corn sauce, baby back ribs with tangy mustard sauce, a variety of innovative sandwiches and burgers, fajitas, quesadillas, and salads such as the signature Santa Fe, a combination of corn, black beans, red peppers, and zucchini. The patio faces Gulf Boulevard and offers lovely views of the beachfront across the street at sunset time.

MURPH'S, 2208 Gulf Blvd. Tel. 596-7401.
  Cuisine: SEAFOOD. **Reservations:** Not accepted. **Directions:** Take Fla. 688 west to Gulf Blvd. and turn right; the restaurant is a little over a mile north, on the gulf side between 22nd and 23rd Aves.
$ Prices: Appetizers $2.95–$5.95; main courses $3.95–$6.95 at lunch, $6.95–$13.95 at dinner. MC, V.
  Open: Daily 11:30am–10pm.

This informal indoor-outdoor spot is not directly on the beach, but it is within viewing distance of the gulf from the tables on the outside deck (a prime spot to watch sunsets). The emphasis is on local seafoods, cooked to order over an open wood-fired grill, or blackened, steamed, or fried. Choices include grouper, snapper, swordfish, tuna, and "catch of the day." If you don't mind a little work, try the you-peel-'em shrimp or seasonal specials of Florida lobster and stone crab claws. Top the meal with key lime pie (a family recipe) available by the slice or if you become addicted, buy a whole pie. Lunch items include fish sandwiches, burgers, gumbo soups, and salads. Beer and wine available.

INEXPENSIVE

CRABBY BILL'S, 401 Gulf Blvd. Tel. 595-4825.
   Cuisine: SEAFOOD. **Reservations:** Not accepted. **Directions:** Take Fla. 688 west to Gulf Blvd. and turn left; the restaurant is one block south on the Intracoastal Waterway side.
$ **Prices:** Appetizers $2.95–$4.95; main courses $3.95–$16.95. MC, V.
   Open: Mon–Thurs 11am–10pm, Fri–Sat 11am–11pm, Sun 1–10pm.

As its name implies, crabs are the specialty at this informal restaurant and seafood market, long a tradition on the beach strip. In 1993, success spawned the opening of a second location—a new and larger branch overlooking the gulf waters at St. Petersburg Beach. For a complete description of the menu, common to both places, see "St. Petersburg Beach," above, in this chapter.

7. CLEARWATER BEACH

EXPENSIVE

BOB HEILMAN'S BEACHCOMBER, 447 Mandalay Ave. Tel. 442-4144.
   Cuisine: AMERICAN. **Reservations:** Recommended. **Directions:** Take Fla. 60 west over Memorial Causeway to Mandalay; turn right and restaurant is two blocks north on the right at Papaya St.
$ **Prices:** Appetizers $2.95–$6.95; main courses $5.95–$12.95 at lunch, $10.95–$25.95 at dinner. AE, DC, MC, V.
   Open: Mon–Sat 11:30am–11pm, Sun noon–10pm.

Even though it doesn't have any water views, this restaurant has been an area mainstay since 1948. The decor in the two dining rooms features unusual murals and lots of leafy plants. The menu presents a wide variety of fresh seafood, from Everglades frogs' legs to Maine lobsters, as well as Atlantic sole and the best of the local catch. Beef is also a specialty here, with aged steaks and prime ribs much in demand. One of the most popular items on the menu is in a class by itself—"back-to-the-farm" fried chicken from an original 1926 recipe. The new 25,000-bottle wine cellar, Cellar in the Sand, is worth a visit before or after a meal.

MODERATE

THE COLUMBIA, 1241 Gulf Blvd. Tel. 596-2828.

Cuisine: SPANISH. **Reservations:** Recommended. **Directions:** From Clearwater Beach, take the toll bridge south to Sand Key; the restaurant is next to the Radisson Hotel on the harbor side.

$ Prices: Appetizers $1.95–$4.95; main courses $4.95–$7.95 at lunch, $7.95–$14.95 at dinner. AE, CB, DC, MC, V.

Open: Sun–Thurs 11am–10pm, Fri–Sat 11am–11pm.

Situated just south of the main Clearwater Beach strip, this restaurant is the newest offshoot of the famous Tampa landmark. This branch manages to meld the old and the new with great success—lovely wide-windowed views of Clearwater Harbor and a decor of dark woods, old Spanish tiles, Don Quixote prints, and intricate wrought ironwork. See Chapter 10, "Tampa Dining: Ybor City," for a description of the cuisine.

THE FLAGSHIP, 20 Island Way. Tel. 443-6210.

Cuisine: SEAFOOD. **Reservations:** Recommended. **Directions:** Take Fla. 60 west to Memorial Causeway and turn right on Island Way.

$ Prices: Appetizers $2.99–$8.99; main courses $4.99–$7.99 at lunch, $9.99–$22.99 at dinner. AE, MC, V.

Open: Sun–Thurs 11:30am–9:30pm, Fri–Sat 11:30am–10pm.

Decorated with brassy nautical fixtures and seascape art, this is one of the area's best-known dining spots. Located just east of the main beach strip, it sits on the waterfront in a well-landscaped two-acre setting, next to the Clearwater Marine Science Center.

The menu is similar at lunch and dinner, with a wide variety of seafood as well as chicken, beef, and pastas; sandwiches and salads are available at lunch. The seafood selections include a half-dozen daily specials ranging from amberjack to mahimahi and scrod to salmon, all cooked to order—blackened, charbroiled, broiled, or fried. Other choices range from Danish lobster tails, snow crab, lobster tails, and shrimp in various styles, to prime rib (in the evening only).

LEVEROCK'S, 551 Gulf Blvd. Tel. 446-5884.

Cuisine: SEAFOOD. **Reservations:** Not accepted.

$ Prices: Appetizers $1.95–$3.95; main courses $3.95–$6.95 at lunch, $6.95–$14.95 at dinner. AE, CB, DC, DISC, MC, V.

Open: Daily 11:30am–10pm. **Closed:** Thanksgiving and Christmas.

 Formerly Fisherman's Wharf, this restaurant is one of the newest branches in the Leverock's group, a local chain known for the freshest of seafood at affordable prices. Set on a 2.75-acre waterfront site, this location is one of the most scenic—on the southern tip of Clearwater Beach, at the foot of the Sand Key bridge, overlooking the waters of Clearwater Pass. But with expansive views and excellent seafood at affordable prices, it's very popular, so come at off-peak dining times to avoid waiting for a table. Even if you do have to wait, it's well worth it.

For a description of the menu, see "South of Downtown," earlier in this chapter.

RAJAN'S, 435 Mandalay Ave. Tel. 443-2100.

    Cuisine: SEAFOOD. **Reservations:** Recommended. **Directions:** Take Fla. 60 west across Memorial Causeway to Mandalay Ave. and turn right; the restaurant is two blocks north on the right at Papaya St.

$ **Prices:** Appetizers $3.95–$10.95; main courses $2.95–$7.95 at lunch, $7.95–$22.95 at dinner. MC, V.

    Open: Mon–Sat 11:30am–11pm, Sun noon–10pm.

Named for its owners (Ray and Jan), this informal Florida-style eatery is across the street from the beach. Using a seafood-by-the-seashore theme, the menu offers several types of oysters, as well as soft-shell or stone crabs, butterflied shrimp, scallops scampi, grouper Oscar, and filet of sole. You can also make your own platters with a choice of two or three types of seafood. Steaks and chicken round out the dinner menu, and at lunch you can also order seafood sandwiches, croissant-wiches, soups, burgers, and omelets.

SEAFOOD & SUNSETS AT JULIE'S, 351 S. Gulfview Blvd. Tel. 441-2548.

    Cuisine: SEAFOOD. **Reservations:** Recommended. **Directions:** Take Fla. 60 across the Memorial Causeway; keep left, follow the road to the end, and turn left onto S. Gulfview Blvd.; the restaurant is on the left opposite the public beach.

$ **Prices:** Appetizers $1.95–$6.95; main courses $3.95–$7.95 at lunch, $6.95–$17.95 at dinner. AE, MC, V.

    Open: Daily 11am–10pm.

A Key West–style atmosphere prevails at this beach-house eatery on the main thoroughfare. And yes, there is a Julie (Julie Nichols), who is

---

Ⓕ FROMMER'S COOL FOR KIDS: RESTAURANTS

Balloon Palace *(see p. 89)* Dozens of miniature hot-air balloons float across the ceiling, and the menu offers barbecued choices or finger foods, just right for small appetites.

Chuck E. Cheese's *(see p. 84)* A restaurant designed for children—rides, songs, video games, puppets, animated animals—and lots of pizza, too!

Island House *(see p. 100)* An extensive menu just for kids, and a free balloon for each youngster who finishes dinner.

94th Aero Squadron *(see p. 101)* Old planes and World War I memorabilia fascinate kids of every age, as do the views of planes taking off from the adjacent airport.

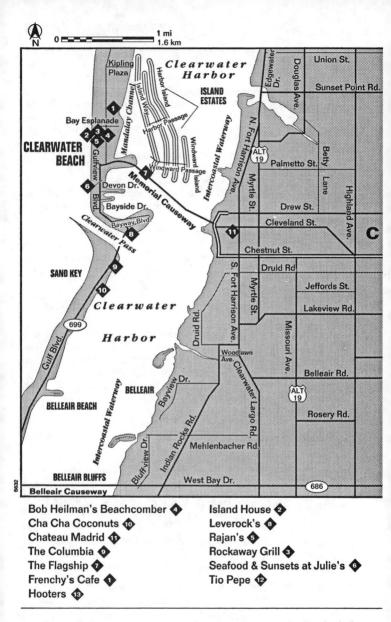

usually on the scene. Seating is indoors or on an umbrella-shaded patio, ideal for sunset-viewing each evening. And just to make sure no one misses this spectacular sight, sunset time is posted on a blackboard every day.

Dinner items range from Florida lobster tails, stone crabs, conch, grouper and other fish (prepared charbroiled, blackened, fried, or broiled) to steaks, surf-and-turf, and chicken. In addition, sandwiches, salads, burgers, fish-and-chips, you-peel-'em shrimp, and

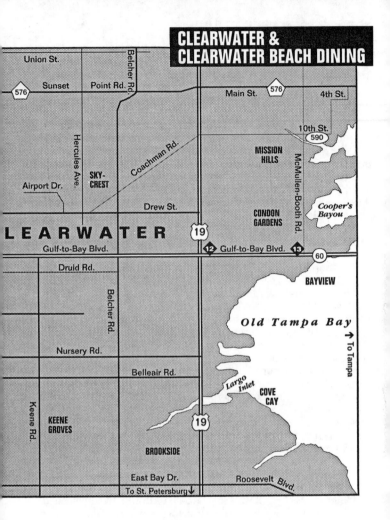

other finger foods are sold throughout the day, to go or to stay. Beer
and wine available.

INEXPENSIVE

CHA CHA COCONUTS, 1241 Gulf Blvd., Clearwater. Tel.
596-6040.
Cuisine: AMERICAN. **Reservations:** Not required. **Direc-**

tions: From Clearwater Beach, take the toll bridge south to Sand Key; the restaurant is next to the Radisson Hotel on the left.
$ Prices: Appetizers $1.95–$4.95; main courses $3.95–$7.95 at lunch or dinner. AE, CB, DC, MC, V.
Open: Mon–Thurs 11am–midnight, Fri–Sat 11am–1am, Sun noon–11pm.

This informal tropical bar and grill sits beside the Columbia restaurant overlooking Clearwater Harbor, with both indoor and outdoor deck seating along the boardwalk. It's a great vantage point from which to watch the passing sailboats and yachts or to sip a tropical drink as the sun sets. Live music is usually on tap after dark. See the entry for Cha Cha Coconuts under "Downtown," above in this chapter. For the Tampa branch, see Chapter 10, "Tampa Dining: Harbour Island."

FRENCHY'S CAFE, 41 Baymount St. Tel. 446-3707.

Cuisine: SEAFOOD. **Reservations:** Not accepted.
$ Prices: Appetizers $1.95–$4.95; main courses $2.95–$14.95. MC, V.
Open: Mon–Thurs 11:30am–11pm, Fri–Sat 11:30am–midnight, Sun 1–11pm.

A casual eatery nestled on a side street across from the beachfront, off Mandalay Avenue, across the street from the Clearwater Beach Hotel, this is Clearwater Beach at its most relaxed. A U-shaped bar dominates the small interior, with a sprinkling of square tables, booths, nautical fixtures, and an overworked jukebox.

Ignore the noise and come for the grouper burgers, famous in their own right, as are the "crabby shrimp" sandwiches. Other items on the menu range from smoked fish spreads and crackers to oysters, mussels, and clams in the shell, as well as Greek-style salads and Louisiana shrimp gumbo soup, boiled shrimp, and Florida stone-crab claws. A second location is two blocks away at 419 Poinsetta Ave. (tel. 461-6295).

ISLAND HOUSE, 452 Mandalay Ave. Tel. 442-2373.

Cuisine: SEAFOOD/GREEK. **Reservations:** Recommended.
Directions: Take Fla. 60 west across Memorial Causeway to Mandalay Ave. and turn right; the restaurant is one block north on the left.
$ Prices: Appetizers $1.95–$5.95; main courses $6.95–$12.95. AE, MC, V.
Open: Dinner only, Tues–Sun 4–10:30pm.

A local favorite since 1963, this restaurant is run by the Houllis family, who have incorporated many recipes from Greece into the menu. The choices include Greek salads, moussaka, Greek spaghetti (spaghetti with browned butter, sautéed onions, and Romano cheese), and lamb and seafood kebabs. In addition, there's a wide variety of seafood, from pan-fried catfish to mountain trout, snow crab, frogs' legs, conch-and-squid combo, and surf-and-turf. Steaks and prime rib are also featured. Children are particularly welcome here, and each youngster who finishes his or her dinner gets a free balloon.

ROCKAWAY GRILL, 7 Rockaway St. Tel. 446-4844.

Cuisine: SEAFOOD/FLORIDA. **Reservations:** Not accepted.

$ Prices: Appetizers $2.95–$6.95; main courses $3.95–$13.95 at lunch or dinner. MC, V.

Open: Sun–Thurs 11am–midnight, Fri–Sat 11am–1am.

With an uncovered outdoor deck extending out into the white sands, this casual restaurant between Bay Esplanade and Ambler Street, next to the Palm Pavilion Hotel, radiates a beach-party atmosphere. It is understandably popular with sun-seekers during the day and in the evening at sunset-watching time. Grouper sandwiches are the prime feature of the menu but other popular dishes include she-crab soup, beef and tuna burgers, seafood platters, barbecued ribs, steaks, and chargrilled chicken. If it's too sunny on the open deck, you can also dine indoors in air-conditioned comfort.

8. NEARBY DINING

MODERATE

CHATEAU MADRID, 415 Cleveland St., Clearwater. Tel. 447-2211.

Cuisine: SPANISH/CONTINENTAL. **Reservations:** Recommended.

$ Prices: Appetizers $3.95–$5.95; main courses $4.95–$7.95 at lunch, $8.95–$18.95 at dinner. AE, CB, DC, MC, V.

Open: Lunch Tues–Fri 11:30am–2:30pm; dinner Tues–Thurs 5–10pm, Fri–Sat 5–11pm, Sun 3–9pm.

As its name implies, this restaurant is a bastion of Spanish hospitality and cuisine, nestled on the main thoroughfare in downtown Clearwater, between Fort Harrison Avenue and Osceola Boulevard. With a decor of rich reds and wrought-iron trim, the dining room conveys a relaxing Iberian atmosphere.

For details of the dinner menu, see the description of its sister restaurant of the same name at Indian Shores, earlier in this chapter. Lunch, available only at this downtown Clearwater location, includes pastas, fish, and meat dishes plus Spanish-style sandwiches and salads. On Friday and Saturday evenings a flamenco guitarist serenades diners at this branch.

94TH AERO SQUADRON, 94 Fairchild Dr., Clearwater. Tel. 536-0409.

Cuisine: AMERICAN. **Reservations:** Recommended.

$ Prices: Appetizers $2.95–$7.95; main courses $4.95–$7.95 at lunch, $11.95–$19.95 at dinner. AE, DC, MC, V.

Open: Mon–Thurs 11am–10pm, Fri 11am–10:30pm, Sat 5–11pm, Sun 10:30am–2:30pm and 4:30–10pm.

Off Roosevelt Boulevard between the St. Petersburg-Clearwater airport and Boatyard Village, overlooking Old Tampa Bay, this restaurant is designed to resemble a World

War I French farmhouse. On the front lawn you'll see an authentic 1917 Sopwith Camel, a collector's item, and inside is a decor of sandbag walls, military artifacts and equipment, old pictures and posters, and antique bottles and books lining the four fireplaces. But that's only part of the setting—the building also overlooks the runways of the airport, so you can enjoy water views or watch the planes land as you dine.

The dinner menu offers steaks, prime rib, Colorado lamb, pastas, and stir-fry dishes, as well as a variety of local seafoods. Lunch items include soups (the beer-cheese soup is a specialty), sandwiches, and light and unusual main courses such as blue crab quesadilla. It's a fun place for all ages, and a change from the beach scene.

TIO PEPE, 2930 Gulf-to-Bay Blvd., Clearwater. Tel. 799-3082.

   Cuisine: SPANISH/INTERNATIONAL. **Reservations:** Recommended.

$ Prices: Appetizers $2.95–$6.95; main courses $3.95–$15.95 at lunch, $11.95–$22.95 at dinner. AE, MC, V.

   Open: Lunch Tues–Fri 11am–2:30pm; dinner Tues–Thurs 5–11pm, Fri–Sat 5–11:30pm, Sun 4–10pm.

Situated along the busy thoroughfare between Clearwater Beach and Tampa airport, between McMullen-Booth Road and U.S. 19, this restaurant stands out beside the road with a tile roof and white-washed facade. The interior is equally Iberian with rich red tones, wrought-iron fixtures, and romantic little alcoves with tables for two. The aroma of freshly baked breads greets you as you enter.

The dinner menu offers Spanish specialties, such as gambas suprema (jumbo shrimp wrapped in bacon) or paella valenciana, as well as local and international dishes including whole Florida lobster, pompano en papillote, trout a la rusa, duckling with red-currant sauce, pork chop in prune-and-garlic sauce, chateaubriand, and rack of lamb. Lunchtime features sandwiches, salads, and steaks, as well as daily specials that provide very good value, from Spanish beef stew to chicken and yellow rice.

INEXPENSIVE

HOOTERS, 2800 Gulf-to-Bay Blvd. Tel. 797-4008.

   Cuisine: AMERICAN. **Reservations:** Not accepted.

$ Prices: Appetizers $1.95–$4.95; main courses $2.95–$14.95 at lunch or dinner. AE, MC, V.

   Open: Mon–Fri 11am–midnight, Sat 11am–1am, Sun noon–10pm.

This is the original Hooters; branches also thrive in St. Petersburg, (see "North of Downtown," above in this chapter) and Tampa (see Chapter 10, "Tampa Dining"). Though located along a busy thoroughfare between Clearwater Beach and Tampa airport, opposite the Clearwater Mall between McMullen-Booth Road and U.S. 19, and far from the surf and sand, it's a relaxed eatery. Step in and enjoy—the jukebox blares "golden oldies" and the finger-food menu is designed to give you a laugh or two.

Hooters is definitely not the choice for an evening of fine dining, but it is a fun place, especially if you're fond of chicken wings, steak sandwiches, steamed shrimp, or oyster roasts (oysters roasted in the shell and served with drawn butter). It's hard to spend more than $10 on a meal, but if you really want to splurge, there's one tongue-in-cheek selection designed for a group of friends: the "Gourmet Chicken Wing Dinner" (20 wing pieces with a bottle of Dom Perignon for $100.01).

9. RESTAURANTS BY CUISINE

KEY TO ABBREVIATIONS: *E* = Expensive; *I* = Inexpensive; *M* = Moderately Priced; *VE* = Very Expensive; * = an Author's Favorite; $ = Super-Special Value

AMERICAN
A.J.'s Deli Café, downtown (*I*), 80
Apropos, downtown (*M*), 75
Balloon Palace, Madeira Beach (*M*), 89
Bob Heilman's Beachcomber, Clearwater Beach (*E**), 95
Captain Kosmakos, Treasure Island (*M*), 88
Cha Cha Coconuts, Clearwater Beach (*I*), 99
Cha Cha Coconuts, downtown (*I*), 80
Chuck E. Cheese's, north of downtown (*I*), 84
The Friendly Tavern, Redington Shores (*I*), 92
Heritage Grille, downtown (*E**), 75
Hooters, Clearwater (*I*), 102
Hooters, north of downtown (*I*), 85
Jasmine's Gulffront Steak House, North Redington Beach (*M*), 91
Keystone Club (*M*), 78
Mulligan's Sunset Grill, St. Petersburg Beach (*M*), 87
94th Aero Squadron, Clearwater (*M**), 101
Ollie's Grille (*M*), 79
Outback Steakhouse, north of downtown (*M*), 84
Sunset Beach Café, Treasure Island, (*I*), 89
Tavern on the Green, downtown (*I*), 80
Leverock's Waterfront Steak House, north of downtown (*M$*), 83

AUSTRALIAN
Outback Steakhouse, north of downtown (*M*), 84

CARIBBEAN
Cha Cha Coconuts, downtown (*I*), 80

CONTINENTAL
Basta's Cantina d'Italia Ristorante, downtown (*E*), 74
The Good Times, south of downtown (*M*), 81
Le Grand Café, downtown (*M*), 78
The Wine Cellar, North Redington Beach (*E**), 91

FLORIDA
Rockaway Grill, Clearwater Beach (*I*), 101

GERMAN
Omi's Bavarian Inn, Madeira Beach (*I*), 90

GREEK
Island House, Clearwater Beach (*I*), 100

INTERNATIONAL
Captain Kosmakos, Treasure Island (*M*), 88
Tio Pepe, Clearwater (*I*), 102

ITALIAN
Basta's Cantina d'Italia Ristorante, downtown (*E*), 74
Nick's on the Water (*M*), 79

JAPANESE
Arigato, north of downtown (*M$*), 82
Kinjo, St. Petersburg Beach (*M*), 86

REGIONAL
Silas Dent's, St. Petersburg Beach (*M*), 87

SCANDINAVIAN
Scandia, Indian Shores (*M*), 93

SEAFOOD
Crabby Bill's, Indian Rocks Beach (*I$*), 95
Crabby Bill's, St. Petersburg Beach (*I*), 87
The Flagship, Clearwater Beach (*M*), 96
Fourth Street Shrimp Store, north of downtown (*I$*), 85
Frenchy's Café, Clearwater Beach (*I*), 100
Friendly Fisherman, Madeira Beach (*M*), 90
Guppy's on the Beach, Indian Rocks Beach (*M*), 94
Hungry Fisherman, Indian Shores (*I*), 93
Hurricane, St. Petersburg Beach (*M$*), 86
Island House, Clearwater Beach (*I*), 100
Leverock's, Clearwater Beach (*M*$*), 96
Leverock's, Madeira Beach (*M*$*), 90
Leverock's, south of downtown (*M*$*), 81
Leverock's, St. Petersburg Beach (*M*$*), 86
Lobster Pot, Redington Shores (*E**), 91
Murph's, Indian Rocks (*M*), 94
Pep's Sea Grill, north of downtown (*I*), 85
Rajan's, Clearwater Beach (*M*), 97
Sea Critters Café, St. Petersburg Beach (*I*), 88
Seafood & Sunsets at Julie's, Clearwater Beach (*M*), 97
Shells, Redington Shores (*I$*), 92
Silas Dent's, St. Petersburg Beach (*M*), 87

SMOKED SEAFOOD
Ted Peter's Famous Smoked Fish, south of downtown (*I*), 82

SPANISH
Chateau Madrid, Clearwater (*M*), 101
Chateau Madrid, Indian Shores (*M*), 93
The Columbia, Clearwater Beach (*M*), 96
The Columbia, downtown (*M*$*), 78

WHAT TO SEE & DO IN ST. PETERSBURG

From downtown to the beaches, St. Petersburg is a city with a myriad of outdoor and indoor activities. It would take months to see and do it all, but if you only have a week or less, here are some suggestions to help you choose what is most appealing.

Suggested Itineraries

If You Have 1 Day   Explore the newly rejuvenated downtown area, starting with the Pier on Tampa Bay—browsing in the shops, touring the aquarium, sampling the variety of foods, and savoring the panoramic views. Continue to the nearby Museum of Fine Arts, the St. Petersburg Historical and Flight One Museum, Beach Drive with its string of fine boutiques, and along the bayfront to the Dalí Museum. Walk through the city along the wide corridor of Central Avenue, ending at the newly built sports/entertainment center, the St. Petersburg ThunderDome.

If You Have 2 Days   Do the downtown area and add a few more nearby attractions, from Sunken Gardens to Great Explorations or Fort DeSoto Park. Take a relaxing boat cruise in the afternoon on Tampa Bay or Boca Ciega Bay, or go to the greyhound races, or perhaps a baseball game or concert.

If You Have 3 Days   After taking in the downtown sights for the first two days, spend a full day on nearby St. Petersburg Beach or Pass-A-Grille Beach, with swimming and sunning and perhaps a little fishing or a parasail ride.

If You Have 5 Days or More   Branch out from St. Pete to the nearby beaches and visit the Suncoast Seabird Sanctuary at Indian Shores, John's Pass Village on Madeira Beach, Redington Long Pier at Redington Shores, Heritage Park at Largo, or the Marine Science Center of Clearwater. Spend a day or two exploring Treasure Island, Indian Rocks Beach, the Intracoastal Waterways, or Boca Ciega Bay.

Soak up the sunshine, cast a fishing line, board a cruise boat, watch the pelicans diving for dinner or the sandpipers scurrying on the water's edge, see the sun set from a different vantage point each evening, or just relax and have the time of your life in this gulf coast paradise.

1. THE TOP ATTRACTIONS

THE PIER, 800 Second Ave. NE, St. Petersburg. Tel. 821-6164.

⭐ The focal point of the city's recent downtown rejuvenation, this festive waterfront sightseeing/shopping/entertainment complex extends one-quarter of a mile into Tampa Bay. Dating back to 1889, it was originally built as a railroad pier, but over the years it was redesigned in various ways until it took its present shape of an inverted pyramid in 1988.

Today it's the city's prime playground, with five levels of shops and restaurants, plus an aquarium, tourist information desk, observation deck, catwalks for fishing, boat docks, a small bayside beach, miniature golf, water-sport rentals, and sightseeing boats. Best of all are the views—sweeping panoramas of the bay, the marina, and the St. Petersburg skyline. A free trolley service and a motorized surrey operate between the Pier entrance and the nearby parking lots.

Adjacent to the Pier is Straub Park, a scenic 36-acre waterfront park that runs along Beach Drive, between First and Fifth Avenues NE. It's ideal for a stroll after visiting the Pier, a place to sit on a bench and watch the swirl of activity.

Admission: Free to all the public areas and decks; donations welcome at the aquarium; parking is $1.

Open: Most shops, Mon–Sat 10am–9pm, Sun 11am–7pm; restaurants, daily 11am–11pm; lounges, daily 10am–1am; aquarium, Mon and Wed–Sat 10am–9pm, Sun 11am–7pm.

FLORIDA INTERNATIONAL MUSEUM, 101 Third St. N. Tel. 824-6734.

⭐ As we go to press, it has been announced that the former Maas Brothers department store, once an area landmark but standing idle for the past few years, has been earmarked for a $2 million renovation converting it into a block-long museum with a cultural focus. Slated for completion in early 1995, the new museum will mark its inauguration with a major art exhibition from Russia, "Treasures of the Czars" (January 11 to July 11, 1995), one of the largest collections of royal family treasures ever to leave Russia.

On loan from Kremlin Museums in Moscow, the exhibit contains approximately 250 pieces from the 300-year rule of the Romanoff family including 17th- and 18th-century coronation costumes spun of gold and silver thread; ambassadorial attire and memorabilia; and religious chalices and vestments; and mother-of-pearl muskets. Subsequent annual international exhibits are currently being finalized for 1996 through 1998.

St. Petersburg

6633

ST. PETERSBURG SIGHTS

590
60
6
7
Courtney Campbell Causeway
19

O l d

275
To Tampa

St. Petersburg-Clearwater International Airport
Howard Frankland Bridge

686
8

T a m p a

Ulmerton Rd.
688
686
Gandy Bridge
92

693

B a y

694
275
Pinellas Park
74th Ave.
54th Ave.
49th St.
595
38th Ave.
19

9
Coffeepot Bayou

Treasure Island Causeway
Downtown
10
11
12
St. Petersburg
13
ALT 19
Central Ave.
375
14
S. Pasadena
Gulfport
15
22nd Ave. S.
175
16
Albert Whitted Municipal Airport
St. Petersburg Beach Causeway
17
Big Bayou
699
Lake Maggiore
Coquina Key
19
18
Pinellas Bayway
54th Ave. S.
Little Bayou
Beach
682
Long Key
Bird Key

I n t r a   c o a s t a l
W a t e r   w a y

Bush Key
Cabbage Key
20
T a m p a
Shell Key
679
B a y
The Reefs
Madelaine Key
19
275
679

21
Mullett Key

Airport

Admission: Tickets, which will be sold at the museum for a specific day and a time, are expected to be priced at $11 adults, $3 students.

Open: Details of hours are not final at press time. Check with the St. Petersburg–Clearwater Area Convention & Visitors Bureau, 1 Stadium Dr., Suite A, St. Petersburg, FL 33705 (tel. 813/821-7892), for latest information. **Directions:** Downtown, three blocks west of the bayfront area, between First and Second Avenues North.

ST. PETERSBURG THUNDERDOME, 1 Stadium Dr., St. Petersburg. Tel. 825-3100.

The skyline of St. Petersburg changed dramatically with the opening of this new $110-million slant-roofed dome in March 1990. An attraction in itself, it was built on a 66-acre downtown site (between 10th and 16th Streets South, from First Avenue South to Fourth Avenue South) to host major concerts, sports competitions, and conventions, and, foremost, as a home for a major-league baseball team. As we go to press, no team has yet signed on to play from this base, but city officials are working feverishly to make that a reality by the time you read this guidebook.

The stadium has a translucent roof that is the first cable-supported dome of its kind in the U.S. and one of the largest of its type in the world. The secret to the building's versatility is a series of movable stands that slide, section by section, on pneumatic tires, then lower into place hydraulically. Seating capacities range from 12,000 to 55,000, depending on the event. In addition to sports and entertainment, the dome is also the venue for ethnic folk fairs, garden shows, and other general-interest daytime activities. On nonevent days, guided tours are available.

Admission: $4–$35, depending on the event.

Open: Box office open Mon–Fri 10am–5pm. Performance times vary, depending on the event.

SALVADOR DALÍ MUSEUM, 1000 Third St. S., St. Petersburg. Tel. 823-3767.

Nestled on Tampa Bay just south of the Bayfront Center and the Pier, this starkly modern museum houses the world's largest collection of works by the renowned Spanish surrealist. Assembled over a 40-year period, the collection was donated in 1982 by a Cleveland industrialist, A. Reynolds Morse, and his wife, Eleanor R. Morse, who were friends of Dalí and his wife, Gala. Although Dalí never set foot here himself, it is said that the St. Pete harbor site was chosen because of its resemblance to the artist's favorite Iberian haunt, the Bay of Cadaques.

Valued at over $150 million, the collection includes 94 oil paintings, over 100 watercolors and drawings, and 1,300 graphics, plus posters, photos, sculptures, and objets d'art, and a 2,500-volume library with works on Dalí and surrealism. A new touch-screen computer system lets visitors view paintings and photos with quotes from Dalí.

You can see the museum at your leisure or join one of the guided tours that are conducted daily for the public (the schedule varies according to demand; call for exact times). The museum store offers

---

⭐ **FROMMER'S FAVORITE ST. PETERSBURG EXPERIENCES**

Swimming, Sunning, Shelling Take your choice, along 28 miles of wide, sandy, clean, and safe beaches.

Sunset Time Vivid vistas of red, pink, yellow, or golden hues on the western horizon—everywhere along the gulf beaches.

Gliding Above Gulf Waters Look down on St. Petersburg Beach from the heights of a parasail.

Casting a Line From a boat, shoreline, or pier, take your time and hook a grouper, snapper, or other "big catch" of the day.

Watching Wild Seabirds Soar Into the Sky Marvel as previously injured birds take to the sky every day after being restored to health at the Suncoast Seabird Sanctuary.

Dining with the "Early Birds" Enjoy three or four courses of top-class cuisine at bargain-basement prices.

Music in the Air Listen to an open-air band concert or watch live Shakespeare performances along the bayfront.

---

over 100 reproductions of Dalí's work, as well as Dalí-related T-shirts, jewelry, books, and gift items.

Admission: $5 adults, $4 seniors, $3.50 students, free for children under 10.

Open: Tues–Sat 9:30am–5:30pm, Sun–Mon noon–5pm. **Closed:** Thanksgiving, Christmas, and New Year's Day. **Directions:** Follow the signs from I-275 and other parts of downtown; the museum is on Bayboro Harbor adjacent to the Bayboro Campus of the University of South Florida.

MUSEUM OF FINE ARTS, 255 Beach Dr. NE, St. Petersburg. Tel. 896-2667.

⭐ Resembling a Mediterranean villa on the waterfront, at the foot of the approach to the Pier, just north of Second Avenue NE, this museum houses a permanent collection of European, American, pre-Columbian, and Far Eastern art, with works by such artists as Fragonard, Monet, Renoir, Cézanne, and Gauguin.

Other highlights include period rooms with antiques and historical furnishings, plus a gallery of Steuben crystal, and world-class rotating exhibits.

Admission: $5 adults, $3 seniors, $2 students. Free admission on Sun.

Open: Tues–Sat 10am–5pm, Sun 1–5pm; third Thurs of each

month 10am–9pm. Guided tours, Tues–Fri at 11am and 2pm, Sat–Sun at 2pm.

FORT DESOTO PARK, 3500 Pinellas Bayway S., (Fla. 679), St. Petersburg. Tel. 866-2484.

One of the oldest sections of St. Petersburg, this is the largest and most diverse park in the area, made up of five islands south of the mainland (Mullet Key, Madelaine Key, St. Jean Key, St. Christopher Key, and Bonne Fortune Key), all nestled between the waters of Tampa Bay and the Gulf of Mexico. With a total of 900 acres, 7 miles of waterfront, and almost 3 miles of beaches, the islands are connected by roads and bridges. A public park for over 25 years, it also offers fishing piers, shaded picnic sites, a bird and animal sanctuary, and 235 campsites.

Historical accounts indicate that Mullet Key gained significance from the visits by Juan Ponce de León, who anchored his ship here in 1513. However, the island is most often associated with Hernando de Soto, for whom Fort DeSoto, on the southwest tip of the island, is named.

Now listed on the National Register of Historic Places, this fort was built in 1898 as an artillery installation to protect Tampa Bay during the Spanish-American War. It was armed with 12-inch mortars, which, incidentally, never fired a single shot at any enemy. Today you can explore the fort; its lookout point offers great views, especially at sunset.

Admission: Free, except for tolls totaling 85¢.

Open: Daily sunrise–sunset. **Directions:** Take I-275 south to the Pinellas Bayway (Exit 4) and follow signs.

SUNCOAST SEABIRD SANCTUARY, 18328 Gulf Blvd., Indian Shores. Tel. 391-6211.

Among the attractions outside the immediate downtown area, this one is well worth a special trip. Founded in 1971 by zoologist Ralph Heath, Jr., it's the largest wild-bird hospital in the U.S. It's dedicated to the rescue, repair, and recuperation of sick and injured birds, which are released when rehabilitated.

Situated right on the edge of the beach, this facility daily treats an average of 18 to 20 seabirds that have been injured by a variety of causes, from fish hooks and fishing lines to gunshot wounds. Unfortunately, approximately 90% of all injuries are directly or indirectly attributable to humans. At any one time, there are usually in excess of 500 sea and land birds living at the sanctuary, from cormorants, white herons, and birds of prey to the ubiquitous brown pelican. Most of these birds are returned to their natural habitat when they are well, but some, particularly those that have lost an eye or a limb, remain in permanent residence; some of these produce offspring, which are then released.

Visitors are free to wander around this tree-lined open-air sanctuary, photograph and observe the wide variety of birds, and look in the bird hospital and various other facilities. You can also tag along as Ralph Heath or one of his staff takes a bucket of small fish down to the beach to feed the passing pelicans, often finding injured birds in the process. Tours of the entire operation are given on Wednesday and Sunday at 2pm.

Admission: Free, but donations are welcome.

Open: Daily 9am–dusk. **Directions:** North of downtown, take I-275 to Fla. 694 (Exit 15) west, cross over the Intracoastal Waterway to Gulf Blvd. and turn left; the sanctuary is a quarter of a mile south.

JOHN'S PASS VILLAGE AND BOARDWALK, 12901 Gulf Blvd., Madeira Beach. Tel. 391-7373.

 Named after Juan (John) Levique, a sea-turtle fisherman who lived here in the 19th century, this rustic Florida fishing village lies on the southern edge of Madeira Beach, where the waters of Boca Ciega Bay meet the gulf. It is composed of a string of simple wooden structures topped by tin roofs, all resting on pilings 12 feet above sea level and connected by a 1,000-foot boardwalk. Most of the buildings have been converted into shops, art galleries, and restaurants.

The focal point is the large fishing pier and marina, where you can see the commercial and charter fishing boats unloading their daily catch, or sign up for a day's fishing trip on a party boat. Stroll the boardwalk and you're bound to find a good spot to watch the pelicans skimming the tops of the waves in search of fish or the dolphins playing in the tidal currents. This is also the home port of the *Europa Fun Kruz* cruise ship, and the base for many other water-sports activities.

Admission: Free.

Open: Daily 9am–6pm or later for shops and activities, 7am–11pm for most restaurants. **Directions:** From downtown, take Central Ave. west via Treasure Island Causeway to Gulf Blvd., turn right, go north for 20 blocks, and cross over the bridge.

SUNSHINE SKYWAY BRIDGE, I-275 and U.S. 19, St. Petersburg. Tel. 823-8804.

Spanning the mouth of Tampa Bay, this 4.1-mile-long bridge connects Pinellas and Manatee Counties and the city of St. Petersburg with the Bradenton/Sarasota area. Built at a cost of $244 million over a period of five years (1982–87), this is Florida's first suspension bridge, soaring 183 feet above the bay. The bridge's cables are painted yellow and illuminated at night. The approaches to an older bridge, which still stand to the west, are now used as fishing piers.

Admission: $1 toll each way.

Open: Daily 24 hours.

2. MORE ATTRACTIONS

ST. PETERSBURG HISTORICAL AND FLIGHT ONE MUSEUM, 335 Second Ave. NE, St. Petersburg. Tel. 894-1052.

Located on the approach to the Pier, this museum features a permanent interactive exhibition chronicling St. Petersburg's history. The thousands of items on display range from prehistoric artifacts to documents, clothing, and photographs. There are also computer stations enabling visitors to "flip through the past." Walk-through exhibits include a prototype general store and post office (ca. 1880) and a replica of the Benoist airboat, suspended "in flight" from a 25-foot ceiling and commemorating the first scheduled commercial flight in the world, which took off from St. Petersburg in 1914.

Admission: $4.50 adults, $3.50 seniors, $1.50 children 7–17, free for children 6 and under.

Open: Mon–Sat 10am–5pm, Sun 1–5pm.

SUNKEN GARDENS, 1825 Fourth St. N., St. Petersburg. Tel. 896-3186.

One of the city's oldest attractions, this seven-acre tropical-garden park north of downtown between 18th and 19th Streets North, dates back to 1935. It contains a vast array of 5,000 plants, flowers, and trees, including trails, walkways, and bridges. In addition, there's an aviary and over 500 rare birds, many of which perform in bird shows throughout the day. The complex also contains a huge gift shop and a wax museum depicting biblical figures.

Admission: $11 adults, $6 children 3–11, free for children under 3.

Open: Daily 9am–5pm.

FLORIDA MILITARY AVIATION MUSEUM, 16055 Fairchild Dr., Clearwater. Tel. 535-9007.

In a delightful location beside Old Tampa Bay and in the shadow of modern airplanes taking off from the adjacent airport, this outdoor museum features military aircraft, many dating from World War II. The aircraft range from patrol bombers to supersonic jet fighters from all branches of the military forces.

Admission: $2 adults, $1 children under 16.

Open: Tues, Thurs, and Sat 10am–4pm, Sun 1–5pm. **Directions:** Take Fla. 686; the museum is between St. Petersburg–Clearwater airport and the Boatyard Village shopping complex.

KOPSICH PALM ARBORETUM, North Shore Dr., St. Petersburg. Tel. 893-7335.

Although palm trees abound in Florida, this is one place where you'll see a great variety of the graceful trees—over 200 palms and cyades representing more than 45 species from around the world. Situated on the bayfront at the foot of 10th Avenue NE, just north of the Stouffer Vinoy Hotel, this two-acre park was developed in 1976, thanks to a grant provided by Gizella Kopsich, an Austrian-born local resident who died in 1980 at the age of 103. In addition to the great array of native, new, and exotic palms, the park also includes a gazebo, conversation corners with wooden benches, and red-brick paving. Guided walks are also available by appointment.

Admission: Free.

Open: Daily dawn–dusk.

HERITAGE PARK, 11909 125th St. N., Largo. Tel. 582-2123.

This 21-acre turn-of-the-century historical park features 20 of Pinellas County's oldest existing historic homes and buildings, "transplanted" to this pine-tree-shaded site north of St. Petersburg off U.S. Alt. 19, between Walsingham Road and Ulmerton Road, east of Indian Rocks Beach. The attractions include the oldest homestead in the county—the McMullen-Coachman log house—as well as a church, school, barn, store, bandstand, and train depot. There are periodic demonstrations of crafts such as rug hooking, wool spinning, blacksmithing, and weaving on a loom.

Admission: Free, but donations are accepted.

Open: Tues–Sat 10am–4pm, Sun 1–4pm.

CLEARWATER MARINE SCIENCE CENTER AQUARIUM, 249 Windward Passage, Clearwater. Tel. 447-0980.

On an island in Clearwater Harbor, this facility is dedicated to the rescue, rehabilitation, and release of marine mammals and sea turtles. Visitors can view a 320-pound sea turtle, an Atlantic bottle-nosed dolphin, a 50,000-gallon mangrove/seagrass habitat, and many marine animals.

Admission: $4.25 adults, $2.75 children 3–11, free for children under 3.

Open: Mon–Fri 9am–5pm, Sat 9am–4pm, Sun 11am–4pm.

Directions: From the mainland, turn right at Island Way; the center is one mile east of Clearwater Beach on Island Estates.

PORT ROYAL SUNKEN TREASURE MUSEUM, 5501 Gulf Blvd., St. Petersburg Beach. Tel. 360-4141.

Focusing on historic shipwrecks and adventures at sea, this new museum presents permanent exhibits and hands-on displays of sunken treasures. The objects include a replica of one of the first diving bells used to recover treasure from shipwrecks, as well as antiques and priceless valuables, such as Ming vases and gold and silver objects, recovered from the Sunken City of Port Royal. The museum also houses a collection of sand sculptures by Paul Dawkins.

Admission: $6.50 adults, $5 seniors and students, $3.50 children 6–12, free for children under 6.

Open: Daily 10am–9pm. **Directions:** Take the Pinellas Bayway, turn right at Gulf Blvd., and museum is between 55 and 56th Aves.

SAFETY HARBOR MUSEUM OF REGIONAL HISTORY, 329 S. Bayshore Blvd., Safety Harbor. Tel. 726-1668.

This small museum, in a residential bayfront community one block south of Safety Harbor resort, between Iron Age and Scott Streets, focuses on local history, with particular emphasis on the 16th century when Hernando de Soto discovered five mineral springs here. Safety Harbor also gained attention in 1842 when Count Phillipe Odet, a former surgeon in the French navy under Napoléon, settled here and established the first grapefruit plantation in Florida. Exhibits also include a collection of local Native American artifacts and photographs showing Safety Harbor at the turn of the century when visitors were flocking to the mineral springs. The grounds include an early Seminole burial gravesite and a well made of tabby, a kind of cement that the Spaniards used, comprised of oyster shells and lime.

Admission: $1 per person, 50¢ children under 12.
Open: Tues–Fri 10am–4pm, Sat–Sun 1–4pm.

3. COOL FOR KIDS

GREAT EXPLORATIONS, 1120 Fourth St. S., St. Petersburg. Tel. 821-8885.

With a variety of "hands-on" exhibits, this museum welcomes visitors of all ages, but it's most appealing to children, especially on a rainy day. To name just a few of the activities, kids can explore a long, dark tunnel; measure their strength, flexibility, and fitness; paint a work of art with sunlight; and play a melody with a sweep of the hand. It's south of downtown, one block west of the bayfront and the Dalí Museum.

Admission: $5 adults, $4.50 seniors, $4 children 4–17, free for children under 4.
Open: Mon–Sat 10am–5pm, Sun noon–5pm.

BOYD HILL NATURE PARK, 1101 Country Club Way S., St. Petersburg. Tel. 893-7326.

Located at the south end of Lake Maggiore, this 216-acre city park has six scenic trails and boardwalks that meander through natural subtropical vegetation and native trees. Each loop averages 15 minutes of walking time, for a total of 1½ hours. Children are especially delighted to see birds, young reptiles, and other native species along the paths. There is also a library and nature center with exhibits, four aquariums, an observation beehive, and changing exhibits, as well as a picnic area and children's playground.

Admission: $1 adults, 50¢ children 17 and under.
Open: Daily 9am–5pm; Apr–Oct, Tues and Thurs to 8pm.
Directions: Travel south on Ninth St. S. to Country Club Way and bear right to the entrance.

MOCCASIN LAKE NATURE PARK, 2750 Park Trail Lane, Clearwater. Tel. 462-6024.

This 51-acre wildlife preserve has a 5-acre lake, nature trails, an aviary, and exhibits on animals, birds of prey, plants, and energy sources. There is also an assortment of live native reptiles, fish, and aquatic reptiles. Solar energy provides some of the park's electrical power. It's located inland, northeast of Clearwater Beach, east of U.S. 19 and north of Gulf-to-Bay Boulevard.

Admission: $2 adults, $1 children 3–12, free for children under 3.
Open: Tues–Fri 9am–5pm, Sat–Sun 10am–6pm.

4. ORGANIZED TOURS & CRUISES

Take to the road or the water to see the sights of the St. Petersburg area—and beyond.

DRIVING TOUR

SCENIC DRIVE/Historic Sites and Local Lore, St. Petersburg Chamber of Commerce, 100 Second Ave. N., St. Petersburg. Tel. 821-4715.
Although there are no guided walking or driving tours of the city at present, the local chamber of commerce offers a self-guided and signposted driving-tour leaflet. You can follow the route at your leisure in your own vehicle, learning a bit of history and seeing the main sights along the way. The route starts downtown at the chamber office and then swings southward, passing attractions such as the Salvador Dalí Museum and Great Explorations. The trail then turns northward along the bayfront, passing waterfront parks, marinas, museums, galleries, The Pier, the Stouffer Vinoy Hotel, and other attractions. Highlights northeast of the bayfront include Coffee Pot Boulevard, a winding tree-lined street of brick pavement dating back to the 1920s, and the Snell Isle Bridge, a Venetian-style bridge opened in 1925.
Price: Free.

WATER TOURS

One of the most enjoyable ways to see the St. Petersburg area is to board a boat and view the skyline and harborsides from the various bays and gulf waters. There are a variety of boats, from paddle wheelers and old fishing vessels to pirate ships and pontoons, all of which take passengers for an hour or two, or longer. Many offer lunch or dinner cruises, often with dancing and entertainment. Here are a few to whet your appetite:

THE ADMIRAL TOUR BOAT, Slip 59/60, Clearwater Beach Marina, Clearwater Beach. Tel. 462-2628, or toll free 800/444-4814.
This air-conditioned triple-decker craft provides two options for afternoon cruises on Clearwater Bay—a 1½-hour sightseeing cruise or a 2-hour luncheon/sightseeing cruise. In addition, there's an evening dinner/dance cruise with live band and full

sit-down dinner. Boarding is half an hour before departure time. Reservations are required for the meal cruises.

Prices: Sightseeing cruise, $6 adults, $4 children; lunch/ sightseeing cruise, $6.95 adults, $4.95 children (lunches $5.25– $6.75); dinner/dance cruise, $18.45–$23.45.

Open: Sightseeing cruise, Tues and Thurs 2–3:30pm; lunch/ sightseeing cruise Wed and Fri–Sat noon–2pm; dinner/dance cruise, Tues–Fri and Sun 7–10pm, Sat 7–10:30pm. **Directions:** Take Fla. 60 west to the Clearwater Beach Marina; it's next to the Bait House.

CAPTAIN MEMO'S PIRATE CRUISE, Slip 3, Clearwater Beach Marina, Clearwater Beach. Tel. 446-2587.

This is a cruise that's particularly fun for those looking for a bit of "adventure" at sea. Decorated with all the trappings of an authentic pirate ship, the *Pirate's Ransom,* an authentic reproduction, offers swashbuckling cruises, under the direction of fearless Captain Memo (Bill Wozencraft) and his crew. The cruise goes along the Intracoastal Waterway and into the Gulf of Mexico near Clearwater Beach, with frequent sightings of dolphins and maybe a few pirates along the way. The price includes complimentary beer, wine, or soft drinks, and champagne on the evening departure.

Prices: $25–$28 adults, $18 seniors and children 13–17, $15 children 2–12, free for children under 2.

Open: Cruises, daily 10am–noon, 2–4pm, and 4:30–6:30pm; also 7–9pm Apr–Sept. **Directions:** Take Fla. 60 west to the Clearwater Beach Marina.

CLEARWATER FERRY SERVICE, W. Drew St., Clearwater. Tel. 442-7433.

Launched in 1990, this new catamaran boat service, on the waterfront of downtown Clearwater at the Drew Street Dock, just west of the offices of the Greater Clearwater Chamber of Commerce, offers a six-hour excursion from downtown Clearwater via the Intracoastal Waterway and Anclote River to Tarpon Springs, a town of predominantly Greek heritage that's famous for its sponge-diving industry. The trip includes lunch at a Greek restaurant overlooking the water, and ample time for shopping at the open-air markets. In addition, this company operates a regularly scheduled ferry service to Caladesi Island, a state park on a barrier island north of Clearwater Beach. Reservations are required for the Tarpon Springs excursion but not for the Caladesi Island ferry.

Prices: Round-trip cruise to Tarpon Springs with lunch, $26.10; ferry to Caladesi Island, $6.05 round-trip.

Open: Tarpon Springs cruise, Tues and Sat 9am–3pm; Caladesi Island ferry, Tues–Sun, schedule varies.

DOLPHIN ENCOUNTER CRUISES, W. Drew St., Clearwater. Tel. 442-7433.

Departing from the West Drew Street dock in downtown Clearwater, these cruises are operated via the 125-passenger double-deck catamaran *Clearwater Express.* The 1½-hour trip goes out into the Gulf of Mexico along the beaches and shoreline for a first-hand view of dolphins frolicking in their natural surroundings. Seabirds are also on view, and bird feeding is allowed (the boat company provides the food). There is a snack bar and cocktail service on board.

Admission: $7.95 adults, $4.70 children 3–12.

Schedule: Mid-March to May and Sept to Oct, Tues–Sun 10am and 3:30pm; June–Aug, Tues–Sun 10am, 1pm, 3:30pm.

THE LADY ANDERSON, St. Petersburg Beach Causeway, 3400 Pasadena Ave. S., St. Petersburg. Tel. 367-7804, or toll free 800/533-2288.

Docked between St. Petersburg and the beach area, this three-deck boat plies the waters of Boca Ciega Bay and the Gulf of Mexico. Cruises are operated at lunch and dinner times, with buffet meal service and dance music, as well as cocktail service (at an extra charge). Boarding for all trips is half an hour before departure and reservations are required. On certain evenings, cruises with special themes, such as gospel music, are offered; check in advance for exact schedules.

Prices: lunch cruise, $14.50 adults, $12.50 children under 10; dinner cruise, $19.50–$24.50 adults, $12.50–$14.50 children.

Open: Oct to mid-May, lunch cruise Tues–Fri 11am–1pm; dinner cruise, Tues and Thurs–Sat 7–10pm. **Directions:** From downtown St. Pete, take Central Ave. west to St. Petersburg Beach Causeway and follow the signs.

SHELL KEY SHUTTLE, 801 Pass-A-Grille Way, St. Petersburg Beach. Tel. 360-1348.

If you feel like escaping to a nearby unspoiled island south of St. Petersburg, here's the way. This company offers regular shuttle service to Shell Island on a 57-passenger catamaran. The ride takes 15 minutes and you can return when you wish, on the next shuttle or on the last one of the day. Once on the island, you can go shelling, swimming, fishing, or observe the local birds and wildlife. On some days there's also a half-hour sunset cruise (by reservation only).

Prices: $10 adults, $5 children 12 and under.

Open: Daily at 10am, noon, 2pm, and (summer only) 4pm. **Directions:** Take the Pinellas Bayway to St. Petersburg Beach, turn left on Gulf Blvd., and go south to Eighth Ave. at Pass-A-Grille Way.

SHOW QUEEN, Slip 18, Clearwater Marina, 25 Causeway Blvd., Clearwater Beach. Tel. 461-3113.

With a *Showboat*-style exterior, this 150-passenger triple-deck riverboat offers two- to three-hour sightseeing and meal cruises of the Clearwater area with views of shoreline homes and opportunities to see seabirds and dolphins at play. Boarding is 30 minutes before each departure.

Prices: Lunch cruise, $8 adults, $4 children 4–10; summer sunset cruise (with buffet and entertainment), $19.95 adults, $9.95

children 4–10; dinner/dance cruise, $25 adults for cruise, meal, and entertainment, $15 for cruise only.

Open: Lunch cruise, Tues–Sat at noon and 2:30pm, Sun at 1pm; sunset cruise, June–Sept, at 7pm; dinner/dance cruise, Oct–May, at 7pm.

Directions: Take Fla. 60 west to the Clearwater Beach Marina.

SEA SCREAMER, Kingfish Wharf, Treasure Island. Tel. 367-2996.

Touted as the world's largest speedboat, this 73-foot turbocharged twin-engine vessel provides two rides on one trip—an exhilarating spin in the Gulf of Mexico waters and a leisurely narrated cruise around Treasure Island with opportunities to view birds and marine life along the way. On certain days of the week, the *Sea Screamer* departs from Clearwater Beach Marina, Slip 48.

Prices: $9 adults, $6 children 6–12.

Schedule: From Treasure Island, Wed–Sat at noon, 2pm, and 4pm; from Clearwater Beach, Sun–Tues 11am, 2pm, and 4pm.

STARLITE PRINCESS, Hamlin's Landing, Fla. 688, Indian Rocks Beach. Tel. 595-1212.

✪ Docked at Hamlin's Landing, a condo/shopping development north of St. Petersburg at the west end of Fla. 688, on the Intracoastal Waterway near Indian Rocks Beach, this authentic 106-foot, three-deck paddle wheeler offers four different types of cruises—sightseeing only (with optional lunch), a luncheon/dance cruise, a dinner/dance cruise, and a six-hour excursion to the Pier of St. Petersburg (offered once a week). Most of the trips follow a scenic itinerary along inland waters, but the St. Petersburg excursion also goes under the Sunshine Skyway Bridge. Reservations are required for all cruises except the sightseeing-only option. There is a snack bar on board, as well as optional cocktail service. Boarding is half an hour before departure.

Prices: Cruise only, $8.75 adults, $5.75 children 2–12; cruise with lunch, $14.70–$17.50 per person; cruise with dinner, $23.95–$31.45 per person; St. Petersburg excursion with breakfast and lunch, $35 per person.

Open: Cruise only (lunch optional), Tues and Fri–Sat noon–2pm; luncheon/dance cruise, Wed noon–3pm; dinner/dance cruise, Tues–Wed and Fri–Sun 7:30–10:30pm; cruise to St. Petersburg, Thurs 10am–3:30pm.

MINI-CRUISES

EUROPA FUN KRUZ, John's Pass Marina, John's Pass Village, Gulf Blvd. at 129th St., Madeira Beach. Tel. 393-5110, or toll free 800/688-PLAY.

Cruise by day or night in the waters of the Gulf of Mexico on board this 300-passenger three-deck luxury ship. The price includes full tableside meal, Las Vegas–style casino gambling, live entertainment, dancing, games, contests, and a children's program (on Saturday and Sunday mornings). Reservations are required.

Prices: Day cruises, $39.95; night cruises, $39.95–$49.95, plus port charges and tax. *Note:* Reduced rates often apply in off-season

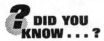

and on additional "after-midnight" cruises on weekends, Fri–Sun from $19.95.

Open: Mon–Wed 10am–4pm and 6:30pm–midnight, Thurs–Sat 10am–4pm and 6:30pm–12:30am, Sun 11am–5pm and 6:30pm–midnight; Fri–Sun "after-midnight" cruises from 1:15–6:15am.

EMPRESS CRUISE LINES, Kingfish Wharf, John's Pass, Treasure Island. Tel. 895-DEAL, or toll free 800/486-8600.

The *Crown Empress,* a three-deck cruise ship, offers daily six-hour "cruise-to-nowhere" trips into the Gulf of Mexico. The price includes a buffet meal, dancing to a live band, karaoke, bingo, horse-racing games, and access to a bi-level casino and a duty-free gift shop. In addition to daily departures from Kingfish Wharf, a sister ship, the 600-passenger *Majestic Empress,* offers trips from Clearwater Bay Marina, 198 Seminole St., Clearwater.

Prices: From $25 plus $12 port charges.

Open: Sun–Thurs 11am–5pm and 7pm–midnight; Fri–Sat 11am–5pm, 7pm–1am, and 1:30–6am.

5. SPORTS & RECREATION

SPECTATOR SPORTS

BASEBALL

Baseball and St. Petersburg have been linked for over 80 years. Al Lang, one of the city's early mayors, was an avid baseball fan and actively promoted St. Petersburg as a base for spring training. The St. Louis Browns were the first to come, in 1914, and over the years they were followed by the Philadelphia Phillies, Boston Braves, New York Yankees, and New York Mets.

Currently, St. Petersburg is the winter home of the **St. Louis Cardinals** and, at least temporarily, the **Baltimore Orioles.** Nearby Clearwater and Dunedin also serve as training grounds to two other major-league teams, the **Philadelphia Phillies** and the **Toronto Blue Jays,** respectively.

Up until 1990, the Al Lang Stadium was the major baseball venue in downtown St. Petersburg. With the recent opening of the St. Petersburg ThunderDome, however, baseball will be bigger than ever in this city. What follows is a rundown on the baseball scene at present.

ST. PETERSBURG THUNDERDOME, 1 Stadium Dr., St. Petersburg. Tel. 825-3100.

⭐ This is St. Petersburg's new centerpiece, a $110-million domed stadium with a seating capacity of 43,000 for baseball, as well as 37,400 for football, 28,900 for boxing, and 35,000 for basketball. As we go to press, this facility is still searching for a major-league baseball team. More than 22,000 season tickets have been reserved, with deposits, in anticipation of the inaugural year of regular-season major-league baseball in St. Pete. Exact schedules and prices will be announced when arrangements for a team are finalized.

The dome is between 10th and 16th Streets South, off First Avenue South (Exit 9 off I-275).

AL LANG STADIUM, 180 Second Ave. SE, St. Petersburg. Tel. 822-3384.

This is the winter home of the St. Louis Cardinals and (at least temporarily) the Baltimore Orioles, who hold their spring training here in February and March. The crack of the bat can also be heard at other times, with major-league exhibition games in the spring, followed by the St. Petersburg Cardinals, a Class A minor-league team (April through September).

The stadium is downtown, between the Pier and Bayfront Center.
Admission: $3–$7.
Open: Year-round.

JACK RUSSELL STADIUM, 800 Phillies Dr., Clearwater. Tel. 442-8496.

The Philadelphia Phillies play their spring training season at this 7,000-seat stadium. It's north of St. Petersburg, less than a mile northeast of downtown Clearwater, and 3½ miles west of U.S. 19, between Palmetto Street and Greenwood Avenue.
Admission: $7–$8.
Open: Mid-Feb to Apr.

GRANT FIELD, 373 Douglas Ave., Dunedin. Tel. 733-0429.

This field is the winter home of the Toronto Blue Jays. It's located 3 miles north of Clearwater and 3½ miles west of U.S. 19, just south of Main Street.
Admission: $6–$8.
Open: Mid-Feb to Apr.

DOG RACING

DERBY LANE, 10490 Gandy Blvd., St. Petersburg. Tel. 576-1359.

Founded in 1925, this is the world's oldest continually operating greyhound track, with indoor and outdoor seating, and standing areas. Facilities include restaurants and a cocktail lounge. It's north of downtown, half a mile east of Fourth Street North.

Admission: $1 adults, $2.50 for Derby Club level; free self-parking, $3 for valet parking.

Open: Jan–June, Mon–Sat at 7:30pm; matinees Mon, Wed, and Sat at 12:30pm.

HOCKEY

TAMPA BAY LIGHTNING, St. Petersburg ThunderDome, 1 Stadium Dr. Tel. 825-3334.

Tampa Bay Lightning is the southernmost franchise of the National Hockey League. For the 1994–95 season, the team is headquartered at St. Petersburg's ThunderDome, but for the 1995–96 season, it is scheduled to move to Tampa into a new $110 million downtown arena (see "Sports and Recreation," in Chapter 11).

Admission: Tickets, $8–$50.

Open: Playing season is Oct–Apr, but schedule varies.

SOFTBALL

KIDS & KUBS, Northshore Park, Eighth Ave. NE at the bayfront, St. Petersburg. Tel. 345-1066 or 866-6551.

As a city often associated with senior citizens, St. Petersburg is a natural home ground for the Three-Quarter Century Softball Club (usually referred to as the "Kids & Kubs"), a group of amateur softball players, primarily in their 70s and 80s, who play a full six-month schedule of exhibition games. Founded in 1930, the club is often featured in the national and international media to show that life in St. Petersburg is synonymous with longevity and activity.

Admission: Free.

Open: End Oct–early Apr, Tues, Thurs, and Sat at 12:45pm.

STOCKCAR RACING

SUNSHINE SPEEDWAY, 4500 Ulmerton Rd. (Fla. 688), St. Petersburg. Tel. 573-4598 or 573-4660.

Car-racing fans gather weekly at this large track, located just south of the St. Petersburg–Clearwater airport.

Admission: $8 adults, $4 children 6–12, free for children under age 6; parking is free.

Open: End Feb–end Nov, Sun at 7pm.

OTHER SPORTS

FOOTBALL   See Chapter 11, "What to See and Do in Tampa."

HORSE RACING   See Chapter 11, "What to See and Do in Tampa."

JAI-ALAI   See Chapter 11, "What to See and Do in Tampa."

POLO   See Chapter 11, "What to See and Do in Tampa."

RECREATION

With year-round sunshine and 28 miles of coastline along the Gulf of Mexico, the St. Petersburg area offers a wide choice of participatory sporting activities.

One of the newest developments, of benefit to walkers, bicyclists, joggers, and nature lovers, is the new **Pinellas Trail**, a 47-mile-long and 15-foot-wide path, stretching from St. Petersburg to Tarpon Springs. The trail's first 5-mile segment opened in late 1990, and the trail is still being extended, currently at 23 miles in length from Tarpon Springs to Seminole. When it's complete in the mid-1990s, it will be the longest trail of its kind in the eastern U.S. For more information or a brochure, contact the Pinellas County Park Department, 631 Chestnut St., Clearwater, FL 34616 (tel. 813/581-2953 or 462-3347).

When visiting St. Petersburg, you can get up-to-the-minute recorded information about the city's sports and recreational activities by calling the **Leisure Line** (tel. 893-7500). Below is a sampling of some of the things you can do.

BICYCLING

With miles of flat terrain, St. Petersburg is ideal for biking. One of the prime routes is along the bayfront, and around Straub Park where there is a signposted biking trail. Other recommended areas include Fort DeSoto Park and Pass-A-Grille.

A countywide system of bike trails is currently being developed. Check with the chamber of commerce for the latest information at the time of your visit. Bikes can be rented from the following:

BEACH CYCLIST, 7517 Blind Pass Rd., St. Petersburg Beach. Tel. 367-5001.

On the northern tip of St. Pete Beach, off 75th Avenue and west of the St. Petersburg Beach Causeway, this place offers several types of bikes, from a beach cruiser (allowed on the beaches at Treasure Island and Madeira Beach), to a selection of standard racing bikes.

Prices: From $10 for 4 hours, $12 for 24 hours, $39 per week.
Open: Mon–Sat 10am–6pm.

TRANSPORTATION STATION, 645 Bayway Blvd., Clearwater Beach. Tel. 443-3188.

At the southern end of Clearwater Beach, on the bay side off Gulf Boulevard, this place rents all types of bikes, from single speed to racers, tandems, mountain bikes, and one- and two-passenger scooters. Helmets and baby seats are also available.

Prices: Bicycles, $5–$8 per hour, $14.95–$21.95 for overnight special, $44–$66 per week; scooters, $13–$18 per hour, $39.95–$54.95 for overnight special, $109–$169 per week.
Open: Daily 9am–7pm.

FISHING

With over 300 varieties of fish in Tampa Bay and the Gulf of Mexico waters, fishing is a year-round sport in the St. Petersburg area.

Saltwater fishing is particularly popular along the gulf shoreline, with catches ranging from grouper and snapper to trout, flounder, pompano, sea bass, tarpon, sailfish, snook, redfish, kingfish, and mackerel. Fishing can be done from the shore itself, as well as from piers, bridges, and boats. A popular option for visitors is to join a "party boat," a large seagoing craft that accommodates a number of customers for full- or half-day trips at a moderate per-person cost.

Visitors are required to have a license for all saltwater fishing, from land or sea. The cost is $30 per year or $15 for a seven-day license. A stamp for taking crayfish (sometimes called Florida lobster) is an additional $2, as is a stamp for catching snook. Children under 16 are exempt from the fees.

The licenses are available at all county tax collectors' offices and at many bait-and-tackle shops, with a $1.50 and 50¢ surcharge, respectively. Most captains of charter fishing fleets have licensed vessels for saltwater fishing, so guests on those boats do not need a separate license. Always check in advance, as infractions carry a $500 fine.

The St. Petersburg area also offers freshwater fishing for sunfish, catfish, speckled perch, and bass. This, too, requires a license for nonresidents at a cost of $30 per year or $15 for seven days. For more information, call the Florida Game and Freshwater Fish Commission (tel. 904/488-4676) or Saltwater Fish Commission (tel. 904/488-7326).

Here is a sampling of companies that cater to visitors:

DOUBLE EAGLE'S DEEP SEA FISHING BOATS, Slip 50, Clearwater Beach Marina, 25 Causeway Blvd., Clearwater Beach. Tel. 446-1653.

This company offers a change from the usual fishing boat, using two modern catamarans, 83 feet and 65 feet in length. The vessels go 20 to 25 miles offshore into the gulf on four- or seven-hour day trips, with bait provided.

Prices: $20–$30 adults, $16–$25 children; $4 for tackle.

Sailings: Daily 8am–noon, 1–5pm, or 9am–4pm. **Directions:** Take Fla. 60 west to the Clearwater Beach Marina.

CAPT. HUBBARD'S MARINA, 150 128th Ave., Madeira Beach. Tel. 393-1947 or 392-0167.

Known as a "fish famous" spot, this marina is the focal point of John's Pass, a huge recreational village perched on pilings where Boca Ciega Bay meets the gulf. From here, you can try all types of fishing, from the dock and catwalks, or on party boats. Capt. Wilson Hubbard, who has been overseeing the operations since 1929, claims that John's Pass fishing boats catch more fish on 9 out of 10 days than any other boats on the Florida coast. It's not unusual for over 4,000 pounds of grouper to be landed in a day. Reservations are required for the longer trips.

Prices: $19.50 half day, $37.50 full day, $95 overnight (including the use of a bunk). Fishing poles can be rented for $5–$7.50.

Sailings: Daily: half-day trips, 8am–1pm and 1–6pm; full-day trips, 8am–6pm; overnight trips, Tues and Fri departing 8pm.

CAPTAIN KIDD, 801 Pass-A-Grille Way, St. Petersburg Beach (Mailing address: 3062 E. Vina del Mar Blvd, St. Petersburg Beach, FL 33706). Tel. 360-2263.

Departing from the southern end of St. Petersburg Beach, this 63-foot twin-diesel-powered fishing vessel offers half- and full-day fishing trips in the gulf. On-board facilities include a full-service galley and free fishing instruction for beginners; fish-cleaning service is also available.

Prices: $24–$33.50 adults, $21–$31.50 seniors and children.

Sailings: Mon–Fri 8am–noon and 1–5pm, Sat–Sun 8:30am–4pm. **Directions:** From downtown St. Petersburg, take the Pinellas Bayway to Gulf Blvd., turn left, and go south to Eighth Ave.

CAPT. DAVE SPAULDING'S QUEEN FLEET, Slip 52, Clearwater Beach Marina, 25 Causeway Blvd., Clearwater Beach. Tel. 446-7666.

One of the largest party-boat fishing fleets in the Clearwater area, this company offers trips of varying durations. Bait is furnished but rod rental is extra. Private charters for evenings are also available. Reservations are encouraged but not required.

Prices: $20 half day, $30–$32 three-quarters of a day; $5 for rods.

Sailings: Daily 8am–noon, 1–5pm, 9am–4pm, or 8am–5pm. **Directions:** Take Fla. 60 west to the Clearwater Beach Marina; the fleet is at the eastern dock.

MISS PASS-A-GRILLE, Dolphin Landings Charter Boat Center, 4737 Gulf Blvd., St. Petersburg Beach. Tel. 367-4488 or 360-7411.

Conveniently docked at a location in the heart of the St. Pete Beach hotel strip, behind the Dolphin Landings Shopping Center, at 47th Avenue, this fishing boat offers daily trips into Tampa Bay and the gulf, for either a half day (four hours) or a full day (seven hours).

Prices: $24.95 for four hours, $37.95 for seven hours.

Sailings: Tues–Wed and Fri at 8am and 1pm, Thurs and Sat–Sun at 9am.

Pier Fishing

REDINGTON LONG PIER, 17490 Gulf Blvd., at 175th Ave., Redington Shores. Tel. 391-9398.

Extending 1,021 feet into the Gulf of Mexico, this pier is a favorite with fishermen and sightseers alike. For the best fishing, according to the local authorities, come early in the evening, from about an hour before sunset until midnight, especially if the tide is incoming. Fishing is also recommended early in the morning, from before dawn until about daybreak, particularly if the tide is coming in. The pier offers a snack bar, restrooms, rod rentals, bait, tackle, shelters and benches, and fish-cleaning facilities.

Prices: Fishing charges, $5 adults, $4 children; rod rental, $4 plus $5 deposit; spectators or walk-ons, 50¢.

Open: Daily 24 hours.

PIER 60, west end of Fla. 60, Clearwater Beach. Tel. 462-6466.

A fixture for over 40 years, this fishing pier in the center of the Clearwater Beach strip is currently undergoing renovation, but will remain open as changes and extensions are made. Current facilities include a snack bar, bait-and-tackle shop, rod rental, restrooms, and observation deck with telescopes.

Prices: Fishing charges, $3.75; spectators or walk-ons, 50¢.

Open: Daily 24 hours.

GOLF

There are over 40 golf courses and schools in the St. Petersburg area. Many of these facilities welcome visitors. Here are a few suggestions:

AIRCO FLITE GOLF COURSE, 3650 Roosevelt Blvd., Clearwater. Tel. 573-4653.

Adjacent to the St. Petersburg–Clearwater airport and behind the Showboat Dinner Theater, this is an 18-hole, par-72 course, with driving range, clubhouse, restaurant, lounge, and snack bar. Lessons and golf-club rentals are also available. Bookings can be made up to six days in advance.

Prices: $27 per person including cart.

Open: Daily 7am–6pm.

BARDMOOR NORTH GOLF CLUB, 7919 Bardmoor Blvd., Largo. Tel. 397-0483.

Often the venue of major tournaments, this public club offers an 18-hole course, par 72, plus a driving range designed by Tom Fazio, and a restaurant, lounge, and snack bar. Lessons and rental clubs are also available. The course is north of St. Petersburg, off Starkey Road and south of Fla. 688.

Prices: Greens fees, $55 Mon–Fri, $59 Sat–Sun, with cart.

Open: Daily 7am–dusk.

CHI CHI RODRIGUEZ GOLF CLUB, 3030 McMullen-Booth Rd., Clearwater. Tel. 725-2945.

Newly opened in 1989, this is an 18-hole, par-69 course, with a snack bar. Rental clubs are also available. The course is northeast of Clearwater, and a quarter mile north of Fla. 580.

Prices: $28 Mon–Fri, $30 Sat–Sun, with cart.

Open: Daily 7am–6pm.

INNISBROOK GOLF INSTITUTE, Innisbrook Hilton Resort, 36750 U.S. 19 N., off Klosterman Rd., Tarpon Springs. Tel. 813/942-2000, ext. 5383, or toll free 800/456-2000.

★ Play on the Copperhead, one of Florida's top-rated courses, as part of this program. A typical four-day/three-night program includes 12 hours of individual instruction, videotape analysis, on-course supervision, personal lockers for storing clubs, overnight accommodations, play and greens fees on Innisbrook's three championship 18-hole courses, unlimited range balls, breakfast and lunch daily, cocktail reception, and all related service charges. See Chapter 5, "St. Petersburg Accommodations," for more information on Innisbrook. The resort is between U.S. 19 and U.S. Alt. 19, five miles north of Clearwater.

Prices: $1,200 single or double for the four-day program.
Open: Jan–May and Sept–Dec, Thurs–Sun and Sun–Wed.

LARGO MUNICIPAL GOLF COURSE, 12500 131st St., Largo. Tel. 587-6724.

A popular course with local residents, this is an 18-hole, par-62 public course, within two miles of Indian Rocks Beach, four blocks north of Fla. 688.

Prices: Greens fees, $11 before 2pm, $9 after 2pm.
Open: Daily 7am–dark.

MANGROVE BAY GOLF COURSE, 875 62nd Ave. NE, St. Petersburg. Tel. 893-7797.

★ One of the top 50 municipal golf courses in the U.S., this course hugs the inlets of Old Tampa Bay in the northeast corner of St. Petersburg, one mile east of Fourth Street North, and offers 18-hole, par-72 play. Facilities include a driving range and snack bar; lessons and golf-club rentals are also available. Reserved tee times may be made up to seven days in advance (tel. 893-7797).

Prices: $18 with no cart, $28 with cart.
Open: Daily 6:30am–6pm.

PARASAILING

CAPT. WAYNE'S SKYRIDER, Slip 22, Clearwater Municipal Marina, Clearwater Beach. Tel. 449-0007.

Glide over the waters of Clearwater Harbor on board a parasail built for two, designed with an aerial recliner seat accommodating two passengers. All takeoffs and landings are launched and retrieved from a fixed powerboat platform. The entire trip takes one hour, with a full 15 minutes in the air.

Prices: $40 for one person only, $37.50 each for two passengers.
Open: Daily 9am–6pm.

SUNSPORTS UNLIMITED, 3400 Gulf Blvd., St. Petersburg Beach. Tel. 360-1881, ext. 163.

Parasail rides lifting passengers up to 400 feet over the Gulf of Mexico are the specialty of this firm, located on the grounds of the Don CeSar Resort. Waverunner rentals are also available.

Prices: Parasail rides $40 for eight minutes per person; Waverunners $35 per half-hour, $65 per hour per person.
Open: Daily 10am–6pm.

SAILING

Whether you want to perfect your sailing skills or learn from scratch, this area offers many opportunities to practice and participate. Clearwater, in particular, is a mecca for sailboat rides and rentals. Here are a few suggestions:

ANNAPOLIS SAILING SCHOOL, 6800 34th St. S., St. Petersburg. Tel. 813/867-8102, or toll free 800/237-0795. Learn to sail or perfect your sailing skills at this branch of the famous Maryland-based school. Various courses are offered for two, five, or eight days. Depending on the course you take, you'll overnight at the adjacent Days Inn Marina Beach Hotel or on board one of the cruising sloops.

Prices: $185–$1,655 per person, depending on season and length of course.

Open: Daily year-round. **Directions:** From downtown, take I-275 south to Pinellas Point Dr. (Exit 3); school is on the left.

***KAI LANI,* Clearwater Beach Marina, Slip 49, Clearwater Beach. Tel. 446-6778.**
This 50-foot catamaran under sail offers two-hour trips along the Clearwater Beach coast, during the morning or afternoon, and again at sunset hour. The sunset cruise includes complimentary beer, wine, and soft drinks. Reservations are recommended.

Prices: Morning or afternoon sails, $20 adults, $12 children; sunset sail, $25 adults, $12 children.

Sailings: Daily 10am, 2pm, and sunset hour (time varies).

***OPA,* Clearwater Beach Marina, Slip 21, Clearwater Beach. Tel. 442-8030.**
Come aboard this 41-foot sailboat for a relaxing 2½-hour sail with Captain Dan along the waters of Clearwater Beach and the Gulf of Mexico. Maximum of six people per cruise. Longer trips to Tarpon Springs or overnight can also be arranged.

Prices: $17–$20 per person.

Sailings: Daily 10am, 1:30pm, and sunset.

***PHOENIX,* Dolphin Landings, 4737 Gulf Blvd., St. Petersburg Beach. Tel. 813/360-7411** or 367-4488.
Based on Boca Ciega Bay, this 41-foot sailing ketch offers trips to various Gulf of Mexico ports, including nearby natural barrier islands and Egmont Key. Most trips are two to eight hours in duration and include complimentary soft drinks. Reservations are required. The *Phoenix* is directly behind the Dolphin Village Shopping Center, between 47th and 48th Avenues.

Prices: $20–$60 adults, $10–$30 children.

Sailings: Daily at 8:15am, 9:30am, noon, 1:15pm, and 2:15pm, and sunset, but departures vary according to demand.

***SOUTHERN ROMANCE,* Slip 16, Clearwater Beach Marina, 25 Causeway Blvd., Clearwater Beach. Tel. 813/461-6148.**

This is a 40-foot ocean racing/cruising yacht that takes a maximum of 12 passengers at a time for a two-hour sailing in Clearwater Harbor and gulf waters. Advance reservations suggested.

Prices: $16 per person.

Sailings: Daily at 10am, 1:30pm, and 4pm. **Directions:** Take Fla. 60 west to the Clearwater Beach Marina.

SUNCOAST SAILING CENTER, Clearwater Beach Marina, Slip 10, Clearwater Beach. Tel. 813/581-4662.

Sail aboard a 65-foot windjammer or a 38-foot racing yacht. You can be part of the crew or just relax for 2½ hours and enjoy the views of the gulf waters. Rentals of small sloops and sailing lessons also available. Reservations required.

Prices: $17.50–$20 adults, half price for children.

Sailings: Daily at 10am, 1:30pm, and 4:30pm. **Directions:** Take Fla. 60 west to the Clearwater Beach Marina.

SWIMMING

Edged by dozens of sugar-white sandy beaches, the St. Petersburg area is ideal for swimming, sunning, or just walking along the shore. There's never a fee for using a beach, but there are charges for metered parking, usually 25¢ for each half hour. Most beaches have restrooms, refreshment stands, and picnic areas.

Many of the hotels sit right on the beach, so you can just step outside the door and wiggle your toes in the sand. In case your accommodations are not beachfront, or if you just want to sample a different beach or two each day, here's a rundown of prime swimming areas that offer public access:

✪ **St. Petersburg Beach**   The prime beach of St. Pete's gulf coast shores, it's three miles long, just west of Gulf Boulevard. Public access and parking areas include 46th Street (Belle Vista Beach), 68th Street (Upham Beach), and at Pass-A-Grille, on Eighth Avenue.

✪ **Fort DeSoto Park**   South of St. Petersburg, this string of islands offers three miles of beaches with shorelines fronting Tampa Bay as well as the Gulf of Mexico. There are also extensive picnic and camping facilities here, with no parking charges.

Treasure Island   North of St. Pete Beach, this small island has 45 dune walkovers and street ends, giving pedestrian access to gulf beaches between 77th and 127th Avenues, with some parking meters at 77th, 90th, 100th, 112th, 120th, and 126th Avenues.

Madeira Beach   Sea oats and sand dunes add to the beach scene here, with 1½ miles of natural beachfront off Gulf Boulevard, on the southern end of Sand Key Island. The best access and parking are at the Madeira Beach County Park, along 141st to 148th Avenues, at Archibald Memorial Beach at 152nd Avenue, and near John's Pass at 129th Avenue.

Redington Beaches   A largely residential area, these gulf beaches (Redington Beach, North Redington Beach, and Redington Shores) offer numerous public accesses but little parking except at the fishing pier at 175th Avenue at Redington Shores.

Indian Rocks Beach   Here are three miles of gulf beaches, with street parking access between 15th and 27th Avenues and First and Eighth Avenues. Parking is limited but free.

Sand Key Park   This is the area's largest and newest beach park, situated at the north tip of Sand Key Island. It offers a beachfront overlooking the Gulf of Mexico or the boating channel of Clearwater Pass. Ample parking is available.

✪ Clearwater Beach   Equally distant from St. Petersburg or Tampa (22 miles in either direction), this wide and sandy 4-mile stretch is the largest of all the beaches in the Tampa Bay area. The major points of access and parking (over 800 parking spaces) are along Gulfview Avenue at the south end of the island.

TENNIS

There are more than 200 private and public tennis courts in the St. Petersburg area. Many resorts, hotels, and motels have their own tennis courts on site and offer court time to guests on a complimentary or reduced-rate basis. Here are a few tennis facilities.

HURLEY PARK, 1600 Pass-A-Grille Way, Pass-A-Grille, St. Petersburg Beach.

There's just one court here, opposite the beach, open on a first-come, first-play basis.

Prices: 25¢ for 15 minutes (quarters only).

Open: Daily 8am–10pm. **Directions:** Take Pinellas Bayway to Gulf Blvd., turn left and go to 15th Ave., then turn right.

McMULLEN PARK, 1000 Edenville Ave., Clearwater. Tel. 462-6144.

This inland facility southeast of Clearwater Beach, off U.S. 19 between Gulf-to-Bay Drive and Belleair Road, offers 17 lighted courts, a pro shop, and a locker room; lessons are also available. Reservations recommended.

Prices: $2.50 before 6pm, $3 after 6pm per hour per court.

Open: Mon–Fri 8am–10pm, Sat 8am–8pm, Sun 8am–4pm.

ST. PETERSBURG TENNIS CENTER, 650 18th Ave. S., St. Petersburg. Tel. 894-4378.

Just south of downtown, in Bartlett Park, five blocks from Lassing Park and Tampa Bay, this facility offers 15 Har-Tru tennis courts, as well as snack bar, locker rooms, and showers. Private lessons and clinics are available.

Prices: $6.40 per person per hour.

Open: Daily 8am–9pm.

WATER SPORTS

In addition to fishing, sailing, and swimming, the St. Pete area offers an abundance of other water-related activities. Just step on the beach or go near the bay and you'll see a myriad of inviting craft, from aquacycles to Aqua-Ray boats, catamarans to kayaks, pontoon or paddleboats to parasails, and Waverunners or Windsurfers to water skis, just to mention a few. Here are a few good sources for renting equipment:

BOATING ZONE, Slips 5 and 6, Clearwater Beach Marina, Clearwater Beach. Tel. 446-5503.

If you can handle a boat yourself, this company rents crafts equipped with 70hp to 175hp motors. Sizes range from 17 to 20 feet, carrying four to seven persons. Eight-foot miniboats with 6hp engines, ideal for two people, can also be rented by the hour.

Prices: $20 per hour; miniboats, $14 per hour.

Open: Daily 9am–5pm. **Directions:** Take Fla. 60 west to the Clearwater Beach Marina.

BLUE WATER WAVE RUNNERS, Holiday Isles Marina, 545 150th Ave., Madeira Beach. Tel. 393-4566.

Situated next to Leverock's restaurant on the west side of the Tom Stewart Causeway, this company specializes in renting Waverunners of various sizes.

Prices: $35–$45 per hour.

Open: Daily 9:30am–5:30pm or later.

CAPTAIN DAVE'S WATERSPORTS, 9540 Blind Pass Rd., St. Petersburg Beach. Tel. 367-4336.

This company at the north end of St. Petersburg Beach—beside Blind Pass Bridge in the Lighthouse Point Shopping Center, next to Mulligan's restaurant—offers Waverunner and powerboat rentals, parasail rides, snorkel trips to Egmont Key, and sailing and shelling trips.

Prices: Waverunner rentals, from $35 per half hour, $60 per hour; powerboat rentals, $50 and up for one hour, $70 and up for two hours, $135 and up per day; parasail rides, $30–$35; snorkel trips, $35; sailing and shelling trips, $25.

Open: Daily 9am–5pm or later.

CAPT. MIKE'S WATERSPORTS, 6300 Gulf Blvd., St. Petersburg Beach. Tel. 360-1998 or 360-1053.

Located on the beach behind the Colonial Gateway Inn, off 63rd Avenue, this company offers parasailing rides, pontoon boats, snorkeling equipment, boat rentals, waterski rentals and lessons, and shelling trips. "Early bird" reduced rates ($5 off) are available between 9 and 10am. A second location is behind the Dolphin Beach Hotel at 4900 Gulf Blvd.

Prices: From $35 for parasailing, $25 for waterskiing; $30 for lessons; shelling trips, $20 adults, $12 children.

Open: Daily 8am–6pm or later.

DOLPHIN LANDINGS CHARTER BOAT CENTER, 4737 Gulf Blvd., St. Petersburg Beach. Tel. 367-4488 or 360-7411.

From this boat dock at 47th Avenue, behind the Dolphin Village Shopping Center, you can arrange for a number of water-sports activities including sailing/shelling trips for three or four hours on board 37- to 41-foot yachts, as well as two-hour dolphin-watch tours, and sunset sailing excursions. Reservations are recommended.

Prices: Shelling trips, $20 adults, $12 children; dolphin-watching trips, $20 adults, $10 children; sunset sailing, $20 adults, $10 children.

Open: Daily, shelling/sailing trips 8:15am–sunset; schedules vary. Dolphin-watch trips at 1:30pm, sunset sailing at 4:30pm.

FUN RENTALS, Municipal Marina, Slip 300, 150th Ave., Madeira Beach. Tel. 397-0276.

This company at the south side of the Tom Stewart Causeway, behind Leverock's Restaurant, rents 22-foot pontoon boats (seating 10) for fishing, sightseeing, or plying the waters of the Intracoastal Waterway.

Prices: $90 per half day, $150 per full day.
Open: Daily 9:30am–5:30pm.

ISLAND MARINE, 11045 Gulf Blvd., Treasure Island. Tel. 367-2132.

This company rents a variety of equipment, from 17- to 19-foot powerboats and 24-foot catamarans, to Waverunners, waterskis, beach cruiser bikes, and rods and reels for fishing.

Prices: Powerboats from $30 per hour, $100 per half day, and $160 per full day; pontoons from $40 per hour, $140 per half day, and $200 per day; Waverunners from $30 per half hour and $50 per hour; waterskis from $8 per half day, $15 per full day; beach cruiser bikes from $6 per half day and $10 per full day; rods and reels from $5 per half day and $8 per full day.
Open: Daily 8am–6pm or later.

SHERATON SAND KEY RESORT, 1160 Gulf Blvd., Clearwater Beach. Tel. 395-1611.

At the northern tip of Sand Key Island, next to Sand Key Park, this is one of the largest water-sports centers on the entire beach strip, with rentals for glass-bottom paddleboats, Hobie Cats, Windsurfers, and cat boats. Lessons are also available for windsurfing.

Prices: $12–$35 per half hour or hour, depending on equipment rented; windsurfing lessons, $10.
Open: Daily 7:30am–6:30pm or later.

SUNCOAST BOAT RENTAL, Holiday Isles Marina, 545 150th Ave., Madeira Beach. Tel. 391-5266.

Located on the west side of the Tom Stewart Causeway next to a Leverock's restaurant, this company rents four- to 10-person powerboats for fishing, waterskiing, or cruising in the nearby waters. Boats range in size from 16 to 24 feet.

Prices: $49–$89 for two hours, $59–$125 for four hours, $99–$225 per day.
Open: Daily 8am–dusk.

WATERWORKS RENTALS, The Pier, St. Petersburg. Tel. 363-0000.
Headquartered on the south side of the main entrance of the Pier, this firm rents Waverunners and boats from 12 to 22 feet for use along the bayfront. A second location is at 200D 150th Ave., Madeira Beach (tel. 399-8989).

Prices: Waverunners from $25 per half hour, boats from $15 per hour.

Open: Daily 9am–6pm or later.

WALKING TOUR — DOWNTOWN ST. PETERSBURG

Start: St. Petersburg ThunderDome.
Finish: The Pier.
Time: Allow approximately two hours.
Best Times: Weekends.
Worst Times: Weekday morning or evening rush hours.

FROM THE THUNDERDOME TO THE CARNEGIE LIBRARY   Start your tour at the:

1. **St. Petersburg ThunderDome,** 1 Stadium Dr. (between 10th and 16th Streets, off First Avenue South), the city's new stadium/showplace on 66 acres. You may wish to walk the grounds or just admire the huge slant-roofed dome from First Avenue South, a good picture-taking vantage point. Next, head one block north to Central Avenue and stop at the:

2. **Gas Plant Antique Arcade,** 1246 Central Ave. (between 12th and 13th Streets North). This four-story complex, housed in a former gas plant, is the largest antiques mall on Florida's west coast, with more than 100 dealers displaying their wares.

   Continue along Central Avenue for five blocks to Seventh Street North. This stretch still has some empty stores and a few pawn shops, although the advent of the ThunderDome is beginning to perk up the area. Stop to look at the:

3. **Green-Richman Arcade,** 689 Central Ave. Built in 1923, this Mediterranean Revival–style shopping arcade displays a style of architecture that was popular in the 1920s. A forerunner of the modern shopping mall, this arcade once housed a major boom-era real-estate firm. The building adjacent, at 687 Central Ave., is the recently restored State Theater, a former movie house.

   At Seventh Street, head north and go two blocks to Arlington Avenue. Cross Arlington, turn right, and go one block to Mirror Lake Drive. On your left is the:

4. **Unitarian Universalist Church,** 719 Arlington Ave., built in 1926. The design was inspired by the mission churches of the Spanish Colonial period. Turn left on Mirror Lake Drive and take time to admire:

5. **Mirror Lake,** the city's first source of drinking water. Landscaped in the early 1900s as a park with shady palm trees and

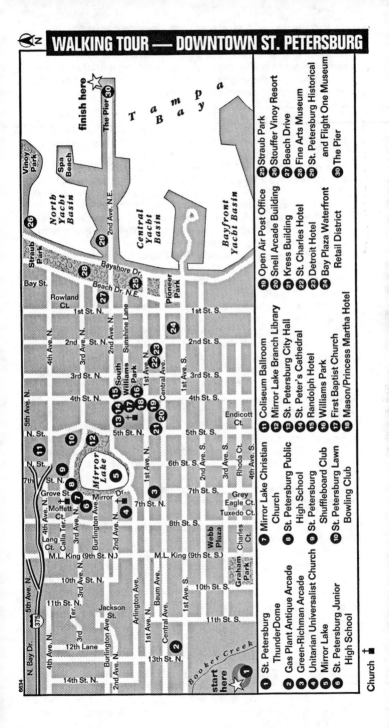

WALKING TOUR — DOWNTOWN ST. PETERSBURG

N

finish here
The Pier 30

Tampa Bay

Vinoy Park
Spa Beach
North Yacht Basin
2nd Ave. N.E.
26
29
Straub Park
28
Bayshore Dr.
Bay St.
Rowland Ct.
Beach Dr. N.E.
27
1st St. N.
Central Yacht Basin
Pioneer Park
1st St. S.
4th Ave. N.
3rd St. N.
Sunshine Lane
2nd Ave. N.
2nd St. N.
2nd St. S.
2nd Ave. S.
24
Bayfront Yacht Basin

5th Ave. N. St.
3rd St. N.
South Williams Park
22 23
1st St. N.
Central Ave.
1st St. S.
3rd St. S.
3rd Ave. S.
15 16
13 14 7
18 19
4th St. N.
4th St. S.
Endicott Ct.
17
5th St. N.
21 20
5th St. S.
5th Ave. N.

11
10
12
N. St.
9
N. St.
Mirror Lake
5
1st Ave. N.
2nd Ave. S.
3rd Ave. S.
Rhoda Ct.
4th St. S.
7th St. N.
Grove St.
8
Mirror Dr.
7th St. N.
Grey Eagle Ct.
Tuxedo Ct.
7th
St. N.
7
6
Mirror Dr.
3
8th St. S.
Moffett Ct.
4
Burlington Ave.
2nd Ave. N.
Webb Plaza
Charles Ct.
Lang Ct.
Calla Terr.
4th Ave. N.
3rd Ave. N.
M.L. King (9th St. N.)
M.L. King (9th St. S.)
Graham Park
N. Bay Dr.
5th Ave. N.
375
10th St. N.
3rd Ave. N.
10th St. S.
11th St. N.
Ter. 3rd 3rd Ave. N.
1st Ave. N.
11th St. S.
Jackson St.
Arlington Ave.
Baum Ave.
Central Ave.
12th Lane
13th St. N.
2
Burlington Ave.
1st Ave. N.
Booker Creek
start here
1
14th St. N.
4th Ave. N.
2nd Ave. S.

1 St. Petersburg ThunderDome
2 Gas Plant Antique Arcade
3 Green-Richman Arcade
4 Unitarian Universalist Church
5 Mirror Lake
6 St. Petersburg Junior High School
7 Mirror Lake Christian Church
8 St. Petersburg Public High School
9 St. Petersburg Shuffleboard Club
10 St. Petersburg Lawn Bowling Club
11 Coliseum Ballroom
12 Mirror Lake Branch Library
13 St. Petersburg City Hall
14 St. Peter's Cathedral
15 Randolph Hotel
16 Williams Park
17 First Baptist Church
18 Mason/Princess Martha Hotel
19 Open Air Post Office
20 Snell Arcade Building
21 Kress Building
22 St. Charles Hotel
23 Detroit Hotel
24 Bay Plaza Waterfront Retail District
25 Straub Park
26 Stouffer Vinoy Resort
27 Beach Drive
28 Fine Arts Museum
29 St. Petersburg Historical and Flight One Museum
30 The Pier

Church ✝

6634

benches, it soon became St. Pete's first lovers' lane. Today it's a tranquil spot to rest and enjoy the birdsong and reflections of the fine houses that surround the lake. Continue north three blocks, passing the lake. On the southwest corner of Mirror Lake Drive and Third Avenue North is:

6. **St. Petersburg Junior High School,** 296 Mirror Lake Dr., a Mediterranean Revival structure built in 1924 (now an adult learning center). Cross Third Avenue, continuing east, and you'll see two more Mediterranean Revival buildings: the

7. **Mirror Lake Christian Church** (1926), and

8. **St. Petersburg Public High School,** 709 Mirror Lake Dr. (1919) (now condos and apartments). Continue east across Seventh Street and the adjacent parking lot to the:

9. **St. Petersburg Shuffleboard Club** (1924), the largest shuffleboard club in the world. Walk through the grounds to Fourth Avenue North. Turn right and see the:

10. **St. Petersburg Lawn Bowling Club,** 536 Fourth Ave. N. (1926), one of the oldest clubs for this sport in the country. Directly across the street is the:

11. **Coliseum Ballroom,** 535 Fourth Ave. N. (1924), one of the oldest continually operating big-band-era dance halls in the United States. Continue east on Fourth Avenue to Fifth Street North, turn right and continue south till you cross Third Avenue North. On your right is the:

12. **Mirror Lake Branch Library,** 300 Fifth St. N. Dating back to 1915, this beaux arts structure was the city's first library building and was financed by a grant from the Carnegie Foundation.

REFUELING STOP   The best place for refreshment in this area is the **Heritage Grille,** 234 Third Ave. N., at the corner of Second Street, two blocks east of the Mirror Lake Branch Library. The restaurant is housed in the Heritage/Holiday Inn, a restored inn that was originally known as the Martha Washington Hotel when it was built in the early 1920s. It's a bright and airy café, with a menu of light regional cuisine.

FROM ST. PETERSBURG CITY HALL TO STRAUB PARK   From the Mirror Lake Branch Library, continue south on Fifth Street, across Mirror Lake Drive (it now becomes Second Avenue North). Make a left, crossing Fifth Street, and on your right is:

13. **St. Petersburg City Hall,** 175 Fifth St. N. Built in 1939, this Mediterranean Revival structure was one of the last buildings of this style built in the city. Backtrack a few steps and make a right onto Second Avenue North, then turn right onto Fourth Street to see:

14. **St. Peter's Cathedral,** 140 Fourth St. N., dating back to 1899 and one of the first Episcopal houses of worship in the city. On the opposite side of the street is the:

15. **Randolph Hotel,** 200 Fourth St. N., a good example of an art

deco–style hotel in the downtown area. Half a block farther down Fourth Street is:

16. **Williams Park,** dating back to 1888 and laid out as the city's main square when St. Petersburg was plotted. It's named after John Williams, one of the city's founders. Across from the park is the neoclassical:

17. **First Baptist Church,** 136 Fourth St. N., dating back to 1924 (now no longer operating). Next door is the:

18. **Mason/Princess Martha Hotel,** 401 First Ave. N. Dating back to 1923–24, this neoclassical-style hotel was one of the largest built during the boom era. Cross First Avenue North and you'll see the:

19. **Open Air Post Office,** 400 First Ave. N., dating back to 1917. The world's first open-air post office, it was built so that boxholders could take advantage of St. Pete's mild climate. It is now partially enclosed. Cross the adjacent alley south to the:

20. **Snell Arcade Building,** 405 Central Ave. Built in 1926 by real-estate developer Perry Snell, it was designed primarily as an office building, but it also had an arcade of shops on the ground level and a rooftop restaurant on the third floor.

Now back on Central, there are a number of landmarks worth a look, including the glazed terra-cotta:

21. **Kress Building,** 475 Central Ave., built in 1925–27 and originally a five-and-dime store, now renovated as offices. Continuing east, between Second and Third Streets, is the:

22. **St. Charles Hotel,** 241–45 Central Ave., dating back to 1903 and now the site of Jannus Landing, a small shopping/entertainment complex. For a contrast, look across the street at the new Barnett Tower, 200 Central Ave., at 26 stories the city's tallest building. The city's first hotel, built in 1888, is the:

23. **Detroit Hotel,** 215 Central Ave. Named after the hometown of John Williams, this vintage building is now known for its bars and rock music concerts. Across the street is Phase I of the:

24. **Bay Plaza Waterfront Retail District,** a new shopping and commercial development that will rejuvenate the streetscapes of downtown St. Pete. Target date for opening is 1995–96.

Leaving Central Avenue now, turn left onto Second Street and go north to: First Avenue North and walk two blocks east to Beach Drive. Cross over Beach Drive at First Avenue NE and you're now at:

25. **Straub Park,** named in honor of William Straub, a local newspaper editor who led a campaign for public ownership of the city's waterfront in the early 1900s. Look to the north end of the park for a sweeping view of a newly restored landmark, the:

26. **Stouffer Vinoy Resort.** Walk one block north to Second Avenue NE. You are now in the heart of the city's bayfront district and have a number of options to complete your tour—visit some of the fashionable shops along the adjacent:

27. **Beach Drive,** stop at the:

28. **Fine Arts Museum** or:

29. **St. Petersburg Historical and Flight One Museum,** both just steps away, or turn right and head to:

30. The Pier, the city's unique shopping/dining/entertainment complex on the water.

REFUELING STOP   For something light, head to **The Pier,** where the choice includes Nick's on the Water and a fast-food court on the ground level, or Cha Cha Coconuts, known for its tropical drinks as well as basic American fare, on the rooftop. On the fourth floor is a branch of the famous Spanish restaurant, the Columbia.

---

6. SAVVY SHOPPING

Although the St. Pete area offers a wide selection of souvenirs and gifts, ranging from antiques and art to all kinds of crafts, some of the best buys are indigenous and synonymous with the locale—i.e., beach and swim wear, resort clothes, nautical items, and citrus products. Senior craft centers (in downtown St. Petersburg and downtown Clearwater) are also special finds, and the area is also home to Haslam's, Florida's largest book emporium.

Most downtown shops are open Monday through Saturday from 9am or 10am until 5pm or 6pm. Department stores, malls, shopping villages, and shops along the beach strip are usually open daily, from 9am or 10am until 8pm or 9pm Monday through Saturday and from noon until 5pm or 6pm on Sunday. In the busy winter season (December through April), longer hours are often in effect along the beach strip.

All purchases are subject to 7% sales tax.

During 1995–96, plans call for the opening of the Bay Plaza Waterfront Retail District, a new upscale midtown shopping development in a Mediterranean-style open-air layout. Located just west of the Pier, this new retail complex is expected to greatly revitalize the downtown shopping scene.

MALLS, MARKETS & SHOPPING CLUSTERS

BAY AREA OUTLET MALL, 15525 U.S. 19, Clearwater. Tel. 535-2337.

Known for selling well-known brand names at bargain prices, this huge 80-unit complex at East Bay/Roosevelt Boulevard and U.S. 19, is spread over four wings. Manufacturers represented range from Bass and Johnston and Murphy shoes to Leggs, T. J. Maxx, Swim Mart, and Bookland Book Outlet. Also on sale are records, ribbons, jewelry, toys, and affordable art. Open Monday through Saturday from 10am to 9pm and on Sunday from noon to 6pm.

BAYSIDE SHOPS, 5501 Gulf Blvd., St. Petersburg Beach. Tel. 367-2784 or 367-4485.

This cluster of shops next to Silas Dent's restaurant and opposite the TradeWinds Resort, between 55th and 56th Avenues, offers resort and tropical clothing, swimwear, hats, T-shirts, hand-painted clothing, and nautical crafts. Plans also call for the reopening of the wax museum that was on this site for many years. Open daily from 10am to 9pm.

DOLPHIN VILLAGE, 4615 Gulf Blvd., St. Petersburg Beach. Tel. 367-3138.

Situated on Boca Ciega Bay in the middle of St. Pete Beach, at 46th Avenue, this is a large two-story art deco–style shopping center with a glass-enclosed elevator. There are over 50 stores, restaurants, and boutiques including a charter boat center, a grocery store, and beauty and barber salons, as well as shops specializing in shells, books, leatherwork, sports equipment, beach rentals, swimsuits, and imports. Open daily from 9am to 6pm or later.

GAS PLANT ANTIQUE ARCADE, 1246 Central Ave., St. Petersburg. Tel. 895-0368.

Housed in a former gas plant two blocks from the ThunderDome this four-story complex is the largest antiques mall on Florida's west coast. More than 100 dealers display their wares, from buttons to breakfronts, as well as a wide range of jewelry, toys, art glass, perfume bottles, Hummels, bronzes, quilts, and paintings. Open Monday through Saturday from 10am to 5pm and on Sunday from noon to 5pm.

JOHN'S PASS VILLAGE AND BOARDWALK, 12901 Gulf Blvd., Madeira Beach. Tel. 391-7373.

Situated on the water at the southern tip of Madeira Beach, this converted fisherman's village houses over 100 shops, selling everything from antiques and arts and crafts to beachwear, resort wear, sporting goods, woodwork, glasswork, and jewelry. There are also several art galleries, including the Bronze Lady, which is the largest single dealer in the world of works by Red Skelton, the comedian-artist. This shop stocks prints from his limited-edition canvas-transfer collection, plus his storybooks, collector plates, figurines, radio cassettes, drawings, pastels, and paintings. Open daily from 9am to 6pm or later.

THE PIER, 800 Second Ave. NE, St. Petersburg. Tel. 821-6164.

Ever since it was reopened in 1988, this has been the hub of shopping for the downtown area, with more than a dozen boutiques, eateries, and other attractions in a panoramic waterside setting north of the Bayfront Center on Tampa Bay. Most of the major shops are indoors on the ground level of the building, but there is also an outdoor marketplace with two rows of pavilions and carts lining the driveway that leads from the parking areas to the Pier entrance. Items on sale range from hats, clothing, and jewelry to toys, country crafts, and artwork, as well as a fudge-and-candy shop and a flag-and-kite emporium.

The Pier also leads to Beach Drive, one of the most fashionable strolling and shopping streets in the downtown area, with a string of shops offering everything from contemporary art to nautical and imported gifts. Open Monday through Saturday from 10am to 9pm, and on Sunday from 11am to 7pm.

THE SHOPPES AT SAND KEY, 1261 Gulf Blvd., Clearwater Beach. Tel. 595-5998.

One of the most delightful shopping settings in the area, this cluster of stores at the north end of Sand Key Island, beside the Radisson Suite Resort, lines an open deck along the Intracoastal Waterway, with views of the water and passing boats from most units. Goods featured range from nautical and shell crafts and beach-wood art to resort wear, fine art, jewelry, and wines. There is also a hairdressing salon, bank, and deli. Open daily from 10am to 9pm.

TYRONE SQUARE MALL, 6901 22nd Ave. N., St. Petersburg. Tel. 345-0126.

Northwest of downtown, at the intersection of Tyrone Boulevard and 66th Street North, this is one of the oldest and largest air-conditioned malls in the area, with a six-theater movie complex, food court, tourist information desk, and 150 stores including Burdine's, Dillard's, Sears, and J.C. Penney. Other outlets include jewelry shops, fashion boutiques, sporting-goods stores, and booksellers, such as B. Dalton and Waldenbooks. A "Wellness Walker" mall walker program also operates here. Open Monday through Saturday from 10am to 9pm and on Sunday from noon to 6pm.

WAGON WHEEL FLEA MARKET, 7801 Park Blvd. (Fla. 694), Pinellas Park. Tel. 544-5319.

The area's largest and most popular open-air market, offering curios, collectibles, and crafts of all kinds, with over 2,000 booths and stalls, and vendors from near and far. It's north of St. Petersburg, at the intersection of 78th Street North and Park Boulevard (Fla. 694). Open on Saturday and Sunday from 8am to 4pm.

SPECIALTY STORES

ART

EVELYN COBB GALLERIES, 222 Beach Dr. NE, St. Petersburg. Tel. 822-8288.

Between Second and Third Avenues North, opposite Straub Park, this shop specializes in fine art, graphics, and crafts by Tampa Bay artists. It also offers the largest collection on the west coast of Florida of the work of Edna Hibel, including stone lithographs, fine art reproductions, porcelains, hand-carved wooden dolls, and more. Open Monday through Friday from 10am to 6pm and on Saturday from 10am to 4pm. On Thursday the galleries are open till 8pm.

P. BUCKLEY MOSS, 190 Fourth Ave. NE, St. Petersburg. Tel. 894-2899.

This downtown gallery/studio opposite Straub Park features the works of one of Florida's most individualistic artists, with a style combining abstraction and realism. She is best known for her portrayal of the Amish and Mennonite people. In addition to paintings, graphics, and offset lithographic reproductions, the gallery offers porcelain plates, figurines, and collector dolls. Open Monday through Saturday from 10am to 5pm, and September to April, also on Sunday from noon to 5pm.

WELLINGTON HALL, 210–214 Beach Dr. NE, St. Petersburg. Tel. 896-5717.

This large bayfront shop downtown between Second and Third Avenues North, across from the Museum of Fine Arts, contains three galleries of art, antiques, and collectibles including porcelain, china, sterling, silverplate, lamps, rugs, glass, jewelry, paintings, books, prints, stamps, autographs, enameled insignia, and engravings. Open Monday through Friday from 9am to 5pm; Saturday and Sunday hours vary.

BEACHWEAR

SWIMWORKS, 431 Corey Ave., at Blind Pass Rd., St. Petersburg Beach. Tel. 360-3146.

All the major brands of swimsuits, from Catalina and Cole to Jantzen and Bill Blass, are sold here at outlet prices, as are other beachwear and sportswear products. Open Monday through Saturday from 9am to 5pm.

WINGS, 6705 Gulf Blvd., St. Petersburg Beach. Tel. 367-8876.

If you forgot your swimsuit or need a new one, this huge block-long emporium at the intersection of 67th Avenue and Blind Pass Drive is hard to beat for price and selection. In addition to swimwear, you'll find hats, sunglasses, lotions, T-shirts, and decals to make your own design on a T-shirt. Open daily from 9am to 10pm.

Other locations are John's Pass Village, 12900 Gulf Blvd., Madeira Beach (tel. 392-9211), 400 Pointsetta Ave., Clearwater Beach (tel. 449-2710) and 646 S. Gulfview Blvd., Clearwater Beach (tel. 441-1042).

BOOKS/NEWSPAPERS

BAYBORO BOOKS, 121 Seventh Ave. S., St. Petersburg. Tel. 821-5477.

Situated next to the University of South Florida Bayboro campus, this small shop offers everything from the classics, academic texts, and technical books to children's books, best-sellers, cookbooks, and mysteries, as well as maps and calendars. Open Monday through Friday from 10am to 6pm and on Saturday from 11am to 3pm.

HASLAM'S, 2025 Central Ave., St. Petersburg. Tel. 822-8616.

★ Although the St. Pete area has lots of book shops (including such chains as B. Dalton and Waldenbooks), this huge downtown emporium between 20th and 21st Streets North claims to be Florida's largest, with over 300,000 books—new and used, hardcover and paperback. Founded in 1933, this family-run business is an attraction in itself, almost like a library, with plenty of bargains on every topic from antiques to zoology. Open Monday through Thursday and on Saturday from 9am to 5:30pm, on Friday from 9am to 9pm.

SCOTTIES, 310 Corey Ave., St. Petersburg Beach. Tel. 360-6700.
If you crave news from back home, this shop stocks a wide variety of newspapers and magazines from around the U.S. and the world. You can also phone in advance to reserve the paper of your choice. Horse-racing and dog-racing forms and programs are also available. It's open daily from 8am to 5pm.

FOOD

DOOLEY GROVES, 6400 Gulf Blvd., at 64th Ave., St. Petersburg Beach. Tel. 360-7421.
Situated in the heart of the beach strip, this handy shop offers a variety of citrus products for buying on the spot or shipping back home. Other items for sale include candies, nuts, marmalades, tropical citrus jellies, and fruit butters. Open daily from 9am to 5pm or later.

YELLOW BANKS GROVES, 14423 Walsingham Rd., Largo. Tel. 595-5464, or toll free 800/722-4590.
Famous for its citrus products, the St. Pete area is home to dozens of groves and fruit stores, selling a variety of grapefruits, oranges, tangerines, and tangelos. This establishment on Fla. 688, 1¼ miles east of Gulf Boulevard, is one of the oldest (over 35 years) and most reliable, and it also will ship fruit for you. You can buy freshly squeezed juice by the glass or container, and fruit by the piece or in bags. In addition, you'll find citrus-related and tropical products, such as grapefruit-cherry marmalade, guava jelly, and jellied candies, as well as coconut patties, pecan log rolls, and shell-art souvenirs. Open November to May, daily from 8am to 5:30pm (closed June to October).

GIFTS & CRAFTS

AGGIE'S ATTIC, in the John's Pass Village shopping complex, 12943 Gulf Blvd. E., Suite 102, Madeira Beach. Tel. 360-4130.
Under the attentive supervision of proprietor Greta Dwyer, this shop at the southern tip of Madeira Beach, at 129th Avenue, is a treasure trove of quality gifts from around the world. You'll find a great selection of local artwork plus imports including handcrafted

birds and fish figurines from Mexico; Delft hand-painted china and jewelry from Holland; Claddagh rings, Belleek and Royal Tara china, and hand-cut crystal from Ireland; goblets from Spain; wood carvings from Africa; and handmade bread boards from Honduras. Open Monday through Saturday from 11am to 6pm.

FLORIDA CRAFTSMEN GALLERY, 237 Second Ave. S., St. Petersburg. Tel. 821-7391.

Founded in 1986, this is a showcase for the works of over 100 Florida artisans and craftspersons. Designed to appeal to serious collectors as well as those seeking moderately priced gifts, the items include both functional and whimsical creations in jewelry, ceramics, woodwork, fiberwork, glassware, paper creations, and metalwork. It's downtown in the historic Wilson Building, adjacent to American Stage Theater. Open Tuesday through Saturday from 10am to 4pm.

FLORIDA SHELL SHOP, 9901 Gulf Blvd., Treasure Island. Tel. 343-8377.

In addition to shells of all sizes and shapes, you'll find a wide selection of shell art, shell holiday decorations, shell wind chimes, shell baskets, shell jewelry, and sand dollars. The shop is two blocks north of Blind Pass Road at 99th Avenue. Open Monday through Thursday from 10:30am to 6pm, on Friday and Saturday from 10:30am to 9pm, and on Sunday from 11am to 6pm.

GLASS CANVAS GALLERY, 233 Fourth Ave. NE, St. Petersburg. Tel. 821-6767.

Located just off Beach Drive, this modern gallery features a dazzling array of glass sculpture, tableware, art, and craft items, many of which have a sea, shell, or piscine theme. Open Monday to Wednesday and Friday from 10am to 6pm, Thursday from 10am to 8pm, Saturday from 10am to 5pm, and Sunday from noon to 5pm.

RED CLOUD, 208 Beach Dr. NE, St. Petersburg. Tel. 821-5824.

Situated directly opposite the Museum of Fine Arts, this shop is an oasis for Native American crafts, from jewelry and headdresses to sculpture and art. Open Monday through Wednesday and Friday and Saturday from 10am to 6pm, and Thursday from 10am to 8pm.

SENIOR CITIZEN CRAFT CENTER GIFT SHOP, 940 Court St., Clearwater. Tel. 442-4266.

Opened over 30 years ago, this is one of the area's most fascinating gift shops—an outlet for the work of about 400 local senior citizens/consignors. Each craftsperson must be 55 years or older to participate; in turn, 80% of the sale price of each object goes to the person who made it. The items for sale, many of which are one-of-a-kind, include knitwear, crochetwork, sweaters, woodwork, stained glass, clocks, hand-etched scrimshaw, jewelry, pottery, shell art, dolls, afghans, wreaths, tile work, ceramics, quilts, baby clothes, and hand-painted clothing. It's well worth a visit, even though it's a little off the usual tourist track in downtown Clearwater, between Prospect and Greenwood Streets. Open June to August, Monday through Friday from 10am to 4pm; September to May, Monday through Saturday from 10am to 4pm.

THE SHELL STORE, 440 75th Ave., St. Petersburg Beach. Tel. 360-0586.

This shop between Gulf Boulevard and Blind Pass Road specializes in corals and shells, and an on-premises mini-museum illustrates how they both live and grow. In addition to shells and corals of all types, you'll also find a good selection of shell decorations, shell hobby supplies, shell art, shell planters, and shell jewelry. Also, classes are conducted in basic and advanced levels of shell craft and information is available on local shelling. Open Monday through Saturday from 9:30am to 5:30pm.

THE STRAW GOAT, 130 Beach Dr. NE, St. Petersburg. Tel. 822-4456.

This well-stocked little shop overflows with the work of American and European artisans, with particular emphasis on Scandinavian gifts and cooking utensils. Items range from crystal chandeliers, ceramics, and chimes to wall plates and wall hangings, flowers, baskets, glassware, silver, and decorative stationery. The Straw Goat is downtown, between Second Avenue NE and Sunshine Lane NE, opposite Straub Park. Open Monday through Saturday from 10am to 5pm.

SUNSHINE GIFT SHOP, 330 Fifth St. N., St. Petersburg. Tel. 893-7101.

All the items for sale at this shop are handmade by senior citizens of the area. The choices range from baby clothes and toys to shell crafts, sweaters, quilts, afghans, greeting cards, household items, beadwork, jewelry, ceramics, stained glass, woodwork, and ornaments. The shop is downtown, between Third and Fourth Avenues North. Open Monday through Friday from 9am to 4pm, and sometimes also on Sunday (call to check).

JEWELRY

EVANDER PRESTON CONTEMPORARY JEWELRY, 106 Eighth Ave., St. Petersburg Beach. Tel. 367-7894.

If you're in the market for some one-of-a-kind jewelry, visit this unique gallery/workshop, housed in an 80-year-old building on Pass-A-Grille. A celebrated character in the St. Pete area, the bearded Preston creates striking hand-hammered pieces that reflect European classic styles as well as 20th-century contemporary art. Among his most famous works is a tiny toy train, the *EP Express,* with an 18-karat gold electrically powered locomotive, platinum wheels, a one-half-carat diamond headlight, and cargo car that includes an emerald, a sapphire, and a ruby, plus gold nuggets. It took four months to make, and is often on display in the gallery here, a room with suede-covered walls, contemporary paintings and sculpture, and primitive African art. Open Monday through Saturday from 10am to 5:30pm and Sunday from 11am to 5pm. To get here, take the Pinellas Bayway to Gulf Boulevard, turn left, and go south to Eighth Avenue, between Pass-A-Grille and Gulf Ways.

7. EVENING ENTERTAINMENT

From Broadway shows and ballroom dancing to rock and roll, reggae, and dinner theater, the St. Petersburg area offers a varied selection of nighttime entertainment. And don't forget the option of an evening cruise on the bay or gulf waters (see "Organized Tours and Cruises," above in this chapter).

The best way to keep abreast of what's on is to read the **St. Petersburg Times,** the city's award-winning daily newspaper. In particular, don't miss the Friday edition's "Weekend" supplement, packed with information on theaters, shows, nightclubs, festivals, and all sorts of local activities.

Another excellent publication is **Tampa Bay,** a monthly magazine that covers all facets of the lively arts in the area. It's on sale at local newsstands. Unlike some cities, St. Petersburg does not have a central ticket booth for reduced-rate, same-day performances. If you can't make it to a particular box office, you can reserve tickets to shows at TicketMaster outlets at the Bayfront Center, the Pier, and other locations in major shopping malls throughout the city, or by calling 813/287-8844.

THE PERFORMING ARTS

MAJOR CONCERT/PERFORMANCE HALLS

BAYFRONT CENTER, 400 First St. S., St. Petersburg. Tel. 892-5767.

Downtown, south of the Pier between Fourth and Fifth Avenues South, this is the city's waterfront showplace, featuring the 8,100-seat Bayfront Arena and the 2,000-seat Mahaffey Theater. Between them, they host a variety of major concerts, Broadway shows, national touring companies, big-band festivals, ice shows, the circus, and sporting events. The box office is open Monday through Friday from 10am to 6pm. The curtain for evening events is usually at 7:30 to 8pm; for matinees it's at 3 or 3:30pm.

Admission: Tickets, $5–$40, depending on the event.

ST. PETERSBURG THUNDERDOME, 1 Stadium Dr., St. Petersburg. Tel. 825-3100.

Built at a cost of $110 million, this giant arena opened in 1990 with a Kenny Rogers extravaganza including a cast of 5,000 performers, a laser show, and fireworks. The dome has a capacity of 50,000 for concerts, although its primary purpose is to provide a home for a new baseball team. Other large-scale events are slated year-round. Evening performances usually start at 7:30pm, but the schedule varies depending on the event.

To get here, take I-275 downtown to Exit 9 (First Avenue South); the dome is between 10th and 16th Streets South.

Admission: Tickets, $15–$30, depending on the event.

RUTH ECKERD HALL, in the Richard B. Baumgardner Center for the Performing Arts, 1111 McMullen-Booth Rd., Clearwater. Tel. 791-7400.

North of St. Petersburg, east of Clearwater Beach, and a mile north of Fla. 60, this 2,200-seat auditorium is the major venue for a varied program of Broadway shows, ballet, drama, symphonic works, popular music, jazz, and country music. The box office is open Monday through Saturday from 10am to 9pm and on Sunday from noon to 5pm. Evening performances begin at 7:30 or 8pm; matinees, on Wednesday and Saturday at 2pm, and on Sunday at 1 or 3pm. The gift shop is open Monday through Saturday from 10am to 3pm.

Admission: Tickets, $10–$55, depending on the event.

THEATERS

AMERICAN STAGE, 211 Third St. S., St. Petersburg. Tel. 822-8814.

Downtown, between Second and Third Avenues South, this is St. Petersburg's resident professional theater, presenting contemporary dramas and comedies, as well as children's theater. In May the company performs free Shakespeare in the Park outdoors at Demens Landing on the waterfront and at Plant Park, Tampa. The box office is open October to June, Monday through Friday from 9am to 5pm, and also on Saturday and Sunday when a play is running. Curtain time Wednesday through Friday is at 8pm, on Saturday at 2 and 8pm, and on Sunday at 7:30pm.

Note: From mid-April through mid-May, the American Stage moves outdoors to present an annual open-air Shakespeare Festival at Demens Landing, First Avenue and Bayshore Boulevard SE. Performances are at 8pm, Tuesday through Sunday. Tickets are $6 for adults, no charge for children under 12.

Admission: Theater tickets, $12–$22.

FRANCIS WILSON PLAYHOUSE, 302 Seminole St., Clearwater. Tel. 446-1360.

Founded in 1930, this small community theater is located in a garden setting in downtown Clearwater, close to the ferry dock. It presents a variety of classic and current Broadway musicals and comedies, with performances at 8:15pm Wednesday or Thursday through Saturday, and 2:15pm on Saturday and Sunday.

Admission: Tickets, $7–$10.

ROYALTY THEATRE, 405 Cleveland St., Clearwater. Tel. 443-6647.

For almost 25 years, this downtown community theater has been

presenting a variety of Broadway musicals and comedies. Performances are Thursday through Saturday at 8pm, Sunday at 2:15pm.
Admission: Tickets, $8–$11.

ST. PETERSBURG LITTLE THEATER (SPLT), 4025 31st St. S., St. Petersburg. Tel. 866-1973.

This is the city's community theater, presenting six plays or variety shows a year. The season runs from September to May, with performances Thursday through Saturday at 8pm and Sunday matinees at 2pm.

To get here, take I-275 to 22nd Avenue South (Exit 6) and follow the signs to 31st Street South.
Admission: Tickets, $9–$10.

DINNER THEATER

BELLS' SHOWBOAT DINNER THEATER, 3405 Ulmerton Rd., Clearwater. Tel. 573-3777.

Designed with a vintage showboat facade, this inland theater is located on Fla. 688, a busy east-west thoroughfare off I-275 north of downtown St. Petersburg next to the St. Petersburg–Clearwater airport. It presents a variety of Broadway comedies and musicals, with major stars, along with buffet meals. The box office is open on Monday and Tuesday from 9am to 6pm and Wednesday through Saturday from 9am to 9pm. There are dinner performances Wednesday through Saturday (dinner at 6:30pm and show at 8pm) and on Sunday (dinner at 4:30pm and show at 6pm), and lunchtime matinees on Wednesday, Thursday, and Saturday (lunch at 11:30am and show at 1pm).
Admission: $34.95 evenings, $27.90 matinees.

MYSTERY DINNER THEATER. Tel. 584-3490.

Solve a murder mystery while enjoying a four-course dinner at one of three venues in the St. Petersburg/Clearwater area—the Kapok Tree, 923 McMullen-Booth Rd., Clearwater; Belleview Mido Resort, 25 Belleview Blvd., Belleair; or the Sea Wake Inn, 691 S. Gulfview Blvd., Clearwater Beach. Reservations are required (phone 584-3490 for all three venues). The program includes clue packets, bribe money, audience participation, and prizes. The schedule is Thursday and Sunday at 7pm and Saturday at 1pm at Kapok Tree; Friday and Saturday at 7pm at Belleview Mido and Sea Wake.
Admission: Dinner/show $32–$42.

TIDES DINNER THEATER, in the Bath Club complex, 16720 Gulf Blvd., North Redington Beach. Tel. 393-1870.

Billing itself as the only dinner theater on the beach strip, this facility between 167th and 168th Avenues presents classic Broadway musicals performed by the local Seminole Players. The box office is open Monday through Friday from 9am to 2pm, or you can make reservations by phone. The season runs from November to April, with dinner performances on Friday and Saturday (cocktails at 6pm,

dinner at 6:45pm, and show at 8pm) and on Sunday (cocktails at 4pm, dinner at 4:45pm, and show at 6pm), and lunchtime matinees on Saturday (cocktails at 11am, lunch at 11:45am, and show at 1pm).
Admission: Tickets, $25–$30.

THE CLUB & MUSIC SCENE

NIGHTCLUBS/LOUNGES

BALI HAI, 5250 Gulf Blvd., St. Petersburg Beach. Tel. 360-1811, ext. 2130.
Set atop the St. Petersburg Hilton Inn in the center of St. Pete Beach, between 52nd and 53rd Avenues, this is a revolving rooftop lounge, featuring live music, mostly of the contemporary genre. It's a romantic spot, particularly at sunset time. Mixed drinks cost $2 to $5 and Polynesian drinks are also available. Open Tuesday through Saturday from 8:30pm to 12:30am.

CELEBRITY LOUNGE, 3600 34th St. S., St. Petersburg. Tel. 867-6070.
This lively lounge, in the Howard Johnson Hotel south of downtown St. Pete, presents a variety of entertainment, from karaoke on Tuesday, blues or reggae on Wednesday, and rock or Top 40 music on Friday and Saturday. The music runs from 9:30pm to 1am nightly.
Admission: No charge–$5.

MANHATTANS, 11595 Gulf Blvd., Treasure Island. Tel. 363-1500.
Aiming to bring the varied musical appeal of the Big Apple to the beach strip, this club offers dancing to the music of live contemporary and classic rock bands, as well as oldies music on Monday and country on Tuesday. It's open seven nights a week from 8pm to 2am.
Admission: No cover charge.

REFLECTIONS, 5500 Gulf Blvd., St. Petersburg Beach. Tel. 367-6461.
This is a relaxing piano lounge at the Trade Winds Resort, in the heart of St. Pete Beach between 55th and 56th Avenues, overlooking waterways, an outdoor deck, and a gazebo. In addition to cocktails (drinks $2 to $5), fine wines are available by the glass. Open daily from 5pm to 2am; entertainment starts at 9pm.

TEN BEACH DRIVE, 10 Beach Dr., St. Petersburg. Tel. 823-1247.
Billed as St. Petersburg's oldest piano bar, this downtown spot offers live piano music Monday through Saturday from 7pm till 1am and Sunday from 5 to 10pm. It's located at the corner of Central Avenue. Drinks run $2 to $4.
Admission: No cover charge.

THE WINE CELLAR, 17307 Gulf Blvd., North Redington Beach. Tel. 393-3491.

Home of an award-winning restaurant, this elegant lounge on the beach strip, on the bay side of Gulf Boulevard between 173rd and 174th Avenues, is an attraction in itself. Easy-listening music, and sometimes jazz and blues, is featured by live combos. Drinks run $3 to $6. Open Tuesday through Thursday from 7:30 to 11:30pm and Friday and Saturday from 8:30pm to 1am.

COMEDY CLUBS

COCONUTS COMEDY CLUB, 6110 Gulf Blvd., St. Petersburg Beach. Tel. 360-NUTS, 360-6887, or 360-4545.

One of the oldest and best-known comedy spots on the beach strip, next to the Sandpiper Beach Resort between 61st and 62nd Avenues, this club features an ever-changing program of live stand-up comedy acts. Shows are at 9pm Wednesday and Thursday, and at 9 and 11pm on Friday and Saturday.

Admission: $7 cover charge, plus a two-drink minimum.

RON BENNINGTON'S COMEDY SCENE, in the Howard Johnson Hotel, 20967 U.S. 19, at Fla. 60, Clearwater. Tel. 791-4477.

Nationally known comedians perform at this popular club; dinner/show packages are available. Reservations suggested. Shows are at 8:30pm Tuesday through Thursday, and at 8:30 and 10:45pm on Friday and Saturday.

Admission: $5–$8 cover charge, plus a two-drink minimum.

ROCK/TOP 40

THE BIG CATCH, 9 First St. NE, St. Petersburg. Tel. 821-6444.

This casual downtown club features live and danceable rock and Top 40 hits, as well as darts, pool, and hoops. Open Thursday through Saturday from 9pm to 2am.

Admission: Cover charge usually $3–$5.

CALYPSO BAY CAFE, 2516 Gulf-to-Bay Blvd., Clearwater. Tel. 726-3225.

East of the Clearwater Beach area, at the intersection of U.S. 19, this is one of the best spots for rock music, both live and with a DJ. On Sunday the beat changes to jazz format. Open Monday through Saturday from 9:30pm to 1:30am and on Sunday from 5:30 to 9:30pm.

Admission: $3 cover charge.

CHA CHA COCONUTS, 800 Second Ave. NE, St. Petersburg. Tel. 822-6655.

Situated on the rooftop of the Pier, this spot offers live rock and Top 40 (and sometimes jazz, blues, or western) music, with tropical drinks and panoramic views of the St. Pete skyline. Drinks run $1.95 to $4.95. Open Sunday through Thursday from 7 to 11pm, on Friday and Saturday from 7pm to midnight.

There are additional locations at 1241 Gulf Blvd., Clearwater Beach (tel. 596-6040), and on Harbour Island, Tampa (tel. 223-3101); see Chapter 11, "What to See and Do in Tampa".

ETCHINGS, in the Colonial Gateway Inn, 6300 Gulf Blvd., at 63rd Ave., St. Petersburg Beach. Tel. 360-0889.

There is always something on tap at this contemporary and popular lounge, with a variety of live entertainment: jazz or blues on Monday, karaoke on Tuesday, and Top 40s dance music Wednesday through Sunday. The club is open daily from 5pm to 2am, with music from 8:30pm to 1:30am. Drinks cost $1 to $4.

JAZZ/BLUES/COUNTRY/REGGAE

CRACKER'S, 5501 Gulf Blvd., St. Petersburg Beach. Tel. 360-6961.

Although there is contemporary music on most nights at this rustic lounge, there is usually reggae on Saturday and Sunday. It stands in the middle of St. Petersburg Beach, in the upstairs room at Silas Dent's restaurant, between 55th and 56th Avenues. Drinks cost $2 to $4. It's open every night, with music on tap from 9pm to 1am.

Admission: $2 cover charge.

DUKE'S COUNTRY & WESTERN LOUNGE, 4601 34th St. S., St. Petersburg. Tel. 867-3131.

Located in the Holiday Inn south of downtown, this lounge offers country dance music from 8pm to 1am on Tuesday, Thursday, and Friday, with free adult country dance lessons on Tuesday and Thursday from 8:30 to 10pm. In addition, there is karaoke on Wednesday and Saturday from 9pm to 1am.

Admission: Cover varies, from no charge to $4 for some special events.

THE HURRICANE LOUNGE, 807 Gulf Way, St. Petersburg Beach. Tel. 260-4875.

Considered as one of the three best places for jazz on either side of the bay, this beachside spot has a "long-term, unwavering commitment to jazz." Drinks go for $2 to $4. It's open on Sunday and Wednesday from 9pm to 1am, and on Friday and Saturday from 9:30pm to 1:30am.

To get here, take Pinellas Bayway to Gulf Boulevard, turn left, go to Eighth Avenue, then turn right to Gulf Way.

RINGSIDE CAFE, 2742 Fourth St. N., St. Petersburg. Tel. 894-8465.

Housed in a renovated boxing gymnasium north of Sunken Gardens, between 27th and 28th Avenues, this informal neighborhood café has a definite sports theme, but the music focuses on jazz (on Wednesday) and blues (Thursday through Sunday). Drinks cost $1 to $4. Open Monday through Saturday from 11am to 2am and on Sunday from noon to 1am.

Admission: $2–$8 cover charge Fri–Sat.

DANCE CLUBS/DISCOS

CLUB DETROIT, in the Hotel Detroit, 16 Second St. N., St. Petersburg. Tel. 896-1244.

Housed in this landmark hotel in the heart of the city, between Central and First Avenues, this lively (and sometimes noisy) spot includes a lounge, Channel Zero, and an outdoor courtyard, Jannus Landing. Look for blues, reggae, and progressive DJ dance music indoors and live rock concerts outdoors (Thursday through Saturday). There's also a pool table, darts, and other barroom games.

Admission: Cover charge, $2 and up indoors, $10–$18 for outdoor concerts.

JAMMIN'Z DANCE SHACK, 470 Mandalay Ave., Clearwater Beach. Tel. 441-2005 or 442-5754 (recorded information).

This nightclub offers a beachy atmosphere and a dance floor with state-of-the-art sound, light, video, and laser effects. A DJ spins Top 40 tunes from 8pm to 2am nightly.

Admission: $3–$5.

STORMY'S, 807 Gulf Way, Pass-A-Grille. Tel. 367-7571.

Located on the second floor of the famous Hurricane Restaurant, at the southern tip of St. Petersburg Beach, between Eighth and Ninth Avenues, this spot offers continuous dance music with a DJ. The setting overlooks the gulf beachfront. Open daily from 9pm to 2am.

Admission: $2 cover Fri–Sat for those under 30.

SURF CLUB, in the Holiday Inn Surfside, 400 Mandalay Ave., Clearwater Beach. Tel. 461-3222.

On the beach, this is one of the newer and trendier nightspots, featuring a multilevel dance floor with the latest in lighting, state-of-the-art sound systems, and multiscreen videos. Drinks run $2 to $5. The club is open Tuesday through Saturday from 9pm to 1:30am.

To get here, take Fla. 60 west to the beach and turn right on Mandalay Avenue; the hotel is at the corner.

BALLROOMS

COLISEUM BALLROOM, 535 Fourth Ave. N., St. Petersburg. Tel. 892-5202.

Dating back to 1924, this landmark Spanish-style building is an attraction in itself, and was featured in the motion picture *Cocoon*. With a 13,000-square-foot maple dance floor (one of the nation's largest), it's *the* place to go in downtown St. Pete for an evening of dancing to big-band, country, ballroom, and other kinds of music. Frequent concerts are also given by the local pops orchestra and other musical groups. No liquor is served, but you may bring your own. It's open on Monday through Saturday from 8pm to midnight, although starting time varies with each event.

To get here, take I-275 downtown to Exit 10; the ballroom is between Fifth and Sixth Streets North.

Admission: $4–$15.

JOYLAND, 11225 U.S. 19, Clearwater. Tel. 573-1919.

One mile south of Ulmerton Road (Fla. 688), north of St. Petersburg, this is the area's only country-and-western ballroom, featuring live bands and well-known performers. Free dance lessons are offered at 7:30pm each night. It's open Tuesday through Sunday from 4 to 11pm or later.

Admission: $3–$10.

THE BAR SCENE

BEACH NUTTS, 9600 W. Gulf Blvd., Treasure Island. Tel. 367-7427.

On the lower half of Treasure Island, at 96th Avenue, this is the quintessential beach bar, a wooden beach cottage perched atop a stilt foundation on the Gulf of Mexico. The open-air bar is a delightful place to unwind. The light music is lively, ranging from good-time songs and reggae to Top 40 hits and rock. Open daily from 5pm to 1am. There's never a cover.

CHARLIE AND DICK'S OASIS PUB, 678 75th Ave., St. Petersburg Beach. Tel. 360-5294.

This casual place is known for its accordion sing-alongs and nostalgic music nightly at 8pm. On Sunday afternoons, there is usually a jam session. Drinks go for $1.30 to $4. The pub is open Tuesday through Thursday from 8pm to 1am, on Friday and Saturday from 8pm to 2am, and 7pm to midnight on Sunday. It's one block west of Gulf Boulevard, at Sunset Way, opposite the beach.

Admission: Free, but there's a two-drink minimum Fri–Sat.

GATORS ON THE PASS, 12754 Kingfish Dr., Treasure Island. Tel. 367-8951.

Located at Kingfish Wharf on the northern tip of Treasure Island, this place claims to have the world's longest waterfront bar, with a huge deck overlooking the waters of John's Pass. The complex also includes a no-smoking sports bar and a three-story tower with a top-level observation deck for panoramic views of the Gulf of Mexico. There is live music, from acoustic and blues to rock, most nights from 7pm to 1am.

Admission: Cover charge $2 for most acts.

HARP AND THISTLE PUB, 650 Corey Ave., St. Petersburg Beach. Tel. 360-4104.

You don't have to be Irish to love this little bit of the auld sod on the beach west of the St. Petersburg Causeway between Coquina and Sunset Ways. It's a popular spot to hear authentic Irish folk music, as well as for sipping draft Guinness and other Irish brews. Drinks are $2 to $5. Open Monday through Saturday from 10am to 2am and on Sunday from 1pm to 2am.

Admission: Usually free, occasional $2 cover charge.

HORSE AND JOCKEY, 1155 Pasadena Ave., at Gulfport Blvd., South Pasadena. Tel. 345-4995.

For a taste of Old London, here in the Pasadena Square shopping center is a typically British pub. You can try your hand at a game of darts, imbibe a few of the 11 British beers on tap, or come in the afternoon and sample a traditional "high tea"—with finger sand-wiches, scones, sherry trifle, and a brimming pot of English tea—served Monday through Friday from 3 to 5pm (24-hour notice and reservations required). Drinks run $2 to $5, and high tea goes for $7.95. Open daily from noon to midnight.

To get here from downtown, take Central Avenue west and turn left on Pasadena Avenue.

GETTING TO KNOW TAMPA

1. ORIENTATION
• **WHAT'S SPECIAL ABOUT TAMPA**
2. GETTING AROUND
• **FAST FACTS: TAMPA**

Just as Walt Disney World put Orlando on the tourism map, Busch Gardens is the main draw for most first-time visitors to Tampa. But after arriving, most travelers find there's a lot more to Tampa than the famous Anheuser-Busch theme park.

Sitting on the Hillsborough River and rimmed by Hillsborough Bay and Tampa Bay, Tampa is a city of many waterfront views and activities—a natural mecca for vacationers. This metropolis of nearly 300,000 people is also a major business hub on Florida's west coast. The base for many financial, manufacturing, shipping, agricultural, and high-tech industries, Tampa is the seventh-largest port and one of the fast-growing cities in the U.S.

Like neighboring St. Petersburg, Tampa is both old and new. The Spanish architecture, Cuban foods, and flamenco music of Ybor City hark back to an earlier time, while the sleek mirrored-glass skyscrapers of the downtown district and the state-of-the-art workings of the airport have given Tampa a head start into the 21st century.

1. ORIENTATION

ARRIVING

BY PLANE The **Tampa International Airport,** off Memorial Highway and Fla. 60, Tampa (tel. 813/870-8700), situated five miles northwest of downtown Tampa, is the gateway for all scheduled domestic and international flights. See Chapter 4, "Getting to Know St. Petersburg," for a description of the airport's services.

Getting Into Town The **Hillsborough Area Regional Transit Authority/HARTline** (tel. 254-HART) operates service between the airport and downtown on its no. 31 bus. This is not an airport express bus, but a local route that makes stops at the airport daily between the hours of 6am and 8:15pm. Look for the HARTline bus sign outside each airline terminal; the fare is $1, and the ride takes 25 to 30 minutes.

Central Florida Limo (tel. 813/396-3730) operates van service between the airport and downtown hotels. No reservations are necessary; just proceed to the transport booth outside each baggage-claim area. For early-morning or late-night service, it's best to make a

✔ WHAT'S SPECIAL ABOUT TAMPA

Architectural Highlights

☐ The Hyde Park National Register Historic District, a showcase of American architecture from colonial to Victorian.

☐ The Columbia Restaurant, Ybor City (1905), with hand-painted tiles, stained-glass windows, and other antique accoutrements.

Museums

☐ The Henry B. Plant Museum, once part of a landmark hotel, now a showcase of antiques and Old Tampa grandeur.

☐ Museum of African-American Art, the first of its kind in Florida and home of the U.S.'s foremost collection of African-American art.

☐ Ybor City State Museum, for a look at the development of Tampa's Latin Quarter.

Events/Festivals

☐ Gasparilla Festival, Tampa's traditional annual frolic, with modern-day pirates, parades, concerts, and more.

☐ Florida State Fair, a two-week fest of the best in Florida and Tampa.

For the Kids

☐ Busch Gardens, for up-close views of 3,000 animals in natural settings, and thrilling rides and activities.

☐ Museum of Science and Industry, for a look at a simulated space-shuttle operation, ham radio center, and weather station.

☐ Lowry Park Zoo, a 24-acre parklike facility of animals in their natural settings including an aviary, wildlife center, habitat for nocturnal animals, and a manatee hospital.

Activities

☐ Viewing the Tampa skyline from an authentic gondola, as it floats along the channels and under the bridges of Tampa Bay and the Hillsborough River.

☐ Running, walking, or driving along the world's longest continuous sidewalk on Bayshore Boulevard.

☐ Exploring Harbour Island's indoor and outdoor activities.

Shopping

☐ Old Hyde Park Village, Tampa's "Rodeo Drive."

☐ Ybor City, a cluster of antiques and craft shops in the city's Latin Quarter.

---

reservation in advance; otherwise, vans make continuous pickups at least every half hour. The ride takes about 20 minutes and the fare is $7 to $15 for up to two passengers, depending on destination.

For taxi service to downtown Tampa and its environs, **Yellow Cab** (tel. 253-0121) and **United Cabs** (tel. 253-2424) line up outside the baggage-claim areas 24 hours a day. Average fare from the airport to downtown Tampa is $12 to $14, and the trip takes about 15 minutes.

BY TRAIN   Amtrak trains from points north terminate at the Tampa Amtrak Station, 601 Nebraska Ave. N., Tampa (tel. 813/221-7600).

BY BUS   Greyhound/Trailways buses from destinations around the United States arrive at the carrier's downtown depot at 610 Polk St., Tampa (tel. 813/229-2174).

BY CAR   The Tampa area is linked to the Interstate system and is accessible from I-275, I-75, I-4, U.S. 19, U.S. 41, U.S. 92, U.S. 301, and many state roads.

TOURIST INFORMATION

For free brochures and helpful advice while you're in Tampa, plan to stop in at the **Visitor Information Center of the Tampa/ Hillsborough Convention and Visitors Association (THCVA),** 111 Madison St., Suite 1010, Tampa, FL 33602-4706 (tel. 813/223-2752, or toll free 800/44-TAMPA). Open Monday through Saturday from 9am to 5pm, it's located downtown, on the ground level of the First Florida Tower building, at the corner of Ashley and Madison Streets. In addition, the THCVA also maintains unstaffed **information/brochure carts** at the convention center, on Harbour Island, and at Ybor Square. Before your arrival, call toll free 800/44-TAMPA for a visitor information guide and to make hotel reservations.

A good source of on-the-spot information north of downtown in the Busch Gardens area is the **Tampa Bay Visitor Information Center,** 3601 E. Busch Blvd., Tampa, FL 33612 (tel. 813/985-3601). It offers free brochures about attractions in Tampa and other parts of Florida as well as a sightseeing-tour booking service. Hours are Monday to Saturday from 9am to 6pm and Sunday from 10am to 6pm.

CITY LAYOUT

Tampa's downtown district is laid out according to a grid system. **Kennedy Boulevard (Fla. 60),** which cuts across the city in an east-west direction, is the main dividing line for north and south street addresses. **Florida Avenue** is the dividing line for east and west street addresses. The two major arteries bringing traffic into the downtown area are **I-275,** which skirts the northern edge of the city, and the **Crosstown Expressway,** which extends along the southern rim.

All the streets in the central core of the city are one way, with the exception of **Franklin Street,** which has been transformed into one continuous pedestrian mall. From the southern tip of Franklin, you can also board the People Mover, an elevated tram to Harbour Island.

One of the streets of most interest to visitors is **Ashley Street,** a wide thoroughfare that runs along the west corridor of the city close to the Hillsborough River. Ashley Street is the location of the Tampa Bay Performing Arts Center, the Tampa Public Library, Tampa Museum, the new $130-million Tampa Convention Center, and the

Visitor Information Office of the Tampa/Hillsborough Convention and Visitors Association, as well as major banks and businesses.

One-way streets are not quite as prevalent in other parts of Tampa, although certain sections, such as Ybor City and parts of Hyde Park, have a predominance of one-way traffic.

Finding an Address Since the streets in Tampa's downtown district all have names instead of numbers, there's no simple way to find an address as there is in St. Petersburg. The Tampa/Hillsborough Convention and Visitors Association can supply you with a basic map of major streets; the best way to master the layout of streets is to get the map and walk or drive around a bit.

The streets of Ybor City are numbered, which makes getting around that area comparatively easy, but in most other areas— including Hyde Park, Busch Gardens, and West Shore—streets are named, not numbered. Most of the locals will gladly give directions, however, based on the address's proximity to a familiar point of reference: "five blocks east of Busch Gardens," for example, or "two miles west of the airport." In many cases, directions will start with the exit of I-275 that's closest to the place you're trying to reach. If you use I-275 as a focal point, chances are you'll be able to find almost any address.

NEIGHBORHOODS IN BRIEF

Downtown This is the core of Tampa, a compact business and financial hub. There are dazzling bank buildings at every turn, from Citizens and Chase to Barnett, First National, First Union, NationsBank, Southeast, and Sun.

Although there are a few hotels, there is very little midtown residential housing, not even the apartment complexes or condominiums you might expect to see along the river. Most of the skyscrapers are new, and indeed much of downtown Tampa has been built in the past 30 years. No doubt, more housing will spring up in the downtown area in the next few years, but, for the moment, the streets tend to be relatively quiet at night and on weekends, except around the hotels or the performing arts center.

Harbour Island South of the downtown business district and linked by an elevated People Mover to the mainland, this is the city's waterfront playground, sort of a small-scale version of Baltimore's Inner Harbor. Surrounded by water, it's home to the luxurious Wyndham Hotel, dozens of fine shops, restaurants, the Tampa Players Theater, and all sorts of riverfront activities from gondola rides to paddleboats. There is also a marina for private craft, several blocks of condominiums, and an athletic club. The island was built 85 years ago on reclaimed land, and from 1909 to 1972 it was used to transfer cargo from ships to waiting railroad cars. It was transformed to its present glamorous state in 1985.

Hyde Park Just west of downtown, this is the city's classiest residential neighborhood, sort of the Beverly Hills of Tampa. Its development was spurred a century ago when Henry Plant built his spectacular Tampa Bay Hotel (now the University of Tampa) on the west bank of the Hillsborough River in 1891. Hyde Park rapidly

drew prominent citizens who built homes south of the hotel, often with views of Hillsborough Bay. Many of these homes remain today, and are part of a National Register Historic District reflecting a host of architectural styles—from colonial and federal revival, to neoclassical, Italian Renaissance, Gothic Revival, Tudor Revival, Queen Anne, Mediterranean Revival, American Foursquare, and pure Victorian.

In the center of the district is Old Hyde Park Village, an upscale

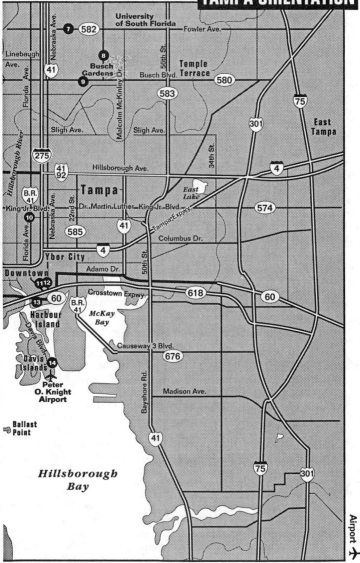

University of South Florida
Fowler Ave.

582
7

Nebraska Ave.
Linebaugh Ave.

41

8
Busch Gardens

9

Florida Ave.

Busch Blvd.

Temple Terrace

580

75

583

Malcolm McKinley Dr.

56th St.

301

East Tampa

Sligh Ave.

Sligh Ave.

Hillsborough River

275

41
92

Hillsborough Ave.

34th St.

4

B.R.
41
King Jr. Blvd.

10

Tampa

Dr. Martin Luther King Jr. Blvd.

East Lake

574

Florida Ave.

Nebraska Ave.

22nd St.

41

585

Tampa Expwy.

Columbus Dr.

50th St.

4

Ybor City

Downtown

1 12

Adamo Dr.

Crosstown Expwy.

618

60

13

60

B.R.
41

McKay Bay

Harbour Island

Davis Blvd.

Causeway 3 Blvd.

676

Davis Islands

14

Madison Ave.

Bayshore Rd.

Peter O. Knight Airport

Ballast Point

41

75

301

Hillsborough Bay

Airport

shopping development designed to retain all the original charm of the neighborhood. On the southern edge of Hyde Park is palm-tree-lined Bayshore Boulevard, rimming Hillsborough Bay with the longest continuous sidewalk in the world. Between the Hyde Park area and Harbour Island is yet another residential district, known collectively as Davis Islands; to the south of Hyde Park are more fine residential clusters (such as Palma Ceia and Sunset Park) and the MacDill Air Force Base.

The West Shore   West of Hyde Park, this is the most southwesterly part of the city, approaching Old Tampa Bay. Roughly speaking, it runs from Tampa International Airport southward, particularly along Westshore Boulevard. The success of the airport has been a prime factor in developing this neighborhood into a commercial and financial hub. Huge office towers, banking centers, and commercially oriented hotels have sprung up along this corridor, making it a prime place to stay as well as to do business. The Dale Mabry Highway (part of U.S. 92), a busy commercial strip offering a string of restaurants and nightspots (and home to the Tampa Stadium), also rims this area.

Courtney Campbell Causeway   This small strip runs west of the airport—where Kennedy Boulevard (Fla. 60) crosses Old Tampa Bay—and continues over to the gulf beaches. It's not really a neighborhood, per se, but it's a popular place for visitors, with a cluster of fine hotels, many waterfront restaurants, a beach, and water-sports centers. The International Shrine Headquarters is also here.

The Busch Gardens Area   This area surrounds the theme park of the same name north of downtown. Busch Boulevard, which runs from east to west, is a busy commercial strip just south of the Busch Gardens entrance. It is lined with motels, restaurants, and other enterprises. The major road running north of Busch Gardens is Fowler Avenue, an equally commercialized strip that is also home to the University of South Florida–Tampa campus. Surrounding residential neighborhoods of note include Carrollwood and Temple Terrace.

Ybor City   East of downtown, this is Tampa's Latin Quarter, an enclave founded more than 100 years ago when Don Vincent Ybor (pronounced *Eee*-bor) settled here and started a cigar factory. Ybor City eventually became "the cigar capital of the world," and thousands of Cuban cigar workers poured into this corner of Tampa. Although the factory has since been converted into a shopping complex (Ybor Square), many vestiges of Ybor City's heyday remain, including the landmark Columbia restaurant, famous for its Spanish cuisine and flamenco dancing, and several ethnic mutual-aid societies such as the Cuban Club, the Spanish Club, and the Italian Club. In recent years, local artists have also set up studios in many of the buildings, adding a bohemian charm and ambience to the area.

East Tampa   A mostly residential area, has a popular focal point where I-4 meets I-75. As might be expected, various commercial enterprises have sprung up here, including a huge bingo parlor on the site of the Seminole Native American Reservation. This is also the home of the Florida State Fairgrounds, venue for major annual events and fairs. From I-4, many visitors also head farther east to neighboring destinations such as Plant City (spring training grounds of the Cincinnati Reds), or set out for Walt Disney World and other Orlando-area attractions, just over an hour away.

MAPS

The Tampa/Hillsborough Convention and Visitors Association is a good source for up-to-date maps of the Tampa area. The newsstands and gift shops at Tampa International Airport and the bookstores in and around the city also carry current maps, but the best general map store in the region is **A World of Maps,** 6820 N. Florida Ave., Tampa, FL 33604 (tel. 813/237-1711, or toll free 800/226-2771). They also sell maps by mail, in case you want to study one before you arrive.

2. GETTING AROUND

BY PUBLIC TRANSPORTATION

BY BUS The **Hillsborough Area Regional Transit/ HARTline** (tel. 254-HART) provides regularly scheduled bus service on more than 45 routes between downtown Tampa and the suburbs. The service is geared mainly to commuters, although visitors staying at downtown hotels certainly can use a bus to get to the airport or major shopping centers. It would not be practical, however, to depend totally on bus service to reach most attractions, hotels, and restaurants.

Fares are $1 for local service, $1.50 for express routes; correct change is required.

Many buses start or finish their route downtown at the new Marion Street Transit Parkway, between Tyler and Whiting Streets. It provides well-lit open-air terminal facilities, including 40-foot-long shelters with copper roofs, an informational kiosk, benches, newsstands, and 24-hour security.

BY TRAM The **People Mover** is a motorized tram on elevated tracks connecting downtown Tampa with Harbour Island. It operates from the third level of the Fort Brooke Parking Garage, on Whiting Street between Franklin and Florida Streets. Travel time is 90 seconds, and service is continuous Monday through Saturday from 7am to 2am and on Sunday from 8am to 11pm. The fare is 25¢ each way and exact change is required to purchase tokens from machines.

BY TAXI

Taxis in Tampa do not normally cruise the streets for fares, but they do line up at hotels, the performing arts center, and bus and train depots. If you need a taxi, it's best to ask at your hotel or call either **Yellow Cab** (tel. 253-0121) or **United Cabs** (tel. 253-2424). Both companies also provide vans for small groups or families.

BY CAR

The Tampa/Hillsborough County area encompasses over 1,000 square miles of land, crossed by three major highways, I-275, I-4, and the Crosstown Expressway. Nearly every attraction is within five miles of I-275 (which runs in a north-south direction) or I-4 (which goes east-west), neither of which charges any tolls. The Crosstown Expressway stretches from Gandy Boulevard east through downtown to the suburb of Brandon and costs from 50¢ for shorter distances to $1.25 to drive its entire length (exact change required). Most locals use I-275 as their thoroughfare of choice, and most directions are given with I-275 as the major point of reference.

RENTALS Although the downtown area can be easily walked, it is virtually impossible to see the major sights and enjoy the best restaurants of Tampa without a car. Most visitors step off a plane and pick up a car right at the airport for use throughout their stay.

Five major firms are represented on the grounds of Tampa International Airport: Avis (tel. 813/396-3500), Budget (tel. 813/877-6051), Dollar (tel. 813/396-3640), Hertz (tel. 813/874-3232), and National (tel. 813/396-3782). Most of these companies also maintain offices downtown and in other parts of Tampa.

In addition, many smaller firms and local companies have premises just outside the airport along the corridor that includes Westshore Boulevard, Spruce Street, and Cypress Street. These firms, which provide van transportation to and from the airport and often post the most competitive rates, include Alamo (tel. 813/289-4323), A-Plus (tel. 813/289-4301), Enterprise (tel. 813/282-1680), Payless (tel. 813/289-6554), Thrifty (tel. 813/289-4006), and Value (tel. 813/289-8870).

Note: Under Florida law, rental-car agencies are required to charge drivers $2.05 per car per day (or part of a day) to help finance drug education for young people and for law enforcement. This rule applies to all rentals up to a maximum of 30 days.

PARKING Because so many of the locals use their own cars to get to work or for sojourns downtown, Tampa has plenty of parking. You have a choice of enclosed garages, attended and metered lots, or metered on-street parking. Average parking charges in garages are 60¢ to $1 per hour, $3.60 to $5.50 per day; in lots, 30¢ to $1 per hour, $2.50 to $4 per day; and at street meters, 50¢ to $1 per hour. The majority of meters take quarters only, although some accept dimes and nickels. It's wise to carry quarters if you plan to use metered parking. Meter rules are enforced Monday through Friday from 8am to 5pm. Fines for parking violations range from $10 to $100, depending on the infraction.

The City of Tampa publishes a handly leaflet with the latest parking locations and prices. To obtain the leaflet or to ask a question about parking in the city, contact the Parking Office, 107 N. Franklin St., Tampa (tel. 223-8177).

If you drive over to Harbour Island, covered parking under the shops is free for the first three hours, then costs $1 per hour, up to a daily maximum of $5.

DRIVING RULES The speed limit in residential or business districts is 30 m.p.h. Right turns at red lights are legal, after a full stop, except when a sign indicates otherwise. Pedestrians at crosswalks have the right of way; automobiles must yield to them. Seat belts are mandatory for front-seat passengers; children 5 or younger must be in protective seats.

FAST FACTS / **TAMPA**

Airports   See "Orientation," in this chapter.

Area Code   Tampa's telephone area code is 813.

Babysitters   With a few hours' advance notice, most hotels can arrange for babysitters. Otherwise, call the Baby Sitter's Agency Bureau and Registry (tel. 681-2002).

Buses   See "Getting Around," in this chapter.

Business Hours   See "Fast Facts: St. Petersburg," in Chapter 4.

Car Rentals   See "Getting Around," in this chapter.

Climate   See "When to Go," in Chapter 2.

Currency and Exchange   See "Fast Facts: For the Foreign Traveler," in Chapter 3.

Dentist   For information about dentists in the area, call Dental Referral Services (tel. 224-0073).

Doctor   Most hotels have a doctor on call; if not, contact the Doctor Referral Service of the Hillsborough County Medical Association (tel. 253-0471) or the 24-hour Ask-A-Nurse/Physician Referral Service of St. Joseph's Hospital (tel. 870-4444).

Documents Required   See Chapter 3, "For the Foreign Traveler."

Driving Rules   See "Getting Around," in this chapter.

Drugstores   Eckerd Drugs is one of the leading pharmacy groups in the area, with over 35 stores throughout downtown and the suburbs, including 24-hour branches at 11613 N. Nebraska Ave. (tel. 978-0775) and 3714 Henderson Blvd. (tel. 876-2485). Other chains with a large presence in the area include Rite-Aid and Walgreens. Consult the yellow pages under "Pharmacies" for complete listings.

Embassies and Consulates   See "Fast Facts: For the Foreign Traveler," in Chapter 3.

Emergencies   For police, fire, or ambulance emergency, dial 911 (free at pay phones).

Eyeglasses   Many national chains operate in the Tampa area, including LensCrafters, Pearle Vision Center, and Sears Optical. Consult the yellow pages under "Optical Goods: Retail" for the nearest branch.

Hairdressers and Barbers   Hair-care businesses for men and women are plentiful, with some of the best shops located in department stores such as J. C. Penney or Montgomery Ward, and at the various shopping malls. Chains with several locations include Cost-Cutters, Fantastic Sam's, HairCrafters, andManTrap. Consult the yellow pages under "Barbers," "Beauty Salons," and "Hair Styling" for the numbers of the locations nearest to you.

Holidays   See "When to Go," in Chapter 2, and also "Fast Facts: For the Foreign Traveler," in Chapter 3.

Hospitals   Transitional Hospital of Tampa, 4801 N. Howard

Ave., Tampa (tel. 874-7575); St. Joseph's Hospital, 3001 W. Dr. Martin Luther King, Jr., Blvd., Tampa (tel. 870-4000); Shriners Hospitals for Crippled Children, 12502 N. Pine Dr., Tampa (tel. 972-2250); Tampa General Hospital, Davis Islands (tel. 251-7000); and University Community Hospital, 3100 E. Fletcher Ave., Tampa (tel. 971-6000).

Information   See "Orientation," in this chapter.

Laundry and Dry Cleaning   Most hotels supply same-day laundry and dry-cleaning service. Two local chains, each with at least half a dozen locations spread throughout the Tampa area, include Pioneer (tel. 253-3323) and Sterling (tel. 221-8055).

Libraries   The main branch of the Tampa Public Library is downtown at 900 N. Ashley St., Tampa (tel. 273-3652), with a north branch at 8916 North Boulevard, Tampa (tel. 975-2111).

Liquor Laws   For general information, see "Fast Facts: St. Petersburg," in Chapter 4. In Tampa, most lounges serve alcohol until 3am.

Lost Property   If an article is lost or found at a hotel, restaurant, shop, or attraction, contact the management; if lost or found in public areas, contact the police.

Mail   The main post office is at Tampa Airport, 5201 W. Spruce St. (tel. 879-1600), open daily 24 hours.

Maps   See "Orientation," in this chapter.

Money   See "Currency" in "Fast Facts: For the Foreign Traveler," in Chapter 3.

Newspapers and Magazines   The *Tampa Tribune* is the daily newspaper; the best periodical covering the area is *Tampa Bay*, a monthly magazine.

Photographic Needs   Eckerd Express Photo Services offers one-hour processing at over half a dozen convenient Tampa locations, including one at Hyde Park Village, Swann and Dakota Avenues (tel. 251-2211) and another at the Hillsboro Plaza Shopping Center (tel. 875-8665). For equipment repairs, try the Camera Barn, 100 E. Hillsborough Ave., Tampa (tel. 238-7777).

Police   See "Emergencies," above. To report lost or stolen goods, call 223-1515.

Radio and TV   See "Fast Facts: St. Petersburg," in Chapter 4.

Religious Services   There are hundreds of houses of worship in the Tampa area; inquire at the front desk of your hotel or consult the yellow pages under "Churches," "Religious Organizations," and "Synagogues."

Restrooms   All hotels, restaurants, attractions, and shopping centers have restrooms available for customers. Most public or government buildings also have visitor restrooms.

Safety   Be mindful of money and valuables in public places; do not leave wallets or purses unattended on the beach; lock car doors and trunks at all times.

Shoe Repairs   Two handy downtown locations are Florida Shoe Hospital, 406 E. Zack St., Tampa (tel. 223-1020), and Palace Shoe Repair, 905 N. Tampa St., Tampa (tel. 223-5886).

Taxes   Local taxes can add quite a bit to your costs, so keep them in mind when you figure your budget. There's a 10.5% tax on hotel room charges, a 6.5% tax on restaurant bills, and a 6.5%

general sales tax on purchases. If you leave the area by plane on an international flight, you'll be hit with a $6 airport departure tax.

Taxis   See "Getting Around," in this chapter.

Time Zone   Eastern. For more information, see "Fast Facts: For the Foreign Traveler," in Chapter 3.

Tipping   See "Fast Facts: St. Petersburg," in Chapter 4.

Transit Information   Dial 254-HART.

CHAPTER 9

TAMPA ACCOMMODATIONS

This city's greatest hotel, the legendary Tampa Bay Hotel, was opened more than a century ago, in 1891. The creation of railroad magnate Henry B. Plant, the 511-room hotel was the first large fully electrified building in Tampa. It was also the most extravagant, costing an astonishing (for those days) $2 million.

Set on the western shore of the Hillsborough River, the Tampa Bay Hotel was modeled after the Alhambra Palace in Spain. It was 1,200 feet long, topped by 13 silver minarets, and filled with priceless art and impeccable furnishings. A trendsetter in every way, the hotel had a casino, heated indoor swimming pool, golf course, and racetrack, as well as two ballrooms, a grand salon, two writing and reading rooms, a solarium, billiard room, hair salon, and gentleman's bar. Rickshas were used to carry guests through the tropical gardens and long hallways. The guest list was a veritable who's who of the times—from Teddy Roosevelt and William Jennings Bryan to Babe Ruth, John Drew, and Anna Pavlova.

Sadly, this great landmark—the social center of Tampa—ceased to operate as a hotel in 1930. And there hasn't been anything like it since.

Today Tampa is a city of relatively new hotels, all built in the last 25 years or so, and most within the last decade. The architecture is decidedly modern, and the skyline is sleek.

Unlike many major cities, the downtown sector of Tampa is not full of hotels—banks outnumber hotels by at least two-to-one. This may change dramatically with the opening of Tampa's new convention center, but for the time being, the downtown hotels are limited mostly to a handful of familiar chain names.

The greatest concentration of Tampa's hotels is west of downtown, near Tampa International Airport. These properties are within a mile or two of the airport and its adjacent business corridor, primarily along Westshore Boulevard and the Courtney Campbell Causeway. Like their downtown cousins, these hotels cater to a largely commercial clientele, at least during the week.

The third-largest cluster of lodgings is found north of downtown in the Busch Gardens area. These hotels and motels are geared more to vacationers and families.

The high season for prices is January through April, but rates do not vary as dramatically here as they do along the beaches surrounding St. Petersburg. The prices of Tampa's larger business-oriented hotels—downtown and west of the city—are pretty much the same throughout the year. The big price breaks come on weekends—all year long—when rates drop as much as 50%. A room or suite that costs $149 on weeknights can be as low as $69 on weekends.

The only exception is the Busch Gardens area, where hotels and motels are just as busy, if not busier, on weekends as on weekdays. By and large, rates do not dip on weekends, and they can be slightly higher on holiday weekends or during special events.

This is balanced, however, by the fact that overall rates in the Busch Gardens area tend to be at least 30% to 40% lower than at hotels in other parts of the city. Services are more limited at these properties and you won't get water views, but, if you want the lowest rates, this is where you'll find them. Many of the motels here also offer two- and three-day packages that include admission tickets to Busch Gardens.

The rates that we cite below give you the broad spectrum of the regular weekday rates. When you call, be sure to inquire about weekend rates and inclusive packages. These change with the seasons, but can often be real bargains.

In addition, at all times of the year you'll pay an extra **10.5% tax** on the price of a room—6.5% for Florida sales tax and 4% for city and resort tax, otherwise known as "bed tax" or "occupancy tax." Tipping is normally at your own discretion for daily maid service, valet parking, concierge arrangements, etc., unless otherwise specified.

The following price categories for Tampa area hotels are based on per-night, double-occupancy rates:

Very Expensive	Over $175
Expensive	$125–$175
Moderate	$65–$125
Inexpensive	Under $65

Reservations are a *must* in the high season and strongly recommended at other times. Tampa hotels are often booked up with meetings and groups at all times of the year, so it's never wise to leave anything to chance. You can shop around before you go—and compare prices—by using the toll-free reservations numbers provided by most hotels.

1. DOWNTOWN/ HARBOUR ISLAND

EXPENSIVE

HYATT REGENCY TAMPA, 211 N. Tampa St., Tampa, FL 33602. Tel. 813/225-1234, or toll free 800/233-1234. Fax 813/273-0234. 519 rms. A/C TV TEL

$ Rates: $117–$150 single; $142–$175 double. AE, CB, DC, DISC, MC, V. **Parking:** Valet parking $7, self-parking $4.

⭐ Standing out on the city skyline, with a striking mirrored facade, this 17-story tower is situated on the corner of Tampa and Jackson Streets, in the heart of downtown at Tampa City Center, adjacent to the Franklin Street Pedestrian Mall and the People Mover monorail station, and within three blocks of the convention center. Currently Tampa's largest hotel, it is popular with convention and meeting groups. The interior is dominated by an eight-story atrium lobby with a two-story cascading waterfall, lots of foliage, and a resident macaw. Guest rooms have a contemporary decor with light woods and coastal colors, and many units on the upper floors have bay or river views.

Dining/Entertainment: Seafood (lunch only) is featured at Saltwaters Bar and Grille on the lobby level. Meals are available throughout the day and evening at Pralines, a café with indoor and outdoor patio seating overlooking the mall area (see Chapter 10, "Tampa Dining"). For libations with piano music, take the escalator to Breeze's Lounge on the second floor of the atrium.

Services: Airport courtesy shuttle, 24-hour room service, concierge, valet laundry.

Facilities: Outdoor heated swimming pool, whirlpool, health club, meeting rooms, car-rental and airline desks.

WYNDHAM HARBOUR ISLAND HOTEL, 725 S. Harbour Island Blvd., Harbour Island, Tampa, FL 33602. Tel. 813/229-5000, or toll free 800/822-4200. Fax 813/229-5322. 280 rms, 20 suites. A/C MINIBAR TV TEL **Directions:** Take the Franklin Street Bridge or People Mover to Harbour Island.

$ Rates: $169 single; $189 double; $275–$875 suite. AE, CB, DC, MC, V. **Parking:** $6.

⭐ If location is everything, then this 12-story luxury property has a distinct advantage—it's just a minute or two from the bustle of the business district, yet it sits tranquilly on Harbour Island, surrounded by the channels linking the Hillsborough River and Hillsborough Bay. Easily accessible from downtown, it is likewise connected to the shops and waterside activities of the Harbour Island complex. It also offers its customers all the perks of living on the island, including guest privileges at the Harbour Island Athletic Club and use of 20 tennis courts, five racquetball courts, and two squash courts (a $10 basic fee per adult applies, plus hourly court fees).

The spacious guest rooms, all of which have views of the water, are furnished in dark woods and floral fabrics, and each has a well-lit marble-trimmed bathroom, executive desk, coffee maker, and work area. Suites, many of which have corner locations, also have wet bars.

Dining/Entertainment: Watch the yachts drift by as you dine at the Harbour View Room (see Chapter 10, "Tampa Dining"), or enjoy your favorite drink in the Bar, a clubby room with equally good views, both located on the lobby level. Snacks and tropical drinks are available throughout the day at the Pool Bar, accessible from the third floor.

Services: Courtesy airport shuttle, room service, concierge, secretarial services, notary public, bed turndown service, valet laundry.

Facilities: Outdoor heated swimming pool and deck, 50 boat slips, meeting rooms, newsstand/gift shop.

MODERATE

HELNAN RIVERSIDE HOTEL–TAMPA, 200 Ashley Dr., Tampa, FL 33602. Tel. 813/223-2222, or toll free 800/288-2672. Fax 813/273-0839. 265 rms. A/C MINIBAR TV TEL
$ Rates: $75–$85 single or double. AE, CB, DC, MC, V. **Parking:** Valet $4.50.

Ideally located on the Hillsborough River, between Jackson and Washington Streets and within two blocks of the convention center, this six-story property was formerly the Tampa Hilton. Purchased in late 1989 by Helnan International, the entire hotel was renovated and revamped in 1989–90 at a cost of $6 million.

The refurbished guest rooms have a contemporary decor with dark woods and pastel tones; most units have private balconies with river views. The modern bathrooms have extra perks, such as a makeup mirror, hairdryer, and phone.

Dining/Entertainment: Choices include The River Deli for light fare all day and The Lounge for libations.

Services: Airport courtesy shuttle, room service, valet cleaning service (weekdays).

Facilities: Heated outdoor swimming pool, exercise room, gift shop, car-rental desk, meeting rooms.

HOLIDAY INN–ASHLEY PLAZA, 111 W. Fortune St., Tampa, FL 33602. Tel. 813/223-1351, or toll free 800/HOLIDAY. Fax 813/221-2000. 311 rms. A/C TV TEL **Directions:** Take I-275 to Exit 25; the hotel is at the corner of Ashley and Fortune Sts.
$ Rates: $72.50–$92.50 single; $82.50–$102.50 double. AE, CB, DC, DISC, MC, V. **Parking:** Free.

Perched along the Hillsborough River, this modern 14-story hotel is next to the Tampa Bay Performing Arts Center and is also within walking distance of most of the city's top attractions, including the Tampa Museum and the Franklin Street Pedestrian Mall. Guest rooms are spacious, with dark-wood furnishings, rose or aqua-toned fabrics, and full-length wall mirrors. Most rooms on upper floors have views of the river, and 22 rooms have kitchenettes.

Dining/Entertainment: The lobby level offers three choices: the Backstage Restaurant, for moderately priced beef, seafood, and pasta dishes in a theatrical setting; the Deli for light fare; and the Encore lounge for drinks and occasional live music.

Services: Airport courtesy shuttle, room service, valet laundry.
Facilities: Outdoor heated swimming pool, whirlpool, fitness

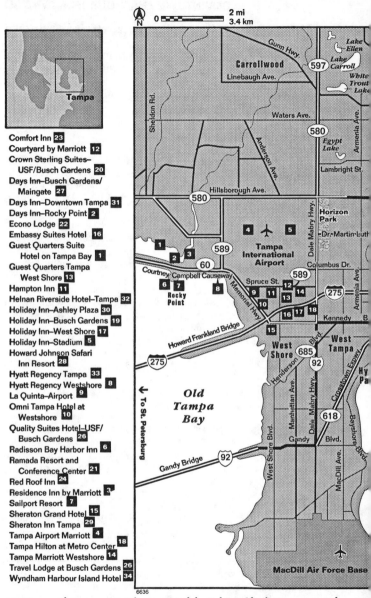

Comfort Inn 23
Courtyard by Marriott 12
Crown Sterling Suites–
  USF/Busch Gardens 20
Days Inn–Busch Gardens/
  Maingate 27
Days Inn–Downtown Tampa 31
Days Inn–Rocky Point 2
Econo Lodge 22
Embassy Suites Hotel 16
Guest Quarters Suite
  Hotel on Tampa Bay 1
Guest Quarters Tampa
  West Shore 13
Hampton Inn 11
Helnan Riverside Hotel–Tampa 32
Holiday Inn–Ashley Plaza 30
Holiday Inn–Busch Gardens 19
Holiday Inn–West Shore 17
Holiday Inn–Stadium 5
Howard Johnson Safari
  Inn Resort 28
Hyatt Regency Tampa 33
Hyatt Regency Westshore 8
La Quinta–Airport 9
Omni Tampa Hotel at
  Westshore 10
Quality Suites Hotel–USF/
  Busch Gardens 26
Radisson Bay Harbor Inn 6
Ramada Resort and
  Conference Center 21
Red Roof Inn 24
Residence Inn by Marriott 3
Sailport Resort 7
Sheraton Grand Hotel 15
Sheraton Inn Tampa 29
Tampa Airport Marriott 4
Tampa Hilton at Metro Center 18
Tampa Marriott Westshore 14
Travel Lodge at Busch Gardens 26
Wyndham Harbour Island Hotel 34

room, meeting rooms, coin-operated laundry, gift shop, car-rental desk.

INEXPENSIVE

DAYS INN–DOWNTOWN TAMPA, 515 E. Cass St., Tampa, FL 33602. Tel. 813/229-6431, or toll free 800/ DAYS-INN. Fax 813/228-7534. 180 rms. A/C TV TEL

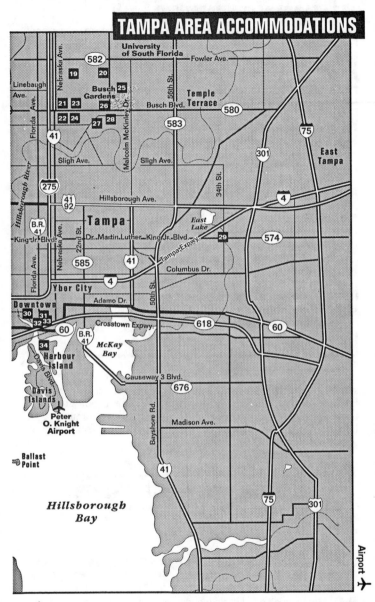

TAMPA AREA ACCOMMODATIONS

$ Rates: $29–$54 single; $34–$54 double. AE, DC, DISC, MC, V.
Parking: Enclosed, free.

If you want to stay downtown on a limited budget, this is the best choice, although it's not in a thriving part of the city. As long as you don't mind walking past a few boarded-up buildings, this eight-story hotel is situated at the corner of Cass and Marion Streets, within five blocks of the Tampa Bay Performing Arts Center and two blocks from the Franklin Street Mall. It's also next to the Greyhound bus

---

(F) FROMMER'S SMART TRAVELER: HOTELS

VALUE-CONSCIOUS TRAVELERS SHOULD TAKE ADVANTAGE OF THE FOLLOWING:

1. Off-season discounts from May to December.
2. Discounts sometimes available (to seniors, travel-club members, etc.).
3. Special weekend rates at hotels downtown or along a business corridor.
4. Reduced-rate packages at hotels near Busch Gardens.

QUESTIONS TO ASK IF YOU'RE ON A BUDGET

1. Is there a parking charge? In Tampa, many downtown hotels charge $3 to $6 a night, although others, particularly in the Busch Gardens and Courtney Campbell Causeway area, provide free parking.
2. Is the 10.5% hotel tax included in the price quoted?
3. Is continental breakfast included in the price quoted?
4. Is there a surcharge on local and long-distance calls? At some hotels, local telephone calls are free.
5. Is there a discount for cash payment?

---

station and the Marion Street Transitway, making it an ideal location if you're using public transport to get around. Guest rooms offer the usual amenities, and dining is limited to a small restaurant serving lunch (Monday to Friday only). Guest facilities include an outdoor swimming pool on the second-floor level.

2. AIRPORT/WEST SHORE

EXPENSIVE

GUEST QUARTERS TAMPA WEST SHORE, 4400 W. Cypress St., Tampa, FL 33607. Tel. 813/873-8675, or toll free 800/433-4600. Fax 813/879-7196. 263 suites. A/C TV TEL
$ Rates (including full breakfast and evening cocktail party): $89–$149 single or double. AE, CB, DC, MC, V. **Parking:** Free, outdoors.

With an exterior of salmon-toned Spanish-style architecture, this eight-story building one mile from Tampa airport, at Cypress Street and Westshore Boulevard, adds old-world charm to an area filled with modern glass-and-concrete structures. The interior includes a plant-filled atrium with cascading waterfalls and a tropical garden courtyard. The guest units are suites with separate bedroom and living areas, contemporary furniture, muted color schemes, and wet bar. All have sofa beds, microwave ovens, coffee makers, and private patios or balconies.

Dining/Entertainment: Regional dishes and local seafoods are the specialties at the St. James Bar & Grill, adjacent to the greenery-filled atrium.

Services: Airport courtesy shuttle, room service, valet laundry.

Facilities: Indoor swimming pool, sauna, steam room, gift shop, meeting rooms.

EMBASSY SUITES HOTEL, 555 N. Westshore Blvd., Tampa, FL 33609. Tel. 813/875-1555, or toll free 800/ EMBASSY. **Fax 813/286-3664. 221 suites. A/C TV TEL**
$ Rates (including full buffet breakfast and evening cocktail reception): $89–$139 single or double; $149–$209 two-bedroom suite. AE, CB, DC, DISC, MC, V. **Parking:** Free.

This 16-story property less than two miles from Tampa airport, between Fla. 60 and I-275 (Exit 21), stands out in the Westshore business district with a striking facade of white stucco and glass. The interior is equally appealing, with arched corridors and walls decorated with Florida seabird art. Each guest unit offers a separate bedroom and living area with contemporary pastel-toned furnishings and a fully equipped kitchen. Some two-bedroom suites are available.

Dining/Entertainment: An art deco theme prevails at the Bay Café, a bright and brassy eatery and lounge on the second level. Outdoor dining is available at the Terrace, overlooking fountains, a three-tier waterfall, and the pool.

Services: Airport courtesy shuttle, concierge, valet laundry.

Facilities: Heated outdoor swimming pool, sun deck, saunas, whirlpool, exercise room, library, newsstand/gift shop, meeting rooms.

OMNI TAMPA HOTEL AT WESTSHORE, 700 N. Westshore Blvd., Tampa, FL 33609. Tel. 813/289-8200, or toll free 800/THE-OMNI. Fax 813/289-9166. 272 rms. A/C TV TEL
$ Rates: $99–$140 single; $114–$175 double. Omni Club level, $145 single, $160 double. AE, CB, DC, MC, V. **Parking:** Free, outdoors.

A favorite hotel with traveling executives, this 11-story property is part of Austin Center South, a mixed-use business complex one mile from Tampa airport, between Cypress Street and Fla. 60. The skylit lobby sets the tone of the hotel's "European look"—marble, mirrors, and palms, amid restful tones of gray, beige, and rust.

Guest rooms, accessible by computer-card keys, are decorated in rich dark tones of green, contrasted with pale grays and light oak, with mirrored closet doors and executive desks. Spacious bathrooms offer every amenity, including hairdryers. The entire 11th floor is the Omni Club, with private lounge, concierge, and added equipment such as a second telephone in the bathroom.

Dining/Entertainment: Seasons, the lobby-level restaurant noted for its regional cuisine and local seafood, is traditional in style, with a decor rich in mahogany and fine tapestries; the adjacent lounge offers relaxing piano music each evening.

Services: Airport courtesy shuttle, room service, valet laundry.

Facilities: Heated outdoor swimming pool, whirlpool, two saunas, fitness equipment, meeting rooms.

SHERATON GRAND HOTEL, 4860 W. Kennedy Blvd., Tampa, FL 33609. Tel. 813/286-4400, or toll free 800/ 325-3535. Fax 813/286-4053. 325 rms, 23 suites. A/C TV TEL

$ Rates: $99–$129 single; $109–$139 double; $149–$500 suite. AE, CB, DC, MC, V. **Parking:** Garage free; valet parking $7.

This contemporary-style 11-story property is part of Urban Center, a financial office complex in the heart of the Westshore business district and across from the Westshore Plaza Shopping Mall, two miles from the airport, at the intersection of Fla. 60 and Westshore Boulevard. In addition to its steady business clientele, it attracts vacationers who enjoy the panoramic views from the three glass elevators, and the bright and airy atriums filled with indoor greenery and cascading fountains.

The guest rooms are equally attractive, with soft-toned color schemes, traditional dark-wood furnishings, writing desks, easy chairs, full-length mirrors, built-in armoires, roomy closets, and marble-finished bathrooms. Rooms on the upper floors have distant views of Old Tampa Bay.

Dining/Entertainment: For continental recipes and fresh Florida seafood, try J. Fitzgerald's, on the lobby level. Other public areas include the Atrium Lobby Lounge, where there is piano music Monday through Saturday evening, and the Courtyard Café for light meals in an indoor/outdoor setting, and the Grand Slam Sports Bar for food and beverages.

Services: 24-hour room service, courtesy airport shuttle, concierge, valet laundry.

Facilities: Outdoor heated swimming pool, meeting rooms, car-rental desk, gift shops, travel agency, florist, two banks, news/ tobacco shop, rooms equipped for the disabled.

TAMPA AIRPORT MARRIOTT, Tampa International Airport, Tampa, FL 33607. Tel. 813/879-5151, or toll free 800/228-9290. Fax 813/873-0945. 296 rms. A/C TV TEL **Directions:** Follow the signs for HOTEL at the airport; the hotel is connected to departure terminals by an indoor walkway.

$ Rates: $100–$160 single or double; $139–$155 concierge level. AE, CB, DC, DISC, MC, V. **Parking:** Valet $4, self-parking free. Wedged between the terminals, this is the only on-site hotel at Tampa's busy airport and a good specimen for those who thrive on the excitement of overnighting near the jetways. Guest rooms are well soundproofed, decorated in contemporary style with dark woods and fabrics of cheery pastel tones. The sixth floor is the concierge level with larger executive-style rooms that include wet bars and added amenities.

Dining/Entertainment: An express elevator takes you to the seventh floor and CK's, the hotel's revolving rooftop restaurant and lounge, a popular attraction for those in transit and locals alike (see

Chapter 10, "Tampa Dining"). On the lobby level is the Garden Café for light fare and the Flight Room for cocktails and large-screen TV.

Services: Concierge, babysitting, valet laundry.

Facilities: Outdoor heated swimming pool, health club, gift shop, airline desk, car-rental desk, meeting rooms, rooms equipped for disabled guests.

MODERATE

COURTYARD BY MARRIOTT, 3805 W. Cypress St., Tampa, FL 33607. Tel. 813/874-0555, or toll free 800/ 321-2211. Fax 813/870-0685. 145 rms. A/C TV TEL **Directions:** Take Exit 23B of I-275, three miles east of the airport, at the northwest corner of Dale Mabry Hwy.

$ Rates: $49–$105 single or double. AE, CB, DC, DISC, MC, V. **Parking:** Free.

With a fireplace glowing in the lobby, this contemporary four-story hotel is a quiet oasis tucked beside a busy traffic corridor. Like other properties of this chain, it follows the usual layout, with guest rooms surrounding a well-landscaped central courtyard and gazebo.

The rooms, which offer a choice of a king-size bed or two double beds, feature dark-wood furnishings and pastel-toned fabrics, and have in-room coffee makers. Facilities include a café/lounge, outdoor swimming pool, indoor whirlpool, exercise room, complimentary airport transportation, and guest laundry.

HOLIDAY INN–STADIUM, 4732 N. Dale Mabry Hwy. (U.S. 92), Tampa, FL 33614. Tel. 813/877-6061, or toll free 800/HOLIDAY. Fax 813/876-1531. 312 rms. A/C TV TEL

$ Rates: $52–$64 single or double. AE, CB, DC, DISC, MC, V. **Parking:** Free.

When Tampa Stadium hosts a major event, this place (just two blocks north of the stadium) really hops. Otherwise it's a basic one- and two-story motel on a busy commercial corridor east of the airport between Buffalo and Hillsborough Avenues. Rooms have standard furnishings and some kitchenettes are available; rear units face a pond.

Dining/Entertainment: Choices currently include The Greenery for dining in a garden atmosphere and the Casbah lounge for drinks and music, although both are under renovation at press time.

Services: Airport courtesy shuttle, room service, babysitting.

Facilities: Outdoor heated swimming pool, meeting rooms.

HOLIDAY INN–WEST SHORE, 4500 Cypress St., Tampa, FL 33607. Tel. 813/879-4800, or toll free 800/HOLIDAY. Fax 813/873-1832. 500 rms. A/C TV TEL

$ Rates: $84–$112 single; $94–$122 double. AE, CB, DC, DISC, MC, V. **Parking:** Free.

Outside of the downtown area, this is Tampa's largest hotel. Like its neighbors along the Westshore corridor, a mile from Tampa airport between Westshore Boulevard and Lois Avenue, it caters primarily to businesspeople and is a favorite for convention and meeting groups. It's built in a rectangular configuration with three six-story wings and one 10-story wing, all surrounding a central courtyard area with outdoor pool and gardens. The guest rooms, many of which have balconies, are as varied as the architecture. The decor primarily features dark-wood furnishings and fabrics of pink, raspberry, and lavender tones, or beachy beige combinations. Most rooms overlook either the inner courtyard or nearby roadways, but units on the upper floors tower over nearby buildings and provide distant views of the bay.

Dining/Entertainment: The Cypress Café offers American cuisine, Bob's Sports Bar has a large-screen TV for sports and entertainment, and the Gazebo Bar features tropical drinks by the pool.

Services: Airport courtesy shuttle, room service, concierge, babysitting, valet laundry.

Facilities: Outdoor heated swimming pool, Jacuzzi, fitness center with sauna and whirlpool, meeting rooms, gift shop, newsstand.

TAMPA HILTON AT METROCENTER, 2225 N. Lois Ave., Tampa, FL 33607. Tel. 813/877-6688, or toll free 800/ HILTONS. Fax 813/879-3264. 240 rms. A/C TV TEL
$ Rates: $65–$125 single or double; $120–$135 concierge level. AE, CB, DC, DISC, MC, V. **Parking:** Free.

Situated in a commercial corridor a mile from the airport, at the corner of Boy Scout Boulevard and Lois Avenue between the airport and downtown, this 12-story property has an inviting skylit lobby of cherry and lime tones, and is often a focal point for the local business clientele. Guest rooms are contemporary, with light-beige walls and carpets contrasting with deeper tones of red or navy fabrics. Bathrooms have separate vanity areas. The top two floors feature concierge-style rooms with balconies. The entire eighth floor is designated for nonsmokers.

Dining/Entertainment: The main restaurant, Hemingway's, has a Key West atmosphere with ceiling fans, tropical plants, and appropriate background music. The Bay Breeze Lobby Bar overlooks the pool, where there is also a snack bar and gazebo.

Services: Airport courtesy shuttle, room service, babysitting, valet laundry.

Facilities: Outdoor heated swimming pool, hot tub, tennis court, gift shop, meeting rooms, rooms equipped for the disabled.

TAMPA MARRIOTT WESTSHORE, 1001 N. Westshore Blvd., Tampa, FL 33607. Tel. 813/287-2555, or toll free 800/228-9290. Fax 813/289-5464. 312 rms. A/C TV TEL
$ Rates: $119–$135 single or double; $139–$155 concierge level. AE, CB, DC, DISC, MC, V. **Parking:** Free.

Popular with a business clientele, this busy 14-story hotel a mile from the airport, at the corner of Cypress Street and Westshore Boulevard, greets guests with a contemporary skylit lobby. Bedrooms are well maintained, with dark-wood furnishings, full-length wall mirrors, and fabrics of dusty rose or aqua. The top floor is the concierge level, with larger layouts and enhanced amenities.

Dining/Entertainment: The Westshore Grille Restaurant is noted for seafood, and Champions Sports Bar is a popular gathering place each evening, with over a dozen TVs for monitoring sports events and a DJ for contemporary dance music.

Services: Airport courtesy shuttle, valet laundry.

Facilities: Heated indoor/outdoor swimming pool, health club, sauna, whirlpool, games room, gift shop, meeting rooms, rooms equipped for disabled guests.

INEXPENSIVE

HAMPTON INN, 4817 W. Laurel St., Tampa, FL 33607. Tel. 813/287-0778, or toll free 800/HAMPTON. Fax 813/287-0882. 134 rms. A/C TV TEL

$ Rates (including continental breakfast): $52–$69 single; $62–$79 double. AE, DC, DISC, MC, V. **Parking:** Free.

 Opened in the fall of 1988, this six-story hostelry offers very good value in an otherwise high-priced airport/business corridor. It's located a mile from Tampa airport, south of Spruce Street and directly off Westshore Boulevard. Guest rooms are decorated with dark woods set off by pink, peach, and beige tones. Some units offer king-size beds and extra work areas, and a full 50% of the rooms are designated for nonsmoking guests. Services and facilities are limited, but there is an outdoor swimming pool, meeting room, and a courtesy shuttle to the airport.

LA QUINTA–AIRPORT, 4730 W. Spruce St., Tampa, FL 33607. Tel. 813/287-0440, or toll free 800/531-5900. Fax 813/286-7399. 122 rms. A/C TV TEL

$ Rates (including continental breakfast): $53–$65 single; $60–$75 double. AE, CB, DC, DISC, MC, V. **Parking:** Free.

Equally convenient to the airport and the Westshore business district, just outside the Tampa airport exit, between O'Brien Street and Westshore Boulevard, this two-story hacienda-style motel offers a homey alternative to the many sleek high-rise properties in this area. Guest rooms, which surround a central courtyard, are decorated in a contemporary southwestern motif, with light woods, Pueblo art, and fabric tones of muted green, amber, and brown, while bathrooms are well lit with separate vanity areas. Public areas include a living room–style lobby with fireplace and a sun deck with sombrero-shaped umbrellas. There's a complimentary airport shuttle and an adjacent 24-hour restaurant.

3. COURTNEY CAMPBELL CAUSEWAY AREA

VERY EXPENSIVE

HYATT REGENCY WESTSHORE, 6200 Courtney Campbell Causeway, Tampa, FL 33607. Tel. 813/874-1234, or toll free 800/233-1234. Fax 813/870-9168. 445 rms. A/C TV TEL

$ Rates: $169 single; $195 double; $180–$225 single or double on Regency Club level. AE, CB, DC, DISC, MC, V. **Parking:** Self-parking free; valet $7.

Overlooking Old Tampa Bay, this imposing 14-story property is nestled on a 35-acre nature preserve adjacent to the Bayport Plaza Business Complex, convenient to the airport (a mile west) and downtown, and yet sequestered in a world of its own. The lobby provides a warm welcome, with a blend of arches and columns, hand-painted murals, and imported marble flooring.

Seashore colors and light woods dominate the decor of the guest rooms, most of which provide expansive views of the bay and of evening sunsets. The Regency Club level on the 12th floor offers 44 rooms with extra amenities and services such as a complimentary limousine transfer to the Tampa business district.

Dining/Entertainment: On the 14th floor is Armani's, a rooftop Italian restaurant known for its fine food and views, and behind the main hotel a 250-foot boardwalk leads to Oystercatchers, a Key West–style seafood eatery with indoor and outdoor seating overlooking the bay (see Chapter 10, "Tampa Dining," for more information about both). On the lobby level, there is Petey Brown's Café.

Services: Airport courtesy shuttle, 24-hour room service, concierge, babysitting service, valet laundry.

Facilities: Two outdoor swimming pools, two lighted tennis courts, whirlpool, saunas, health club, nature walks and jogging trails, meeting rooms.

EXPENSIVE

GUEST QUARTERS SUITE HOTEL ON TAMPA BAY, 3050 N. Rocky Point Dr. W., Tampa, FL 33607. Tel. 813/888-8800, or toll free 800/424-2900. Fax 813/888-8743. 203 suites. A/C MINIBAR TV TEL

$ Rates: $125–$135 single; $145–$155 double. AE, CB, DC, DISC, MC, V. **Parking:** Free, outdoor.

One of the newest hotels along this strip overlooking Old Tampa Bay, this seven-story property two miles west of Tampa airport, opposite International Shrine Headquarters, has a unique facade in the shape of a trapezoid. The futuristic theme is carried into the lobby, which has a spacious three-story atrium.

Each guest unit is a suite, with separate bedroom and living room/dining area. Rooms have wide windows with views of the bay, dark woods, beige and pastel-toned fabrics, comfortable reclining chairs and ottomans, and little extras such as a mini-TV in the bathroom, full-length mirrored door, coffee/tea maker, and hairdryer.

Dining/Entertainment: The Galerie Restaurant and Lounge overlooks the bay and the pool area.

Services: Airport courtesy shuttle, room service, concierge, nightly turndown service, babysitting service, valet laundry.

Facilities: Heated outdoor swimming pool, whirlpool, sauna, sun deck, exercise room, library, business center with computer access, meeting rooms.

MODERATE

RADISSON BAY HARBOR INN, 7700 Courtney Campbell Causeway, Tampa, FL 33607. Tel. 813/281-8900, or toll free 800/333-3333. Fax 813/281-0189. 260 rms. A/C TV TEL

$ Rates: $59–$99 single or double. AE, CB, DC, DISC, MC, V. **Parking:** Free.

One of the few hotels fronting Old Tampa Bay that actually has a sandy beach of its own, this six-story property two miles west of Tampa airport, between the International Shrine Headquarters building and Ben T. Davis Beach, was constructed to give all rooms a view of the water. To make the most of the views, each room also has a balcony or patio. Guest-room decor, which uses mostly sea-toned fabrics, reflects art deco influences, with rounded furnishings and shell-shaped chairs.

Dining/Entertainment: Views of the water and the beach are prime attractions at the lobby-level Damon's Restaurant and Lounge.

Services: Airport courtesy shuttle, valet laundry.

Facilities: Heated outdoor swimming pool, two lighted tennis courts, exercise room, meeting rooms, hair salons for men and women, gift shop, car-rental desk.

RESIDENCE INN BY MARRIOTT, 3075 N. Rocky Point Dr., Tampa, FL 33607. Tel. 813/281-5677, or toll free 800/331-3131. Fax 813/281-5677, ext. 795. 176 suites. A/C TV TEL **Directions:** Follow the signs two miles west from Tampa airport; the hotel is off the main road behind the Days Inn.

$ Rates (including continental breakfast and evening hospitality cocktail hour Mon–Thurs): $99–$102 studio suite, $139–$142 penthouse suite. AE, DC, MC, V. **Parking:** Free.

For families or for long-term individual stays, this town house–style property offers great value. Set back from the main road, it overlooks the bay amid a well-landscaped community-style setting with its own fishing pier/boat dock. Each unit is a suite with bedroom, living area, and fully equipped kitchen, including microwave oven, coffee maker, and dishwasher. Layouts include one-level studio suites or two-story penthouse suites; the larger units have two bedrooms, two bathrooms, and two TVs; many have fireplaces.

Services: Airport courtesy shuttle, babysitting, grocery-shopping service, valet laundry.

Facilities: Heated outdoor swimming pool, Jacuzzi, court for racquet sports, complimentary pass to nearby health and racquet club, meeting rooms.

SAILPORT RESORT, 2506 Rocky Point Dr., Tampa, FL 33607. Tel. 813/281-9599, or toll free 800/255-9599. Fax 813/281-9510. 219 suites. A/C MINIBAR TV TEL

$ Rates (including continental breakfast): $65–$97 one-bedroom

---

Ⓕ FROMMER'S COOL FOR KIDS: HOTELS

Days Inn–Busch Gardens *(see p. 183)* Has an outdoor pool, children's playground, volleyball court, badminton, tennis courts, and rentals for paddleboats.

Hyatt Regency Westshore *(see p. 177)* Set amid a 35-acre nature preserve, with walking trails and water sports.

Saddlebrook Resort *(see p. 185)* Has a supervised children's program, a tennis school for junior players, plus swimming pool with lifeguard, bicycle rentals, and more.

---

suite, $105–$149 two-bedroom suite. AE, DC, MC, V. **Parking:** Free.

Overlooking Old Tampa Bay two miles west of the airport, off the main road just behind the International Shrine Headquarters, this three-story property offers large suites that are really more like apartments than hotel rooms. Each unit has one or two bedrooms, each with queen-size bed, a fully equipped kitchen, a living room with a queen-size sofa bed, balcony overlooking Tampa Bay, and a stereo system. Other homey touches include some rattan furniture, seascape art, linen closets, and a medicine chest in the bathroom. There are no dining outlets, and check-in is confined to a small office rather than a formal lobby; but basic hotel functions, such as daily maid service and valet laundry service, are provided. Free newspapers are available in the lobby.

Facilities: Heated outdoor swimming pool, lighted tennis court, fishing pier, barbecue grills, meeting rooms, 24-hour grocery/sundries store.

INEXPENSIVE

DAYS INN–ROCKY POINT, 7627 Courtney Campbell Causeway, Tampa, FL 33607. Tel. 813/281-0000, or toll free 800/DAYS-INN. Fax 813/281-1067. 148 rms, 4 suites. A/C TV TEL

$ Rates: $50–$75 single; $55–$90 double; $90–$115 suite. AE, DC, DISC, MC, V. **Parking:** Free.

 Set back from the main road two miles west of Tampa airport off Rocky Point Drive, this motel-style property has a lovely waterfront setting on Old Tampa Bay, and a small strip of beach. The layout encompasses six two-story wings surrounding an outdoor swimming pool with landscaped courtyard, so the bedrooms offer either bay or poolside views. The units have a cheery decor of pink and green tones, brass trim, and basic light-wood furniture.

For dining or imbibing, try the Southern Exposure Waterfront

Café and Sports Bar. Facilities include a heated outdoor swimming pool, two tennis courts, a shuffleboard court, horseshoes, badminton, volleyball court, children's playground, and rentals for paddleboats. There is also a coin-operated guest laundry and meeting rooms.

4. BUSCH GARDENS AREA

MODERATE

CROWN STERLING SUITES HOTEL—USF/BUSCH GAR-DENS, 11310 N. 30th St., Tampa, FL 33612. Tel. 813/971-7690, or toll free 800/433-4600. Fax 813/972-5525. 129 suites. A/C TV TEL **Directions:** Take I-275 north to Fowler Ave. (Exit 34); go east for 1 ½ miles to 30th St., turn right, and cross over the railroad tracks; the hotel is on the right.

$ Rates (including full breakfast and evening cocktail party): $89–$109 suite. AE, CB, DC, DISC, MC, V. **Parking:** Free.

Situated one mile north of Busch Gardens, this three-story all-suite hostelry has a southern mansion ambience, highlighted by well-landscaped grounds, wrought-iron trim, veranda-style outdoor corridors with hanging plants, and a central courtyard with shady palms and outdoor pool.

Each guest unit has a separate bedroom with a king-size bed, living room with dining area/work space, wet bar, microwave oven, refrigerator, coffee maker, and sofa bed. The color scheme blends light-wood furnishings with refreshing peach and lime tones.

Services: Courtesy shuttle service to Busch Gardens.

Facilities: Outdoor heated swimming pool, Jacuzzi, meeting rooms, suites designed for disabled guests.

HOLIDAY INN—BUSCH GARDENS, 2701 E. Fowler Ave., Tampa, FL 33612. Tel. 813/971-4710, or toll free 800/HOLIDAY. Fax 813/977-0155. 395 rms. A/C TV TEL **Directions:** Take I-275 north to Fowler Ave. (Exit 34); go east on Fowler for just over a mile and the hotel is on the right.

$ Rates: $74–$89 single; $84–$104 double. AE, CB, DC, DISC, MC, V. **Parking:** Free.

The largest hotel in the area, this sprawling two-story complex is one mile north of Busch Gardens, and opposite the University of South Florida campus. The main focus here is a central outdoor courtyard with swimming pool, extensive tropical gardens, mini-waterfalls, rock gardens, gazebo, and wooden footbridges.

Guest rooms, most of which face the courtyard, are outfitted with light woods and touches of brass; color schemes vary from mauve and pink to a trio of blue, gray, and aqua.

Dining/Entertainment: Choices include T.G.I. Friday, serving breakfast, lunch, and dinner; Colonel Tidbits Emporium, offering continental breakfast and snacks; and the Cabana Pool Bar for drinks.

Services: Complimentary transport to Busch Gardens, airport courtesy shuttle, room service, babysitting, valet laundry.

Facilities: Outdoor heated swimming pool, health club, meeting rooms.

QUALITY SUITES HOTEL—USF/BUSCH GARDENS, 3001 University Center Dr., Tampa, FL 33612. Tel. 813/971-8930, or toll free 800/786-7446 or 800/228-5151. Fax 813/971-8935. 150 suites. A/C MINIBAR TV TEL **Directions:** Take I-275 north to Busch Blvd. (Exit 33); travel east on Busch for 1½ miles to 30th St., turn left, and drive half a mile north; the hotel is on the right off Bougainvillea Ave.

$ Rates (including full breakfast): $79–$155 single; $84–$160 double. AE, DC, DISC, MC, V. **Parking:** Free.

 Opened in the summer of 1989, this hacienda-style all-suite hotel sits directly behind the Busch Gardens property, although the entrance to the theme park is four blocks away. Besides its proximity to the area's major attraction, it has become a fast favorite with both business travelers and families because of its great value.

Each guest unit has a separate bedroom with built-in armoire, luggage rack, and well-lit mirrored vanity area, and a living/dining room with sofa bed, wet bar, coffee maker, microwave oven, stereo/VCR unit, and a phone system with voice-message and computer-hookup capabilities. The decor relies heavily on rounded art deco–style furnishings, with bright shades of pink, raspberry, or green.

Services: Gift shop/food store, VCR rentals, valet laundry.

Facilities: Outdoor heated swimming pool, Jacuzzi, meeting rooms, coin-operated laundry, suites designed for disabled travelers.

RAMADA RESORT AND CONFERENCE CENTER, 820 E. Busch Blvd., Tampa, FL 33612. Tel. 813/933-4011, or toll free 800/288-4011. Fax 813/932-1784. 255 rms. A/C TV TEL **Directions:** Take I-275 north to Busch Blvd. (Exit 33); turn left at the exit ramp light and the hotel is on the left.

$ Rates: $59–$99 single or double. AE, CB, DC, DISC, MC, V. **Parking:** Free.

Situated two miles west of Busch Gardens, on the main thoroughfare, this two- and four-story hotel attracts a brisk business trade as well as theme-park attendees. The lobby leads to an enclosed skylit atrium-style courtyard with fountains, benches, streetlights, shops, cafés, bars, pool, and other sporting activities. Guest rooms, which surround the courtyard, offer standard furnishings, enlivened by colorful, eye-catching fabrics.

Dining/Entertainment: Apricots Restaurant, off the lobby, features seafood dishes. Charades Nite Club offers live entertainment Tuesday through Saturday, and the atrium offers a café, lounge, and coffee shop.

Services: Courtesy transport to Busch Gardens, concierge, secretarial services, valet laundry.

Facilities: Indoor and outdoor heated swimming pools, two Jacuzzis, sauna, four lighted tennis courts, tennis pro shop, exercise room, games room, coin-operated laundry, gift shop, meeting rooms.

INEXPENSIVE

COMFORT INN, 2106 E. Busch Blvd., Tampa, FL 33612. Tel. 813/931-3313, or toll free 800/221-2222. Fax 813/933-8140. 50 units. A/C TV TEL **Directions:** Take I-275 north to Busch Blvd. (Exit 33) and go east on Busch for one mile; the hotel is on the left at 21st St.

$ Rates: $36–$75 single; $41–$75 double; $45–$75 efficiency. AE, DISC, MC, V. **Parking:** Free.

Situated about half a mile west of Busch Gardens, this relatively new three-story motor inn offers a choice of accommodations. Most rooms are standard doubles, and some have only a shower instead of a full bath. In addition, there are larger rooms with king-size beds and full baths; and over a third of the units are also outfitted with small kitchenettes. Facilities are limited, but there is an outdoor heated swimming pool.

DAYS INN–BUSCH GARDENS/MAINGATE, 2901 E. Busch Blvd., Tampa, FL 33612. Tel. 813/933-6471, or toll free 800/DAYS-INN. Fax 813/931-0261. 176 rms. A/C TV TEL **Directions:** Take I-275 north to Busch Blvd. (Exit 33); go east on Busch for just over 1 ½ miles; the hotel is on the right at 30th St.

$ Rates: $32–$59 single; $37–$64 double. AE, DC, MC, V. **Parking:** Free.

Within walking distance of Busch Gardens, this sprawling two-story motel is popular with families. Although the registration office is just off the main thoroughfare, most of the guest rooms are set back in a quieter environment surrounding an outdoor swimming pool. Rooms offer colorful standard furnishings, with two double beds. In addition to the pool, on-site facilities include a children's playground, a 24-hour chain restaurant, and coin-operated laundry.

ECONO LODGE, 1701 E. Busch Blvd., Tampa, FL 33612. Tel. 813/933-7681, or toll free 800/424-4777. Fax 813/935-3301. 240 rms. **Directions:** Take I-275 north to Busch Blvd. (Exit 33); go east on Busch for about three-quarters of a mile and the hotel is on the right.

$ Rates: $32–$52 single; $38–$58 double. AE, CB, DC, DISC, MC, V. **Parking:** Free.

This two- and three-story motel is laid out with a central courtyard, about a mile west of Busch Gardens. Rooms are standard, mostly with two double beds or one king-size bed, a small tiled bathroom with separate vanity area, and a decor of dark woods, blue and green tones, and wildlife art from Busch Gardens on the walls. This property is popular with families for its price level and also because it has a number of connecting units. Facilities include an outdoor swimming pool and a steak house/lounge designed in a railroad car motif.

HOWARD JOHNSON SAFARI INN RESORT, 4139 E. Busch Blvd., Tampa, FL 33617. Tel. 813/988-9191, or toll free 800/GO-HOJO. Fax 813/988-9195. 99 rms. A/C TV TEL **Directions:** Take I-275 north to Busch Blvd. (Exit 33); go east on Busch for just over two miles and the hotel is on the right.

$ Rates: $38–$59 single; $44–$64 double. AE, CB, DC, MC, V. **Parking:** Free.

 Situated almost directly across from the entrance of Busch Gardens, this two-story motel is a favorite with families. The guest rooms, most of which have private balconies or patios, offer standard furnishings in light woods, with wildlife prints on the walls, and bedspreads made of jungle patterns and colors. Most units have two double beds; 10 rooms are larger, with deluxe appointments including king-size bed, wet bar, and refrigerator.

A wildlife theme prevails at the Safari Café and Lounge.

RED ROOF INN, 2307 E. Busch Blvd., Tampa, FL 33612. Tel. 813/932-0073, or toll free 800/THE-ROOF. Fax 813/933-5689. 108 rms. A/C TV TEL **Directions:** Take I-275 north to Busch Blvd. (Exit 33); go east on Busch just over a mile and the hotel is on the right.

$ Rates: $29.99–$33.99 single; $43.99–$57.99 double. AE, DC, DISC, MC, V. **Parking:** Free.

 A half mile west of Busch Gardens, this two-story property is set back from the road in a grassy, well-landscaped setting. The layout consists of two adjacent wings with an outdoor pool and whirlpool in the center. The guest units, outfitted with brightly colored fabrics and standard furnishings, represent good value for the area. The inn serves free coffee.

TRAVEL LODGE AT BUSCH GARDENS, 9202 N. 30th St., Tampa, FL 33612. Tel. 813/935-7855, or toll free 800/255-3050. Fax 813/935-7958. 148 rms, 12 suites. A/C TV TEL **Directions:** Take I-275 north to Busch Blvd. (Exit 33); go east on Busch for 1½ miles, then turn left at 30th St., the hotel is on the left.

$ Rates: $36–$58 single; $40–$62 double; from $70 suite. AE, CB, DC, DISC, MC, V. **Parking:** Free.

Across the street from the west side of the Busch Gardens property, this three-story motel with an attractive mirrored facade is one of the closest to the giant theme park. Guest rooms offer standard amenities, with a few extra touches such as ceiling fans and separate vanity areas. The decor is eclectic, with some green and brown jungle-style tones and other bright purple and pink patterns, designed to delight visiting families. Facilities on the premises include a 24-hour fast-food restaurant, outdoor heated swimming pool in a tropical garden setting, games room, and an all-purpose shop.

5. EAST OF TAMPA

VERY EXPENSIVE/EXPENSIVE

SADDLEBROOK RESORT, 5700 Saddlebrook Way, Wesley Chapel, FL 33543. Tel. 813/973-1111, or toll free 800/ 729-8383. Fax 813/973-4504. 270 rms, 500 suites. A/C MINIBAR TV TEL **Directions:** Take I-275 to I-75 and go north to Exit 58; then travel one mile east on Fla. 54 to the Saddlebrook entrance.

$ Rates: $90–$325 single or double. AE, CB, DISC, MC, V. **Parking:** Valet $4.

Situated on 480 acres of inland woodlands, this secluded resort is 33 miles northeast of Tampa airport. A haven for sports enthusiasts, it's the home of two Arnold Palmer–designed golf courses, world headquarters of the Arnold Palmer golf academy, and the Harry Hopman international tennis school.

Guest units are spread throughout the property in a layout of over 20 two-story villas, offering a choice of standard hotel rooms and one- or two-bedroom suites. Each unit is furnished in a homey, contemporary style, and the suites have fully equipped kitchens, living and dining rooms, private bath for each bedroom, and a balcony or patio.

Dining/Entertainment: The Little Club and Little Club Patio serve American cuisine in a casual setting, while the Cypress Room offers an international menu and ambience. There is dancing and entertainment nightly in the Polo Lounge, and cocktails and snacks are also available at the Superpool Bar.

Services: Airport shuttle service ($17.50), room service, concierge, supervised children's program.

Facilities: Two 18-hole golf courses; 45 tennis courts; outdoor heated swimming pool; fitness center; bicycle rental; massage therapy; meeting rooms; gift, golf, and tennis shops; barber; beauty shop.

MODERATE

SHERATON INN TAMPA, 7401 E. Hillsborough Ave., Tampa, FL 33610. Tel. 813/626-0999, or toll free 800/ 325-3535. Fax 813/622-7893. 276 rms. A/C TV TEL **Directions:** Take I-275 north to I-4, and I-4 east to Orient Rd. (Exit 5); the hotel is at the intersection of Orient Rd. and Hillsborough Ave.

$ Rates: $95–$105 single; $105–$115 double. AE, CB, DC, MC, V. **Parking:** Free.

Ten minutes from downtown, this two-, three-, and six-story property is situated in a palm-tree-shaded setting, close to the State Fair Grounds and Seminole Bingo. It also makes an ideal base if you're planning day trips to Walt Disney World and other Orlando-area attractions, just an hour away. Guest rooms, many of which surround a central courtyard and pool area, are contemporary in decor, with dark woods, restful tones, brass fixtures, mirrored closets, and floral art. Many units have balconies or patios.

Dining/Entertainment: The lobby area has a lounge bar with an informal atmosphere; or follow a covered walkway to an adjacent building and the Cypress Landing Restaurant and Lounge.

Services: Airport courtesy shuttle, room service, valet laundry, secretarial services.

Facilities: Outdoor heated swimming pool, health club, meeting rooms, gift shop.

TAMPA DINING

From the landmark Columbia with its flamenco dancing to the flamboyant and pricey Bern's Steak House, Tampa offers a wide variety of fine restaurants. The menu choices range from typical American fare to regional southern dishes or Cajun/Créole cooking, as well as the cuisines of Spain, France, Italy, Germany, Mexico, and Asia.

And, like neighboring St. Petersburg, the Tampa area is outstanding for seafood—fresh from Tampa Bay, nearby gulf waters, and beyond. The port of Tampa is home to one of Florida's largest shrimp-boat fleets. Other local favorites include grouper, pompano, snapper, stone crabs, rock shrimp, and crayfish.

Above all, from the channels surrounding Harbour Island to the shores of Tampa Bay, this city is known for its waterfront dining, from romantic rooftop settings to rustic beachside decks. Even Tampa airport, so widely acclaimed as a transportation hub, has a great rooftop restaurant in its own right, the revolving CK's, with ever-changing views of nearby waters and the city skyline.

See Chapter 6, "St. Petersburg Dining," for general guidelines on reservations, tipping policies, alcoholic beverages, price ranges, and "early-bird" dining. Note, however, that the tax charged at Tampa restaurants is only 6.5%, not 7%.

1. DOWNTOWN/ HARBOUR ISLAND/ DAVIS ISLANDS

EXPENSIVE

HARBOUR VIEW ROOM, in the Wyndham Harbour Island Hotel, 725 S. Harbor Island Blvd., Harbour Island. Tel. 229-5001.
   Cuisine: AMERICAN. **Reservations:** Recommended.

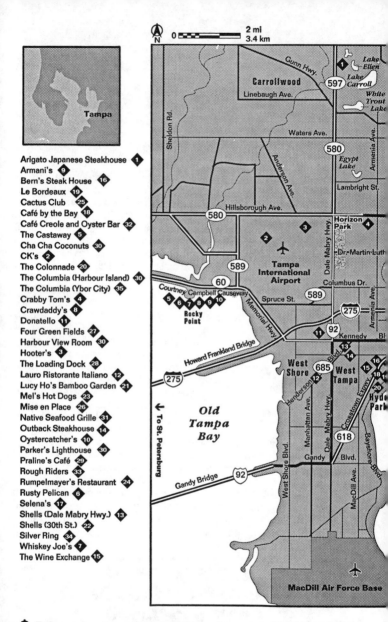

Arigato Japanese Steakhouse 1
Armani's 9
Bern's Steak House 16
Le Bordeaux 19
Cactus Club 25
Café by the Bay 18
Café Creole and Oyster Bar 32
The Castaway 5
Cha Cha Coconuts 30
CK's 2
The Colonnade 20
The Columbia (Harbour Island) 30
The Columbia (Ybor City) 35
Crabby Tom's 4
Crawdaddy's 8
Donatello 11
Four Green Fields 27
Harbour View Room 30
Hooter's 3
The Loading Dock 28
Lauro Ristorante Italiano 12
Lucy Ho's Bamboo Garden 21
Mel's Hot Dogs 23
Mise en Place 26
Native Seafood Grille 31
Outback Steakhouse 14
Oystercatcher's 10
Parker's Lighthouse 30
Praline's Café 29
Rough Riders 33
Rumpelmayer's Restaurant 24
Rusty Pelican 6
Selena's 17
Shells (Dale Mabry Hwy.) 13
Shells (30th St.) 22
Silver Ring 34
Whiskey Joe's 7
The Wine Exchange 15

$ Prices: Appetizers $2.95–$8.95; main courses $5.95–$11.95 at lunch, $16.95–$24.95 at dinner. AE, CB, DC, MC, V.

Open: Lunch Mon–Sat 11:30am–2:30pm, Sun 10:30am–2:30pm; dinner Mon–Sat 6–11pm, Sun 6–10pm.

With wide-windowed views of the waterways surrounding Harbour Island, subdued lighting, and classical music playing in the background, this romantic hotel eatery is an attraction in

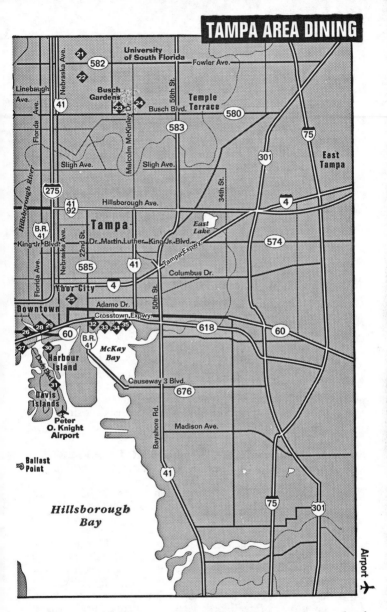

itself. Sit back, relax, watch the yachts glide by, and enjoy local seafoods and such specialties as poached salmon with pecan citrus sauce, herb-grilled lamb chops, or médaillons of veal with crab and béarnaise sauce, as well as prime rib roasted with rock salt and cut to order. Lunch offers these items plus burgers, sandwiches, salads, and pizzas. The wine list is extensive and so are the bottle prices, $16 to $350.

**ⓕ FROMMER'S SMART TRAVELER:
RESTAURANTS**

QUESTIONS TO ASK IF YOU ARE ON A BUDGET

1. Is an "early bird" dinner offered? If so, what are the prices and the hours of service?
2. Is the service charge included in the bill's total?
3. Is the 6.5% state tax included in the total?
4. Are there any specials today? What are the prices?
5. If you're traveling with kids, is there a children's menu?

MODERATE

THE COLUMBIA, 601 S. Harbor Island Blvd., Harbour Island. Tel. 229-2992.
  Cuisine: SPANISH. **Reservations:** Recommended.
$ **Prices:** Appetizers $1.95–$4.95; main courses $4.95–$8.95 at lunch, $7.95–$14.95 at dinner. AE, CB, DC, MC, V.
  Open: Daily 11am–11pm.

 Opened in 1985, this is the downtown version of the famous Ybor City landmark. Here, on Level 1 of the Market complex on Harbour Island, you get expansive views of the harbor instead of the Old Tampa ambience. It's worth sampling both venues for the contrast. For a description of the cuisine, see the entry under "Ybor City," below, in this chapter.

MISE EN PLACE, 420 W. Kennedy Blvd. Tel. 254-5373.
  Cuisine: AMERICAN. **Reservations:** Accepted only for parties of six or more.
$ **Prices:** Appetizers $2.50–$5.50; main courses $4.95–$7.95 at lunch, $9.95–$16.95 at dinner. AE, CB, DC, DISC, MC, V.
  Open: Lunch Mon–Fri 11am–3pm; dinner Tues–Thurs 5:30–10pm, Fri–Sat 5:30–11pm.

 With a fitting French name (meaning "everything in place"), this popular American bistro serves a beautifully presented innovative cuisine with the freshest of local ingredients—at moderate prices. Having built up a devoted following in its original West Platt Street location, it is now situated in swank new quarters three blocks west of downtown in the Grand Central Place complex, directly opposite the University of Tampa. It's easily walkable from most downtown hotels.

The menu changes daily, but dinner main courses often include such choices as roast duck with Jamaica wild-strawberry sauce, grilled swordfish with tri-melon mint salsa, and rack of lamb with hazelnut persillade. Lunch items range from unusual sandwiches, such as curried chicken and chutney or tarragon chicken with smoked

Gouda, sprouts, and lettuce on a croissant, to omelets with such unique fillings as corned beef, Swiss, and grated potatoes.

NATIVE SEAFOOD GRILLE, 238 E. Davis Blvd., Davis Islands. Tel. 254-9660.

Cuisine: FLORIDA/CARIBBEAN. **Reservations:** Accepted for parties of six or more; preferred seating for smaller parties.

$ Prices: Appetizers $2.95–$6.95; main courses $4.95–$6.95 at lunch, $7.95–$13.95 at dinner. AE, DISC, MC, V.

Open: Lunch Mon–Fri 11:30am–2:30pm, dinner Mon–Thurs 5–10pm, Fri 5–11pm; lunch/dinner Sat 11:30am–11pm, Sun 1–9pm.

Located just off Bayshore Boulevard and directly across from Harbour Island, this indoor-outdoor restaurant is in the middle of Davis Islands, a primarily residential area very convenient to downtown. With Caribbean art and music, lots of greenery, and an herbal garden, it exudes a tropical ambience. To add to the authenticity, many of the nuts, grains, spices, fruits, and edible flowers used are obtained from a nonprofit group that works with indigenous tribes around the world, such as Brazilian rain forest workers.

The menu includes jumbo shrimp marinated in a Brazil and macadamia nut pesto; sautéed grouper with sliced bananas and rum sauce; grilled salmon with key lime marinade in watercress dill sauce; crab cakes with mango-papaya salsa; smoked chicken with homemade jerk sauce and goat cheese; South American Churrasco beef with chimichurri marinade; and a variety of fruit and vegetable salads. There is also a fresh-fish market on the premises.

PARKER'S LIGHTHOUSE, 601 S. Harbour Island Blvd., Harbour Island. Tel. 229-3474.

Cuisine: SEAFOOD. **Reservations:** Recommended for dinner.

$ Prices: Appetizers $2.95–$11.95; main courses $6.95–$10.95 at lunch, $10.95–$20.95 at dinner. AE, MC, V.

Open: Lunch Mon–Thurs 11:30am–2:30pm, Fri–Sat 11:30am–2pm, Sun 10:30am–2:30pm; dinner Mon–Thurs 5:30–10pm, Fri–Sat 5:30–10:30pm, Sun 5–10pm.

 Overlooking the channels of the Hillsborough River and the Tampa skyline, this bright and airy restaurant on Level 2 of the Market complex on Harbour Island is a favorite for outdoor dining, but you can also sit indoors with the benefit of full air conditioning and enjoy the views through floor-to-ceiling windows. If you're fond of fish, this place is a must.

Choose from an ever-changing selection that ranges from shark to swordfish, snapper to salmon, sheepshead to Spanish mackerel, or yellowfin tuna to trout. Then decide how you'd like it prepared—sautéed, baked, broiled, or blackened, and with a choice of seasoned butters (from ginger-lime to chive-parsley or pine nut). No precooking here! The menu also includes lobsters, steaks, pastas, and chicken. It's a fun place to watch the boats go by, and the service is enthusiastic. Lunch items range from sandwiches, pastas, and salads to smaller portions of mesquite-grilled seafoods; the lower-level lounge also serves burgers and sandwiches throughout the day and evening.

PRALINES CAFE, Two Tampa City Center. Tel. 225-1234, ext. 7497.

Cuisine: AMERICAN. **Reservations:** Recommended.

$ **Prices:** Appetizers $3–$6; main courses $6.50–$16 at lunch or dinner. AE, CB, DC, DISC, MC, V.

Open: Daily 6:30am–11pm.

Housed on the ground level of the Hyatt Regency Hotel and situated overlooking the Esplanade of the Franklin Street Mall, this indoor-outdoor café is a good spot for some relaxing refreshment in the heart of downtown. The all-day menu features a variety of soups, salads, burgers, sandwiches, pastas, and fajitas, as well as specialty dishes such as rosemary chicken, ginger-orange red snapper, lamb T-bones, and filet mignon with jalapeño butter.

INEXPENSIVE

CHA CHA COCONUTS, 601 S. Harbour Island Blvd., Harbour Island. Tel. 223-3101.

Cuisine: AMERICAN. **Reservations:** Not required.

$ **Prices:** Appetizers $2.95–$6.95; main courses $3.95–$7.95. AE, DC, MC, V.

Open: Mon–Thurs 11am–10pm, Fri–Sat 11am–midnight, Sun noon–9pm.

Billed as a tropical bar and grill, this informal waterfront spot on the Level 1 of the Market complex on Harbour Island, with indoor and outdoor seating, is ideal for lunch or a light meal. The view is entrancing, and live music is often on tap. For details on the cuisine, see Chapter 6, "St. Petersburg Dining."

FOUR GREEN FIELDS, 205 W. Platt St. Tel. 254-4444.

Cuisine: IRISH/AMERICAN. **Reservations:** Not required.

$ **Prices:** Appetizers $1.50–$3.95; main courses $3.95–$8.95. AE, MC, V.

Open: Mon–Thurs 11am–midnight, Fri–Sat 11am–1am, Sun noon–midnight. **Closed:** Mar 18.

⭐ Although this charming whitewashed and thatched-roofed cottage looks like it belongs in the middle of Tipperary, it sits just one block west of the Tampa Convention Center. The menu, which is the same all day, presents salads and sandwiches with an Irish flair or traditional dishes such as fish-and-chips, beef stew braised in Guinness, shepherd's pie, or corned beef and cabbage. There is live Irish music on tap Tuesday through Thursday from 8pm to midnight and Friday and Saturday from 9pm to 1am.

THE LOADING DOCK, 100 Madison St., at Ashley St. Tel. 223-6905.

Cuisine: AMERICAN/DELI. **Reservations:** Not required.

$ **Prices:** All items $1.75–$4.95. No credit cards.

Open: Mon–Fri 8am–8pm, Sat 10:30am–2:30pm.

This midtown eatery is housed in a vintage Tampa building that was once the city's main loading dock for wholesale groceries. The menu plays on the "loading dock" theme, with sandwiches such as the "union boss" (hot corned beef, Swiss, and sauerkraut), the "box car" (salami and provolone), and the "forklift" (all-beef knockwurst with sauerkraut and spicy mustard). Salads and soups are also featured, and wine and beer are available.

A more modern branch is located at Austin Center West, 1408 N. Westshore Blvd. (tel. 289-5666).

---

2. HYDE PARK/BAYSHORE BOULEVARD

VERY EXPENSIVE

BERN'S STEAK HOUSE, 1208 S. Howard Ave. Tel. 251-2421.
    Cuisine: AMERICAN. **Reservations:** Required.
$ Prices: Main courses $13.80–$45. CB, DC, MC, V.
    Open: Dinner only, daily 5–11pm; dessert room open until 1am.

⭐ No visit to Tampa is complete without dinner at Bern Laxer's one-of-a-kind restaurant, an attraction in itself. Many people make reservations weeks in advance. Started on a small scale in 1953, and still totally unpretentious on the outside, it has grown into a two-story seven-room Tampa institution west of downtown at the corner of Marjory Avenue.

Above all, it's a temple of beef, where the motto is "Art in steaks." You order a prime, well-aged steak according to the thickness and weight you prefer, and then it's cut and broiled over charcoal to your exact desire. If beef is not your fancy, lamb or veal are also available. Depending on the season, most vegetables served at Bern's are grown in the restaurant's own organic garden, and the freshest of other ingredients—from creamery butter to coffee beans—are *de rigueur.* All main courses come with onion soup, salad, baked potato, garlic toast, and onion rings. If you'd like a bottle of wine with your meal, you're bound to find a favorite—the phonebook-size wine list offers more than 7,000 selections.

Desserts are yet another event, served upstairs in a unique room with piano bar and dance floor, plus over 40 plush booths built from wine casks, each featuring a TV set and a telephone for placing personal music requests. Choose from over 40 desserts, including bitter chocolate pâté, pistachio cake, and cappuccino parfait, plus cream drinks and "sipping desserts" made with liqueurs, sweet wines, and ports by the glass. It's possible to reserve a booth for dessert only, but preference is given to those who dine. (*Note:* Smoking is prohibited in six of the seven dining rooms.)

EXPENSIVE

SELENA'S, 1623 Snow Ave. Tel. 251-2116.
    Cuisine: CREOLE/SICILIAN. **Reservations:** Recommended.
$ Prices: Appetizers $4.95–$8.95; main courses $4.95–$8.95 at lunch, $7.95–$17.95 at dinner. AE, CB, DC, MC, V.

Open: Mon–Wed 11am–10pm, Thurs 11am–11pm, Fri–Sat 11am–midnight, Sun 11am–9pm.

Step into this charming restaurant west of downtown, in the Old Hyde Park Village shopping complex, and it feels like New Orleans, whether you sit in the plant-filled Patio Room, the eclectic Queen Anne Room, decked out with fireplace, chandeliers, linens, and lace, or the outdoor café. Open the menu and you'll see an interesting blend of dishes, reflecting the owners' family backgrounds. Local seafoods, especially grouper and shrimp, top the menu at dinner, with much of it served Créole style or blackened, as well as broiled and fried. Choices also include pastas, chicken, steaks, and veal. Desserts range from key lime pie to Cajun country bread pudding. Lunch items also include gumbos, salads, po'boy sandwiches, Italian sausages, casseroles, and quiches. In the evenings, jazz enlivens the atmosphere, as musical groups perform upstairs in a 200-seat lounge.

MODERATE

LE BORDEAUX, 1502 S. Howard Ave. Tel. 254-4387.
   Cuisine: FRENCH. **Reservations:** Accepted only for parties of six or more.
$ **Prices:** Appetizers $3–$6; main courses $5–$10 at lunch, $8–$16 at dinner. MC, V.
   Open: Lunch Mon–Sat 11:30am–2:30pm; dinner Mon–Sat 5:30–11pm, Sun 5:30–9:30pm.

Located in a residential neighborhood west of downtown, one block north of Bayshore Boulevard, this bungalow/bistro is a real find, with first-rate French food at affordable prices. The domain of French-born chef/owner Gordon Davis, it offers a homey ambience, with a choice of two dining rooms. The menu changes nightly and is usually confined to 10 main-course choices or fewer, but you can count on homemade pâtés and pastries. Specials often include bouillabaisse, pot au feu, salmon en croûte, veal with wild mushrooms, and filet of beef au Roquefort. Beer and wine only.

THE COLONNADE, 3401 Bayshore Blvd. Tel. 839-7558.
   Cuisine: AMERICAN/SEAFOOD. **Reservations:** Accepted only for large parties.
$ **Prices:** Appetizers $1.95–$5.95; main courses $4.95–$8.95 at lunch, $7.95–$16.95 at dinner. AE, DC, MC, V.
   Open: Sun–Thurs 11am–10pm, Fri–Sat 11am–11pm.

Nestled in a palm-shaded residential neighborhood overlooking Tampa Bay, this is one of the city's loveliest dining spots, with an appealing wood-and-glass decor. Established in 1935, it has grown from a drive-in soda stop to a 300-seat local institution. Popularity has its price, however, and sometimes lines at this no-reservations restaurant can be a bit discouraging. Most folks console themselves by sipping a frozen drink in the adjacent lounge.

Seafood, caught by the restaurant's own fishing fleet, is the big draw here, but prime rib, steaks, and chicken are also available. Specialties include grouper in lemon butter, crab-stuffed flounder, wild Florida alligator, Cajun catfish, broiled Florida lobster, and half a dozen varieties of shrimp dishes (from batter-dipped or crabmeat-stuffed to pecan-fried or scampi style). Combination platters are also popular. The restaurant is west of downtown, between Julia Street and El Prado Boulevard.

THE WINE EXCHANGE, 1611 W. Swann Ave. Tel. 254-9463.

Cuisine: AMERICAN. **Reservations:** Not accepted.

$ Prices: Appetizers $2.95–$5.95; main courses $4.95–$6.95 at lunch, $7.95–$12.95 at dinner. MC, V.

Open: Lunch Sun–Thurs 11:30am–4:30pm, Fri–Sat 11:30am–4:30pm; dinner Sun–Thurs 5:30–10:30pm, Fri–Sat 5:30–11:30pm.

With a European bistro-style atmosphere, this trendy restaurant in Old Hyde Park Village, between Rome and South Dakota Avenues, is a favorite for those who enjoy creative food and fine wines at affordable prices. Main courses at dinner range from five-cheese lasagne and smoked chicken ravioli to grilled chicken breast in Tai peanut sauce, grilled shrimp Cajun style, salmon filet baked in a Dijon mustard crust, and grilled Delmonico steak with roasted garlic. Lunch offers a mix of salads, sandwiches, pastas, and pizzas. Several dozen well-known and boutique wines are available by the glass to accompany the food.

INEXPENSIVE

CACTUS CLUB, 1601 Snow Ave. Tel. 251-4089.

Cuisine: AMERICAN SOUTHWEST. **Reservations:** Not required.

$ Prices: Appetizers $1.95–$5.95; main courses $4.95–$6.95 at lunch, $5.95–$11.95 at dinner. AE, CB, DC, MC, V.

Open: Mon–Thurs 11am–midnight, Fri–Sat 11am–1am, Sun 11am–11pm.

Big and brassy, yet casual and comfortable, this sometimes-noisy café radiates southwestern pizzazz in the heart of Old Tampa, (west of downtown in the Old Hyde Park Village shopping complex). It's an ideal spot to go if you're in the mood for southwestern salads, fajitas, tacos, enchiladas, chili, hickory-smoked baby back ribs, Texas-style pizzas, blackened chicken, or guacamole/green chili burgers.

CAFE BY THE BAY, 1350 S. Howard Ave. Tel. 251-6659.

Cuisine: AMERICAN. **Reservations:** Not required.

$ Prices: All items $2.95–$7.95. DISC, MC, V.

Open: Breakfast/lunch Mon–Sat 7am–2pm, Sun 8am–3pm.

The name may be a little misleading, since there are no water views (the location is west of downtown between Mississippi and Southview Avenues). It's close to the Old Hyde Park Village complex, so it makes a good pre- or postshopping refreshment stop. Early-morning fare includes waffles and omelets of all types. Lunch items range from salads and sandwiches (the Cuban sandwich is one of Tampa's best) to burgers and unusual sandwiches such as Italian Grill (spinach, tomatoes, mushrooms, and provolone), and the Hyde Parker (turkey and lean bacon topped with Cheddar cheese on an onion roll).

3. YBOR CITY

MODERATE

THE COLUMBIA, 2117 Seventh Ave. E., Ybor City. Tel. 248-4961.
Cuisine: SPANISH. **Reservations:** Recommended.
$ **Prices:** Appetizers $1.95–$4.95; main courses $4.95–$10.95 at lunch, $7.95–$16.95 at dinner. AE, CB, DC, MC, V.
Open: Daily 11am–11pm.

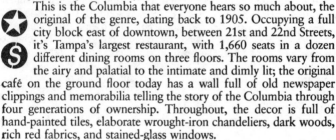

This is the Columbia that everyone hears so much about, the original of the genre, dating back to 1905. Occupying a full city block east of downtown, between 21st and 22nd Streets, it's Tampa's largest restaurant, with 1,660 seats in a dozen different dining rooms on three floors. The rooms vary from the airy and palatial to the intimate and dimly lit; the original café on the ground floor today has a wall full of old newspaper clippings and memorabilia telling the story of the Columbia through four generations of ownership. Throughout, the decor is full of hand-painted tiles, elaborate wrought-iron chandeliers, dark woods, rich red fabrics, and stained-glass windows.

Specialties include red snapper Alicante (baked in a casserole with sweet Spanish onions and green peppers, and topped with almonds, eggplant, and shrimp), filet mignon Columbia (a filet wrapped in bacon, with mushrooms, ham, onions, and green peppers in tomato and burgundy sauce), traditional chicken and yellow rice, and three types of spicy paellas. There are over a dozen other choices, such as red snapper en papillote, if you prefer to go easy on the spices; lobster is also available at higher prices. All main courses come with traditional Cuban bread, yellow rice, or potato. Salads are extra, but especially worth the extra bucks is the legendary "Original 1905 Salad"—lettuce, tomato, smoked ham, Swiss and Romano cheeses, olives, and lots more, with a house garlic dressing. At lunchtime, this salad is offered as a main course, as are mini-paellas, Cuban sandwiches, burgers, soups, omelets, and an assortment of tempting tapas. If you have a choice, though, come for dinner: Besides the legendary food, you'll also get a flamenco show (8:30pm Monday through Saturday; $5 cover charge).

CAFE CREOLE AND OYSTER BAR, 1330 E. Ninth Ave., Ybor City. Tel. 247-6283.
Cuisine: CREOLE/CAJUN. **Reservations:** Recommended.
$ **Prices:** Appetizers $2.95–$8.95; main courses $5.95–$12.95 at lunch, $8.95–$14.95 at dinner. AE, CB, DC, MC, V.
Open: Mon–Tues 11:30am–10pm, Wed–Thurs 11:30am–11pm, Fri–Sat noon–midnight, Sun noon–4pm.

The setting of this restaurant tells quite a tale about Ybor City history. The building, at the corner of Ninth Avenue and 14th Street, dating back to 1896, was originally known as El Pasaje, and was famous as the home of the Cherokee Club, a gentleman's hotel and private club with a casino, restaurant, and bar. Artisans were brought from Spain and Cuba to create spectacular stained-glass windows, wrought-iron balconies, Spanish murals, and marble bathrooms. Among the prominent guests were Theodore Roosevelt, Grover Cleveland, and many of Florida's governors. During the depression and the years after, the building was used variously as a political club, low-rent hotel, and WPA school of music, art, and dance. It was placed on the National Register of Historic Places in 1973, and new owners, the D'Avanza family from New Orleans, restored it in the 1980s as the Café Créole, complete with Louisiana-style cuisine and indoor-outdoor seating.

Specialties include Créole and Cajun dishes, such as red beans and rice with andouille sausage, blackened catfish, seafood gumbo, grouper Bienville, crayfish étouffé, and jambalaya. During the crawfish season (January through June), there is a Louisiana "crawfish and shrimp boil" on Wednesdays. The oyster bar also offers bayou country oysters served half a dozen ways. At lunch, you can also order po'boy sandwiches and salads. On most days, there is outdoor dining in an adjacent courtyard.

ROUGH RIDERS, 1901 13th St., Ybor City. Tel. 248-2756.
  Cuisine: AMERICAN. **Reservations:** Not required.
$ Prices: Appetizers $1.95–$3.95; main courses $3.95–$12.95. AE, MC, V.
  Open: Mon–Thurs 11:30am–midnight, Fri–Sat 11:30am–2am, Sun noon–6pm.

One of half a dozen eateries in the Ybor Square shopping complex at Eighth Avenue and 13th Street, this informal spot commemorates the 1898 visit of Teddy Roosevelt and his band of "Rough Riders" to Ybor City during the Spanish-American War. The theme is reflected in the pictures on the walls and the names of the items on the menu. Don't expect gourmet cuisine, but you'll get good hearty fare—burgers, steaks, prime rib, and sandwiches.

INEXPENSIVE

SILVER RING, 1831 E. Seventh Ave., Ybor City. Tel. 248-2549.
  Cuisine: SPANISH/AMERICAN. **Reservations:** Not required.
$ Prices: $2.25–$4.95. No credit cards.
  Open: Mon–Sat 6:30am–5pm.

Operating since 1947, this is now an Ybor City tradition, sort of an informal museum of life in this corner of Tampa, east of downtown, between 18th and 19th Streets. The walls are lined with old pictures, vintage radios, a 1950s jukebox, fishing rods, deer heads, and globes. Most of all, it is *the* place to come for a genuine Cuban sandwich—smoked ham, roast pork, Genoa salami, Swiss cheese, pickles, salad dressing, mustard, lettuce, and tomato on Cuban bread. At least 400 a day are sold here, and up to 800 on Friday and Saturday. Other items on the menu include Spanish bean soup, deviled crab, and other types of sandwiches. You can also buy some good locally made cigars.

4. AIRPORT/WEST SHORE

EXPENSIVE

CK's, in the Tampa Airport Marriott. Tel. 878-6500.
Cuisine: CONTINENTAL/AMERICAN. **Reservations:** Recommended. **Directions:** Follow the HOTEL signs at the airport; take the express elevator to the eighth floor.
$ Prices: Appetizers $4.95–$6.95; main courses $5.95–$11.95 at lunch, $16.95–$24.95 at dinner. AE, CB, DC, MC, V.
Open: Lunch Mon–Sat 11:30am–2:30pm; dinner Sun–Thurs 5–10pm, Fri–Sat 5–11pm; brunch Sun 10:30am–2:30pm.

In the heart of the airport, this is the only revolving rooftop restaurant in Tampa. Every table offers an ever-changing view spanning the adjacent jetways and more distant vistas of Tampa Bay and the city skyline.

The extensive dinner menu ranges from local seafoods to prime rib, steaks, and filet mignon. Specialties include veal Lemuel (sautéed with lobster, white asparagus, and hollandaise sauce), smoked swordfish, grilled marinated quail with pear brandy sauce, grilled southwest chicken with black bean salsa, and rack of lamb. Lunch items include soups, salads, burgers, omelets, seafood, and steaks.

DONATELLO, 232 N. Dale Mabry Hwy. Tel. 875-6660.
Cuisine: NORTHERN ITALIAN. **Reservations:** Recommended.
$ Prices: Appetizers $5.95–$9.95; main courses $11.95–$12.95 at lunch, $12.95–$23.95 at dinner. AE, CB, DC, DISC, MC, V.
Open: Lunch Mon–Fri noon–3pm; dinner daily 6–11pm.
Closed: Super Bowl Sun, Thanksgiving, and Christmas.

With stucco arches, Italian tile work, and peach-colored linens, this romantic restaurant south of the airport, two blocks north of Kennedy Boulevard (Fla. 60), has a Mediterranean atmosphere, artfully enhanced by soft individual table lighting and an attentive tuxedoed waiting staff.

The menu is similar at lunch and dinner, with slightly larger portions and more choices in the evening. Specialties include linguine with Maine lobster; breast of duck with Curaçao and orange sauce; veal "Dolce Vita," with ham, mushrooms, and truffles; salmon Stromboli, with asparagus, shrimp, and creamy white-wine sauce; and osso bucco alla milanese. All pastas and desserts are made on the premises. As a graceful final touch, each female diner is presented with a long-stemmed red rose. Valet parking.

MODERATE

CRABBY TOM'S OLD TIME OYSTER BAR AND SEAFOOD RESTAURANT, 3120 W. Hillsborough Ave. Tel. 870-1652.

Cuisine: SEAFOOD. **Reservations:** Accepted only for parties of 10 or more.

$ Prices: Appetizers $1.95–$5.95; main courses $4.99–$16.99. AE, DISC, MC, V.

Open: Mon–Thurs 11am–10pm, Fri–Sat 11am–11pm, Sun 4–9pm.

 As its name suggests, this informal eatery northwest of the airport, between Dale Mabry Highway and Armenia Avenue, is affiliated with Crabby Bill's of Indian Rocks Beach in the St. Pete area. Like its counterpart, this spot lacks waterside views and an impressive decor, but it puts major emphasis on the "crab" in Crabby. Sit back, relax, and crack open a pile of stone crab claws, Alaska snow crab claws, or king crab legs.

If you tire of crab, there's always a lobster from the 140-gallon tank, or an array of other seafood, from grouper, flounder, and catfish to shrimp, scallops, and mahimahi, as well as clams and oysters on the halfshell, or a "seafood feast" that presents a sampling of almost everything. Chicken, pasta, and barbecued ribs are also on the menu, but this is really a place for seafood lovers, with at least half a dozen daily or weekly maritime specials, usually announced by hand-made signs on the walls. As long as you don't mind a noisy down-on-the-dock atmosphere, picnic-table seating, and paper place-mat/menus, the prices are hard to beat anywhere. Wine and beer available.

OUTBACK STEAKHOUSE, 3304 Henderson Blvd. Tel. 875-4329.

Cuisine: AUSTRALIAN/AMERICAN. **Reservations:** Not accepted.

$ Prices: Appetizers $1.95–$5.95; main courses $7.95–$16.95. AE, DC, MC, V.

Open: Lunch Mon–Fri 11:30am–4pm; dinner Sun–Thurs 4–10:30pm, Fri–Sat 4–11:30pm.

For a description of the cuisine at this Aussie-style restaurant, south of the airport, east of Dale Mabry Highway, between Horatio and DeLeon Streets, see the entry in Chapter 6, "St. Petersburg Dining." A second Tampa branch is located north of the airport in the Carrollwood section of the city at 11620 N. Dale Mabry Hwy. (tel. 969-4329), open for dinner only, Sunday through Thursday from 4:30 to 10:30pm and on Friday and Saturday from 4:30 to 11:30pm.

LAURO RISTORANTE, 3915 Henderson Blvd. Tel. 281-2100.

Cuisine: ITALIAN. **Reservations:** Recommended.

$ Prices: Appetizers $3.95–$7.95; main courses $7.95–$9.95 at lunch, $7.95–$17.95 at dinner. AE, CB, DC, MC, V.

Open: Lunch Mon–Fri 11:30am–2:00pm, dinner Mon–Sat 6–11pm.

With a classic decor, soft music, tuxedoed waiters, and a kitchen presided over by award-winning chef Lauro Medaglia, this restaurant is a little off the beaten track, but well worth a detour southwest of downtown and west of the Dale Mabry Highway. The menu includes six different veal dishes; steak flamed in a cream sauce of brandy and green peppercorns; chicken breast with eggplant, mozzarella, and tomatoes; sweetbreads with prosciutto; and jumbo marinated grilled shrimp; as well as over a dozen freshly made pastas such as fettuccine Alfredo, cannelloni, tortellini, and gnocchi con Gorgonzola (potato dumplings with Gorgonzola cream sauce).

INEXPENSIVE

HOOTERS, 4215 W. Hillsborough Ave. Tel. 885-3916.
Cuisine: AMERICAN. **Reservations:** Not accepted.
$ **Prices:** Appetizers $1.95–$4.95; main courses $2.95–$14.95. AE, MC, V.
Open: Mon–Fri 11am–midnight, Sat 11am–1am, Sun noon–10pm.

Though it's located far from the beach, north of the airport between Westshore Boulevard and Dale Mabry Highway, a year-round beach-party atmosphere prevails at this typical Tampa Bay eatery. For a description of the decor and the menu, see the entry for the original Hooters across the bay in Clearwater (Chapter 6, "St. Petersburg Dining"). Beer and wine served.

SHELLS, 202 S. Dale Mabry Hwy. Tel. 875-3467.
Cuisine: SEAFOOD. **Reservations:** Not accepted.
$ **Prices:** Appetizers $1.95–$4.95; main courses $4.95–$13.95. AE, MC, V.
Open: Dinner only, Sun–Thurs 5–10pm, Fri–Sat 5–11pm.
Closed: Thanksgiving and Christmas.

 In the Tampa Bay area, Shells is a local institution, known for fresh seafood at low prices. Founded in 1985, this restaurant has since been cloned in over 20 other locations in Florida and as far away as Atlanta and Nashville. This inconspicuous spot, south of the airport and two blocks south of Kennedy Boulevard, between Azelle and Platt Streets, is the original, the one that set the standards for the others—simple seafood menu, no frills, no reservations, and, above all, no strain on the budget. You'll probably have to wait at least a half hour to be seated, and then you'll eat at picnic-style tables, but the food is worth it.

The menu features hefty portions of Alaskan king crab legs and claws, Dungeness crab clusters, snow crab, scallops, shrimp, grouper, cod, and pasta combinations such as shrimp with cheese tortellini. More elaborate dishes range from shrimp Fra Diablo to seafood Newburg. Nightly specials often include Maine lobsters or baby-lobster pasta. There are a few beef and chicken choices. Beer and wine available.

Other locations in the Tampa area: 14380 N. Dale Mabry Hwy. (tel. 968-6686), north of the airport, with a full bar; and 11010 N. 30th St. (tel. 977-8456), in the Busch Gardens area, serving beer and wine.

5. COURTNEY CAMPBELL CAUSEWAY AREA

EXPENSIVE

ARMANI'S, in the Hyatt Regency Westshore Hotel, 6200 Courtney Campbell Causeway. Tel. 281-9165.
Cuisine: NORTHERN ITALIAN. **Reservations:** Recommended. **Directions:** Follow Fla. 60 west of the airport to the hotel; the restaurant is on the 14th floor.
$ **Prices:** Appetizers $4–$8.50; main courses $10.75–$24.75. AE, CB, DC, DISC, MC, V.
Open: Dinner only, Mon–Thurs 5–10pm, Fri–Sat 5–11pm.
Overlooking Old Tampa Bay, this romantic rooftop restaurant is a favorite with the locals as well as hotel guests. Most of the windows face west, making it an ideal place to watch sunsets while savoring fine cuisine with impeccable service.

Veal selections are particularly notable, such as scaloppine with mushroom-cream cognac and black-and-white truffle sauce, or veal chop with Frangelico cognac, sun-dried tomatoes, and cream. Other specialties include Black Angus filet mignon with three peppercorns; filet of Norwegian salmon; and lobster Fra Diablo. The antipasto bar and the wine list are extensive, and all pastas and gourmet pizzas are made on the premises. Free or valet parking.

RUSTY PELICAN, 2425 Rocky Point Dr. Tel. 281-1943.
Cuisine: CONTINENTAL/SEAFOOD. **Reservations:** Recommended. **Directions:** Follow Fla. 60 west of the airport to Courtney Campbell Causeway; turn left at Rocky Point Dr.
$ **Prices:** Appetizers $2.95–$8.95; main courses $13.95–$20.95 at dinner. AE, CB, DC, MC, V.

Ⓕ FROMMER'S COOL FOR KIDS: RESTAURANTS

CK's (see p. 198) A revolving rooftop restaurant with views of airplanes taking off and landing.

Mels' Hot Dogs (see p. 205) For hot dogs of all styles, topped with anything a little heart desires.

Parker's Lighthouse (see p. 191) Offers great views of the passing boats and balloons for little diners.

Rough Riders (see p. 197) For burgers, steaks, and sandwiches amid pictures portraying the escapades of Teddy Roosevelt and his troops during the Spanish-American War.

Open: Dinner Mon–Sat 5–11pm, Sun 5–10pm; brunch Sun 11am–3pm.

 Situated on Old Tampa Bay at the south end of Rocky Point Drive, this is the top spot in a cluster of three restaurants that also includes Crawdaddy's and Whiskey Joe's. The decor, which features two huge stone fireplaces, ceiling-high potted trees, fine crystal, and pastel-toned linens, is enhanced by views of the water in a relaxing and romantic setting. As at all the restaurants along this strip, the sunset hour is prime time here.

The innovative menu features such seafood main courses as shrimp chardonnay, Florida mixed grill (shrimp, lobster, and tuna over pasta), and scallops with linguine, as well as specialty dishes, like steak Diane, charbroiled lamb chops, and chicken Jack Daniels.

MODERATE

THE CASTAWAY, 7720 Courtney Campbell Causeway. Tel. 281-0770.
　　Cuisine: AMERICAN/POLYNESIAN/SEAFOOD. **Reservations:** Accepted for dinner, with seating at the first available table at the time requested. **Directions:** Follow Fla. 60 west of the airport; the restaurant is visible on the left after Rocky Point Dr.
$ Prices: Appetizers $2.95–$10.95; main courses $5.95–$12.95 at lunch, $13.95–$19.95 at dinner. AE, CB, DC, MC, V.
　　Open: Lunch Mon–Fri 11am–4pm, Sat–Sun 11am–4pm; dinner Mon–Thurs 5–10pm, Fri–Sat 5–midnight, Sun 5–10pm; brunch Sun 9:30am–2:30pm.
Situated just east of the Ben T. Davis Municipal Beach, the Castaway bills itself as Tampa's only beachfront restaurant. The building rests on stilts over the waters of Old Tampa Bay, making the views hard to equal.

The menu is a blend of seafaring specials with a Polynesian influence. Choices at dinner range from seafood brochettes, bouillabaisse, and stir-fry dishes, to shrimp curry, coconut shrimp, and scallops chardonnay. Nonseafood selections include Hawaiian chicken, pastas, prime ribs, and steaks. Salads, sandwiches, burgers, and seafood platters are available at lunch.

CRAWDADDY'S, 2500 Rocky Point Dr. Tel. 281-0407.
　　Cuisine: REGIONAL/SEAFOOD. **Reservations:** Recommended. **Directions:** Follow Fla. 60 west of the airport to Courtney Campbell Causeway and turn left on Rocky Point Dr.
$ Prices: Appetizers $2.95–$6.95; main courses $4.95–$10.95 at lunch, $10.95–$17.95 at dinner. AE, CB, DC, MC, V.
　　Open: Lunch Mon–Fri 11am–3pm; dinner Mon–Thurs 5–10pm, Fri–Sat 5pm–midnight, Sun 5–10pm.

Situated on Old Tampa Bay in the same cul-de-sac as the Rusty Pelican, this more informal spot is named after Beauregard "Crawdaddy" Belvedere, a Roaring '20s tycoon. He owned a fish camp on this site that attracted guests from near and far for dining and entertainment. The decor here has not changed much since those days—there are seven dining rooms, spread over three levels, all bedecked with Victorian furnishings, books, pictures, and collectibles, and all sharing wide-windowed views of the bay.

The "down home"—style menu ranges from beer-battered shrimp-and-fish camp fry (shrimp, scallops, and fresh fish, deep-fried in corn crisp and almond coating, with jalapeño hush puppies) to fried grouper fingers, beer-battered shrimp, prime rib, and steaks. Lunch fare includes soups, salads, sandwiches, burgers, pastas, and seafood. Stir-fry dishes, raw-bar selections, and jambalayas are also featured at both lunch and dinner.

OYSTERCATCHERS, 6200 Courtney Campbell Causeway. Tel. 281-9116.

Cuisine: SEAFOOD. **Reservations:** Recommended. **Directions:** Follow Fla. 60 west of the airport to the Hyatt Regency Westshore Hotel; restaurant is behind the hotel on the water.

$ Prices: Appetizers $3.95–$7.95; main courses $7.95–$11.95 at lunch, $13.95–$20.95 at dinner. AE, CB, DC, DISC, MC, V.

Open: Lunch Mon–Fri 11:30am–2:30pm, Sun 10:30am–3pm; dinner Sun–Thurs 6–10:30pm, Fri–Sat 6–11pm.

Nestled on the edge of a 35-acre nature preserve overlooking Old Tampa Bay, this restaurant is housed in a freestanding Key West–style building, connected by a 250-foot boardwalk to the Hyatt Regency Westshore complex. The atmosphere is casual, with indoor and outdoor seating and a decor of light blue and green sea tones, white patio-style furniture, and wide windows that give every table a view of the water.

The lunch menu offers salads, seafoods, and specialty dishes such as mesquite-grilled fish, hibachi chicken, lobster pita, and seared peppered tuna. Dinner choices focus primarily on "catch-of-the-day" seafoods, prepared in a variety of ways, from mesquite-grilled to blackened, sautéed, or poached. Local favorites include rock shrimp in snail butter and parchment-baked red snapper. There's also a variety of steaks, plus rack of lamb, and duck.

INEXPENSIVE

WHISKEY JOE'S, 2500 Rocky Point Dr. Tel. 281-0577.

Cuisine: REGIONAL/AMERICAN. **Reservations:** Accepted only for parties of 10 or more. **Directions:** Follow Fla. 60 west of the airport to Courtney Campbell Causeway and turn left on Rocky Point Dr.

$ Prices: Appetizers $2.95–$5.95; main courses $4.95–$11.95 at lunch or dinner. AE, CB, DC, MC, V.

Open: Lunch Mon–Fri 11:30am–2:30pm; dinner Sun–Thurs 5–11pm, Fri–Sat 5–1am; brunch Sun noon–3pm.

Adjacent to Crawdaddy's, this casual spot looks like an old shack on the outside, and isn't much better within, but that's part of its appeal. Peanut shells clutter the floor, the piped-in music can be a bit loud, and the menu is limited, but a relaxed, "let's-have-fun" atmosphere prevails. It does offer a choice of indoor or outdoor seating overlooking Old Tampa Bay. Favorite items on the menu include conch chowder, beer-cheese soup, burgers, peel-and-eat shrimp, conch fritters, buffalo wings, mesquite-broiled fish, and barbecued baby back ribs.

6. BUSCH GARDENS AREA

MODERATE

ARIGATO JAPANESE STEAKHOUSE, 13755 N. Dale Mabry Hwy. Tel. 960-5050.
Cuisine: JAPANESE. **Reservations:** Recommended on weekends.
$ Prices: Appetizers $2.95–$4.95; main courses $8.95–$17.95. AE, CB, DC, DISC, MC, V.
Open: Dinner only, Mon–Thurs 5–10pm, Fri–Sat 5–10:30pm, Sun 4–9pm.

This restaurant northwest of Busch Gardens in the Carrollwood section, one block north of Fletcher Avenue, is a favorite in the Tampa Bay area and has won many local awards. For a full description, see Chapter 6, "St. Petersburg Dining."

LUCY HO'S BAMBOO GARDEN, 2740 E. Fowler Ave. Tel. 977-2783.
Cuisine: CHINESE. **Reservations:** Accepted only for parties of five or more.
$ Prices: Appetizers $1.95–$9.95; main courses $5.95–$19.95; lunch buffet $6.50. AE, DC, DISC, MC, V.
Open: Mon–Sat 11:30am–10pm, Sun 11:30am–9pm.

A standout in the Asian-cuisine category, this restaurant usually comes out on top in reader polls taken by local newspapers and magazines. There are two branches, but this one is the original and well worth trying. The menu features a blend of Mandarin, Cantonese, and Szechuan dishes, such as Mongolian beef, cashew chicken, pepper steak, and whole fish Hunan-style. Chinese alcohol and beer are also available. The restaurant is northwest of Busch Gardens in University Collection Shopping Center, just west of the USF campus.

The second branch is located in the Greenhouse Shopping Center at 3611 W. Hillsborough Ave., at Dale Mabry Highway (tel. 874-8818).

RUMPELMAYER'S RESTAURANT, 4812 E. Busch Blvd. Tel. 989-9563.
Cuisine: GERMAN/EUROPEAN. **Reservations:** Recommended.
$ Prices: Appetizers $2.95–$6.95; main courses $3.95–$9.95 at lunch, $7.50–$17.50 at dinner. AE, CB, DC, DISC, MC, V.
Open: Daily 11am–11pm.

Eight blocks east of Busch Gardens at 48th Street, in the Ambassador Square Shopping Center, this small (60-seat) old-world restaurant is presided over by Lou Rumpelmayer, a former chef on the *Delta Queen* steamboat and at various Hilton hotels throughout the world. He has aptly paired his culinary experience and native background to create an authentic bit of Bavaria within walking distance of Busch Gardens.

Tasty and traditional main courses range from Heringsalat (a cold plate of North Sea herring with red beets, apples, and onions), to assorted wursts, wienerschnitzel, sauerbraten, Hungarian stuffed cabbage, and Polish kolbaszi. Seafood lovers take delight in the smoked mackerel from the North Sea, Garnalen (shrimp scampi with Moselle wine), and Dutch flounder sautéed in brown butter. All come with German potato salad and a choice of kraut. Live German music is usually on tap, as are more than 20 European beers and wines.

INEXPENSIVE

MEL'S HOT DOGS, 4136 E. Busch Blvd. Tel. 985-8000.
   Cuisine: AMERICAN. **Reservations:** Not accepted.
$ **Prices:** All items $3–$6. No credit cards.
   Open: Mon–Sat 10am–10pm, Sun 11am–9pm.

If you crave an old-fashioned Chicago-style all-beef hot dog before or after a foray into the African atmosphere of Busch Gardens, look no further. Considered the "big daddy" of hot-dog eateries, this informal establishment a block east of Busch Gardens at 42nd Street, specializes in hot-dog dishes, from "bagel dogs" to bacon, Cheddar or corn dogs. Most choices are served on a poppy-seed bun, and most come with french fries and a choice of coleslaw or baked beans. Even the decor is dedicated to wieners, with walls and windows lined with hot-dog memorabilia. Just in case hot-dog mania hasn't won you over, there are a few alternative choices (sausages, chicken breast, and burgers). But the biggest attraction is Mel himself (Mel Lohn), an enthusiastic Tampa entrepreneur who is invariably on the scene—greeting guests at the door, manning the order desk, or mingling among the tables. Beer and wine available.

SHELLS, 11010 N. 30th St. Tel. 977-8456.
   Cuisine: SEAFOOD. **Reservations:** Not accepted.
$ **Prices:** Appetizers $1.95–$4.95; main courses $3.95–$6.95 at lunch, $4.95–$13.95 at dinner. AE, MC, V.
   Open: Sun–Thurs 11:30am–10pm, Fri–Sat 11:30am–11pm.
   Closed: Thanksgiving and Christmas.

This Shells is north of Busch Gardens, between Bougainvillea and Fowler Avenues. For a full description, see the main branch listing under "Airport/West Shore," above in this chapter.

7. RESTAURANTS BY CUISINE

AMERICAN

Lauro Ristorante (*M*), 199
Selena's, Hyde Park (*E*), 193

JAPANESE
Arigato Japanese Steakhouse, Busch Gardens area (*M*), 204

POLYNESIAN
The Castaway, Courtney Campbell Causeway area (*M*), 202

REGIONAL
Crawdaddy's, Courtney Campbell Causeway area (*M$*), 202
Whiskey Joe's, Courtney Campbell Causeway area (*I*), 203

SEAFOOD
The Castaway, Courtney Campbell Causeway area (*M*), 202
The Colonnade, Bayshore Boulevard (*M$*), 194
Crabby Tom's Old Time Oyster Bar and Seafood Restaurant, airport
  (*M$*), 198
Crawdaddy's, Courtney Campbell Causeway area (*M$*), 202
Oystercatchers, Courtney Campbell Causeway area (*M**), 203
Parker's Lighthouse, Harbour Island (*M$*), 191
Rusty Pelican, Courtney Campbell Causeway area (*E**), 201
Shells, Busch Gardens area (*I$*), 205
Shells, West Shore & airport area locations (*I$*), 200

SPANISH
The Columbia, Harbour Island (*M$*), 190
The Columbia, Ybor City (*M$**), 196
Silver Ring, Ybor City (*I*), 197

KEY TO ABBREVIATIONS: *E* = Expensive; *I* = Inexpensive;
M = Moderately Priced; *VE* = Very Expensive; * = an Author's
Favorite; $ = Super-Special Value

WHAT TO SEE & DO IN TAMPA

A business and recreational hub, Tampa is a city of many parts. From the sleek skyscrapers downtown and near the airport, to the historic districts of Ybor City and Hyde Park or the exotic habitats of Busch Gardens, this city offers much to see and do.

Suggested Itineraries

If You Have 1 Day Take your pick— Busch Gardens or downtown Tampa. It's hard to narrow the choice to one or the other, but the theme park offers so many activities, shows, and sights, that it takes at least eight hours to do it justice. Since Busch Gardens is one of the top tourist attractions in Florida, it's obvious that most visitors head there as a top priority. If you prefer to see what makes Tampa tick as a city, however, explore downtown. Walk the Franklin Street Mall. Visit the new Florida Aquarium, Tampa Bay Performing Arts Center, and the Tampa Museum of Art. Tour the convention center, and then take the People Mover over to Harbour Island for some shopping, a meal overlooking the water, and perhaps a gondola ride to cap the day.

If You Have 2 Days Take the first day to explore downtown and Harbour Island and the next day head up to Busch Gardens. Plan to spend part of a day in Ybor City, Tampa's Latin Quarter, winding up at the landmark Columbia restaurant in time to see its famous flamenco show.

If You Have 3 Days Assuming you've seen the best of downtown, Harbour Island, and Busch Gardens, take a drive to some of the nearby attractions, such as the H. B. Plant Museum, Bayshore Boulevard, or Old Hyde Park Village. If you want to take a stroll on a nearby beach or see the sun set over Old Tampa Bay, head to the Courtney Campbell Causeway area. You might prefer to spend an afternoon at Tampa Bay Downs, the Tampa Greyhound Track, Tampa Jai-Alai, or Seminole Bingo.

If You Have 5 or More Days There's lots more to see, from Lowry Park Zoo to the Seminole Indian Village, or the Museum of Science and Industry. Take time to browse at the many area shopping malls. Check the local papers to see if there's a game or major concert on at Tampa Stadium or the USF Sun Dome, or take a drive to Plant City to watch the Tampa Bay Polo Club play at Walden

Lake. From Tampa, it's just a half-hour drive westward to St. Petersburg and the gulf coast beaches. You can also head inland to such nearby attractions as Walt Disney World and Disney–MGM Studios, EPCOT Center, Cypress Gardens, and Universal Studios–Florida.

1. THE TOP ATTRACTIONS

BUSCH GARDENS, 3000 E. Busch Blvd., Tampa. Tel. 987-5000 or 987-5082 for recorded information.

Founded 35 years ago as a hospitality garden for the local Anheuser-Busch brewery, this 300-acre family entertainment center has grown to become the most popular attraction on Florida's west coast. Designed to reflect the atmosphere of turn-of-the-century Africa, the park contains one of the largest collections of free-roaming wild animals in the U.S., as well as dozens of rides, live entertainment, restaurants, and shops. It's divided into eight distinct sections:

Timbuktu, an ancient desert trading center, features African artisans at work, a shopping bazaar, and a theater featuring dolphin shows, plus a "sandstorm" ride, boat swing ride, roller coaster, and electronic-games arcade. This area also contains one of the best places to eat, Das Festhaus, a 1,200-seat dining hall with German-style food, music, and dancing.

Morocco is a walled city with elaborate tilework and exotic architecture, Moroccan craft demonstrations, a sultan's tent with snake charmers, and the Moroccan Palace Theater, which presents an extravagant ice show.

Serengeti Plain, a serene and open area, is home to hippos, buffalo, impala, gazelles, reticulated giraffes, black rhinos, elephants, and ostriches. Visitors can observe the animals, without disturbing them, from a passing steam locomotive or via overhead skyrides and monorails.

Nairobi is home to Myombe Reserve: The Great Ape Domain, a natural habitat for various types of gorillas and chimpanzees, and a baby-animal nursery, as well as a petting zoo, reptile displays, and Nocturnal Mountain, where a simulated environment allows visitors to observe animals that are active in the dark.

Stanleyville, a prototype African village, features a shopping bazaar and live entertainment, as well as two water rides—the Tanganyika Tidal Wave and Stanley Falls. **The Congo** features Kumba, the largest steel roller coaster in the southeastern U.S., and Claw Island, a display of rare white Bengal tigers in a natural setting, plus white-water raft rides. **Bird Gardens,** the original core of Busch Gardens, boasts rich foliage, lagoons, and hundreds of exotic birds including golden and American bald eagles, hawks, owls, and falcons, as well as a walk-through, free-flight aviary. And **Crown Colony,** the newest area of the park, is the home of a team of Clydesdale horses as well as a multilevel restaurant, an old-world gift shop, and the Anheuser-Busch hospitality center. The newest attraction, Questor, a flight simulator, is also located in this area.

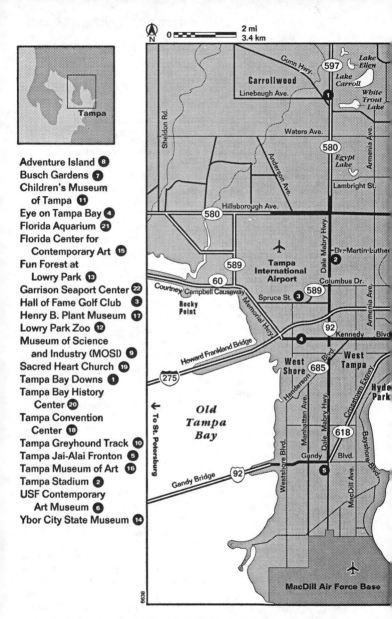

In total, there are more than 3,700 animals, birds, and reptiles and
many types of live entertainment. All this, plus the Anheuser-Busch
brewery tour (self-guided) to observe the beer-making process and an
opportunity to sample the famous brews.

To get the most from your visit, arrive early and allow at least eight
hours. Start the day by taking one or two of the rides that circle the
park (the air-conditioned monorail, open-air skyride, or the train) to
get a feel for the scope and location of the various attractions. The

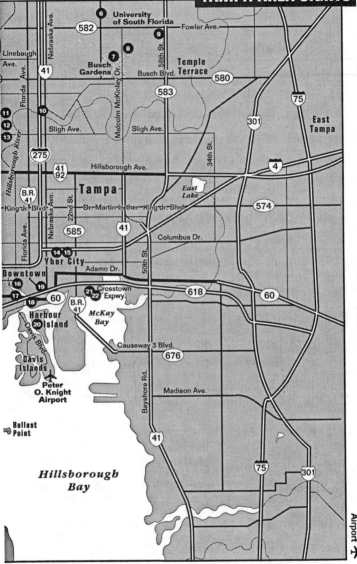

admission price covers all rides, shows, and attractions except arcade or video games.

Admission: $31.90 adults, $25.50 children 3–9, free for children 2 and under. Parking is $3.

Open: Daily 9am–6pm, with extended hours in summer and during holiday periods. **Directions:** Take I-275 to Busch Blvd. (Exit 33), and go east two miles to the park entrance on 40th St. (McKinley Dr.).

✪ FROMMER'S FAVORITE TAMPA EXPERIENCES

A Gondola Trip Cruise by Tampa's landmarks along the Hillsborough River and Tampa Bay on board an authentic gondola.

Strolling Down the Franklin Street Mall A relaxing respite in an oasis of trees, flowers, and waterfalls, amid the skyscrapers of downtown Tampa.

Taking a Ride on the People Mover Whisk your way between downtown Tampa and Harbour Island in 90 seconds.

Along Bayshore Boulevard Drive, walk, or run along the 6.3-mile scenic sidewalk overlooking Hillsborough Bay.

Skating in the Streets Follow or join the Radiant Rollers as they glide through the streets of Tampa on Friday and Saturday nights.

Meandering in Ybor City Listen to the Spanish melodies in the air, peek into artists' studios, sip a cup of strong Cuban coffee in a café, or just savor the diverse aromas—from freshly baked breads to hand-rolled cigars.

Down on the Docks Watch the shrimp boats unload a day's catch at Hooker Point, off the 22nd Street Causeway in South Tampa.

FLORIDA AQUARIUM, 300 S. 13th St., Tampa. Tel. 229-8861.

✪ With a shell-shaped glass dome, this new $84 million aquarium stands out along the newly developing strip of waterside attractions between downtown and Ybor City. Slated to open in April 1995, it tells the story of Florida's water, from underground source to open sea. The exhibits—which contain over 4,300 animals and plants representing 550 species native to Florida—focus on the state's wetlands, beaches, bays, saw grass marshes, swamps, mangrove forests, and the Everglades, along with a signature half-million gallon Coral Reefs Exhibit.

Admission and opening hours: Not final at press time, but expected to be approximately $12 adults. **Directions:** From downtown convention center, turn east on Platt St.; go approximately half a mile to aquarium.

GARRISON SEAPORT CENTER, Port of Tampa, 13th and Platt Sts., Tampa. Tel. 248-1924.

⭐ Rising on the Tampa skyline adjacent to the Florida Aquarium, this facility is a new hub of waterfront activity for downtown Tampa. Slated for a spring 1995 opening, it is comprised of two new passenger cruise terminals serving the various lines that offer cruise trips from Tampa—including Holland America, Regency Cruises, OdessAmerica, Carnival Cruise Lines, and American Family Cruises (see "Cruises," below in this chapter).

Entertainment also plays a large part at this new center, with a 16,000-seat music amphitheater, a music-themed restaurant, a comedy hall of fame and comedy club, nightclub, recording studios, music superstore, music-oriented shops, and food court.

To familiarize visitors with these developments at the Port of Tampa, there are two-hour tours of the seaport area, departing each Wednesday at 10am from the Garrison Cruise Terminal. Tours are free, but space is limited; reservations suggested.

Admission and opening hours: Not final at press time. **Directions:** From downtown convention center, turn east on Platt St.; go approximately half a mile to aquarium.

TAMPA MUSEUM OF ART, 601 Doyle Carlton Dr., Tampa. Tel. 223-8130.

⭐ Situated on the east bank of the Hillsborough River south of the Tampa Bay Performing Arts Center, off Ashley Drive, this visual arts complex offers seven galleries with changing exhibits ranging from classical antiquities to contemporary art, sculpture, photography, and crafts. Permanent exhibits include the Joseph Veach Noble Collection of Greek and Roman antiquities, and the C. Paul Jennewein sculpture collection.

Admission: $3.50 adults, $3 seniors, $2.50 children 6–18, free for children under 6. Free for everyone Sat 10am–1pm.

Open: Tues and Thurs–Sat 10am–5pm, Wed 10am–9pm, Sun 1–5pm; tours Wed and Sat–Sun at 1pm. **Directions:** Take I-275 to Exit 25 (Ashley Dr.).

HENRY B. PLANT MUSEUM, 401 W. Kennedy Blvd. (Fla. 60), Tampa. Tel. 254-1891.

⭐ A unique vision along the Tampa skyline, this landmark was modeled after the Alhambra Palace in Spain, with distinctive Moorish architecture topped by 13 silver minarets. It was built as the 511-room Tampa Bay Hotel in 1891, at an outrageous cost (for those days) of $2 million, by railroad tycoon Henry B. Plant, who filled it with priceless art and furnishings from Europe and Asia.

Although it ceased to operate as a hotel in 1930, the building was saved by the University of Tampa and was declared a National Historic Landmark in 1977. Today the ground-floor rooms have been converted into a museum, filled with elegant displays of Victoriana, Venetian mirrors, Wedgwood china, Louis XV and XVI furniture, and other original art objects and fashions that hark back to the hotel's heyday.

Admission: Suggested donation $3 adults, $1 children 12 and under.

Open: Tues–Sat 10am–4pm, Sun noon–4pm.

TAMPA BAY HISTORY CENTER, 601 S. Harbour Island Blvd., Harbour Island. Tel. 228-0097.

Located on the second level of The Shops on Harbour Island complex, this attraction is still in the development stages. At the moment, you can visit a "preview center" or planning facility, giving a sampling of what is to come. The completed center, projected for a 1996–97 debut, will be a full-size regional history museum and education center. The present mini-museum contains exhibits on the history of Hillsborough County and the Tampa Bay region from the 1500s to today. Lectures, workshops, and presentations on history, archeology, antiques, and collectibles are held monthly; call for the schedule.

Admission: Free.
Open: Mon–Sat 10am–9pm, Sun 1–4pm.

FLORIDA CENTER FOR CONTEMPORARY ART, 1513 E. Eighth Ave., Ybor City. Tel. 248-1171.

This is Tampa's avant-garde showplace, a gallery for alternative visual arts and the hub of a growing creative colony in Ybor City, northeast of downtown between 17th and 18th Streets. Members of the Artists Alliance who exhibit at this nonprofit space offer many of their works for sale.

Admission: Free.
Open: Wed–Sat 1–4pm.

USF CONTEMPORARY ART MUSEUM, Building FAM 101, University of South Florida, 4202 E. Fowler Ave., Tampa. Tel. 974-2849.

Northeast of downtown, one block north of Busch Gardens, between Fowler and Fletcher Avenues, on West Holly Drive on the western side of the campus, this 10,630-square-foot facility spotlights artists and artworks from around the world. In particular, there are valuable collections of pre-Columbian and African artifacts, as well as contemporary prints from the southeastern United States.

Admission: Free.
Open: Mon–Fri 10am–5pm, Sat 1–4pm.

YBOR CITY STATE MUSEUM, 1818 Ninth Ave., Ybor City. Tel. 247-6323.

The focal point of Ybor City, this museum is housed in the former Ferlita Bakery (1896–1973), a century-old yellow brick building northeast of downtown, between 18th and 19th Streets. Various exhibits in the museum depict the political, social, and cultural influences that shaped this section of Tampa. There is particular emphasis on the cigar industry and the fact that Ybor City was once known as the "cigar capital of the world."

You can take a self-guided tour around the museum, which includes a collection of cigar labels, cigar memorabilia, and works by local artisans. Adjacent to the museum is Preservation Park, the site of three renovated cigar workers' cottages, furnished as they were at the turn of the century. Other historic sights nearby include Ybor Square, formerly the largest cigar factory in the world and now converted into a shopping plaza (see "Savvy Shopping," below in this

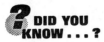

chapter); El Pasaje Hotel, a splendid example of Spanish-American architecture and now the Café Créole (see Chapter 10, "Tampa Dining"), the Cuban Club, a social and fraternal society that dates back to 1902; and José Martí Park, a small plot of land dedicated in honor of a Cuban revolutionary hero.

Admission: Museum, $1 adults and children 6 and up, free for children under 6; tours of cigar workers' cottages, $1 extra per person.

Open: Tues–Sat 9am–noon and 1–5pm.

SEMINOLE INDIAN VILLAGE, 5221 N. Orient Rd., Tampa. Tel. 621-7349.

Located on Tampa's Seminole Reservation, this museum is designed to trace the history of the Seminoles in the area. It's laid out in an eight-sided-star configuration, representing the eight clans of the tribe. The structures include chickees (thatched huts built in the style of 150 years ago), which shelter skilled Seminole craftspeople as they practice beadwork, wood carving, basketmaking, and patchwork sewing. Other more lively demonstrations include alligator wrestling and snake handling. The grounds also serve as a natural habitat for Florida black bears, panthers, otters, bobcats, and deer. The gift shop is a good source for turquoise jewelry, moccasins, sweetgrass baskets, and beadwork.

Admission: $6 adults, $5 children 3–12.

Open: Mon–Sat 9am–5pm, Sun 10am–5pm; tours every hour on the half hour, with last tour at 3:30pm. **Directions:** Take I-4 to Exit 5.

MUSEUM OF AFRICAN AMERICAN ART, 1308 N. Marion St., Tampa. Tel. 272-2466.

Located on the northern edge of downtown off Exit 26 of I-275, between Scott and Laurel Streets, this museum is the first of its kind in Florida, and one of only 10 in the U.S. It houses the Barnett-Aden African-American art collection, valued at $7.5 million, and considered to be the country's foremost collection of African-American art. The works, which include 32 pieces of sculpture and 106 paintings, depict the history, culture, and lifestyle of African-Americans from the 1800s to the present. More than 80 artists are represented in the collection.

Admission: $2 suggested donation.

Open: Tues–Sat 10am–4:30pm, Sun 1–4:30pm.

TAMPA CONVENTION CENTER, 333 S. Franklin St., at Platt St., Tampa. Tel. 223-8511.

Although not technically open as a public attraction, this is the city's focal point for conventions, meetings, and occasional concerts. Even if you are not attending a function inside, it's worth a look at the impressive exterior of this $140-million building owned and operated by the City of Tampa. Situated on a 14-acre site overlooking the Hillsborough River and Harbour Island, it has 2,000 feet of riverfront views and lush landscape. In the front of the center is a $1.7-million park with a spectacular six-ton fountain, *Shamayim—Fire & Water* by Yaacov Agam.

SACRED HEART CHURCH, Florida Ave. and Twiggs St., Tampa. Tel. 229-1595.

Often referred to as Tampa's ecclesiastical jewel, this huge domed church was erected between 1898 and 1905 at a cost of $250,000 as the mother church of the Jesuit missions in Florida. Sitting on the site of an earlier (1858) church, it stands out on the Tampa skyline as an elaborate token of Gothic architecture amid a maze of glassy skyscrapers. Step inside and view a gracious panorama of stained-glass windows, marble arches and columns, carved statuary, hand-painted plasterwork, and a recently restored Moeller pipe organ.

Admission: Free.

Open: Daily 7am–6pm or later. **Directions:** In the heart of downtown, one block west of the Franklin Street Mall.

EYE ON TAMPA BAY, WTVT/Channel 13 Studios, 3213 W. Kennedy Blvd., Tampa. Tel. 870-9650.

If you've always wanted to be on TV, you can get your chance while visiting Tampa. This daytime talk show is the local equivalent of "Oprah" or "Geraldo," with a format that invites guests to air opinions on controversial issues, meet famous stars of stage and screen, and generally be part of the broadcast. Tickets must be reserved in advance by phone.

Admission: Free.

Open: Mon–Fri at 12:30pm. **Directions:** From downtown, follow Fla. 60 (Kennedy Blvd.) west to studios.

2. COOL FOR KIDS

MUSEUM OF SCIENCE AND INDUSTRY [MOSI], 4801 E. Fowler Ave., Tampa. Tel. 987-6300.

An educational attraction for all ages, this museum offers exhibits on industry, technology, and the physical and natural sciences. The Challenger Learning Center has a space-shuttle simulator and memorial to the seven Challenger astronauts who perished in 1986. Recent additions to the museum have included a permanent exhibit about water resources and conservation; an interactive butterfly garden featuring dozens of free-flying butterflies; and a 100-seat planetarium.

As we go to press, MOSI is undergoing a $35 million expansion that will triple its size to become the largest science center in the Southeast. The centerpiece of the expansion will be a 350-seat, 85-foot domed Omnimax theater—Florida's first.

Admission: $5.50 adults, $2 children 3–15, free for children under 3; planetarium admission is an additional $1.50 per person.

Open: Sun–Thurs 9am–4:30pm, Fri–Sat 9am–9pm. **Directions:** Head north of downtown, one mile east of Busch Gardens.

ADVENTURE ISLAND, 4545 Bougainvillea Ave., Tampa. Tel. 987-5660.

Adjacent to Busch Gardens and owned and operated by Busch Entertainment Corp., this is a separate 36-acre outdoor water theme park. A favorite with kids and teens, it has three swimming pools and several water-slide/play areas with names like River of No Return, Gulf Scream, Everglides, Courageous Falls, and Tampa Typhoon. There is also an outdoor café, picnic and sunbathing areas, games arcade, volleyball complex, and dressing-room facilities. Wear a bathing suit and bring towels.

Admission: $16.95 adults, $14.95 children 3–9, free for children under 3. Lockers $1.

Open: Apr–Oct, Mon–Fri 10am–5pm, Sat–Sun 9:30am–6pm; hours extended in summer months. **Closed:** Nov–Mar. **Directions:** Take I-275 to Busch Blvd. (Exit 33), go east two miles to 40th St. (McKinley Dr.), make a left, and follow the signs.

LOWRY PARK ZOO, 7530 North Blvd., Tampa. Tel. 935-8552.

Recently renovated and expanded with lots of greenery, bubbling brooks, and cascading waterfalls, this 24-acre zoo houses animals in settings that closely resemble their natural habitats. Among the major attractions are a 45-foot aviary in a subtropical forest setting; a wildlife center, showcasing Florida's native plants and animals; and a Florida at Night building, specializing in rare nocturnal animals. The zoo offers insight into breeding and rehabilitation through its aviary nursery and manatee hospital. There are also areas devoted to primates, Asian animals, and a children's petting zoo.

Admission: $6.50 adults, $5.50 seniors, $4.50 children 4–12, free for children 3 and under.

Open: Apr–Sept, daily 9:30am–6pm; Oct–Mar, daily 9:30am–5pm. **Directions:** Take I-275 to Sligh Ave. (Exit 31) and follow the signs to Lowry Park.

FUN FOREST AT LOWRY PARK, Sligh Ave. at North Blvd., Tampa. Tel. 935-5503.

Founded over 30 years ago and rejuvenated in 1990, this old-fashioned park offers a dozen traditional kiddie rides, from a big Ferris wheel and merry-go-round to bumper cars. It has a small-town atmosphere and is a favorite with the locals who usually combine a visit here with the adjacent zoo and other attractions.

Admission: Free; coupons for rides 50¢ each; coupon books $12.

Open: Summer, Mon–Sat 11am–6pm, Sun noon–6pm; the rest of the year, Mon–Sat 11am–5pm, Sun noon–5pm. **Directions:** Take I-275 to Sligh Ave. (Exit 31) and follow the signs to Lowry Park.

CHILDREN'S MUSEUM OF TAMPA, 7550 North Blvd., Tampa. Tel. 935-8441.

Geared for those aged 3 to 10, this museum invites children to touch and test, explore and examine, pretend and play in exhibits that are designed to increase curiosity and imagination. Activities range from grocery shopping to blowing giant bubbles or paper making. A visit here can also be combined with a tour of **Safety Village,** a satellite of the museum, that presents Tampa in miniature. Kids can have the run of this scaled-down city, and learn the rules of safety, with miniature traffic lights, buildings, and paved streets.

Admission: $2.50 adults and children 2 and over, $1.75 seniors, free for children under 2.

Open: Tues–Sat 10am–5pm, Sun 1–5pm. **Directions:** Take I-275 to Sligh Ave. (Exit 31) and follow the signs to Lowry Park.

3. ORGANIZED TOURS

WATER & LAND TOURS

GONDOLA GETAWAY CRUISES, Waterwalk, Harbour Island (mailing address: 6412 Sawyer Rd., Tampa, FL 33614). Tel. 888-8864.

See the skyscrapers and other downtown highlights as you float across the waters of Tampa Bay and the lower Hillsborough River in an authentic 70-year-old Venetian gondola. Local boating enthusiast Keith Ziegler, a former social worker/therapist, has restored three 30-foot gondolas, each capable of carrying up to four passengers on 35- to 45-minute trips. With Ziegler or one of his family steering the craft and providing a commentary on downtown sights, you'll drift along channels and under bridges as fish jump in the sparkling waters and Italian opera plays on a cassette player on board. Ziegler will even supply a bucket of ice and glasses if you want to bring your own champagne or wine. Close your eyes and you'll think you're in Venice, but instead it's the ideal way to get your bearings in Tampa—a unique and delightful tour.

Prices: $20 per couple, $5 each for third and fourth passengers; (maximum of four per cruise).

Open: Mon–Sat 6pm–midnight, Sun noon–9pm; other times by appointment; reservations accepted 9am–7pm.

GREEN BANANA EXCURSIONS, Whiting and Ashley Sts., Tampa. Tel. 237-2352.

Based downtown on the Hillsborough River near the convention center, this company offers floating excursions on the Tampa Bay waterways via six-passenger pontoon boats. Cruises last from one to three hours.

Prices: $10 per person for one hour, $20 per person for two hours, $30 per person for three to four hours; $5 extra per person for sunset and weekend cruises.

Open: Year-round, daily by reservation.

SEA TRADER CRUISES, Harbour Island Marina, Harbour Island. Tel. 286-8512.

This "downeast"-style 38-foot cutter-rigged sloop offers sightseeing and sunset cruises, with Capt. Tom Kester at the helm. Advance reservations are required.

Prices: $100 per couple, $35 each for three to six people; or $70 per hour for a minimum two-hour sail, $400 for six hours.

Schedule: Year-round, by appointment.

SWISS CHALET TOURS, 3601 E. Busch Blvd., Tampa. Tel. 985-3601.

Located opposite Busch Gardens, this company operates guided full- and half-day bus tours of Tampa, Ybor City, and environs. Reservations are required at least 24 hours in advance; passengers are picked up at major hotels and various other points in the Tampa/St. Petersburg area. Tours to Sarasota, Bradenton, and other destinations can also be booked.

Prices: Full-day tours $45 adults, $35 children; half-day tours $35 adults, $20 children.

Schedule: Full-day eight-hour tours Tues and Fri; four-hour half-day tours Mon and Thurs.

YBOR CITY WALKING TOURS, Ybor Sq., 1901 N. 13th St., Ybor City. Tel. 223-1111, ext. 46.

Led by enthusiastic local volunteer guides, these tours are the ideal way to acquaint yourself with the highlights of Ybor City, Tampa's Latin Quarter. The route, which starts at Ybor Square and ends at Preservation Park, concentrates primarily on Seventh and Ninth Avenues in the heart of the district. It covers dozens of historic buildings, clubs, theaters, galleries, crafts shops, and restaurants. The tour takes about 1½ hours; reservations are suggested.

Prices: Free.

Open: June–Sept, Tues, Thurs, and Sat at 11am; Oct–May, Tues, Thurs, and Sat at 1:30pm. **Directions:** Assemble at the Information Desk of Ybor Sq., between Eighth and Ninth Aves.

CRUISES

With the development of the Garrison Seaport Center, Tampa is rapidly growing into a major port for the cruise industry. As we go to press, the following cruise lines are offering or planning to offer cruises from Tampa.

AMERICAN FAMILY CRUISES, Port of Tampa. Tel. toll free 800/322-3130.

Beginning in December 1994, American Family Cruises will commence seven-day cruises designed for family travel. The 1,500-passenger ship, *American Pioneer,* will depart from Tampa for the

western Caribbean ports of Playa del Carmen, Cozumel, Buccaneer Bay, Jamaica, and Grand Cayman.
   Prices: $795–$1,995 adults, $395 children 2–17.
   Sailings: Dec–Apr, departing on Sun.

CARNIVAL CRUISE LINES, Port of Tampa. Tel. toll free 800/327-7373.

Commencing October 1994, Carnival Cruise Lines will introduce seven-day cruises of the western Caribbean and the French Quarter on board the 1,022-passenger ship MS *Tropicale*. Ports of call will include Grand Cayman, Cozumel, and New Orleans.
   Prices: $1,149–$2,479 per person.
   Sailings: Year-round, departing on Sun.

HOLLAND AMERICAN LINE, Port of Tampa. Tel. toll free 800/426-0327.

For many years, this cruise company has sailed its 1,214-passenger luxury ship, MS *Nieuw Amsterdam*, on seven-day cruises from Tampa. It cruises to Key West, Playa del Carmen/Cozumel, Ocho Rios, Montego Bay, and Grand Cayman.
   Prices: $1,660–$2,650 per person.
   Sailings: Oct–Apr, departing on Sat.

ODESSAMERICA, Port of Tampa. Tel. toll free 800/221-3254.

In late 1993, this Ukrainian-registered company launched cruises from the Port of Tampa on board its 400-passenger ship, MV *Gruziya* (Georgia), for seven-day Mayan world trips to Puerto Cortés, Honduras; Belize City, Belize; and Cancún, Mexico.
   Prices: $1,695–$2,445 per person.
   Sailings: Oct–June, departing on Sat.

REGENCY CRUISES, Port of Tampa. Tel. toll free 800/388-5500.

This company is the only cruise line to operate two- and five-day cruises from Florida's west coast. The 960-passenger SS *Regent Rainbow* offers two-day weekend party cruises into the Gulf of Mexico and five-day Yucatán cruises that call to Key West, Cozumel, and Playa del Carmen.
   Prices: $139–$299 per person for weekend cruises; $495–$975 per person for five-day cruises.
   Sailings: Year-round, two-day cruises depart on Fri, five-day cruises depart on Sun.

4. SPORTS & RECREATION

SPECTATOR SPORTS

BASEBALL

For more baseball venues within a half-hour drive, see Chapter 7, "What to See and Do in St. Petersburg."

PLANT CITY STADIUM, Park Rd., Plant City. Tel. 752-7337.

About a half-hour drive from downtown Tampa, this is the winter home of the Cincinnati Reds, who hold their spring training here each year.

Admission: $4–$7.

Open: Mid-Feb to Apr. **Directions:** Take I-4 east, 25 miles to Park Rd. (Exit 14), and follow the signs.

DOG RACING

TAMPA GREYHOUND TRACK, 8300 Nebraska Ave., Tampa. Tel. 932-4313.

A modern, climate-controlled, fully enclosed facility, this track features 13 races daily, with eight dogs competing in each. Facilities include a restaurant, lounge, and closed-circuit TVs for viewing the races and playbacks.

Admission: $1 grandstand, $2–$3 clubhouse. Free self-parking, $3 for valet parking.

Open: July–Dec, Mon and Wed–Sat at 7:30pm; matinees Mon, Wed, and Sat at noon, Sun at 1pm. **Closed:** Jan–June. **Directions:** Take I-275 north of downtown to Bird St. (Exit 32).

FOOTBALL, SOCCER, ETC.

TAMPA STADIUM, 4201 N. Dale Mabry Hwy., Tampa. Tel. 872-7977.

Home base for the Tampa Bay Buccaneers football team and the Tampa Bay Rowdies soccer team, this 74,301-capacity stadium north of downtown and east of the airport, at Martin Luther King, Jr., Boulevard, caters to sporting events of all sizes and calibers from the Super Bowl to horse shows and motor sports, as well as world-class concerts. The stadium also hosts the Hall of Fame Bowl each New Year's Day, the Florida Classic, and a wide range of other events.

Prices: $5–$35 or higher, depending on the event.

Open: Box office, Mon–Fri 9am–5pm; call in advance for particulars or reserve through TicketMaster (tel. 871-2993) outlets. Times of games and events vary.

HOCKEY

TAMPA BAY LIGHTNING, 501 E. Kennedy Blvd., Tampa. Tel. 229-8800.

Tampa Bay Lightning, the southernmost franchise of the National Hockey League, is still based at St. Petersburg's ThunderDome as we go to press, but is scheduled to move to downtown Tampa, starting with the 1995–96 hockey season (Oct–Apr). The team will be housed in a new 20,000-seat arena on an 18-acre parcel of land located between the Tampa Convention Center and the new Florida Aquarium. For complete details at the time of your visit, call the number above.

Admission: $8–$50.

Open: Playing season is Oct–Apr, but schedule varies.

HORSE RACING

TAMPA BAY DOWNS, 11255 Racetrack Rd., off Fla. 580, Oldsmar. Tel. 855-4401.

The only Thoroughbred oval horse-race course on Florida's west coast, this is the home of the Tampa Bay Derby, a key test for Triple Crown hopefuls. The program features 10 races a day, and facilities include a restaurant, a lounge, and a gallery with big screens where replays are shown. The 1995–1996 season marks the 49th consecutive year of racing here.

Admission: $1.50 grandstand, $3 clubhouse. Free grandstand admission for seniors on Thurs and for women on Fri. Parking: $1.

Open: Year-round. Live racing, Dec–May, Tues and Thurs–Sun, doors open 11:30am. June–Nov simulcasts only.

JAI-ALAI

TAMPA JAI-ALAI FRONTON, 5125 S. Dale Mabry Hwy., at Gandy Blvd., Tampa. Tel. 831-1411.

Having originated in Spain, and bearing similarities to racquetball, this is considered the world's fastest ball game (the ball can split the breeze at more than 180 m.p.h.). Professional players volley the lethal *pelota* with a long, curved glove called a *cesta*. Facilities include a restaurant and pari-mutuel wagering.

Admission: $1–$3 per person. Parking $1 or free.

Open: Year-round, Mon–Wed and Fri–Sat at 7pm; matinees Mon, Wed, and Sat at noon.

POLO

CHEVAL POLO CLUB, 3939 Cheval Trail, Lutz. Tel. 948-4000.

The horses canter and the mallets are swung at this club, north of downtown, eight months out of the year.

Admission: $5 per person.

Open: Oct–May, Sun at 2pm. **Directions:** Follow Dale Mabry Hwy. north to Van Dyke Rd.; the club entrance follows on the left.

TAMPA BAY POLO CLUB, Walden Lake Polo and Country Club, 2001 Clubhouse Dr., Plant City. Tel. 752-8731.

Touted as the oldest team sport, polo is played regularly at this sylvan site east of Tampa.

Admission: $3.

Open: Mid-Jan to May, Sun at 2pm. **Closed:** June to mid-Jan. **Directions:** Take I-4 to Exit 11 and follow the signs south.

RECREATION

BICYCLING/SKATING

Tampa is prime bicycling territory, from the seven-mile-long stretch of Bayshore Boulevard to the quiet neighborhoods of Hyde Park.

Bicycle rentals are available from **Blades and Bikes,** 201 W. Platt St., Suite A, Tampa (tel. 251-0178). Prices range from $8 an hour to $14 a day for most bikes. This firm also rents skates, categorized as sport blades and high-performance blades, from $10 an hour or $16 a day. All bike prices include helmet and lock, and skate prices include helmet, wrist guards, and elbow and knee pads. Open Monday through Friday from 9am to 8pm, Saturday and Sunday from 8am to 8pm.

BINGO

This low-energy activity is big business in the Tampa Bay area. There are at least three dozen local organizations (church groups, fraternal orders, ethnic groups) that sponsor bingo sessions each week. Of all the bingo venues, however, two of the most popular are owned and operated by the Seminole Tribe of Florida, located side by side seven miles east of downtown Tampa.

SEMINOLE BINGO OF TAMPA, 5223 N. Orient Rd., Tampa. Tel. 621-1302.

Opened in 1982, this facility offers continuous high-stakes bingo all week long. There are four sessions every day, with seating for 1,500 persons. Prices depend on which session is played and what package is purchased. Instant bingo is also available, as are smoke-free areas.

Prices: $8–$15 matinees, $20–$85 evening, $5–$13 night owl; discounts are offered at some Tues, Thurs, and Sun matinees.

Open: Daily 11am–midnight; matinee sessions at 11am and 2:15pm; evening sessions at 7 and 10:30pm. **Directions:** From downtown, take I-4 to Orient Rd. (Exit 5), and go north 500 yards to the entrance.

SEMINOLE GAMING PALACE, 5223 N. Orient Rd., Tampa. Tel. 621-1302.

Opened in 1988, this casino-style facility offers several unique types of bingo. Totally different from the traditional games played at charity locations, these games are extremely fast and offer large prize jackpots.

Prices: 25¢–$2.

Open: Daily 24 hours. **Directions:** From downtown, take I-4 to Orient Rd. (Exit 5) and go north 500 yards to the entrance.

FISHING

Like the St. Petersburg area, Tampa offers many opportunities for casting a line. Unlike St. Pete, however, Tampa does not have a huge coast along the Gulf of Mexico, so Tampa-area fishing is confined mainly to lakes, rivers, and bays. Tampa fishing is also more informal, with no organized programs or fleets of party boats lined up along local marinas to offer day trips to visitors.

According to local experts, you'll find good freshwater fishing for trout in Lake Thonotosassa, east of the city, or for bass along the Hillsborough River. Pier fishing on Hillsborough Bay is also available from Ballast Point Park, 5300 Interbay Blvd. (tel. 831-9585).

For information on required licenses, see "Sports and Recreation," in Chapter 7.

GOLF

HALL OF FAME GOLF CLUB, 2222 N. Westshore Blvd., at Spruce Ave., Tampa. Tel. 876-4913.

You can literally step off the plane and play a round of golf at this 18-hole par-72 course, situated adjacent to Tampa airport. Facilities include a driving range and golf-club rentals. Lessons are also available.

Prices: $18–$22, including cart.
Open: Daily 7am–dusk.

ROCKY POINT GOLF MUNICIPAL GOLF COURSE, 4151 Dana Shores Dr., Tampa. Tel. 884-5141.

Situated two miles west of Tampa airport, off Memorial Highway, between the airport and Old Tampa Bay, this is an 18-hole par-71 course with pro shop, practice range, putting greens, snack bar, and lounge. Lessons and golf-club rentals are also available.

Prices: $20–$25 with cart.
Open: Daily 7am–dusk.

ROGERS PARK MUNICIPAL GOLF COURSE, 7910 N. 30th St., Tampa. Tel. 234-1911.

On the Hillsborough River in north Tampa, this 18-hole par-72 championship course has a lighted driving range, practice range, snack bar, and lounge. Lessons are available, as are clubs for rent.

Prices: $22.50–$25, including cart.
Open: Daily 7am–dusk. **Directions:** Take I-275 north to Sligh Ave. (Exit 31), then turn east to 30th St.

UNIVERSITY OF SOUTH FLORIDA GOLF COURSE, 4202 Fowler Ave., Tampa. Tel. 974-2071.

Located just north of the USF campus, this 18-hole par-72 course is nicknamed "the Claw" because of its challenging layout. It offers lessons, club rentals, and a snack bar.

Prices: $18; with cart, $30.
Open: Daily 7am–dusk. **Directions:** From downtown, take I-275 to Fletcher Ave. (Exit 35) and go east for two miles.

BABE ZAHARIAS MUNICIPAL GOLF COURSE, 11412 Forest Hills Dr., Tampa. Tel. 932-8932.

Situated north of Lowry Park between the Carrollwood and Temple Terrace areas, this is an 18-hole par-70 course. It has a pro shop, putting greens, driving range, and snack bar. Golf-club rentals and lessons are available.

Prices: $14.50–$18.50; with cart $20–$25.
Open: Daily 7am–dusk. **Directions:** From downtown, take I-275 north to Fowler Ave. (Exit 34) and go west half a mile to Forest Hills Dr.

RUNNING

Bayshore Boulevard, a 7-mile stretch along Hillsborough Bay, is famous for its 6.3-mile sidewalk. It is reputed to be the world's longest continuous sidewalk, and is a favorite for runners, joggers, walkers, and cyclists. The route goes from the western edge of downtown in a southward direction, passing stately old homes, condos, retirement communities, and houses of worship, and ending at Gandy Boulevard.

In addition, you might try some of the local Hillsborough County parks, such as the 240-acre **Lettuce Lake,** 6920 Fletcher Ave. at the Hillsborough River (tel. 987-6204), northeast of downtown. Launched in 1982, it's one of the area's newest parks and a hub for outdoor enthusiasts. There's a jogging trail, with a fitness course, plus a bicycle path and picnic areas.

For more information on recommended running areas, contact the **Parks Department,** 7525 North Blvd., Tampa (tel. 931-2121).

SWIMMING

The nearest public beach to downtown is the **Ben T. Davis Beach** on the Courtney Campbell Causeway (Fla. 60), on Old Tampa Bay. If you keep driving, the Campbell Causeway will lead you to Clearwater Beach and the many other gulf beaches in neighboring Pinellas County (see "Sports and Recreation," in Chapter 7).

TENNIS

CITY OF TAMPA TENNIS COMPLEX, Hillsborough Community College, 4001 Tampa Bay Blvd., Tampa. Tel. 870-2383.

Situated east of the airport, at the intersection of Martin Luther King, Jr., Blvd., and Dale Mabry Highway, across from Tampa Stadium, this is one of two tennis sites in the area recently awarded the U.S. Tennis Association's national facility award. It's the largest public complex in Tampa, with 16 hard courts and 12 clay courts. It also offers racquetball courts, plus a pro shop, locker rooms, showers, and lessons. Reservations recommended.

Prices: $1.50–$4.50 per person per hour.
Open: Mon–Thurs 8am–9pm, Fri and Sat–Sun 8am–6pm.

MARJORIE PARK, 59 Columbia Dr., Davis Islands, Tampa. Tel. 253-3997.

Located on Davis Islands, southwest of downtown off Bayshore Boulevard, on the water and overlooking Harbour Island, this complex has eight clay courts. It is one of two tennis complexes in the area that were recently awarded the U.S. Tennis Association's national facility award. Reservations are required.

Prices: $4.50 per person per hour.
Open: Mon–Fri 8am–9pm, Sat–Sun 8am–6pm.

RIVERFRONT PARK, 900 North Blvd., Tampa. Tel. 223-8602.

This facility is located at the north end of the University of Tampa, across the river from the Tampa Bay Performing Arts Center. There are 11 courts here, and visitors are welcome to use them on a first-come basis, although reservations can also be made up to a day in advance. The courts are lit until 10pm and there's no charge for lights. There are 10 other unstaffed facilities such as this spread throughout the city. For locations, call 223-8602.

Prices: $2.25–$4.50 per hour per person.
Open: Daily 7am–10pm.

HARRY HOPMAN/SADDLEBROOK INTERNATIONAL TENNIS SCHOOL, 100 Saddlebrook Way, Wesley Chapel. Tel. 973-1111, or toll free 800/729-8383.

If you're serious about your tennis, this place allows you to build a whole vacation around the sport. Founded by the late Harry Hopman, one of the most successful captain-coaches in Davis Cup history, this well-equipped school, with 45 tennis courts, caters to beginners and skilled players of all ages.

The basic five-day/six-night instructional package includes 25 hours (minimum) of tennis instruction, unlimited playing time, match play with instructors, audiovisual analysis, fitness and agility exercises, and accommodations at the Saddlebrook resort. A similar program for juniors (aged 9 to 20) is also available, including meals. For more information on the resort, see Chapter 9, "Tampa Accommodations." The resort is off I-75, 25 miles north of Tampa.

Prices: $630–$1,035 per person, based on double occupancy, for adults; $660–$720 for junior program.

WATER SPORTS

CANOE ESCAPE, 9335 E. Fowler Ave., Thonotasassa, Tampa. Tel. 986-2067.

Paddle a canoe along the Hillsborough River amid 16,000 acres of rural lands in Wilderness Park, the largest regional park in Hillsborough County. The trips last two hours to a full day, covering approximately two to three miles each hour. All trips are downstream, in two- to four-person canoes, passing through forested land with a chance to observe wading birds, turtles, alligators, deer, and wild turkey.

Prices: $24 for two-hour trips, $28 for four- or six-hour trips.
Open: Mon–Fri 9am–5pm, Sat–Sun 8am–6pm. **Directions:** Take I-75 north of Tampa to Exit 54; the entrance is half a mile east.

CLUB NAUTICO, Waterwalk, Harbour Island. Tel. 223-2107.

Captain your own craft on the waters of Tampa Bay. This company rents powerboats and pontoons.

Prices: Half-day rentals $99–$179 for powerboats, $119–$259 for pontoon boats.
Open: Daily noon–6pm or later, depending on season.

TRIDENT BOAT RENTALS, Waterwalk, Harbour Island. Tel. 223-4168.
Rent a small electric paddleboat or a three-passenger electric boat and ply the waters of Garrison's Channel or the Hillsborough River around Harbour Island. All prices are based on half-hour rentals.
   Prices: $6 (two passengers) in paddleboats, $10 for electric boats.
   Open: Fri 6pm–midnight, Sat 1pm–midnight, Sun 1–7pm.

WALKING TOUR — DOWNTOWN TAMPA

Start: University of Tampa.
Finish: Harbour Island.
Time: Approximately two hours.
Best Times: Weekends.
Worst Times: Weekday morning or evening rush hours.

FROM UNIVERSITY OF TAMPA TO FRANKLIN STREET MALL   Start just west of the downtown business district at the:

1. **Henry B. Plant Museum,** 401 W. Kennedy Blvd., originally the site of the Tampa Bay Hotel built in 1891 by railroad magnate Henry B. Plant and now part of the campus of the University of Tampa (see "The Top Attractions," above in this chapter). Stroll around the beautifully landscaped University of Tampa campus and then cross the John F. Kennedy Boulevard Bridge (originally the Lafayette Street Bridge) to the hub of Tampa's downtown business district.
   After crossing the river, you come to Ashley Street, a prime north-south thoroughfare, lined with hotels, banks, office towers, and many of the city's attractions, including the new:
2. **Tampa Convention Center.** A visit would require a detour to the most southerly tip of Ashley.
   At Ashley Street and Kennedy Boulevard, head north (left) for one block to Madison and, if you wish, stop for a visit at the new ground floor offices of the:
3. **Tampa/Hillsborough Convention and Visitors Association,** 111 Madison St., at the corner of Ashley and Madison. You may want to ask specific questions or stock up on brochures and other travel information about the Tampa area.
   Continue north on Ashley, passing the NationsBank Plaza on the left, to the Ashley Street entrance of the:
4. **Tampa Museum of Art,** 601 Doyle Carlton Dr. (see "The Top Attractions," above in this chapter). Return to Ashley and stroll north for the next five blocks, passing various bank buildings and modern office towers and the:
5. **Riverfront Park,** currently under development and slated for 1995 completion. The next building of interest along Ashley is the main branch of the:
6. **Tampa Public Library,** 900 N. Ashley St., between Cass and Tyler Streets, with a small fine-arts gallery featuring rotating

exhibitions of local artists. Behind the library, on Ashley Drive, is a 25-foot red steel sculpture, *America, America,* by Barbara Neijna.

At Tyler, take a left and visit the:

7. **Tampa Bay Performing Arts Center,** a modern $57-million riverfront entertainment complex. Guided tours are conducted each Wednesday and Saturday at 10am. Directly north of the arts center, off Fortune Street, is the:

8. **Holiday Inn,** one of Tampa's contemporary downtown hotels.

REFUELING STOP   If you'd like some refreshment amid an artsy decor, try the **Backstage Restaurant** of the Holiday Inn, or, for lighter fare, the **Deli** of the same hotel.

Return to Ashley Street and retrace your steps two blocks to Cass Street. Go east on Cass two blocks to Franklin Street and turn right. You are now on the Franklin Street Mall, a largely pedestrianized area and the focal point of downtown Tampa. Stroll in a southward direction, and, after crossing the intersection of Polk Street, look to the east side for the:

9. **Tampa Theatre,** 711 N. Franklin St., a restored 1926 building that is listed on the National Register of Historic Places. The interior is noted for its ornate colonnades, balconies, and replicas of Greek and Roman statuary. Across the street, to the west, is:

10. **TECO (Tampa Electric Company) Plaza,** 702 N. Franklin St., with a public gallery used to showcase the works of Tampa Bay area artists. On the northwest corner of Franklin and Zack Streets, be sure to note *Solaris,* a solar-powered hanging sculpture by William Severson. Continue southward along Franklin. Between Twiggs and Madison, notice a mural on the east side of Franklin Street, *Franklin Street 1925,* by Carl Cowden III and Randall Williams.

Continue to Zack Street and turn east (left). Walk one block to Florida Avenue and you will come to:

11. **Sacred Heart Church,** at Florida Avenue and Twiggs Street, built 1898–1905 and considered Tampa's finest church. It is well worth a visit inside this Gothic-style domed building to see the stained-glass windows, marble columns and arches, and elaborate plasterwork. Returning to Zack Street, continue one more block east to the corner of Marion Street to the:

12. **First Presbyterian Church,** 412 Zack St., known foremost as the home of the **One World Gift Shop** (see "Tampa Shopping," below in this chapter), a treasure house of crafts from Third World countries and Tampa's most altruistic shopping experience (entrance to the shop is around the corner on Polk Street). Retrace your steps two blocks back to the corner of Franklin and Zack Streets.

Continue southward along Franklin, crossing over Kennedy Boulevard and Jackson Street. The latter is considered the "Wall Street of Tampa" and the site of the:

13. **Tampa Financial Center.** Between Jackson and Washington

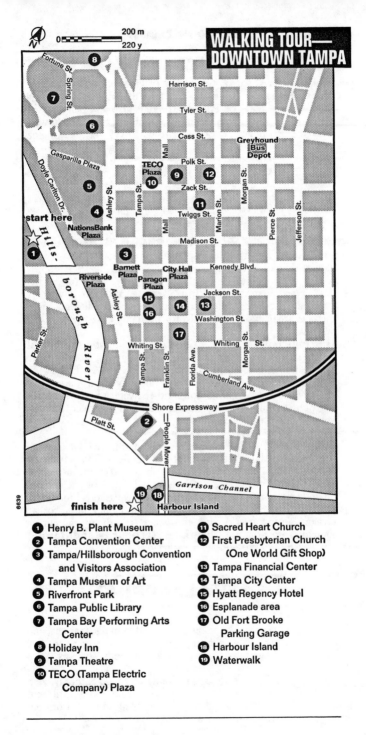

WALKING TOUR—
DOWNTOWN TAMPA

0 ——— 200 m
——— 220 y

Fortune St.
Spring St.
Harrison St.
Tyler St.
Cass St.
Gasparilla Plaza
Mall
Greyhound
Bus
Depot
Polk St.
TECO
Plaza
Zack St.
Morgan St.
Twiggs St.
Ashley St.
Tampa St.
Marion St.
Pierce St.
Jefferson St.
start here
Hills-
NationsBank
Plaza
Madison St.
borough
Barnett
Plaza
Riverside
Plaza
City Hall
Plaza
Kennedy Blvd.
Paragon
Plaza
River
Ashley St.
Jackson St.
Parker St.
Washington St.
Whiting St.
Tampa St.
Franklin St.
Whiting St.
Florida Ave.
Morgan St.
Cumberland Ave.
Shore Expressway
Platt St.
People Mover
Garrison Channel
finish here
Harbour Island
Waterwalk

6639

- ❶ Henry B. Plant Museum
- ❷ Tampa Convention Center
- ❸ Tampa/Hillsborough Convention and Visitors Association
- ❹ Tampa Museum of Art
- ❺ Riverfront Park
- ❻ Tampa Public Library
- ❼ Tampa Bay Performing Arts Center
- ❽ Holiday Inn
- ❾ Tampa Theatre
- ❿ TECO (Tampa Electric Company) Plaza
- ⓫ Sacred Heart Church
- ⓬ First Presbyterian Church (One World Gift Shop)
- ⓭ Tampa Financial Center
- ⓮ Tampa City Center
- ⓯ Hyatt Regency Hotel
- ⓰ Esplanade area
- ⓱ Old Fort Brooke Parking Garage
- ⓲ Harbour Island
- ⓳ Waterwalk

Streets on Franklin, you'll see a number of the city's new developments, including the:

14. **Tampa City Center,** to the east of Franklin, and the:
15. **Hyatt Regency Hotel,** to the west of Franklin. Beside the Tampa City Center on Franklin, there is also an open-air:
16. **Esplanade area,** with waterfalls, fountains, trees, and flowers. This site was once part of Fort Brooke (1835–42), the original U.S. Army settlement around which Tampa grew up.

REFUELING STOP   If you'd like to take a break, the **Esplanade** offers a number of cafés, coffee shops, and fast-food outlets most of which have outdoor seating under the trees, including Pralines, (see Chapter 10, "Tampa Dining").

FRANKLIN STREET MALL TO HARBOUR ISLAND   After a refreshing stroll through the Esplanade area, you're now at the entrance to the:

17. **Old Fort Brooke Parking Garage** and the downtown terminal for the People Mover (on the third floor). It takes 25¢ in exact change, and 90 seconds, for the People Mover to whisk you over to:
18. **Harbour Island.** Once on Harbour Island, you can browse among the interesting shops, offering everything from fashions and resort wear to arts and crafts and jewelry. Along the:
19. **Waterwalk** outside, you can also arrange to take a gondola ride or rent a paddleboat, among other water-sports activities. Harbour Island is a destination in itself and a perfect finale for your walking tour of Tampa.

REFUELING STOP   If you've waited till now for a bit of refreshment, then you have lots of choices. The **Harbour Island Food Court** offers burgers, pizza, and ethnic fast foods. Restaurants in the complex include a branch of the famous Spanish restaurant the Columbia, as well as Parker's Lighthouse for seafood and Cha Cha Coconuts for lighter fare. For an elegant setting overlooking the water, try the restaurant or lounge of the adjacent **Wyndham Harbour Island Hotel.**

5. SAVVY SHOPPING

Much of the Tampa area shopping is clustered in malls, markets, and themed shopping villages, although there are also some very fine specialty shops downtown and in neighborhoods such as Ybor City.

In general, retail shops are open Monday through Saturday, 9am until 6pm, while the malls are usually open from 10am until 9pm Monday through Saturday, and from 11am or noon until 5 or 6pm on Sunday. Some shops in Ybor City are closed Sunday and Monday and/or Tuesday at off-peak times of the year. Outdoor markets operate on weekends only.

Best buys include cigars and cigar-related arts and crafts. Swim suits, hand-painted T-shirts, and resort wear offer good value, too.

A 6.5% sales tax applies to all purchases.

MALLS, MARKETS & SHOPPING CLUSTERS

BIG TOP FLEA MARKET, 9250 E. Fowler Ave., Tampa. Tel. 986-4004.

One of the area's newest flea markets, this place is home to over 600 tempting vendors who sell everything from western boots and athletic footwear to designer fashions, casual apparel, tools, jewelry and gems, arts and crafts, fresh produce, and confections. Open on Saturday and Sunday from 8am to 5pm.

To get here, take I-75 north of downtown to Exit 54 and proceed 500 yards east.

OLD HYDE PARK VILLAGE, 1509 W. Swann Ave., Hyde Park. Tel. 251-3500.

★ Located in one of the city's oldest and most historic neighborhoods west of downtown off Swann Avenue, this is the Rodeo Drive of Tampa, a cluster of 50 upscale shops and boutiques arranged in a village atmosphere. The selection includes Ann Taylor, Banana Republic, Brooks Brothers, Crabtree & Evelyn, Godiva Chocolatier, Laura Ashley, Polo–Ralph Lauren, Talbot's, Victoria's Secret, Williams-Sonoma, and a Doubleday bookshop. In addition to the shops, there are half a dozen restaurants, a multiscreen movie theater, and three free parking garages (on Oregon, Swann, and Rome Avenues). Open Monday through Wednesday and on Saturday from 10am to 6pm, on Thursday and Friday from 10am to 9pm, and on Sunday from noon to 5pm.

THE SHOPS ON HARBOUR ISLAND, 777 S. Harbour Island Blvd., Harbour Island. Tel. 223-9898 or 228-7807.

★ This is Tampa's waterfront marketplace, on an island directly south of downtown and well worth a day's outing. The 20 different shops include art galleries and fashion boutiques, as well as outlets for swimwear, sportswear, sunglasses, candies, collectibles, and Asian treasures. The complex also includes a food court, restaurants, hotel, water-sports activities, gondola rides, and more. It's accessible from downtown via the Franklin Street Bridge or the elevated tram-style People Mover. Open Monday through Saturday from 10am to 9pm and on Sunday from noon to 6pm.

TAMPA BAY CENTER, 3302 W. Dr. Martin Luther King, Jr., Blvd., Tampa. Tel. 870-0876.

Skylights, palm trees, and fountains dominate the decor of this massive 160-store mall across from Tampa Stadium at Dr. Martin Luther King, Jr., Boulevard and Himes Avenue. The complex includes three department stores—Sears, Burdines, and Montgomery Ward—and an assortment of boutiques, known for selling trendy new fashions, jewelry, and accessories. There are also stores for gifts, stationery, arts and crafts, and two booksellers, B. Dalton and Waldenbooks. Open Monday through Saturday from 10am to 9pm and on Sunday from noon to 6pm.

TOP VALUE FLEA MARKET, 8120 Anderson Rd., Tampa. Tel. 884-7810.

Situated in the same 20-acre location for over 25 years, this indoor/outdoor market is a shopper's paradise with its 600 vendors hawking produce, plants, art and antiques, hardware, clothing, sunglasses, souvenirs, and more. Open on Saturday and Sunday from 7:30am to 5pm, it's northwest of downtown at the corner of West Waters Avenue, west of Dale Mabry Highway.

UNIVERSITY MALL, 2200 E. Fowler Ave., Tampa. Tel. 971-3465.

Ideally situated next to the USF campus and a mile north of Busch Gardens, this is Tampa's largest shopping center, with five department stores—J. C. Penney, Dillard's, Montgomery Ward, Burdine's, and Sears—and 130 others selling everything from gifts and souvenirs to jewelry and high fashion. Open Monday through Saturday from 10am to 9pm and on Sunday from noon to 6pm.

To get here, take I-275 north to Fowler Avenue (Exit 34) and travel east one mile to 22nd Street.

WEST SHORE PLAZA, 253 Westshore Blvd., at Kennedy Blvd., Tampa. Tel. 286-0790.

Opened in 1967 and one of the first large regional shopping centers on Florida's west coast, this mall is adjacent to I-275 and within walking distance of many of the major hotels in the West Shore business and banking district. It comprises 100 specialty stores, an international food court, three department stores—Dillard's, Burdine's, and J. C. Penney—and a self-service U.S. post office. Open Monday through Saturday from 10am to 9pm and on Sunday from noon to 5:30pm.

YBOR CITY EUROPEAN MARKET, Centennial Park, Ybor City. Tel. 248-3712.

This colorful open-air market in the heart of Tampa's historic Latin Quarter features a different theme each month. Goods for sale include fresh produce, pastries, flowers, wines, cheeses, coffee, antiques, books, and more. It's open November through March on the third Saturday of each month from 8am to 2pm.

To get here, take I-4 to Ybor City (Exit 1) and follow the signs to the intersection of 18th Street and Eighth Avenue.

YBOR SQUARE, 1901 13th St., Ybor City. Tel. 247-4497.

Listed on the National Register of Historic Places, this complex consists of three brick buildings (dating to 1886) that once comprised the largest cigar factory in the world, employing over 4,000 workers. Today it's a specialty mall, with over three dozen shops and eateries, all housed in a setting of original wooden interiors, hand-blown glass windows, classic brick masonry, and wall-size murals that depict earlier days. The highlights include the Nostalgia Market, a collection of individual antique shops selling everything from rare magazines to clothing, linens, handcrafts, jewelry, quilts, and furniture; and Tampa Rico, an old-world cigar shop where you can purchase hand-rolled cigars and watch them being made. If you're a smoker, it's one place where you're sure to feel welcome—a sign on the wall says THANKS FOR SMOKING. Open Monday through Saturday from 9:30am to 5:30pm and on Sunday from noon to 5:30pm. There are cigar-rolling demonstrations Tuesday through Sunday from noon to 5:30pm.

To get here, take I-4 to Ybor City (Exit 1) and follow the signs to Eighth Avenue and 13th Street.

SPECIALTY STORES

DEAN JAMES GLASS STUDIO, 1401 E. Seventh Ave., Ybor City. Tel. 248-3132.

Step inside this studio and watch artisans making decorative and functional art glass and handcrafted gifts. Open Monday through Saturday from noon to 6pm.

FANCY'S, Harbour Plaza, 410 Knights Run ave., Harbour Island. Tel. 221-5300.

If you are planning a picnic or are in search of gourmet food items, this shop-cum-deli is a must. The shelves are lined with all kinds of cheeses, cookies, sweets, spices, coffees, soups, and baked goods, and there are usually a dozen different salads including grilled chicken Caesar, Caribbean shrimp and orzo, bean and pasta salads, and antipasto. The creative array of sandwiches ranges from Black Forest ham with asparagus and Boursin cheese to roast beef with creamy Rondele cheese on a sourdough baguette. Open Monday through Friday from 8am to 8pm and Saturday and Sunday from 9am to 5pm.

HEAD'S FLAGS, 1923 E. Seventh Ave., Ybor City. Tel. 248-5019.

This unusual store stocks flags from all nations and all states, as well as custom-size flags and banners, ethnic items, T-shirts, and hats. Open Monday through Friday from 9:30am to 5:30pm and on Saturday from 9:30am to 3pm.

To get here, take I-4 to Ybor City (Exit 1) and follow the signs to Seventh Avenue; it's between 19th and 20th Streets.

MARTINEZ DE YBOR ART GALLERY, 2025 E. Seventh Ave., Ybor City. Tel. 247-2771.

Step inside this shop/studio and watch Arnold Martinez paint scenes of Tampa and Ybor City with his unique media—paints and acrylics made of Cuban coffee, tea pigments, and Tampa tobacco. Original paintings, prints, and posters on display are for sale. He's open Wednesday through Saturday 11am to 4pm

Take I-4 to Ybor City (Exit 1), and follow the signs to Seventh Avenue; it's between 20th and 21st Streets.

ONE WORLD GIFT SHOP, 412 Zack St., Tampa. Tel. 229-0679.

Tucked into two rooms of the First Presbyterian Church downtown, on the corner of Marion and Polk Streets, this shop aims to better the world by selling items handcrafted by Third World artisans from Central and South America, Asia, India, and Mexico. In addition to paying the artisans from abroad, profits are also donated to local Tampa charities. Over 500 gifts are featured, from silk wall hangings, African beaded necklaces, and bamboo toy trains to decorative brassware, leather goods, basketry, crocheted sweaters, ceramics, jewelry, alabaster, wood and jade figures, embroidered blouses, and dresses. Open Monday through Friday from 11am to 2pm.

THE PEN STORE, 404 Zack St., Tampa. Tel. 223-3865.

The only store in the Southeast specializing in pens, this unique downtown shop, between the Franklin Street Mall and Florida Avenue, stocks all the major brands (Shaeffer, Cross, Parker, Waterman, and more), as well as desk sets, jeweled pen sets, and inks. It also operates a pen-repair service. Open Monday through Friday from 9am to 5pm and Saturday from 10am to noon.

ST. FIACRE'S HERB SHOP, 1709 N. 16th St., Ybor City. Tel. 248-1234.

Named after the Irish monk who went to France and became the patron saint of gardeners, this unique shop stocks a wide array of fresh herbs, herbal products, fragrances, exotic teas, and books. Open Monday to Thursday 10am to 6pm, Friday and Saturday 10am to 8pm, Sunday noon to 5pm.

WHALEY'S MARKETS, 533 S. Howard Ave. Tel. 254-2904.

This store is a favorite source for Florida Indian River citrus fruit, marmalades, and other local foods including gourmet picnic items. Open Monday through Saturday from 7am to 9pm and Sunday from 7am to 8pm.

6. EVENING ENTERTAINMENT

Whether you're a fan of drama or dance, rock or reggae, comedy or the classics, chances are you'll find it in Tampa. To assist visitors, the Tampa/Hillsborough Arts Council maintains an **Artsline** (tel. 229-ARTS), a 24-hour information service providing the latest on current and upcoming cultural events.

The best way to keep abreast of what's on is to read the **Tampa Tribune,** the city's daily newspaper. In particular, don't miss the Friday edition, which includes "Friday Extra/The Tampa Bay Times," a supplement brimming with information on theaters, shows, nightclubs, festivals, and all sorts of local activities. Another excellent publication is **Tampa Bay,** a monthly magazine that covers all facets of the lively arts in the area. It is on sale at all local newsstands.

Like St. Petersburg, Tampa does not have a central reduced-rate same-day ticket booth, although some venues do offer "rush" tickets, discounted rates for students and seniors at the last minute. If you can't get to an individual box office, **TicketMaster** (tel. 287-8844) will reserve tickets by phone or at one of its outlets (downtown at the Tampa Theatre or throughout the city at Dillard's stores).

THE PERFORMING ARTS
MAJOR CONCERT/PERFORMANCE HALLS

TAMPA BAY PERFORMING ARTS CENTER, 1010 N. MacInnes Place, Tampa. Tel. 222-1000, 221-1045 (box office), or toll free 800/955-1045.

Opened in 1987, this $57-million four-theater complex is the focal point of Tampa's performing-arts scene. With an enviable downtown location on a nine-acre site along the east bank of the Hillsborough River, off Tyler Street one block west of Ashley, it presents a wide range of classical, orchestral, and pop concerts, operas, Broadway plays, cabarets, and special events, in a choice of four venues—the 2,400-seat Festival Hall, 900-seat Playhouse, 300-seat Jaeb Theater, and 150-seat Off Center Theatre.

An attraction in itself, this huge (290,000-square-foot) building sits back from the city's main thoroughfares in a well-landscaped setting, and is connected to a 1,000-car parking garage by a glass-enclosed pedestrian bridge. In conjunction with some performances, especially Broadway shows, you can book a pretheater dinner ($15) through Performing Arts Caterers (tel. 222-1075). The box office is open Monday through Friday from 10am to 5:30pm and on Saturday from noon to 4pm. Evening performances begin at 7:30 or 8pm, matinees at 2 or 2:30pm. Tours are given on Wednesday and Saturday at 10am, and depart from the box office.

Admission: Tickets, $12.50–$45 evening performances, $5–$25 matinees; half-price "rush" tickets available for some events for seniors and students, with some restrictions. Parking: Valet $8, self-parking $2–$5.

TAMPA STADIUM, 4201 N. Dale Mabry Hwy., Tampa. Tel. 872-7977.

Home of Super Bowl XVIII and XXV and many other sporting events, this giant 74,301-seat stadium, north of downtown and east of the airport, at Dr. Martin Luther King, Jr., Boulevard, is the largest venue for public events in the Tampa Bay area. It is frequently the site of world-class concerts, and has recently been the stage for such stars as Paul McCartney, the Rolling Stones, and U2. Box-office hours and days of operation vary; call in advance for information on a particular event, or reserve through TicketMaster outlets.

Admission: Tickets, $10–$35 or higher, depending on the event.

USF SUN DOME, 4202 S. Fowler Ave., Tampa. Tel. 974-3000 or 974-3001 for recorded information.

On the University of South Florida (USF) campus, this huge arena is the site of major concerts, averaging 5,000 to 10,000 in capacity.

It's a frequent venue for touring pop stars, rock bands, jazz groups, and other contemporary artists. The box office is open Monday through Friday from 10am to 5pm; performances are usually scheduled on Friday and Saturday nights beginning at 7:30 or 8pm.

To get here, take I-275 north to Fowler Avenue (Exit 34) and go east two miles to the USF campus.

Admission: Tickets, $15–$35, depending on the event.

THEATERS

OFF CENTER THEATRE, Tampa Bay Performing Arts Center, 1010 N. MacInnes Place. Tel. 972-1200.

The Loft Theatre Production Company presents alternative and contemporary works at this 150-seat facility. The company is a showcase for aspiring bay area creative talent.

Admission: Tickets, $10.

TAMPA PLAYERS THEATER, 601 Harbour Island Blvd., Harbour Island, Tampa. Tel. 221-8587.

This 150-seat theater is the home for the Tampa Players, a well-established local troupe known for performing innovative and contemporary plays. Performances are scheduled Wednesday through Saturday at 7:30pm, Sunday at 2pm. It is located on the upper level of the Shops on Harbour Island complex.

Note: From mid-April to early May, the Tampa Players move outdoors to host the annual American Classics Festival, performing plays by great American authors at the Waterfront Amphitheater on Harbour Island. Festival performances are Wednesday through Sunday at 7:30pm.

Admission: Theater tickets, $13–$17; festival tickets are free for bleacher seats, $3 for folding chairs.

TAMPA THEATRE, 711 N. Franklin St., Tampa. Tel. 223-8981.

On the National Register of Historic Places, this restored 1926 theater, downtown between Polk and Zack Streets, is a showcase of ornate colonnades, balconies, and replicas of Greek and Roman sculpture. There is seating for up to 1,500, with a varied program of classic, foreign, and alternative films, as well as concerts and special events. The box office is open Monday through Friday from 11:30am to 5:30pm. Show times vary, but are usually 5, 7 or 7:30pm, and 9:30 or 10pm.

Admission: Tickets, $5 adults, $3.75 seniors, $2 children 10 and under, except $3 adults and seniors on Tues and on Sat–Sun matinees. Some special events are $15–$20 or more.

WAREHOUSE THEATER, 112 S. 12th St., Ybor City. Tel. 223-3076.

Located in the heart of the city's artsy Latin Quarter, this is one of Tampa's newest theaters, presenting original works by contemporary writers—including mysteries and one-person shows.

Admission: Tickets, $10.50–$12.50.

DINNER THEATER

MYSTERY CAFE, 725 S. Harbour Island Blvd., Harbour Island. Tel. 935-0846.

Audience participation is encouraged at this weekend murder-mystery dinner show, performed in the elegant setting of the Wyndham Harbour Island Hotel. It's on Fridays at 8pm, Saturdays at 7pm.

Admission: Show and dinner, $29.95.

THE CLUB & MUSIC SCENE

COMEDY CLUBS

THE COMEDY WORKS, 3447 W. Kennedy Blvd. (Fla. 60), Tampa. Tel. 875-9129.

An ever-changing program of live comedy gets the audience giggling at this club situated west of downtown between Dale Mabry Highway and MacDill Avenue, at the corner of Himes Avenue. Shows are Sunday and Tuesday through Thursday at 8:30pm, and on Friday and Saturday at 8:30 and 10:45pm.

Admission: $5–$10 cover charge.

SIDESPLITTERS COMEDY CLUB, 12938 N. Dale Mabry Hwy., at Fletcher Ave., Tampa. Tel. 960-1197.

Located northwest of downtown in the Carrollwood section of the city, this club presents live comedy by professional stand-up comedians on most nights. Shows begin Tuesday through Thursday and Sunday at 8:30pm, and on Friday and Saturday at 8 and 10:30pm.

Admission: $6–$8 cover charge.

ROCK & TOP 40

BRASS MUG PUB, 1441 E. Fletcher Ave., Tampa. Tel. 972-8152.

This place features nightly music, from heavy metal to rock and Top 40. There is a jam session on Wednesdays. Pool, darts, and video games are always available. It's open nightly, with music usually starting at 9:30pm.

Admission: $3–$5.

CHA CHA COCONUTS, 601 S. Harbour Island Blvd., Harbour Island. Tel. 223-3101.

This indoor/outdoor setting offers live rock music, harbor views, and tropical drinks. The club is south of downtown; take the Franklin Street Bridge or the People Mover to Harbour Island. Drinks run $1.95 to $4.95. Open Monday through Wednesday from 11am to 10pm, Thursday 11am to 1pm, Sunday noon to 10pm.

MACDINTON'S TAVERN, 405 S. Howard Ave., Tampa. Tel. 254-1661.

Known locally as "Mac's," this place has a rustic neighborhood bar atmosphere and features live high-energy rock entertainment, as well as blues. It's in the Hyde Park area west of downtown, three blocks south of Kennedy Boulevard (Fla. 60), between Azeele and Horatio Streets. It's open Sunday through Wednesday from 9pm to midnight and Thursday through Saturday from 9pm to 2am.

Admission: $2–$3 cover charge.

JAZZ/BLUES/REGGAE

BLUES SHIP, 1910 E. Seventh Ave., Ybor City. Tel. 248-6097.

This club specializes in live blues bands, jazz, and reggae, presented in an informal meeting-house atmosphere in the heart of Tampa's Latin Quarter. Open on Tuesday through Sunday from 5pm to 3am.

To find the Blues Ship, take I-4 to Ybor City (Exit 1); the club is between 19th and 20th Streets.

Admission: $2–$5 cover charge.

BROTHERS LOUNGE, 5401 W. Kennedy Blvd., Tampa. Tel. 286-8882.

A jazz haven for over 20 years and considered one of the top jazz spots in Tampa, this lounge concentrates solely on jazz, seven nights a week. The lounge is west of downtown in the Lincoln Center building, at the corner of Kennedy and Hoover Boulevards. It's open on Monday from 8:30pm to 12:30am, Tuesday through Thursday from 9:30pm to 1:30am, on Friday and Saturday from 9:30pm to 2:30am, and on Sunday from 8pm to midnight.

Admission: $1–$3 cover charge.

CLUB IRIE, 1720 E. Seventh St., Ybor City. Tel. 242-4743.

Blues and reggae are the main attraction at this club, in the heart of the city's Latin Quarter. It's open Wednesday through Sunday from 7pm, but the music usually doesn't get under way until 9:30 or 10pm.

Admission: $3 cover charge.

JAZZ CELLAR, 1916 N. 14th St., Ybor City. Tel. 248-1862.

In the heart of the city's Latin Quarter, this place features the Jazz Cellar Underground Orchestra, which draws jazz fans from near and far. Performances Thursday through Saturday from 9pm to 2am.

Admission: $2–$3.

SELENA'S, 1623 Snow Ave., Tampa. Tel. 251-2116.

In the heart of Old Hyde Park Village, west of downtown between Swan and Morrison Avenues, this trendy spot is ranked as one of the top two jazz meccas in Tampa. Drinks run $2 to $5. It's open on Thursday from 9pm to 1:30am and on Friday and Saturday from 9:30pm to 1:30am.

SKIPPER'S SMOKEHOUSE, 910 Skipper Rd., at Nebraska Ave., Tampa. Tel. 971-0666 or 977-6474.

This is a prime spot for live calypso and Cajun music, reggae, and blues, as well as zydeco, a new sound from southwestern Louisiana that combines Créole music, blues, soul, and more. Open on Tuesday, Wednesday, Saturday, and Sunday from 6:30 to 11pm, and on Friday from 8 to 11pm.

Admission: $3–$8 cover charge, $10 or more for special events.

DANCE CLUBS/DISCOS

THE RITZ, 1503 E. Seventh Ave., Ybor City. Tel. 247-3319.

Housed in the former art deco–style Ritz Theater, this progressive dance club features live rock bands and groups playing the latest alternative hits for a youngish, mostly 20s crowd. Next to the main theater is a smaller room called Apocalypse, a dance club with a DJ who spins alternative music. Open Monday through Saturday from 9pm to 3am.

To put on the Ritz, take I-4 to Ybor City (Exit 1); the theater is at 15th Street and Seventh Avenue.

Admission: $5–$15 for live music, $1–$3 cover charge for DJ music.

YUCATAN LIQUOR STAND, 4811 W. Cypress St., Tampa. Tel. 289-8454.

Situated within walking distance of most hotels in the West Shore district, this club is the nearest thing to a beach bar not on a beach—counters made of old surfboards, tiki-hut trim, mounted fish specimens, and tropically painted booths beckon within. On the outside, there are mounds of sand, palm trees, a volleyball court, and a patio deck. The dance floor is always packed, with music ranging from the Top 40s to reggae, country, or progressive. Drinks begin at $1, and the music is live Wednesday through Friday. Open Monday through Thursday from 4pm to 3am, on Friday from 3pm to 3am, and on Saturday and Sunday from 6pm to 3am.

MORE ENTERTAINMENT

CHAMPIONS, in the Tampa Marriott Westshore Hotel, 1001 N. West Shore Blvd., at Cypress St., Tampa. Tel. 286-2201.

One of a group of over 20 Champions bars scattered throughout the U.S., this sports-themed lounge is unique in the Tampa Bay area, with dozens of TV monitors and walls lined with pennants, trophies, uniforms, magazine covers, and memorabilia. It's an ideal spot to catch a sporting event or just to mix with other sports-minded local fans and players. Drinks run $2 to $4. It's open Monday through Saturday from 11:30am to 2:30am and on Sunday from 11:30am to midnight.

OVO CAFE, 1901 E. Seventh Ave., Ybor City. Tel. 248-6979.

Tucked in the heart of Tampa's Latin Quarter, this is a popular after-dinner gathering spot with both indoor and outdoor seating. People don't flock here for drinks, dancing, or entertainment, however, but for the house specialty dessert—gourmet Belgian waffles topped with yogurt and a splash of liqueur, accompanied by

Cuban coffee, flavored sparkling waters, and iced herbal teas (black currant and herbal hibiscus are favorites). Prices run $2.75 to $7.95 for most desserts. The café is open Wednesday and Thursday from 9am to 11pm, on Friday and Saturday from 10am to 2am, and on Sunday through Tuesday from 10am to 5pm.

To find the Ovo Café, take I-4 to Ybor City (Exit 1); the club is between 19th and 20th Streets.

RADIANT ROLLERS, 201 W. Platt St., Tampa. Tel. 251-0003.

Whether you watch or participate, roller-skating is a unique Tampa tradition. On an average night, 50 to 80 people fasten on their skates and travel as a group through the streets of Hyde Park, Harbour Island, and downtown, for a total skating course of seven miles. The route takes in various nightclubs, where participants usually step inside and dance, with or without their skates. Skating runs are held on Friday and Saturday from 9pm to 1:30am. Skaters assemble west of downtown at the corner of West Platt and South Parker Streets in the Hyde Park area, and registration is one hour before departure.

Admission (including skate rental): $10–$15 per person.

THREE BIRDS, 1518 E. Seventh Ave., Ybor City. Tel. 247-7041.

Although open all day, this bookstore/coffee room comes alive in the evening as a popular gathering spot for the literati of Tampa, particularly at 8:30pm on the first Saturday of every month when "poetry slams" are held. Aspiring poets have a three-minute time limit and judges score in Olympic style. Admission is $2 to $3 per person. It's a bright, airy place, with surrealist paintings and drawings on the walls, interesting music in the background, and lots and lots of books—from volumes on poetry and music to world affairs, gay and lesbian studies, and beat-generation literature. The coffee bar serves imported coffees and teas, fruit smoothies, natural sodas, homemade muffins, and cheesecakes—no alcohol. Prices range from 50¢ to $2.50 for coffee, tea, or baked goods. Open Monday through Thursday from 11am to 6pm, Friday and Saturday from 11am to 10pm, Sunday from 1 to 5pm.

To get to Three Birds, take I-4 to Ybor City (Exit 1); it's located between 15th and 16th Avenues.

TRACKS, 1430 E. Seventh Ave., Ybor City. Tel. 247-2711.

Recognized as Tampa's leading gay nightclub, this huge place has a dance floor, pool room, barroom, lounge area, and video room. There is high-energy dance music most evenings, played by DJs and VJs (video jockeys), and on Tuesday, Friday, and Saturday female impersonators strut their stuff. Tracks is open Tuesday through Sunday from 8pm to 3am.

To get here, take I-4 to Ybor City (Exit 1) and then follow the signs; Tracks is located between 14th and 15th Streets.

Admission: Usually free before 10pm, $3–$5 after 10pm.

EASY EXCURSIONS FROM TAMPA & ST. PETERSBURG

Conveniently located in the heart of central Florida's west coast, the St. Petersburg/Tampa area makes an ideal base for travel to other nearby destinations. Below are a few of our favorite side trips.

Note: Sightseeing bus tours from the St. Petersburg/Tampa area to some of the areas described, such as Sarasota, Sea World, Walt Disney World, and Cypress Gardens, are operated by **Gray Line,** 6890 124th Ave. N., Largo, FL 34641 (tel. 813/535-0208, or toll free 800/282-4051 in Florida).

To find out more about Florida's sightseeing possibilities, we recommend *Frommer's Florida.*

1. DUNEDIN & CALADESI ISLAND

Founded by Scottish settlers in 1870, Dunedin (pronounced Dunn-*eee*-din) is a quiet little town just three miles north of Clearwater. In many ways it is a pocket of old-world charm, with street names such as Brae-Moor, Dundee, Highland, Inverness, McLean, and Scotland. Every April the town celebrates its heritage with a series of traditional **highland games** including bagpipe and drum performances, dancing, and athletic competitions.

WHAT TO SEE & DO

For natural beauty, Dunedin's biggest attractions are its **offshore islands**—Honeymoon and Caladesi. You can drive to Honeymoon Island, a combination of condominium strip and state park, via the Dunedin Causeway (Fla. 586), but Caladesi is more remote, accessible only by passenger ferry from Honeymoon Island.

The ferries are operated by Caladesi Island Ferry Service, at the west end of Fla. 586, Dunedin (tel. 813/734-5263). Reservations are accepted (but not required) for the 15-minute ride. The ferry runs March through November, Monday through Friday hourly from 10am to 5pm, and on Saturday and Sunday every half hour from 10am to 6pm; reduced service December through February. Round-trip fare is $4 for adults and $2.50 for children 12 and under.

The 640-acre **Caladesi Island State Park,** three miles long and half a mile wide, is one of Florida's few remaining undisturbed barrier islands. No cars are allowed. Ideal for swimming, shelling, and scuba diving, the island's beaches front the Gulf of Mexico; there is a mangrove swamp on the bay side, and much of the interior is dominated by virgin pine forest. Sea turtles nest on the beaches during summer nights, and many wading birds and shorebirds seek refuge here. Because Caladesi is surrounded by water, it's always several degrees cooler than the mainland. Facilities include palm-shaded picnic pavilions, snack bar, boardwalks, shower houses and restrooms, playground, and a three-mile nature trail. Hours are 8am to sunset.

For more information about the Dunedin area, which also serves as spring training ground for the **Toronto Blue Jays,** contact the **Dunedin Chamber of Commerce,** 301 Main St., Dunedin, FL 34698 (tel. 813/733-3197).

2. TARPON SPRINGS

Stroll down Dodecanese Boulevard in Tarpon Springs, listen to the Greek music, and smell the freshly baked pastries. It seems like an exotic Greek isle, but it's only 10 miles north of Clearwater and 35 miles from St. Petersburg or Tampa.

First settled in 1876 by Greek immigrants, this town is an enclave of Hellenic traditions, foods, and crafts. It is also the home of a native sponge industry, earning Tarpon Springs the title of "America's Sponge Capital." Here you not only can purchase a wide array of locally harvested sponges, but you can board one of the many excursion boats and watch divers plunge into nearby waters to pull up sponges straight from the sea.

WHAT TO SEE & DO

The **Konger Coral Sea Aquarium,** 852 Dodecanese Blvd., Tarpon Springs (tel. 813/938-5378), features a wide collection of fish that are indigenous to the Gulf of Mexico and the Caribbean Sea. The fish—which range from nurse and lemon sharks to black and red grouper, angel fish, puffers, crevalle jacks, and stingrays—swim freely in a 100,000-gallon main tank that also contains a coral reef. Three smaller tanks display colorful marine life from the Pacific Ocean. Admission is $4.75 for adults, $2.75 for children over 3; the aquarium is open daily from 10am to 5pm.

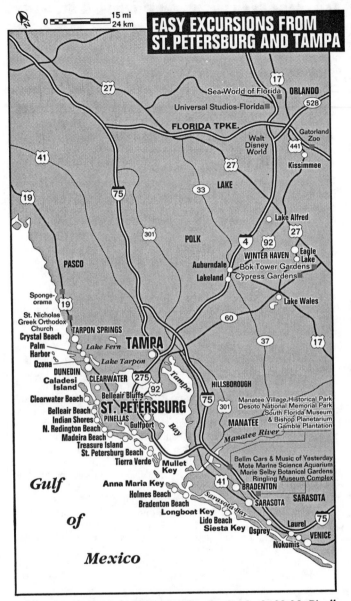

EASY EXCURSIONS FROM ST. PETERSBURG AND TAMPA

15 mi
0
24 km

ORLANDO

17
528

Sea-World of Florida
Universal Studios-Florida

FLORIDA TPKE.

27

Walt
Disney
World

Gatorland
Zoo

441

Kissimmee

27

33

LAKE

301

POLK

Lake Alfred

4   92   27

WINTER HAVEN   Eagle
Lake

Auburndale   Bok Tower Gardens
Lakeland   Cypress Gardens

PASCO

Sponge-
orama   19

St. Nicholas
Greek Orthodox
Church

Crystal Beach
Palm
Harbor
Ozona

TARPON SPRINGS   Lake Fern
TAMPA
Lake Tarpon

Lake Wales

60

37   17

DUNEDIN
Caladesi
Island   **CLEARWATER**   275
92

Tampa

Clearwater Beach   Belleair Bluffs
Belleair Beach   **ST. PETERSBURG**
Indian Shores   **PINELLAS**
N. Redington Beach   **Gulfport**
Madeira Beach
Treasure Island
St. Petersburg Beach
Tierra Verde

HILLSBOROUGH

75

301

Manatee Village Historical Park
Desoto National Memorial Park
South Florida Museum
& Bishop Planetarium
Gamble Plantation

MANATEE

Tampa
Bay   Manatee River

Mullet
Key

Gulf

of

Mexico

Anna Maria Key
Holmes Beach
Bradenton Beach
Longboat Key

41

Sarasota Bay

Bellm Cars & Music of Yesterday
Mote Marine Science Aquarium
Marie Selby Botanical Gardens
Ringling Museum Complex

BRADENTON   **SARASOTA**
SARASOTA

Lido Beach
Siesta Key   Osprey

Laurel

75

Nokomis   **VENICE**

St. Nicholas Greek Orthodox Cathedral, 30 N. Pinellas Ave., Tarpon Springs (tel. 813/937-3540), is a replica of St. Sophia's in Istanbul, and an excellent example of New Byzantine architecture, with an interior of sculptured Grecian marble, elaborate icons, and stained glass. It was built in 1943, replacing a smaller structure erected in 1907 by the community's early settlers. Admission is by donation; the cathedral is open daily from 9am to 5pm.

Spongeorama, 510 Dodecanese Blvd., Tarpon Springs (tel.

813/942-3771), is located on the site of the town's original sponge exchange. This is a museum/theater with exhibits tracing the history of the city's sponge industry and its Greek settlers, and a film demonstrating sponge diving. Admission is free. Spongeorama is open daily from 10am to 6pm.

3. BRADENTON

Heading about an hour south of St. Petersburg or 1½ hours from the Tampa area, you'll know you've reached Bradenton when the sweet aroma of fresh oranges fills the air. As the home of Tropicana, this city of 40,000 people is a major producer of orange juice, as well as of other agricultural products such as tomatoes.

WHAT TO SEE & DO

Set on the Manatee River, Bradenton is also famous as the home of the **Nick Bollettieri Tennis Academy** and as the spring-training ground for the **Pittsburgh Pirates.** Its historic **"Old Main Street"** (12th Street in today's city layout), and many Spanish-style buildings are also well known.

Bradenton's star attraction, however, is **Anna Maria Island,** a 7½-mile stretch of quiet, tree-shaded beaches that rim the Gulf of Mexico. Situated west of downtown Bradenton, the island is accessible by two causeways (Route 64 and Route 684). On the northern end is Anna Maria Bayfront Park, a favorite local haunt for finding unbroken sand dollars and scalloped cockleshells. To the south are Holmes Beach, Manatee County Beach, Cortez Beach (also known as Bradenton Beach), and Coquina Beach, a secluded area at the southern tip of the island lined with sand dunes, pines, and extensive picnic facilities. The Bradenton city line also extends to the top half of neighboring Longboat Key.

For more information on Bradenton, contact the **Greater Bradenton Convention & Visitors Bureau,** P.O. Box 1000, Bradenton, FL 34206 (tel. 813/729-9177, or toll free 800/4-MANATEE). The county also maintains walk-in **Visitor Centers** at the Civic Center, 1 Haben Blvd., off U.S. 301, Palmetto (tel. 813/729-9177) and at 5030 U.S. 301, Ellenton (tel. 813/729-7040), open daily from 8:30am to 5:30pm.

DeSOTO NATIONAL MEMORIAL PARK, 75th St., off Rte. 64, Bradenton. Tel. 813/792-0458.

Commemorating the Spanish explorer Hernando de Soto's 1539 landing in Florida, this park reflects the look and atmosphere of the 1500s. Highlights include a restoration of de Soto's original camp site, and a scenic half-mile nature trail that circles a mangrove jungle and leads to the ruins of one of the first settlements of the area. From December through March, park employees dress in 16th-century costumes and portray the way the early settlers lived, including demonstrations of cooking and musket firing.

Admission: Free.
Open: Daily 9am–5pm.

GAMBLE PLANTATION, 3708 Patten Ave., Ellenton. Tel. 813/723-4536.

Situated on U.S. 301 northeast of downtown Bradenton, this is the oldest structure on the southwest coast of Florida, and a fine example of an antebellum plantation home. Built over a six-year period in the 1840s by Maj. Robert Gamble, it is constructed primarily of a primitive material known as "tabby" (a mixture of oyster shells, sand, molasses, and water), with 10 rooms, verandas on three sides, 18 exterior columns, and eight fireplaces. It is maintained as a state historic site, and includes a fine collection of 19th-century furnishings. Entrance into the house is by tour only, although the grounds may be explored independently.

Admission (including tour): $2 adults, $1 children 6–12.
Open: Thurs–Mon 9am–5pm. Tours given at 9:30 and 10:30am, and 1, 2, 3, and 4pm.

MANATEE VILLAGE HISTORICAL PARK, Sixth Ave. E. and 15th St. E., Bradenton. Tel. 813/749-7165.

A tree-shaded park with a courtyard of hand-laid bricks, this national historic site features restored buildings from the city of Bradenton and the surrounding county. It contains the Manatee County Court House, dating back to 1860 and the oldest structure of its kind still standing on the south Florida mainland; a Methodist church built in 1887; a typical "Cracker Gothic" house built in 1912; a one-room schoolhouse built in 1908; and the Wiggins General Store, dating to 1903 and full of local memorabilia from swamp root and grub dust to louse powder, as well as antique furnishings and an art gallery.

Admission: Free; donations welcome.
Open: Mon–Fri 9am–4:30pm, Sun 1:30–4:30pm. **Closed:** Sun July–Aug.

SOUTH FLORIDA MUSEUM AND BISHOP PLANETARIUM, 201 10th St. W., Bradenton. Tel. 813/746-4131.

The story of Florida's history, from prehistoric times to the present, is told in exhibits including a Native American collection with life-size dioramas; a Spanish courtyard containing replicas of 16th-century buildings; and an indoor aquarium, the home of Snooty, the oldest manatee (or sea cow) born in captivity (1948). The adjacent Bishop Planetarium features a 50-foot hemispherical dome for laser light shows and stargazing activities.

Admission: $5.50 adults, $3.50 children 5–12, free for children under 5.
Open: Tues–Sat 10am–5pm, Sun noon–6pm.

4. SARASOTA

Often referred to as "the circus town," Sarasota is closely associated with circus legend John Ringling, who has left his imprint in many ways. A bright and thriving city of 50,000 people, Sarasota is about a 1½- to 2-hour drive south of the St. Petersburg/Tampa area.

WHAT TO SEE & DO

Sarasota's main attractions, like Bradenton's, are its pristine **beaches,** spread over 20 miles along four keys between Sarasota Bay and the Gulf of Mexico—**Siesta Key,** a quiet and mostly residential island; **Lido Key,** a lively and well-developed island with a string of motels, restaurants, and nightclubs; **St. Armand's Key,** a tiny enclave of lush landscaping, statuary, courtyards, and a fashionable circle of international shopping/dining establishments; and **Longboat Key,** dubbed "the Park Avenue of Sarasota," a narrow stretch of posh resorts and residences. The beaches are connected to the mainland via three causeways, two of which lead to Siesta Key and one to St. Armand's, which connects to Lido and Longboat Keys.

Considered as the cultural capital of Florida's west coast, Sarasota is home to over a dozen theaters and performing arts centers including the state theater of Florida, Florida West Coast Symphony, Asolo Center, and Van Wezel Hall, as well as resident theatrical, operatic, jazz, concert, and ballet companies. To round out the cultural milieu, there are more than 40 art galleries and museums including the centerpiece of the city—the Ringling Museum Complex incorporating the John and Mable Ringling Museum of Art, Florida's official state art museum.

On a sporting note, the city also serves as the winter training ground for the Chicago White Sox.

For more information, contact the **Sarasota Convention & Visitors Bureau,** 655 N. Tamiami Trail (U.S. 41), Sarasota, FL 34236 (tel. 813/957-1877, or toll free 800/522-9799)

BELLM'S CARS & MUSIC OF YESTERDAY, 5500 N. Tamiami Trail (U.S. 41), Sarasota. Tel. 813/355-6228.

This museum displays over 120 classic and antique autos, from Rolls-Royces and Pierce Arrows to the four cars used personally by circus czar John Ringling. In addition, there are over 2,000 antique music machines, from tiny music boxes to a huge 30-foot Belgian organ.

Admission: $7.50 adults, $3.75 children 6–12, free for children under 6.

Open: Daily 9:30am–5:30pm.

MARIE SELBY BOTANICAL GARDENS, S. Palm Ave., off U.S. 41, Sarasota. Tel. 813/366-5730.

A 17-acre museum of living plants, this facility is said to be the only botanical garden in the world to specialize in the preservation, study, and research of epiphytic plants ("air plants") such as orchids, pineapples, and ferns. It is home to more than 20,000 exotic plants, including over 6,000 orchids, and features a bamboo pavilion, a waterfall garden, butterfly and hummingbird garden, medicinal plant garden, a cactus and succulent garden, a fernery, a hibiscus garden, a palm grove, a tropical food garden, and a native shore plant community, plus a museum of botany and the arts.

Admission: $6 adults, $3 for children 6–11, free for children under 6 with an adult.

Open: Daily 10am–5pm. **Closed:** Christmas.

MOTE MARINE AQUARIUM, 1600 Thompson Pkwy., City Island, Sarasota. Tel. 813/388-4441.

Part of the noted Mote Marine Laboratory complex, this facility focuses on the marine life of the Sarasota area. Displays include a living mangrove swamp and seagrass environment, a 135,000-gallon shark tank, loggerhead turtles and their eggs, starfish, lobsters, sea horses, and other inhabitants of both salt and fresh water. In addition, there are many "research-in-progress" exhibits on such topics as the red tide, aquaculture enhancement, cancer research in sharks, and the effects of pesticide and petroleum pollution on the coast. The aquarium is located on City Island, just south of Longboat Key.

Admission: $6 adults, $4 children 6–17, free for children under 6.

Open: Daily 10am–5pm.

RINGLING MUSEUM COMPLEX, 5401 Bay Shore Rd., Sarasota. Tel. 813/355-5101 or 813/351-1660 for recorded information.

The former estate of circus entrepreneur John Ringling, this 66-acre site overlooking Sarasota Bay offers four attractions. Foremost is the John and Mable Ringling Museum of Art, Florida's official state art museum, which houses a major exhibit of baroque art as well as collections of decorative arts and traveling exhibits. Next is the 30-room Ca'd'Zan (House of John), the Ringling winter residence, built in 1925 and modeled after a Venetian palace, and the Circus Galleries, a building devoted to circus memorabilia including parade wagons, calliopes, costumes, and colorful posters. The grounds also include the Asolo Center for the Performing Arts, a professional theater company, plus restaurants and shops.

Admission: $8.50 adults, $7.50 seniors, free for children 12 and under.

Open: Oct–June, Fri–Wed 10am–5:30pm, Thurs 10am–10pm; July–Sept, daily 10am–5:30pm.

5. ORLANDO

Situated about two hours' driving time from the St. Petersburg/ Tampa area, Orlando is one of Florida's fastest-growing destinations, although it is far from the coastal lures of surf and sand. Instead it's a city built on the success of its artificial attractions, especially its theme parks. For an indepth look at this exciting city, we recommend *Frommer's Orlando*.

WHAT TO SEE & DO

GATORLAND ZOO, 14501 S. Orange Blossom Trail, Orlando, FL 32821. Tel. 407/855-5496.
For a close-up look at alligators and crocodiles of every size and species frolicking in a seven-acre lake, spend a couple of hours at this unusual zoo and commercial alligator farm. Visitors are given a 10-minute orientation tour and then permitted to feed the alligators from covered walkways beside the lake. In addition, there are scores of snakes, other reptiles, birds, and animals in 35 acres of natural-habitat settings. It's located south of Orlando, on U.S. 17, 19, and 441.
  Admission: $10.95 adults and children 12 or over, $7.95 children 3–11, free for children under 3.
  Open: Daily 8am–dusk.

SEA WORLD OF FLORIDA, 7007 Sea World Dr., Orlando, FL 32821. Tel. 407/351-3600, or toll free 800/327-2424.
This 150-acre facility focuses on marine life, and is home to hundreds of penguins, seals, dolphins, sea lions, and sharks, not to mention killer whales that perform in special aquatic shows. There are also water-ski shows, a 400-foot observation tower, and a variety of exhibits, plus various marine-themed rides, shops, and Anheuser-Busch hospitality center, and restaurants.
  Admission: $34.95 adults, $29.95 children 3–9, free for children under 3. Parking is $5.
  Open: Daily 9am–6pm or later.

UNIVERSAL STUDIOS–FLORIDA, 1000 Universal Studios Plaza, Orlando, FL 32819. Tel. 407/363-8000, or toll free 800/232-7827.
Opened in 1990, this $680-million, 444-acre attraction includes a full-scale movie and TV production studio, with more than 50 sets, from *Jaws* to a New England Village and New York City's Upper East Side. In addition to viewing behind-the-scenes production work, you can learn about set design, costuming, makeup, filming, editing, mixing, dubbing, animation, sound effects, and special effects. To enhance the ambience, celebrity look-alikes—the likes of Mae West, Charlie Chaplin, Marilyn Monroe, and W. C. Fields—as well as Hanna-Barbera cartoon figures, roam the grounds and interact with

visitors. The park also includes rides, live shows, and over 40 restaurants and shops.

Admission: $35 adults, $28 children 3–9. Parking is $5.

Open: Summer, daily 9am–11pm; the rest of the year, hours vary.

WALT DISNEY WORLD, P.O. Box 10040, Lake Buena Vista, FL 32830-0040. Tel. 407/824-4321.

Located 20 miles southwest of Orlando, this granddaddy of Florida's artificial wonders currently has three theme parks (with plans for another one) spread over 6,600 acres.

The Magic Kingdom, home of Mickey Mouse and Donald Duck, is the 100-acre centerpiece of the Disney domain in central Florida. Opened in 1971, it offers 45 major attractions, restaurants, and shops, all based on favorite Disney themes, from Frontierland and Fantasyland to Adventureland, Tomorrowland, and Mickey's Birthdayland.

EPCOT Center (Experimental Prototype Community of Tomorrow), covering 260 acres, is a permanent scientific and cultural showplace. It consists of Future World, with such areas as Living Seas, Wonders of Life, Universe of Energy, World of Motion, and Spaceship Earth. The second division is the World Showcase, composed of pavilions reflecting the cultures of many countries including the United States, Canada, the United Kingdom, France, Germany, Italy, Norway, Mexico, Japan, China, and Morocco.

Disney–MGM Studios, opened in 1988, is a 135-acre working movie-production facility. Visitors can take a "behind-the-scenes" tour to see feature films, television shows, and Disney animation in production. Other attractions include "Star Tours," a thrill ride into outer space; a "Muppet-Vision" adventure; a "Beauty and the Beast" stage show; opportunities to participate in TV shows and music videos; a sound-effects monster show; a stunt theater; a full-scale re-creation of the famous Chinese Theater of Hollywood; and a variety of movie-related shops and restaurants.

Other on-site Disney World attractions range from **Pleasure Island,** a complex of seven nightclubs, restaurants, and movie theaters, to **Typhoon Lagoon,** a 56-acre water-theme park, as well as hotels, campgrounds, a zoological park, three championship golf courses, scores of other sporting facilities, child-care center, pet-care kennels, shops, and an elaborate internal transport system of monorails, ferries, motor launches, and minibuses.

To get there from the Tampa/St. Petersburg area, take I-4 east. As you approach Walt Disney World, numerous signs will guide you to the massive parking lots.

Admission: One-day/one-park ticket, $36.95 adults, $29.55 children 3–9; four-day pass allowing admission to all three parks, $132 adults, $103.50 children 3–9, free for children under 3. Parking $5 extra.

Open: Daily 9am–7pm, with some sections open later at various times of the year.

6. WINTER HAVEN/LAKE WALES

South of Orlando and directly east of Tampa, the attractions in this area are a little over an hour's drive from Tampa and at least 1½ hours from St. Petersburg.

WHAT TO SEE & DO

BOK TOWER GARDENS, Tower Blvd. and Burns Ave., Lake Wales, FL 33853. Tel. 813/676-1408.
The serene combination of beautiful flowers and carillon bells draws many people to this inland attraction. The layout includes a historic pink-and-gray bell tower with 57 bronze bells that ring on the half hour, and a 128-acre garden, with thousands of azaleas, camellias, magnolias, and other flowering plants, set amid ferns, palms, oaks, and pines. Named for Dutch immigrant Edward W. Bok, who donated the gardens for public viewing in 1929, the site is listed on the National Register of Historic Places and sits on one of Florida's highest points of elevation, at 298 feet.
   Admission: $3 adults and children over 12, free for children under 12.
   Open: Daily 8am–5pm.

CYPRESS GARDENS, 2641 S. Lake Summit Dr. (P.O. Box 1), Cypress Gardens, FL 33884. Tel. 813/324-2111, or toll free 800/237-4826.
Situated off U.S. 27 near Winter Haven, this is a 208-acre botanical-garden theme park, with over 8,000 varieties of plants from 75 different countries, ranging from traditional southern gardenias to bougainvillea, hibiscus, and chrysanthemums, as well as an all-American rose garden, with 500 varieties. Other features include a waterski extravaganza, a butterfly conservatory, an elaborate model railroad, a 153-foot revolving observation tower, and boat rides through a maze of landscaped canals.
   Admission: $24.95 adults, $16.45 children 3–9, free for children under 3.
   Open: Daily 9:30am–5:30pm.

THE AMERICAN SYSTEM OF MEASUREMENTS

LENGTH

1 inch (in.)			=	2.54cm	
1 foot (ft.)	=	12 in.	=	30.48cm	= .305m
1 yard (yd.)	=	3 ft.			= .915m
1 mile	=	5,280 ft.			= 1.609km

To convert miles to kilometers, multiply the number of miles by 1.61 (example: 50 mi. × 1.61 = 80.5km). Also use to convert speeds from miles per hour (m.p.h.) to kilometers per hour (kmph).

To convert kilometers to miles, multiply the number of kilometers by .62 (example: 25km × .62 = 15.5mi.). Also use to convert kmph to m.p.h.

CAPACITY

1 fluid ounce (fl. oz.)			=	.03 liters
1 pint	=	16 fl. oz.	=	.47 liters
1 quart	=	2 pints	=	.94 liters
1 gallon (gal.)	=	4 quarts	=	3.79 liters
	=	.83 Imperial gal.		

To convert U.S. gallons to liters, multiply the number of gallons by 3.79 (example: 12 gal. × 3.79 = 45.48 liters).

To convert liters to U.S. gallons, multiply the number of liters by .26 (example: 50 liters × .26 = 13 U.S. gal.).

To convert U.S. gallons to Imperial gallons, multiply the number of U.S. gallons by .83 (example: 12 U.S. gal. × .83 = 9.95 Imperial gal.).

To convert Imperial gallons to U.S. gallons, multiply the number of Imperial gallons by 1.2 (example: 8 Imperial gal. × 1.2 = 9.6 U.S. gal.).

WEIGHT

1 ounce (oz.)			=	28.35g	
1 pound (lb.)	=	16 oz.	=	453.6g	= .45kg
1 ton	=	2,000 lb.	=	907kg	= .91 metric tons

To convert pounds to kilograms, multiply the number of pounds by .45 (example: 90 lb. × .45 = 40.5kg).

To convert kilograms to pounds, multiply the number of kilograms by 2.2 (example: 75kg × 2.2 = 165 lb.).

TEMPERATURE

°C −18° −10   0   10   20   30   40

°F   0° 10 20 32 40 50 60 70 80 90 100

To convert degrees Fahrenheit to degrees Celsius, subtract 32 from °F, multiply by 5, then divide by 9 (example: 85°F − 32 × 5/9 = 29.4°C).

To convert degrees Celsius to degrees Fahrenheit, multiply °C by 9, divide by 5, and add 32 (example: 20°C × 9/5 + 32 = 68°F).

INDEX

GENERAL INFORMATION INDEX

ACCOMMODATIONS INDEX

ST. PETERSBURG

KEY TO ABBREVIATIONS: *E* = Expensive; *I* = Inexpensive; *M* = Moderately Priced; *VE* = Very Expensive; * = an Author's Favorite; *$* = Super-Special Value

TAMPA

RESTAURANTS BY CUISINE

For a list of Restaurants by Cuisine see pages 103–105 for St. Petersburg and 205–207 for Tampa.

Please Send Me the Books Checked Below:

FROMMER'S COMPREHENSIVE GUIDES
(Guides listing facilities from budget to deluxe,
with emphasis on the medium-priced)

	Retail Price	Code		Retail Price	Code
☐ Acapulco/Ixtapa/Taxco 1993–94	$15.00	C120	☐ Morocco 1992–93	$18.00	C021
☐ Alaska 1994–95	$17.00	C131	☐ Nepal 1994–95	$18.00	C126
☐ Arizona 1993–94	$18.00	C101	☐ New England 1994 (Avail. 1/94)	$16.00	C137
☐ Australia 1992–93	$18.00	C002	☐ New Mexico 1993–94	$15.00	C117
☐ Austria 1993–94	$19.00	C119	☐ New York State 1994–95	$19.00	C133
☐ Bahamas 1994–95	$17.00	C121	☐ Northwest 1994–95 (Avail. 2/94)	$17.00	C140
☐ Belgium/Holland/ Luxembourg 1993–94	$18.00	C106	☐ Portugal 1994–95 (Avail. 2/94)	$17.00	C141
☐ Bermuda 1994–95	$15.00	C122	☐ Puerto Rico 1993–94	$15.00	C103
☐ Brazil 1993–94	$20.00	C111	☐ Puerto Vallarta/ Manzanillo/Guadalajara 1994–95 (Avail. 1/94)	$14.00	C028
☐ California 1994	$15.00	C134	☐ Scandinavia 1993–94	$19.00	C135
☐ Canada 1994–95 (Avail. 4/94)	$19.00	C145	☐ Scotland 1994–95 (Avail. 4/94)	$17.00	C146
☐ Caribbean 1994	$18.00	C123	☐ South Pacific 1994–95 (Avail. 1/94)	$20.00	C138
☐ Carolinas/Georgia 1994–95	$17.00	C128	☐ Spain 1993–94	$19.00	C115
☐ Colorado 1994–95 (Avail. 3/94)	$16.00	C143	☐ Switzerland/ Liechtenstein 1994–95 (Avail. 1/94)	$19.00	C139
☐ Cruises 1993–94	$19.00	C107	☐ Thailand 1992–93	$20.00	C033
☐ Delaware/Maryland 1994–95 (Avail. 1/94)	$15.00	C136	☐ U.S.A. 1993–94	$19.00	C116
☐ England 1994	$18.00	C129	☐ Virgin Islands 1994–95	$13.00	C127
☐ Florida 1994	$18.00	C124	☐ Virginia 1994–95 (Avail. 2/94)	$14.00	C142
☐ France 1994–95	$20.00	C132	☐ Yucatán 1993–94	$18.00	C110
☐ Germany 1994	$19.00	C125			
☐ Italy 1994	$19.00	C130			
☐ Jamaica/Barbados 1993–94	$15.00	C105			
☐ Japan 1994–95 (Avail. 3/94)	$19.00	C144			

FROMMER'S $-A-DAY GUIDES
(Guides to low-cost tourist accommodations and facilities)

	Retail Price	Code		Retail Price	Code
☐ Australia on $45 1993–94	$18.00	D102	☐ Israel on $45 1993–94	$18.00	D101
☐ Costa Rica/Guatemala/ Belize on $35 1993–94	$17.00	D108	☐ Mexico on $45 1994	$19.00	D116
☐ Eastern Europe on $30 1994	$18.00	D110	☐ New York on $70 1994–95	$16.00	D120
☐ England on $60 1994	$18.00	D112	☐ New Zealand on $45 1993–94	$18.00	D103
☐ Europe on $50 1994	$19.00	D115	☐ Scotland/Wales on $50 1992–93	$18.00	D019
☐ Greece on $45 1993–94	$19.00	D100	☐ South America on $40 1993–94	$19.00	D109
☐ Hawaii on $75 1994	$19.00	D113	☐ Turkey on $40 1992–93	$22.00	D023
☐ India on $40 1992–93	$20.00	D010	☐ Washington, D.C. on $40 1994–95 (Avail. 2/94)	$17.00	D119
☐ Ireland on $45 1994–95 (Avail. 1/94)	$17.00	D117			

FROMMER'S CITY $-A-DAY GUIDES
(Pocket-size guides to low-cost tourist accommodations
and facilities)

	Retail Price	Code		Retail Price	Code
☐ Berlin on $40 1994–95	$12.00	D111	☐ Madrid on $50 1994–95 (Avail. 1/94)	$13.00	D118
☐ Copenhagen on $50 1992–93	$12.00	D003	☐ Paris on $50 1994–95	$12.00	D117
☐ London on $45 1994–95	$12.00	D114	☐ Stockholm on $50 1992–93	$13.00	D022

FROMMER'S WALKING TOURS
(With routes and detailed maps, these companion guides point out the places and pleasures that make a city unique)

	Retail Price	Code		Retail Price	Code
☐ Berlin	$12.00	W100	☐ Paris	$12.00	W103
☐ London	$12.00	W101	☐ San Francisco	$12.00	W104
☐ New York	$12.00	W102	☐ Washington, D.C.	$12.00	W105

FROMMER'S TOURING GUIDES
(Color-illustrated guides that include walking tours, cultural and historic sights, and practical information)

	Retail Price	Code		Retail Price	Code
☐ Amsterdam	$11.00	T001	☐ New York	$11.00	T008
☐ Barcelona	$14.00	T015	☐ Rome	$11.00	T010
☐ Brazil	$11.00	T003	☐ Scotland	$10.00	T011
☐ Florence	$ 9.00	T005	☐ Sicily	$15.00	T017
☐ Hong Kong/Singapore/			☐ Tokyo	$15.00	T016
Macau	$11.00	T006	☐ Turkey	$11.00	T013
☐ Kenya	$14.00	T018	☐ Venice	$ 9.00	T014
☐ London	$13.00	T007			

FROMMER'S FAMILY GUIDES

	Retail Price	Code		Retail Price	Code
☐ California with Kids	$18.00	F100	☐ San Francisco with Kids (Avail. 4/94)	$17.00	F104
☐ Los Angeles with Kids (Avail. 4/94)	$17.00	F103	☐ Washington, D.C. with Kids (Avail. 2/94)	$17.00	F102
☐ New York City with Kids (Avail. 2/94)	$18.00	F101			

FROMMER'S CITY GUIDES
(Pocket-size guides to sightseeing and tourist accommodations and facilities in all price ranges)

	Retail Price	Code		Retail Price	Code
☐ Amsterdam 1993–94	$13.00	S110	☐ Montréal/Québec City 1993–94	$13.00	S125
☐ Athens 1993–94	$13.00	S114	☐ Nashville/Memphis 1994–95 (Avail. 4/94)	$13.00	S141
☐ Atlanta 1993–94	$13.00	S112	☐ New Orleans 1993–94	$13.00	S103
☐ Atlantic City/Cape May 1993–94	$13.00	S130	☐ New York 1994 (Avail. 1/94)	$13.00	S138
☐ Bangkok 1992–93	$13.00	S005	☐ Orlando 1994	$13.00	S135
☐ Barcelona/Majorca/ Minorca/Ibiza 1993–94	$13.00	S115	☐ Paris 1993–94	$13.00	S109
☐ Berlin 1993–94	$13.00	S116	☐ Philadelphia 1993–94	$13.00	S113
☐ Boston 1993–94	$13.00	S117	☐ San Diego 1993–94	$13.00	S107
☐ Budapest 1994–95 (Avail. 2/94)	$13.00	S139	☐ San Francisco 1994	$13.00	S133
☐ Chicago 1993–94	$13.00	S122	☐ Santa Fe/Taos/ Albuquerque 1993–94	$13.00	S108
☐ Denver/Boulder/ Colorado Springs 1993–94	$13.00	S131	☐ Seattle/Portland 1994–95	$13.00	S137
☐ Dublin 1993–94	$13.00	S128	☐ St. Louis/Kansas City 1993–94	$13.00	S127
☐ Hong Kong 1994–95 (Avail. 4/94)	$13.00	S140	☐ Sydney 1993–94	$13.00	S129
☐ Honolulu/Oahu 1994	$13.00	S134	☐ Tampa/St. Petersburg 1993–94	$13.00	S105
☐ Las Vegas 1993–94	$13.00	S121	☐ Tokyo 1992–93	$13.00	S039
☐ London 1994	$13.00	S132	☐ Toronto 1993–94	$13.00	S126
☐ Los Angeles 1993–94	$13.00	S123	☐ Vancouver/Victoria 1994–95 (Avail. 1/94)	$13.00	S142
☐ Madrid/Costa del Sol 1993–94	$13.00	S124	☐ Washington, D.C. 1994 (Avail. 1/94)	$13.00	S136
☐ Miami 1993–94	$13.00	S118			
☐ Minneapolis/St. Paul 1993–94	$13.00	S119			

SPECIAL EDITIONS

	Retail Price	Code		Retail Price	Code
☐ Bed & Breakfast Southwest	$16.00	P100	☐ Caribbean Hideaways	$16.00	P103
☐ Bed & Breakfast Great American Cities (Avail. 1/94	$16.00	P104	☐ National Park Guide 1994 (Avail. 3/94)	$16.00	P105
			☐ Where to Stay U.S.A.	$15.00	P102

Please note: if the availability of a book is several months away, we may have back issues of guides to that particular destination. Call customer service at (815) 734-1104.